"Mr. Casey has much in common
seemingly insurmountable dange
and accomplished his dream. The flight of Liberty II will be recorded
in aviation history."

**Slade Gorton**
**U.S. Senator, Washington**

"Since this is a world record
never attempted before, there is
no time limit."

**Everett Langworthy**
**Executive Vice President**
**National Aeronautic Association**

*Tom Casey comes ashore at Lake Abashiri near Memanbetsu, Hokkaido, Japan.*

# William T. Coleman

# Floatplane Odyssey

*Real-life tale of one man's historic quest to circumnavigate the globe, taking off and landing only on water.*

Edited by
John F. Infanger

"FLOATPLANE ODYSSEY"
*Real-life tale of one man's historic quest to circumnavigate the globe,
taking off and landing only on water.*

**Author**
William T. Coleman
3907 NE Sequoia
Lees Summit, MO 64064

**Editor**
John F. Infanger

Includes biographical references
ISBN 978-1-4951-6086-8

Printed in the United States by Rose Printing Company

*Book design by Justin Infanger*

*Dedicated to my English wife, Lady Elaine,*
*who has persevered through many chapters in my life.*

# The State of Washington

## Proclamation

**WHEREAS,** aviation history has been written again in Seattle with Tom Casey's successful around-the-world flight in a single-engine floatplane; and

**WHEREAS,** Washington state has a long history of famous aviation events, including the 1924 attempt by four Douglas Cruiser biplanes to fly around the world, which was successfully completed by two of the airplanes requiring landing on both water and land; and

**WHEREAS,** the Phillips 66-sponsored flight in the Liberty II has set a new world aviation record by being the first flight around the world while landing only on water; and

**WHEREAS,** the flight of the single-engine Liberty II covered more than 27,000 miles and required some 200 take-offs and landings on water, proving that general aviation's newest engine technology, using Cermicrome processed cylinders and Phillips 66 X/C Aviation Oil, can surpass the most rigorous flying tests; and

**WHEREAS,** this event stands as a tribute to man and flying machine;

**NOW, THEREFORE,** I, Booth Gardner, Governor of the State of Washington, do hereby proclaim Sunday, December 18, 1990, as

## Tom Casey and Liberty II Landing Day

in the State of Washington, and I urge all citizens to join me in welcoming Tom Casey home and congratulating him on his world aviation record.

Signed, this 14th day of December, 1990

Booth Gardner

Governor Booth Gardner

# CONTENTS

**"In almost 35 years in naval aviation, I never dreamt I would become part of an adventure like the one pilot Tom Casey led us on ...**

"The U.S. Navy was always there for him, but his journey had countless highs and lows. His plane was almost swamped in Iceland. The Saudis made him a hero and later gave him back surgery to continue his trip. He flew through Desert Shield and was almost destroyed by two typhoons. Off the Japanese coast, he almost got shot down by Russian MiGs and by this time had pissed off a whole lot of U.S. Ambassadors and various foreign government officials (such as biggies like Premier Gorbachev). He had engine trouble in the Orient, and later crashed in the Aleutians before being saved on a 'Top Secret' island. But then again, this great pilot became the first person to fly more than 29,000 miles around the world in a single-engine plane — landing only on water."

*Vice Admiral Richard Dunleavy*
*Deputy Chief of Naval Operations for*
*Air Warfare (Op-05)*

# One

# The Beginning

*as related by*

## Vice Admiral (Ret.) Donald Engen

A man approached me in my Washington, D.C. office, standing with his shoulders arched as if getting ready to make the first pitch of a World Series baseball game. He professed to be the world's greatest seaplane pilot (a notion reinforced by the numerous patches on his jacket).

I stammered a bit. My mind was focused on the events two years prior as this was the same day I left as head of the Federal Aviation Administration.

The gentleman in my office was walking in a hurried gait across the room and, in less than ten seconds, he boldly stood before my desk, leaned forward, and rested both palms on my desk. Most noticeable were his piercing eyes — they radiated confidence.

Hell, I thought to myself, I had commanded an aircraft carrier and later the Second Fleet and this man was cut from the same cloth as a naval aviator. I marveled at his stature. I was 6'4" and we seemed equal in height. I knew he never flew jets due to his height, but I liked his swagger. His cheeks were rosy red (either from sunburn or Jim Beam). His voice was raspy and carried emotions. He started out by introducing himself as one of the great pilots of all time.

He voiced to me that he planned on being as famous as Lindbergh, if given the chance. Today all he asked for was time enough to recount a story and ask for my help to make his dream a reality.

He recounted how an aviation landmark from 1924 was his primary focus. Bubbling with enthusiasm, he told me that a little over 65 years ago the first men to fly around the world took off flying in four Douglas World Cruisers. Nearly six months later, two of their aircraft completed the journey.

Finally, I interrupted the man and asked his name. He looked at me as if I already should have known. "Tom Casey," he answered. Without taking another breath, he continued. He explained that the Douglas pioneers had the entire U.S. Navy supporting them with navigation, communication, and spare engines. They used 30 Liberty engines on the entire trip of 26,345 miles in 176 days. Time in flight was 371 hours, eleven minutes, with an average speed of 70 miles per hour.

Reacting as though I already should have been reading his mind, he blurted out that he wanted to take the same journey — but only in one plane and with one engine. Most importantly, he would land only on water and his trip would take 60 days. He walked around to my side of the desk and spread out a large world map, explaining that he would be flying over mountains, oceans, deserts, glaciers, and icebergs; at the same time, he would be showing people that they can use a private aircraft to go across the country, even around the world, and do it safely and comfortably.

Now standing practically atop my desk, Casey had both his hands waving with excitement and asked if I truly understood the magnitude of the adventure he was planning to undertake. He added that he knew he could do it and it wouldn't end up like his previous try.

That last part stopped me dead in my tracks. "What try?" (Inwardly I wondered what kind of crazy person I had before me. His matter-of-fact, almost blasé tone imparted only one explanation: The dumb bastard had tried this round-the-world adventure once before. I could only imagine the end result was not a world record.)

Casey went on to explain that in the spring of 1989 he had attempted a west-to-east transglobal flight in his aircraft named Liberty

I, a Cessna 185 floatplane. The plane was named after the Liberty engines used in the 1924 adventure. Casey told me that after he had successfully flown 12,000 miles, a vicious gale and subsequent ramming of multiple boats into his aircraft in the Reykjavik, Iceland harbor led to his aircraft being capsized and destroyed.

By now he was slumping into my large leather chair (the one no one ever dared to sit in). His eyes seemed to well up with tears as he related that at that moment in time in Iceland he had lost everything in that venture. He assured me he would never again have an aircraft tied up in an open harbor where it can be exposed to damaging winds.

I was becoming irritated by his intimidating mannerisms. My only recourse was to ask the S.O.B. what the hell he wanted from me. At that point, I had no idea Casey was asking me to help him do this again. To wit, Casey humbly said he wanted another chance to redeem himself and show the world that he was not crazy. His last comment tugged at my aviation soul when he boasted he planned to be in the same record logs as Lindbergh and Earhart.

Yet, the more I listened, the more he had a convincing story. A naval aviator myself, I marveled at his strong emotions; his conviction. Now came the magic words: What could I do to help? Casey ramped up his emotions. First, he wanted my endorsement; and second, he needed a corporate sponsor. I told him I had an idea and would work on it.

Casey restated his goal. Liberty II's circumnavigation of the globe, an accomplishment never before achieved, would be a grueling endurance test for both the pilot and the plane's engine. Almost as if he were standing before the news media, Casey said his flight would encompass many of the human and mechanical stresses of the historic 1986 Rutan Voyager achievement. He estimated that Liberty II would log about the same number of hours as Voyager did, but the endurance flight would add to the stress due to the many planned takeoffs and landings on water.

The preliminaries aside, the journey was about to begin.

– **Vice Admiral (Ret.) Donald Engen**

# Two

# The Playbook

We could hardly keep our eyes open. Shaken out of bed, we had been told to urgently meet in the buffet. Almost the last to arrive, we could see this tall, handsome, and stately man motioning for us to join him.

Vice Admiral Donald Engen's arms were extended outwardly, but he had one finger to his lips as if to caution us to silence. We felt like we were being beckoned aboard Jules Verne's Nautilus submarine for some suspicious and covert adventure. We rapidly took our seats. It was not a second later that the admiral was pumping his arms in the air. He explained these overt gestures were similar to those that Casey had previously made when the two met several months earlier in D.C.

Who the hell was Tom Casey and what was all this about?

It was 6 a.m. on an October morning in 1989 in Atlanta during the annual convention of the National Business Aviation Association (NBAA), and we were meeting for breakfast. The die was about to be cast.

Next to me sat another aviation pioneer, Jack Hammond, head of the Aviation Fuels Division for Phillips 66. Both he and Engen had signed a mutual agreement pact the night before to hang their reputations on one of the boldest plans for making aviation history: Tom Casey's flight of Liberty II.

Also sitting at the table was Engen's assistant David Knight and Tom Geiger, a Phillips 66 business promotions expert. I was seated in a chair next to the food and Hammond.

My name is Bill Coleman, someone who has spent a professional lifetime in public relations and, along the way, aviation. Engen and
Hammond had decided I would be given the playbook for the Casey
flight. Thus, I would be handling one of the greatest aviation flights
of the 20th century.

What made this the adventure of a lifetime? There would
be water-only takeoffs and landings for an around-the-world record.
(Fast-forwarding to the 21st century: To take on such a project, due to
regional conflicts, would soon become impossible.) Casey had convinced Engen that he could complete this task in 60 days.

Continuing with our breakfast, Engen related, "After wreck-
ing his plane the first time, Casey told me he had a new plan." Casey
swore an oath — on his own life — that he and the Liberty II had all
the required flight clearances and entry/exit approvals from the various foreign governments where his aircraft would land, take off from,
fly through, or fly over. Casey was going to leave from Seattle (same as
the 1924 flight) but instead of going west to east like his first venture,
he planned to fly east to west, with the first leg targeting Alaska.
From there he was going to fly across the Aleutian Islands and then
through Russia, landing only on lakes and rivers until he reached the
Baltic States. Then, he would head back to Canada and the United
States to complete the record flight.

Raising my hand, I cautioned, "Gentlemen, let me clarify that
Russia is the Soviet Union, or U.S.S.R. Doesn't a Cold War still exist?"
No one said a word. It was as if I had tried to interrupt a mind-read-
er's séance and was unable to waken anyone.

Admiral Engen continued, explaining that the National Aeronautic Association (NAA), the U.S.-based world record sanctioning
body, was expected to recognize the flight as a new world record. This
same body had recognized Charles Lindbergh's crossing of the Atlantic Ocean as the record for the first person to cross that body of water
in an aircraft.

Normally very reserved, Engen was emotionally charged as
he explained that Casey had a fantastic, well-thought-out, and cost-
effective plan. The admiral was so sure that this was a viable program
for aviation that he had convinced Phillips 66's Hammond to supply

fuel (avgas), aviation oil, funds for landing fees, and a substantial living allowance for the journey — initially $25,000.

For the record, other support was to come from Pan Am and insurance provider Lloyd's of London. (As it later turned out, Pan Am's participation lasted only for a very short time and, in the end, the whole project would fall to Phillips 66 and me. What I didn't like was the fact that if it failed it was likely that I would be the fall guy.)

Hell, in the end various friends also would play critical roles. And, Dave Knight's close contacts with various foreign diplomats in D.C. would prove critical to making this trip happen. As it turned out, we actually had to gain the majority of approvals from every country Casey would fly into or over. So, besides the sponsors, we were forced to forge seemingly impossible relationships with an unlikely cast of characters who either treated us with undoubting support or tried in every way to kick us out of their country.

Some of the key players we would deal with included the U.S. Secretary of State and his staff; U.S. Ambassadors; the Crown Prince of Saudi Arabia plus his personal surgeon; the FAA; highly placed foreign government officials; and many high-ranking U.S. Navy Admirals, Air Force Generals, and Coast Guard Commanders, plus their staffs.

Along the way there would be other characters who would play central roles: Casey's sister Kathleen, who would be his savior later in the flight; Cindy Jones, Casey's personal assistant; and Pan Am Captain Dan Hood.

Hammond was my hero. Early on in our relationship I had learned that he had the undying soul of a true aviator and, through many years of working together, we had flown together all over the United States. Standing six feet tall with a stocky build, he was a true gentleman who also had a forceful personality. He was truly an energetic businessman who loved aviation. He had barnstorming features: ruddy complexion; piercing eyes; and mannerisms in the cockpit that seemed to mirror those of early aviators who made a living flying mail or doing aerobatics at air shows. Hammond had flown with the likes of Jimmy Doolittle and many other greats.

Meanwhile, back at the breakfast planning session, there were marketing and technical issues to address. Hammond felt that the flight would provide a perfect test for the performance limits of a new aircraft engine technology — all predicated on the performance of Phillips 66's aircraft engine oil. To ensure that the engine technology had the best chance to succeed, Hammond demanded that Casey take oil analysis readings at strategic points during the flight. Once a sample was taken, Casey would mail it back to Hammond at Phillips headquarters in Bartlesville, OK for analysis.

As we finished up our Atlanta meeting, Hammond now had his arm around me in a fatherly fashion. He walked with a steady and determined motion. His hands seemed to mirror his verbal expressions. "I'm looking forward to using Casey as a future marketing spokesperson if the flight makes it all the way around the world," he told me. "Casey could tell the world how great our company's oil performed, and we could take the bow for this even happening and then succeeding. And, I hope this son of a bitch is as great a pilot as Engen thinks he is.

"You are going to have to make sure you know where he is at all times. I don't care if you have to fly with him around the world. And if you lose him, you will have to go and find him. My reputation and the Phillips 66 name are in your hands."

As we walked toward our hotel rooms, Hammond grabbed me, saying, "We will have our asses hanging out on this one if it fails." Staring straight into my eyes, he added, "Make it work, Coleman."

With that, the door to his room slammed shut. I stood in the hallway in shock. What in the hell was I going to do? Who were my allies? To make matters worse, after leaving Hammond's room, Tom Geiger (who I reported to directly at Phillips 66) found me. His deep-throated voice abruptly broke my train of thought away from the previous Hammond conversation. Then he said, "I originally turned down Casey's request for any kind of support and I just want that fact to go on record. I even have the correspondence turning down Casey's request."

Oh good; my feeling of shock was being replaced by an eerie isolation.

Later, alone and sitting in my room, I remained somewhat bewildered by the morning's events. Today would be the very first time of many to come that I would ask the question: "Where the hell is Casey?"

In fact, he was back in Seattle teaching young kids how to fly. Casey was coming to New York in January, where I would meet with him. At this point it seemed clear as to what my duties were to be, central of which was promoting this epic flight. But, as I would later find out as this so-called adventure unfolded, more and more responsibilities as well as unfathomable hijinks lurked in the months ahead.

Later that afternoon, as we were leaving the Hyatt Regency in Atlanta, Geiger tried the same feigning tactic while Hammond and I were talking. Hammond's face turned bright red and his cheek muscles bulged, giving the appearance of getting ready to explode. "We're going to do it my way," he exclaimed. "Coleman has the conn and I am fully responsible financially." When I returned to my office in New York, we began to draw up plans for a number of special events for Casey. My team was given the task of promoting the flight. Hammond wanted a big send-off ceremony in Seattle. And, if Casey made it, Hammond said we needed an even bigger event "to welcome his ass back home."

# Three

# Tom Casey – Aviator, Dreamer

At the time of the NBAA Atlanta breakfast meeting, I had yet to meet Tom Casey. While our team in New York was making its initial attack on the PR campaign to come, Casey was on the West Coast working on the coordination details with Pan Am chief pilot Dan Hood.

Hood had originally sold Casey on the idea that Pan Am could help get Russian clearance for Casey to fly from Anchorage across Russia, landing on lakes and rivers. It turned out getting the clearances was not as clear-cut as advertised, as the following telephone discussion indicates.

"Hood, Tom Casey here. What the hell has Pan Am been doing? The Russian clearances – how long is it going to take for Pan Am to get them?

"I've laid my reputation on the line with the business folks as well as the Air Force Generals and Navy Admirals. You told me Russia was in the bag and not to worry."

The Pan Am aviator related that the process was indeed moving along, but there were still obstacles to overcome.

"What? I can't believe my ears," responded Casey. "Pan Am is actually offering to fly me to Moscow to meet with the Russian head of aviation? When?" Hood then told Casey to get his bags packed and that he should plan on being in Russia by the following Wednesday.

"The flight to Moscow was fantastic," Casey would later recall.

"Twelve Scotches and I finally got some shuteye. The Pan Am 747 aircraft seemed roomy. Ha! Well ... a little apples to oranges nowadays. The 2x4x2 configuration back in 1989 is sorta like what Premium Economy is on some carriers today."

Casey's flight took about ten hours. Upon leaving the airport, he was told to take a cab to the Department for Air Transport under the Transportation Ministry in a government building adjacent to the Kremlin.

"I remember entering a very stately building with large pillars," Casey said. "I can't remember if there was a hammer and sickle in the stone archway above the entrance.

"As I entered the buildings there were many photos of dignitaries hanging from one wall. I looked for a receptionist and was directed to the second floor. I recalled everything was painted battleship gray and on the walls was that funny writing. I looked for clues, like a name I was given.

"He was a very polite gentleman but I can't recall his name. He was head of aviation for the Soviet Union and we talked at great length about my proposed trip. He nodded a great deal and finally, after about five vodkas, we shook hands and his interpreter said I would be given approval to fly through Russia.

"The only requirement the Soviet government made to gain its approval was that I had to employ a Russian-speaking navigator who would accompany me in my plane across the Soviet Union. Also, I had to submit my flight plans at least three months prior to leaving.

"To me that sounded easy. I could hire a Russian navigator in Alaska and the flight plans could be drawn up with the help of Pan Am. I was excited. We parted his office with a firm handshake and two more shots of vodka. I now had full Russian approvals."

Casey went home the next day and reported his good fortune to Hood.

Now the whole plan made sense. During his return trip home, his mind pictured vividly the many steps he had taken for reenacting his dream. Initially, for his second attempt, Casey less than six months prior had stopped at Scott Air Force Base and met with General Duane Cassidy in August of 1989. Cassidy was then Commander in Chief of U.S. Transportation Command and Military Airlift Command at Scott.

Cassidy said he would also pursue ensuring Casey had approvals to fly through Russia. He promised that the Air Force would actually track Casey's mission around the world. That meant that with Pan Am's station chief working with the U.S.S.R.'s aviation authority, which also was offering communications links, and the U.S. Air Force actually monitoring every aspect of his trip, nothing could go wrong — at least for now.

He recalled his initial meeting with Admiral Engen. What a first-rate guy, he thought. He promised that the Navy would help if Casey needed it. He would later meet Engen's close friend, Vice Admiral Richard Dunleavy, who would become a major force in making this flight happen. Engen also helped in getting the National Oceanic and Atmospheric Administration to provide equipment for his flight.

Later, from the deck of his home near Seattle, staring out at the long walkway from his back deck to the water's edge, Casey seemed very alone. The ramp led to his seaplane tied down next to a wooden float.

"How did I get here?" he thought. "It was almost a lifetime ago that I was a lifeguard on the Wildwood, New Jersey shores. The biggest event then was the annual boat races. And I was a stud with all the girls. I wasn't alone then."

Casey was a New York City native, and grew up with his sister, father, and mother in Yonkers. After a stint in the Navy, he decided to make Seattle his home. He started his military service as a quartermaster and qualified as a signalman. He always wanted to fly but never qualified to become a naval aviator.

For the next 18 years, his hard work and perseverance earned him both private and instructor's certifications. He also was a master seaplane pilot that earned a healthy living giving lessons.

He always longed for adventure. Having read about the1924 Navy flight, he implored several friends to check his sanity. He asked them, why can't I break a record and fly around the world in a floatplane? Thus, the Liberty I flight concept was born and he spent one year getting funds ready for the trip.

Now, sitting on his deck, he was almost shocked back to reality by vivid unpleasant memories of how that dream ended in Iceland in early 1989 when Liberty I was ravaged by the storm.

Lost in thought, he quickly discovered that his house was littered with flight manuals, maps, and old newspapers. Dishes still remained in the sink and everywhere he looked there were scraps of paper that held notes of supposed importance.

He blamed this chaos on the immediacy of having to get his plane ready for the new Liberty II flight by early April. But what he continued to fixate on was the fact that he had to immediately leave for New York to meet with me and my associates in early January, now two weeks away.

Admiral Engen had told Casey that I was the best at my craft. I was to run the whole PR game and to be a direct contact for Casey, while also helping coordinate Phillips 66's support.

"Coleman is just another spoke in the wheel," he thought. Recognizing how much some guy in a New York office could actually do for the Liberty II flight – well, that was hard to comprehend.

Casey wanted worldwide news coverage, meaning exposure in every newspaper and media outlet in the countries in which he landed. "Until I meet the dude, my gut tells me that Coleman is only thinking about my launch and return events," Casey thought. "I am going to have to shake the trees and get his attention."

At this point, time just wasn't going fast enough for Casey. Meanwhile, his new aircraft floats were being completely refitted with new fuel storage tanks and the muscle engine was also being installed. But the meeting in New York came first.

# Four

# 'Hello' New York

Christmas in Bartlesville, OK is not necessarily my idea of having fun. But I had to meet with Hammond at Phillips 66 to finalize planning. The great adventure was about to begin. Casey would be on my doorstep in New York by mid-January.

That accomplished, time passed quickly once back in New York until "C-Day" arrived. Casey's arrival lived up to all the hype and candid depiction that Admiral Engen had detailed to me. When Casey entered our 45th Street offices, he burst through our eleven-foot-high double doors unannounced; flew past our receptionist; and finally came to a halt outside our conference room. He yelled out in a guttural tone, but in a very loud pitch, "Coleman! I want to meet Coleman."

The man I would meet would eventually become an aviation legend. His journey into history, which likely could not be accomplished today, would equally match the historic flights of Charles Lindbergh and Amelia Earhart.

Casey gave the appearance of Captain America, but without a shield. He brought along his faithful servant and supposed diva, Cindy Jones. She was a 5'1", very busty, controlling, dyed-blonde woman who often tried to take over the conversation and tell us how we should be marketing Casey.

He asked me a million questions. First and foremost: "Are you a pilot?" I said, "Yes."

I was 6'5" and we met at eye level. He had bushy brown hair and looked like a true Irishman after having drunk ten pints. His smile was infectious and his broad shoulders seemed to accentuate his strength of character. He looked like an aviation pioneer with his maps tucked under his armpit and holding an E-6B navigational computer in his right hand. His eyes were fiery and bent on making sure everyone was on his page.

"Have you heard of me?" he asked. Casey, 53, had received both his private and commercial certificates, and added seaplane, instrument, and instructor endorsements by the age of 26. He had logged more than 10,000 hours of flight time in 75 different aircraft. Extolling those numbers, he added, "I have more than 2,000 hours in seaplanes and 2,500 in multi-engine aircraft."

Laughing and whirling his arms in the air like a helicopter ready for takeoff, he added that he had taught physical education and air safety, promoted ski equipment, and spotted fish for Alaskan fishermen.

Jumping subjects, Casey asked me, "Will you be controlling all the arrangements of the inaugural takeoff from Seattle? I mean like the Governor attending and other special guests? How about catering and the media? I want all three TV networks, plus CNN. We need lots of military and perhaps the Russian ambassador. Can you do that?" He eyed me suspiciously.

"Yes to all the arrangements," I said. I told him my job was to promote the flight in the media and we would be inviting special guests. I related that we had spoken with NOAA and they said we could have the event on their Lake Washington ramp.

My staff joined us in the conference room. We explained that we would be sending news stories out to all the media as he flew around the world. Also, we needed to keep in touch with him (if at all possible) at every landing site during his trip. Casey said that getting in touch with me might be difficult while crossing Russia. He pointed out that the U.S. Air Force would be tracking his trip. I kind of wondered about the Air Force tracking him as the Soviets might not like that kind of intrusion.

He also said Pan Am would be able to keep in communication with him. He further informed us that his Pan Am buddy promised to provide worldwide navigation access. Casey would keep in touch with me through both sources. I also wondered if Pan Am had contacts in Siberia. Oh well, I thought, that was not my concern today.

My staff also used the time with Casey to gain background for our news stories. We acknowledged that we had a bare-bones plan and Casey and I needed to keep in touch over the next several months as it was expanded. We used the rest of the meeting to review his planned east-to-west record-making route.

I reminded Casey that he would be attempting to fly over the Soviet Union and not just Russia, per se. Here is where the info from Casey became a bit fuzzy. He had the trip to Alaska all mapped out. His Russian route was primarily the proposed fuel stops. But Casey was not sure that aviation fuel for piston aircraft was available at these stops. He had not yet confirmed this fact with the Russian government.

In fact, up to the day Casey left in May, we had continually tried to no avail to contact Captain Hood at Pan Am. The plan was that his airline was to be the frontline source of radio contact with Casey across Russia. In fact, Pan Am had all the known lines of communication in which to access and subsequently gain final approvals for Casey to fly in Russian airspace. Even Casey seemed a bit hazy on this matter.

In reviewing the U.S. Air Force's support, Casey explained that his mentor, General Cassidy, had retired on September 3, 1989; his new support contact was now Colonel Jim Sills at Scott Air Force Base.

Looking back on the day's events, I couldn't come to any conclusions. My thoughts ran wild. Here is a guy who comes into my office and says he wants to be the first-ever blah, blah, blah. I committed to him we would help pay for the installation of his engine replacement and some other items. I would have a bank account set up for him and wire him money all over the world.

Over the next several months, I began to see a pattern I would experience during this whole trip. Casey at times would just disappear, like when getting his plane retrofitted with floats and a new engine. He was often vague and always said, "I will answer that later." These actions only led to my favorite refrain, one which those around me would frequently hear me crying in frustration: *Where the hell is Casey?*

# Five

# The Plane

In April 1990, Casey planned to arrive at Wipaire, Inc., a company that specializes in floatplanes, in St. Paul, Minnesota, where he would pick up his retrofitted aircraft. "I needed a new plane with a larger engine and floats," Casey explained. "I turned to an old friend, Ben Wiplinger, at Wipaire in Minnesota. This company was world famous for its floats.

'Wip and I bartered and he accepted my offer to provide him my insurance check of $125,000 from the Liberty I accident in Iceland. In exchange, I would get a larger Cessna 206 Stationaire model.

"I also had Wip install a newly designed 4000 float system, plus my new 300-horsepower Teledyne Continental IO-550 robust aircraft engine. Continental Motors donated the engine and other upgrades to the aircraft. Putting this new high technology coating on my cylinders took the most time. Modifying the aircraft left me broke and cost about $150,000." (To offset his empty pockets, Phillips 66 gave him money to help retrofit the plane.)

"Once I circled the globe, the money I would get from selling my plane to the Smithsonian would pay off all my debt and leave me well off," he surmised.

The engine's piston cylinders received a new coating designed to improve lubrication qualities. Engine Components' Cermicrome process impregnates the piston cylinders with microscopic bits of silicon carbide. The result is an extremely hard surface combining the long-wear characteristics of chrome and the low oil consumption of steel, as oil easily forms a film on the piston walls. Originally, Casey's IO-550 used about one liter of oil every four to six hours. With Cermichrome, the engine was expected to use only about one quart every 12 hours.

The retrofitted airplane, a 1977 Cessna, should not be confused with a seaplane like the size of the Yankee Clipper or a PBY of World War II fame. (That would become evident once the journey ensued, when many of the countries involved were completely surprised at the size of the aircraft.)

This was an aircraft of some 28 feet in length with a 39-foot wing span, and interior dimensions of some ten feet in length, four feet in height, and four feet in width. With the addition of floats, Liberty II was capable of remaining buoyant while supporting a weight of 4,000 pounds per float, or a total of slightly more than double the aircraft's maximum weight.

Total usable fuel load for Liberty II was 236 gallons (a 12-hour range). The main (long-range) fuel tank in the wings contained 90 gallons and the wing-tip tanks another 30 gallons. And 116 gallons were carried in special foam-filled fuel bladders located in the float compartments — fuel which can be transferred to the main tank with an electric fuel pump or by a vacuum hand pump.

Navigation equipment installed in Liberty II included: dual NAV/COMs, ADF, DME, autopilot, glideslope, and a high-frequency radio that can furnish communication to military and commercial channels. Other aids included Loran, Trimble Global Positioning System equipment, and a unique moving map display which was programmed to electronically indicate both intended and alternate routes.

Other modifications made to the aircraft included a three-blade McCauley power propeller and the addition of a right-hand co-pilot door (which would later prove to be a lifesaver).

The plan was coming together. "My plane has all the necessary tools to make this journey a success," Casey would say at the time. "Can it meet the conditions I will encounter?"

What could he expect? After all, he was just landing and taking off on water. Most crucial, however, was the latter. Water takeoffs often require a long taxi time while the plane continues to cross the waterway, in order to build up speed for a stepped, full-throttle take-off climb. Casey would make sure his new replacement engine offered the extra power boost he knew he would need in many areas of the world.

*Casey with Liberty II, marked with his sponsor's logo.*

# Six

# Getting Ready for Launch Day

The New York staff diligently began preparing all the press kit materials along with making arrangements for the May launch on Lake Washington. Additionally, newspaper, TV, and radio outlets as well as many dignitaries needed to be locked in for the May 20 event.

George Bukota, our company's vice president in the Seattle office, was to make contact with the governor. He wanted Washington State's Governor Booth Gardner to proclaim the launch date "Tom Casey Day."

My job was to coordinate all launch day events plus interface with the Washington, D.C. crowd. That meant really getting to know Admiral Engen and his assistant, David Knight.

Admiral Engen was a most gracious host. Knight stood 6'2" and was a GQ dresser who was polite but reserved. He had a deep radio voice and came across as a real Washington insider. We spent many dinners over a three-month period, strategizing about how Casey was actually going to get through Russia — in reality the Soviet Union.

Knight opened the right doors to enable us to bring the Washington Governor on board, plus fashioned many introductions with key U.S. officials and other foreign dignitaries. He seemed to know everyone, all the way up to the President. His wife Margo worked for the Smithsonian and was brilliant. I learned firsthand how much she knew about history and politics. How I admired her for all her accomplishments.

Time seemed to be racing. In mid-April, I briefed Phillip 66's Hammond in Bartlesville on the progress to date. Hammond was to be the keynote speaker at Casey's launch, meaning we had to write his speech and hold his hand.

April 20 was now upon us and Casey was on his way to St. Paul to pick up his aircraft. He flew commercial to MSP.

About halfway to St. Paul, the drone of the airliner's jet engines hypnotically narrowed Casey's brain waves, allowing him to mentally review the world record flight plans he had just submitted to the Soviets. He had also hired a Russian-speaking navigator in Anchorage.

The overall flight plan had Liberty II leaving Seattle on May 20, traveling up the Pacific coast to Alaska, and then journeying across the Bering Strait to Russia. The flight would cross the entire 6,000-mile width of the U.S.S.R., to Moscow and Leningrad — landing on 19 lakes and rivers to refuel, then through Scandinavia and Europe on the way to London.

From the British Isles, Liberty II would fly north to Iceland and on to Greenland before reaching North America. Re-entering the U.S. in Maine, the flight would tour the East and South, then up the California coast, finally completing the journey at Seattle, one day prior to the opening of the Goodwill Games on July 21, 1990.

Liberty II would land at more than 80 locations in 21 countries. "My God," Casey thought, "the whole world will know about me. Think of the message I can tell the kids about aviation."

Once reaching Wipaire in St. Paul, Casey watched as his plane came to life. In less than three weeks his floats had been installed and his finely tuned engine was bolted into place. Now came his meticulous inspection of his revitalized aircraft. This took several days and many questions. At last satisfied, he signed off and took possession. He was now set to go back to Seattle.

Right when I desperately wanted to know where Casey was, he called me from St. Paul and said he would be arriving on May 10 at the Seaplane Ramp at Renton Airport. This was at the tip of Lake Washington.

Casey loaded his craft half-full with fuel and left St. Paul. No more than two hours later, he made a deliberate landing and set down on a river in Bismarck, ND to take on a full load of fuel. Why? He wanted to know the time and distance to successfully take off with a full fuel load.

"I couldn't do that in St. Paul as there was too much traffic on the river," he explained. "There was far less traffic here. I steadied myself in my seat and applied full power." Liberty II gracefully gained speed as it skimmed down the river. It took no more than five miles for his aircraft to lift off and gain altitude.

The techniques and skills required to fly a seaplane on and off the water has a way of emphasizing basic airmanship. Floatplane flying is often called "stick and rudder" or "seat of the pants" flying.

Casey reminded himself that his engine only had 2-1/2 hours of actual flight time when he made it to Bismarck. However, upon his arrival in Seattle, he would have logged more than 1,300 miles and his new engine would be fully broken in.

Also, since he had taken on a full load of fuel in Bismarck, Casey could now verify the range of the aircraft. Upon landing in Seattle, he still had a full load of fuel in both floats; that meant he could safely stay aloft for more than 2,000 miles, depending on headwinds.

Meanwhile, there was no more waiting on my end. I hopped a flight on May 7 to Seattle and would meet the next day with our VP Bukota to review the plans for the press event. At about midnight on the night before Casey was to arrive, my phone must have rung 20 times before waking me. "This is Cindy. Are you awake? " I said no and hung up. She called again and began rambling. "Let's map out all the flight's particulars," she said.

This wasn't the first time Cindy had assumed the Royal Majesty stature. In my New York office, while Casey was in St. Paul, Cindy had stopped by to go through all the details. More or less she was making demands. We quickly came to an understanding. It was my way or the highway. I told her to f— herself and slammed the phone down.

When I saw her the next day she was pissed and didn't speak to me as we waited on the dock for most of the day for Casey's arrival. The three of us (Cindy, our photographer Jim Collison, plus me) all waited for Casey. By 3 p.m. we heard his engine roar in the distance.

Liberty II shot out of the clouds like a celestial vision. Central casting would have been elated. Collison got some great shots.

The landing on Lake Washington played into an already preconceived picture I had of Casey. Soon the rest of the world would begin to share the same image of a heroic pilot, especially when they first saw his red, white, and blue aircraft land on a body of water.

Sailing — and I mean sailing — the powerless plane now glided toward the dock. Casey's speed foretold a crash. In the last split second, it seemed, his tail rudder swayed hard right and his sideways craft just slowly nestled up to the dock.

Smiling, he opened the left-hand cabin door and exited the plane. Standing with one foot resting on the float pressed up against the dock, Casey began a soliloquy on the virtues of seaplane flying.

"While the concepts are generally the same as wheeled flying, I found the mindset to be completely different. Land and take off into the wind, of course, but now there was no windsock to guide me and no runway to constrain me. Fly over the water and there is always a runway beneath me. It provides ultimate freedom and the only way to fly," he said.

My job was to place Phillips 66 sponsor decals on his plane and art-direct action photos (airplane taking off, landing, in-air, refueling, and portraits of Casey). These photos were needed for the media kit for the May 20 launch. Right after taking the photos, I would have to return to New York, process film, and select the photos I wanted to use.

Once I left the next day, Bukota was in charge. He went on an adventure and took a test ride. As Bukota would later recall, "The takeoff was really smooth and breathtaking, but once airborne and gaining altitude, we started getting oil sprayed across the windscreen. Oil was gushing out of the top of the left-hand side of the cowling (engine cover) and that made me really nervous.

"Casey was trying to take a matter-of-fact attitude but I could see real concern in his eyes. We circled back and landed on the lake. The whole top of the aircraft, including the wings, was covered in oil."

Casey immediately pulled the engine cover off and in a loud Hulk-like roar said (without taking any blame), "Goddamn, that motherfucking stupid oil cap had not been screwed on properly when someone checked the oil."

Bukota reminded Casey that we had taken photos of him pretending to fill oil in his engine the day before. He had the oil cap off for the photo and must not have tightened it when he replaced it. Pissed off, he told Bukota to mind his own business. "You don't know anything about piston aircraft, so shut your fuckin' mouth," Casey said.

We knew then that Casey could swear the tattoos off any Hells Angel's arm. This same bilious trait would follow him all over the world – in the coming months we would hear about Casey's temper from ambassadors, princes, and many foreign countries' military personnel.

Arriving back in Seattle with completed press kits, I found Casey was practicing. So in the next several days, Bukota and I visited with the media, made arrangements with the people catering the event, and wrote speeches.

And, we visited with The National Oceanic and Atmospheric Administration (NOAA). Their folks provided Liberty II with a multinational search and rescue device. Once activated by an airman in distress, this international device uses a series of satellites and ground stations to send distress signals. (This satellite positioning system would later be Casey's savior in the Aleutian waters).

In related news, Governor Gardner was now on board and a proclamation was being drafted officially honoring Tom Casey on May 20.

# Seven

# One Day and Counting

Jack Hammond was now in Seattle. We went over all the details of the next day's events. He asked about his speech. As he read it out loud, he asked about the beginning quote and particulars about its author, who was a 20th Century writer, famous for *Jonathan Livingston Seagull*. We felt his quote on aviation really signified the course ahead for our hero pilot.

> *"He moves not through distance, but through the*
> *ranges of satisfaction that comes from hauling himself*
> *up into the air with complete and utter control; from*
> *knowing himself and knowing his airplane so well that*
> *he can come somewhere close to touching, in his own spe-*
> *cial and solitary way, that thing that is called perfection."*
> — **Richard Bach,** *A Gift of Wings*

The time had come for Hammond to meet Casey for the first time and see the plane. We all met at the seaplane slip in Renton. Casey and Hammond seemed to really like each other. Casey asked Jack if he might want to take a ride in Liberty II. Hammond, an excellent pilot in his own right, agreed wholeheartedly.

In short order they were bouncing along the lake and as Hammond later told it: "Casey pulled the stick back and we seemed to glide from the water into the air. We got up about 2,000 feet and I immediately heard this crackling sound. It turned out to be my chair busting loose from the floor braces, which then sent my chair flying backwards to the aft of the aircraft.

"Casey took no notice of my predicament, as he was on the radio at that time speaking to Seattle control. As I fell backwards, my headset was yanked from the console and I now laid up against the aft bulkhead trying to use every muscle I had to right myself. Only problem was, I was strapped in by the seat restraints. It must have been at least ten minutes before Casey saw me and yelled out."

"Hey Jack, you need to sit up," he said.

Hammond replied, "You dumb son of a bitch, help me and get this fucking plane on the ground before I kill you!"

As the aircraft turned base, Casey seemed to flip the aircraft on its side. He spun the aircraft around, which aided in a quick return to the seaplane dock. But this maneuver had its consequences, too. Hammond's chair rolled with the turn and he ended up almost face down. Casey, now looking over his shoulder at Jack in a prone position, simply asked if there was a problem. Hammond used his right hand to partially right himself.

Now stunned by Casey's unobservant attitude, Hammond could only recall that all Casey wanted to elaborate on was the dangerous nature of water landings. "I couldn't believe he had the balls. Here I was, pinned against the back of the plane, and he was still talking like nothing was wrong," said Hammond.

"The challenge of water landings," Casey yelled to Hammond over the roar of the engine, "are glassy water landings like today. A lack of depth perception, combined with the failure to set the airplane in the correct attitude, can be deadly. It is an instance in which the pilot must follow procedures. This holds true for our landing today."

Hammond crossed his arms and recoiled as if to appear in the fetal position. He remembered an old aviation truism: "Just experience the moment."

Once safely landed, the plane headed dockside. Casey pulled Hammond's chair upright and then helped him from the plane.

Hammond shouted, "Tom, we are putting up a lot of money on this venture and you try and kill your biggest benefactor. Are you going to make this trip or fuck it up like almost killing me in your faulty seat?"

Casey, putting his hands on either cheek of his face, kept turning it from side to side. He apologized to Hammond.

Later, on our last afternoon together before the big launch day, we all sat having a few beers. Almost out of nowhere, Hammond stared directly at Casey and asked him about his supposed Russian clearances.

"Well, we haven't yet got formal confirmation on clearances from the Russians." Casey said. "When I left the Soviet Union, he (the aviation minister) told me everything was approved."

Hammond bristled and uncomfortably asked Casey how he could have told the whole world that he expected to have the Russians approve his flight plan by the time he left Seattle on May 20.

"Unfortunately," said Casey, "at present, the Russians have nixed me flying my original planned northern route. Why? I was never completely told, but the little information I was privy to was received by Admiral Engen from the AOPA (Aircraft Owners & Pilots Association) group in Russia."

Casey added that the Russians were concerned about the lack of security if he were to fly the northern route. Also, the Russians were unsure about having an adequate supply of avgas.

Interrupting both Hammond and Casey, I explained to everyone that Knight was in continual contact with the Soviet contingent as well as the Russian AOPA group, and in fact his efforts may have saved the day.

Why was Knight's effort important? When Casey sent over his flight plans to the U.S.S.R., it seems that the aviation minister got cold feet. All that was relayed to the Russian AOPA group was, "Nix on the northern route and tell him he has to go south." Without contact with Knight, Casey wouldn't have been able to even consider flying the southern route through Russia.

"So now I am waiting for approval to fly a southern leg," Casey explained. "For this leg, the Russians are still concerned about avgas supply. They have my new flight plans. Additionally, they have received messages through the FAA explaining that my engine can also take marine gas, if avgas is not available. I just don't know why the delay in final approval.

"I will leave Seattle tomorrow and fly to Alaska. There, I will wait for Russian approval. I have my ace in the hole and that is Pan Am's connections with Aeroflot. That should pressure the Russians to let me through."

Hammond took a deep breath and said, "Let's hope tomorrow goes better than today, but I really wish you (Casey) had mentioned this about no Russian clearance before you were ready to leave. Damn, I hope I don't have to tell my management that you fucked up. Casey, I would send Coleman to Alaska with you, but I would be afraid he would never come back. Get your fuckin' act together."

Hammond and I stayed up late that night talking about what might happen if Casey didn't get approvals. We had many "worst-Casey" scenarios. Hammond asked me to provide my candid opinion. My crystal ball opinion was that Casey would hide out in Alaska and no Russia clearance would ever come.

"Jack, we are dealing with the U.S.S.R.," I said. "Disillusioned as I may sound, for the sake of clarity, we are still in a Cold War with them. I just can't place my trust in some Soviet bureaucrat giving approval."

Hammond just shook his head. He wondered how long I thought Casey might wait in Alaska for Russian clearance. My opinion forecasted the waiting period could last as long as two months. During that period, the media would be inquiring where he was.

I added, "Let's hope some enterprising journalist doesn't blow his cover and file a story saying Casey is dead in the water in Alaska and the Russkies are telling him to go home. Then, when the shit hits the fan, we'll have a would-be embarrassed pilot with no place to go. Oh, and our name (Phillips 66) is bill-boarded on the side of his plane.

"Jack, remember that all that time wasted in Alaska we will have been paying for his lodging and meals. At this juncture, I am forecasting Casey will reevaluate his options and then explain about his new plan to make this journey from east to west and reentering the U.S. at Nome, Alaska by leaving from the top of Japan and flying up the coast of the Soviet Union."

Hammond stammered, "For God's sake, Coleman, that change of plans may mean that Phillips 66 will become the primary sponsor." From my perspective, if my crystal ball vision came true, the die was cast. I would be looked upon as the fall guy for Casey's change of plans. The adage 'kill the messenger' would apply. My only grace was that if Casey had to reverse course, he was the best pilot I had ever known.

# Eight

# Casey's Launch to Alaska: 1,460 miles

**Original Day 1.** We rose by 0600 and went to NOAA's seaport ramp on Lake Washington where all the seating had been arranged. Chairs, podium, and catering were now being set up. We were at the historic World War II seaplane training facility and operational base for the Pacific Northwest.

NOAA was now the tenant and we had been given permission to hold the ceremony there. The day was a beautiful sky blue with a perfect breeze from the west.

Turns out, Casey would have the perfect day. He was supposed to be there by 0700, but his plane was nowhere in sight. I went into the NOAA office and tried to reach his plane by radio. Nothing but static. Where the hell is Casey?

We were expecting more than 25 news organizations — all three major TV networks, CNN, plus radio and reporters from six newspapers and wire services from around the world.

By 0930, the press and over 100 guests were all seated. The governor's representative was there ready to proclaim "Tom Casey Day." We had anticipated beginning the conference at that time, but there was still no Casey.

Again: Where's Casey?

At about 1000 we heard this distant sound of a plane coming across the lake and in the next several minutes we saw a red, white, and blue aircraft heading towards us at about 1,000 feet above Lake

Washington. Liberty II swooped majestically over the guests and then wing-waved a salute. Media cameras and TV video captured the moment.

Only two hours earlier, Casey had taken off from Lake Union. At 3,000 feet and climbing to 6,000, the sun appeared as large as an oval silver dollar. His plan: "I will follow that sun to the press briefing."

As if there were a movie director orchestrating the entire chain of events, Casey's plane floated gently until settling on the lake's water and then the craft skimmed the surface towards a landing at the seaplane dock. Friends of Casey moored his floatplane.

As if following a cue from a film director, a giant of a man dislodged himself from the specially built right-hand door that was under the overhead wing of the aircraft. He was dressed in a blue aviator jacket with red and white trim. He wore his Phillips 66 cap with grand distinction. He so looked the part of an adventurer ready to conquer new heights.

Of course, the media ran to the plane and tried to interview Casey. I forcibly pushed through the cameramen and reporters and escorted Casey to the podium. Without hesitation, he grabbed the microphone from my hand and immediately began to speak.

I originally had Hammond scheduled first to speak (Casey knew that) — but not now. Casey told the invited guests and media that he had been up north visiting friends while also doing some tests on the engine. TV cameras were whirling and reporters were milling to get close. "Casey", someone yelled, "tell us how you feel."

"им с нетерпением жду, чтобы сделать много русских друзейus," was his response. (In Russian, that means, "I'm looking to making many new Russian friends.")

Casey was smiling but stunned for a second when one reporter asked him why was he so late. He stood silent, thinking of a response. His mind racing, jumbled thoughts came to him: "No Russian clearance yet. Me, the laughing stock of aviation. Kids — what will they think of me? I've spoken in more than 50 schools to over 10,000 kids. Oh, what will I do if I fail them?"

Pulling himself away from these innermost thoughts, Casey could only laugh at the circumstances. "I was with friends all night."

His response sounded like an alibi on a detective TV show.

Casey never followed the prepared speech. He just wanted to thank all the guests and media for coming. "Sixty days from now I will be back," he said. Then, Casey echoed the words out loud to the media and guests. Everyone clapped.

"This never-before aviation event has been planned for several years. I really want to give my thanks to all the companies, organizations, and individuals which made this flight possible. I want to personally thank Admiral Engen of the AOPA Air Safety Foundation for making this happen.

"And, a special thanks and applause to our major sponsor, the Phillips 66 Company. They are furnishing the aviation oil, all over the world; supplies of fuel; and financial backing. Let me introduce the man who made this possible, Jack Hammond, Phillips 66's head of aviation."

Casey forgot who else he wanted to thank, like Lloyd's of London and NOAA. But what I loved most was seeing Cindy hanging on the arm of Pan Am's Captain Dan Hood.

Hammond talked about the arduous trip and about being the chief sponsor. He then read the State of Washington's Proclamation in which Governor Gardner stated that today was "The Liberty II Flight Day."

The proclamation pointed out that May 20 was the 63rd anniversary of Charles Lindbergh's historic trans-Atlantic flight. Also, Washington State was the launch site for the 1924 historic event that was attempted by four Douglas Cruiser biplanes — to fly around the world — which was successfully completed by two of the airplanes, making both land and water landings, in 176 days.

**10:45 a.m.** Casey had reboarded the aircraft. The media stood three thick at his aircraft and continued to ask their questions. With his body halfway into the aircraft and his left leg straddling the right seat inside the cockpit, Casey looked anxious to leave.

Several editors asked Casey when he was leaving Alaska for Russia. And, will the Russian navigator join him in Alaska, as it said in the news releases? Casey answered neither question and only kept waving, almost imitating President Reagan when he would exit the Air Force helicopter and walk to the White House.

Pulling the rest of his body into the aircraft, Casey poked his head out towards the media and in a forceful tone said, "I hope the Russian navigator can understand this Irishman."

Asked by the NBC reporter if he was nervous, Casey said, "The first takeoff will cure everything."

Nervous as hell, he started to taxi away from his mooring. Oops, big mistake. He forgot to lower the small aft rudders on each float, which actually were the steering mechanisms for the aircraft, so that it can maneuver like a boat on the water.

What happened next was recorded by every TV news agency's film crew. Strong 40 mph wind gusts blew the rudderless Liberty II against the rocks near the NOAA dock as almost everyone shouted helplessly over the roar of his engine: "Oh my God, lower your rudders," he said to himself.

Associated Press writer Tim Klass, who was covering the event, later wrote:

> "*Leaving the dock on Lake Washington, pilot Tom Casey nearly damaged a pontoon because of a fouled rudder line that caused the one-engine plane to run towards the seawall.*
>
> "*Casey turned off the engine quickly, and the plane gently bumped into the rocks. After a moment to free the line, he restarted the engine and was airborne shortly before 11 a.m. PDT.*"

Hammond glared at me and grabbed the lapels of my business suit. "That dumb asshole doesn't know how to fly, and we are sponsoring him. What have we got ourselves into?" I just shrugged and looked for a place to hide.

There was no damage to the aircraft and Liberty II was soon airborne, swooping back over the former U.S. Navy seaplane base with a wave of the wings in salute.

Later, after lunch, Hammond and I both went back to our rooms for an early night. Each of us turned on the TV. Every Seattle channel led off the news hour with Casey. The commentators were all the same:

*"Local resident Tom Casey took off from Lake Washington today in an attempt to be the first person ever to fly around the world in a single-engine floatplane, landing only on water.*

*"For Casey, he had a bit of a rough start today as his aircraft crashed into the seawall at NOAA's seaport* (TV film footage showed the incident). *We wish him well and hope he doesn't crash into anything else. We'll be covering his trip around the world, so stay tuned."*

This abridged news report was the same everywhere. And, Headline News, NBC, CBS, and ABC nightly news all had it playing at different times during their nightly newscasts, plus throughout the night, or so it seemed.

Hammond called me about midnight. Neither one of us could sleep, just listening to the news. "Well, I guess everyone in Bartlesville has seen this news story," Hammond said. "Maybe I will just stay out here on the West Coast for awhile. Right now I don't know when I am going home. No calls from management yet tonight, but there will be tomorrow." Hammond never bothered to say goodnight.

# Pilot takes off to circle globe with a twist

Tom Casey gets a farewell hug and kiss from family friend Lorri Hochhaus before setting out to circumnavigate the globe.

P-I News Services

An Everett pilot took off from Seattle yesterday in a single-engine plane equipped with floats in an attempt to become the first person to fly around the globe landing only on water.

The flight by 53-year-old former Alaska bush pilot Tom Casey began 63 years to the day that Charles Lindbergh set off on his historic solo flight across the Atlantic.

Casey's Cessna 206 floatplane, the "Liberty II," took off from Lake Washington for a 26,000-mile journey expected to take 60 days.

He is scheduled to complete his trip in time for the July 21 opening ceremonies of the Goodwill Games in Seattle.

"It's never been done before," Casey said. "I'm going to be flying over mountains, oceans, deserts, glaciers and icebergs. No one has ever flown around the world in a floatplane before."

Casey planned to pilot his red, white and blue plane over Alaska, the Soviet Union and Europe, touching down on the Moscow River in the Soviet Union, the Seine in France and other major waterways.

However, last-minute negotiations with the Soviet Union may force him alter his route across that country, he told reporters just before cranking up his engine and heading for Alaska.

"I'm 95 percent sure I'll fly over the Soviet Union. I'm just waiting for a navigator," he said.

Casey, who has logged more than 10,000 hours of flight time, will make most of the trip alone but would be required to carry a navigator across the Soviet Union.

"I've always been a sports fan. If there's any good will to be created any place in the world, it's going to be created by sports," Casey said. "To me flying is sport. I'm hoping I'll set the first world record at the Goodwill Games."

Casey's planned route is roughly the same as one taken by the first aircraft to circumnavigate the globe in 1924. However, that flight began with four planes that used floats over water and switched to wheeled landing gear over land. Only two of the aircraft completed that trip.

He expects to make 80 takeoffs and landings on oceans, lakes and rivers.

Casey said he had sunk everything he owns and has borrowed $40,000 more to make the attempt. He estimated total costs at more than $500,000. Sponsors also have contributed to the flight.

Casey's Cessna U206-G Stationaire II was modified with tougher floats and a more powerful engine and propeller.

"The security is my biggest concern. I'm not leaving this plane alone, I'll tell you that," he said. "I'll sleep in it if I have to."

This is not Casey's first bid to set the record. A west-to-east attempt last year ended midway when Liberty I overturned in a windstorm while parked in Reykjavik, Iceland.

"They said it was wind, but I think it was hit by a sailboat," he said. "There was a big hole in the front of the wing."

*Nine*

# The Soviet Dilemma

As he headed for Alaska, clearance through Southern Russia remained an unresolved issue. Knight had been seeking clearance for Casey through an array of channels since the fall of 1989. Knight was the consummate politician, much smoother than me, displaying this asset many times in dealing with ambassadors and other top echelon U.S. Defense and State Department officials.

From the beginning of Casey's adventure, Knight had written formal letters inquiring about Casey's Russian passage. Those higher echelons included the Association for Flight Safety – U.S.S.R.; Aeroflot's managing director; and the Soviet Union's Chairman of International Affairs. He also called and spoke with many lower-level Russian officials and continually discussed how this flight would foster future good relations between the two great countries.

In fact, while Casey waited for Russia clearance, politicians in Washington D.C. were honoring Soviet Premier Mikhail Sergeyevich Gorbachev in strategic talks at a summit with President George H. W. Bush. At that time, forward-thinking Knight even tried to leverage Casey's ardent desire to accomplish this world record feat by speaking with several officials in Gorbachev's party.

To that end, Knight got several shrugs of Soviet shoulders and Knight swears that no one ever actually briefed Gorbachev about Casey. Knight reminded Casey that the Soviet leader was under a tremendous amount of pressure from his own party to take drastic measures that would tighten the noose around democratic freedom demonstrators.

At the time, with Yeltsin shouting "down with Communism" and freedom marchers pursuing changes in other former Soviet-bloc countries, life for Gorbachev was unbearable.

From conversations that Admiral Engen also had with associates, he learned that the Premier would have liked to have stayed in the U.S. The Soviet Union had just ended the nine-year war in Afghanistan in which Gorbachev had taken a major role in ending this bleak chapter in Russian history.

And, after all, why would a great leader like him, with so many political setbacks facing him head on, want or care to know about a U.S. pilot wanting to fly across Russia?

Also, Knight could only imagine that Gorbachev wanted no part of an American flyer entering his history books by flying through Russia. Knight recalled that most of the Russian diplomats he spoke with were always very cordial, but never once wanted to make a commitment.

On May 20, Knight had been alerted, late in the day, by Aeroflot officials that Casey's flight to Russia may not get approved. Casey left Seattle knowing that Aeroflot as well as the Russian politburo were on the fence about the flight through the Southern route. In fact, the only hope Casey might have had in gaining approval now rested with the U.S. government.

On May 21, the Russians had demanded that Casey go through the U.S. Federal Aviation Administration (FAA) to seek clearance. Valery Shelkovnikov, chairman, Association for the Flight Safety Foundation – U.S.S.R., communicated in a telegram to Knight: "Thomas P. Casey (standing by in Anchorage, Alaska) has received word today through Aeroflot that permission for the flight of Liberty II through the U.S.S.R. has been denied due to technical difficulties. The only prequalification would be gained through the FAA."

The die was cast. Knight had to seek approval to fly through Russia by imploring the FAA to request flight clearance by way of Russian officials. Knight called me and said, "We had a better chance of building 100 Phillips 66 gas stations in Russia than getting the FAA to obtain clearance for Casey."

Even Pan Am, with all of its (so-called) relations in Russia, was not making any headway with Aeroflot or Russian aviation officials. This was the first of many times (when we really needed Pan Am's support) in which they let us down.

By the first week of June, while waiting for the Russians to change their mind, the trip across the Soviet Union was dead. Casey had been wasting time and money. His aircraft had been pulled from the water and now reality had slapped him hard.

While sitting in a local pub, friends of his came in with a newspaper that featured a damaging front page story about him and his journey. The *Alaska Flyer* reporter, Kent Lee Woodman, ripped Casey's world record attempt as a farce and said Casey was dreaming if he thought the Russians would give him permission to fly across their country.

The most damaging fact within the story was that the writer claimed Casey was ill prepared for this journey. Woodman, a member of the Alaska Airmen's Association, had just flown over the lakes and rivers Casey hoped to land on. They were all frozen. "How could one possibly plan such a trip without firsthand knowledge of the fuel problems, landing sites, language barriers, and the like?"

The reporter went on to say that Casey could never find fuel or food or lodging in some of the backwater lakes and rivers he proposed on his flight plan. And, he said that Casey's plane lacked the range to attempt this journey. Casey's response: "Liberty II has a non-stop range of 2,000 miles and I planned this trip in Russia to meet any emergency."

Woodman also quoted unnamed sources within the Russian delegation who were visiting Anchorage at the very same time Casey was in Anchorage. The Soviets, looking to open commercial traffic between Alaska and Vladivostok, explained to the reporter that they had too many other important issues to solve than taking on the responsibility for a stupid American pilot seeking fame and fortune. The reporter basically told Casey to go home.

Now Casey had to rethink his game plan and he needed a new direction. Casey called me and first complained loudly about the Woodman story. I had to agree with him. He now felt the Russians had abandoned him but wanted to wait a week or so to find out if the FAA could intercede.

"Every day I got up and tried to call my Russian contact," Casey related. "Failing that, I tried the FAA and then lastly Knight in D.C. I had run out of money and my friends said it was time for me to face reality. I needed a new plan."

He called me on June 12. When asked what his plans were, he responded with an impressive air of confidence. "I'm planning now to fly west to east," he said. "I have been in Alaska since May 2 and for the past 20 days the floats have been out of the water.

"I have been working with my Air Force friends at Elmendorf Air Force Base and we mapped out a plan that will take me around the world in 40 days. I've stopped praying and pacing and I won't give up. See ya soon. I'm leaving tomorrow."

Hammond was told immediately about Casey's revised plan. It now looked as if Phillips 66 was on the hook to support most of this flight. "Phillips 66 had a contract with him for $25,000 and, the way it looks now, we may end up spending more than $150,000 to support his flight in the opposite direction," Hammond said.

A bank account was set up at a New York City bank and I made an initial deposit of $20,000 from which Casey could withdraw.

I called Knight and said we had to plan for a big Washington D.C. sendoff for Casey. Could Knight get clearance for Casey to land on the Potomac? Where do we hold the event?

By this time, my team was already drafting stories for a press kit. Maybe I could get Admiral Dunleavy to send someone from his shop to speak? We needed great media presence. And, from Casey, we needed a flight plan.

# Ten

# Day 1 Redux — West to East

Casey left Alaska on June 13. He arrived late p.m. in Seattle. He swore to follow a path to San Diego; Oklahoma City; St, Augustine, FL; Lancaster, SC; and then Washington DC. By now, he had already accumulated 24 days on this record-breaking adventure.

On June 14 we turned the clock back to Day 1. Hurrah.

The next day, he arrived late in the day at Lake Henshaw in California for fuel. That night when Casey called me he was in a horrible mood. There was a lot of "fuck this and fuck that." He rambled a bit.

I thought his miserable mood came from the no-go on Russian clearance. Not quite — Dan Hood was the culprit as he had robbed him. Casey told me that his short stay in Seattle was very traumatic.

He found out that Dan Hood, part owner in Casey's Cessna 180 aircraft, had taken possession of it while he was in Alaska. Casey said that before he left on May 20 for Alaska, he signed the plane over to Hood. He only did this in case he didn't make it back alive.

But Hood took it a step further and actually registered the plane in his own name. As such, Casey lost his aircraft. This pissed off Casey. Revenge was his ultimate goal and he promised me that he would get Hood one day.

After some words of encouragement, we hung up. Casey was a mess.

We talked again when he touched down in St. Augustine on June 16. He had covered 3,349 miles since leaving Seattle on June 14. He wanted to tell me about his big interview with the local newspaper. He had also stopped at the Ponce de Leon Fountain of Youth and had drunk the water.

Casey never showed me the story, but somehow the Associated Press got hold of the St. Augustine story and suddenly Casey was back in the news again. I left for D.C. that afternoon and, at dinner, Knight and I mapped out the final plans for the news conference on the Potomac.

We were looking to pull off a most spectacular event in D.C. aviation history. We wanted to get approvals to have Casey actually fly down the Potomac, make a sweeping arch, and then land next to the boat dock some 100 feet from the Presidential yacht. We both could not recall if any other floatplane had made a landing on the Potomac so near to the White House.

When Knight actually obtained final approval from the Parks Department, the Secret Service, FAA, and the White House janitor (or so it seemed), he found out that no aircraft had ever attempted such a landing on the Potomac. Casey would be the first.

Casey liked the D.C. press briefing idea. His mind wandered as he left St. Augustine. In his delusional state, the already weary and stressed out pilot thought to himself that his plan now centered on making up time. That meant pushing his aircraft and himself to the fullest extent. He needed to make up the time lost in Alaska waiting for Russian approval.

"I really felt that my revised southern route flight plan should have offered the Russians ample time to complete logistics planning," Casey would later explain. "That allowed them time to schedule fuel stops and obtain weather approvals for landing sites. But the *Alaska Flyer* reporter screwed me and I am going to tell the Washington media that."

The flight up the East Coast was beautiful. Casey could almost imagine people coming out from their homes and waving at his red, white, and blue aircraft. He was thinking about already having completed the record and doing victory laps throughout the U.S. He thought back about being a lifeguard in Wildwood, New Jersey in the summer. (He even knew where I grew up in Sea Isle City, NJ, 25 miles north of Wildwood).

He also reflected on the present — his dad, who lived in New York City, was not feeling well. Casey told himself that everything would be all right until his triumphant return. Hell, he thought, he might even stop in and see his father on the way up north.

As his senses reverted back inside the cockpit, he thought: "Want to check the fuel system. I need to flip the switch over to the floats. How long will it take for the fuel to change over? I know I have done this exercise many times, but I want to check once more. Wow, in less than 20 seconds the fuel from the floats poured into the engine cavity. All the cylinders are humming perfectly. Pressure gauge reads in the green and the moving map display has me now over Georgia."

As he thought about his latest exploit, he began to get more excited. "Just think, I can take a route through Europe, Egypt, India, Thailand, the Philippines, and Japan."

Logic began to sink in. "I will never get any Russian clearance to fly up the East Coast of Russia and cross over at Nome. That is what both Knight and Coleman said." Yet, his delusional mind suffered from renewed optimism. "Russia — there is always a chance they will want to help me to complete this record."

His aircraft now reached Lancaster, SC. "Overnight here, and tomorrow the press briefing in Washington, D.C." He landed at Kirk Air Base Airport (a seaplane base) outside Lancaster.

As his head hit the pillow that night, he reevaluated his belief that the Soviets would help him. Based on the preponderance of evidence, he probably would have to fly from Japan to the U.S. This fact kicked him in the gut. How the hell would he do that? Thinking it through, he tried to map out a plan.

Half asleep, he strategized. Once past the land masses and heading out from Japan to the U.S., he would have to fly over a large stretch of ocean known as the North Pacific. There were no GPS satellites or other navigational aids or land fixes to guide him.

It would test all his flying abilities to reach his final destination point. He would have to fly from the uppermost tip of territorial Japan to Attu in the Aleutian chain — a trip of more than 1,550 miles. "Not much room for error in losing my way and that means running out of fuel," he recognized with a sigh.

Casey recalled what his favorite author, Ernest Gann, had said about the fears faced by many flyers:

> "There are airmen and there are pilots: the first being part bird whose view from aloft is normal and comfortable, a creature whose brain and muscles frequently originate movements which suggest flight.
>
> "And second there are pilots, who regardless of their airborne time remain earth-loving bipeds forever. When these latter unfortunates, because of one urge or another, actually make an ascent, they neither anticipate nor relish the event and they drive their machines with the same graceless labor they inflict upon the family vehicle."

Casey remained restless most of the night and he continued to wonder what the next day in D.C. would be like. He was now in Lancaster and when he arrived in Washington, D.C. he would have flown another 764 miles. Would there be a band playing? Maybe hundreds of people looking skyward to catch a glimpse of the historic plane? Or possibly all the major TV networks filming the arrival? Everyone would want to know why the Soviets wouldn't let him cross Russia. "I will tell them the Cold War was the major reason. They have to believe me," he thought.

"As for Washington, D.C., maybe I will stop and visit the President."

The next morning, Casey's first sign of engine trouble arose during the preflight of the aircraft. He later explained, "On landing the night before, I could feel my engine sputter. Upon further examination, I found that the leads to my magnetos were faulty. I needed to get them replaced. I asked the chief mechanic at Kirk about it and he informed me that I could get the leads replaced in Maryland. I made a call and scheduled a stop after D.C."

Meanwhile, Hammond was given a heads-up that Casey was very close to approaching Washington, D.C. On the PR end, AP wanted to talk to Hammond and we set up an interview for June 17. The reporter asked about his impressions of Casey going to west to east.

"Phillips 66 still totally supports Tom Casey's efforts to fly around the world. It is an unfortunate setback that he had to change his original plan, but we fully expect him to set a record. After all, this is a record of distance, not time or tedium," he answered confidently.

## Eleven

# Setting the Stage

On June 16 I set off to D.C. to see Knight and to ferret out all the projected parameters and obstacles this journey would encompass. This also served as the final execution planning event for the D.C. press conference on June 18th. In no way could I have predicted that this trip to D.C. would be my first of more than 50 subsequent trips, all related to Casey's round-the-world journey.

I would become a veteran of the Trump Shuttle and my frequent visits to the Hyatt Regency Suites on 23rd street in Georgetown would put me on a first name basis with most of the staff.

From D.C., I drove to the AOPA Air Safety Foundation in Frederick, Maryland. This was a beautiful building and its location was not far from Camp David. I entered Knight's inner sanctum and was met immediately by both David and Admiral Engen. We sat in the admiral's executive-styled office and each of us voiced our justification for Casey's attempt.

Engen said it was for all the future aviators. Knight said it raised the image of aviation safety in connection with one of the most arduous feats ever undertaken by one aviator. I said, "I believe Lindbergh would have said that Casey's journey (if he goes on to complete it) would stand as the most complex undertaking in aviation history."

With both arms raised above my head, I changed the direction of the conversation. With firm conviction I aired my trepidations of possible events. "I predict we may face some horrific hurdles along with many unforeseen obstacles in the days and months to come."

Engen downplayed my pessimistic attitude and said we just needed to focus on the present. I told myself that Engen was a pillar of strength. No wonder he was a vice admiral plus Reagan's head of the FAA.

We talked about landing Casey on the Potomac. Knight had all the final approvals. Engen knew Casey would be the first to ever land on the Potomac (so close to the White House and U.S. Capitol). So, we better get great coverage.

The area we planned to land Casey was heavily patrolled by the Secret Service, since the Presidential yacht was moored nearby. And, to our knowledge, only sailboats, not motorcraft, could operate near the Capitol. "Now we land a seaplane. God Bless us all," Engen sharply surmised, as if to say, "God, I hope this goes well."

We finished up the planning session by going through the media invites. I said we probably would have all the major TV, radio, and newspaper outlets and wire services and maybe even *Roll Call*. Knight just laughed.

Engen added he had prearranged an appointment for both Knight and myself to visit the next day, June 17, with Vice Admiral Richard Dunleavy, Deputy Chief of Naval Operations for Air Warfare (OP-05) at the Pentagon. We had met before but that was before Casey had changed his flight plan to west to east. Also, there were many U.S. Navy installations in Casey's path and Dunleavy wanted to discuss this issue.

The next day we were escorted to the Pentagon's "C" Ring and we were met by the most gorgeous Navy Wave I have ever laid my eyes on. Both Knight and I stammered when she asked our names. All we could utter was that we had an appointment with her boss.

Then I hear this voice: "Hey, Coleman, is that you? There could only be one person I know with a crazy project like yours. When I heard this ex-Navy PR man, sponsoring a seaplane world record, was visiting today, I didn't have to think twice on who he was. I told Admiral Dunleavy about you," said Navy Captain Brian Tutterville.

I explained to Dunleavy that Tutterville and I had been shipmates in Aviation Officer Candidate School at Pensacola in 1965 and I guess Tutterville thought I was a bit over-the-top at that time.

Tutterville was the quiet type. Dunleavy wasn't. On entering Dunleavy's office, we stood almost eye-to-eye. He was a handsome naval officer in his dress whites and really had the sea-hardened appearance of an admiral. At about six feet, his football-sized shoulders and ruddy complexion made him seem perfect for a World War II central casting choice as an actor bellowing orders from the carrier's flying bridge. "Hello," he said. His voice was gravelly and deep. He exuded strength and confidence.

In my days in the U.S. Navy, I only met one other officer like Dunleavy and that was Admiral Dick Truly, who made the first night landing at the Cape in the Space Shuttle Challenger.

Dunleavy was courteous but at the same time inquisitive. He wanted to know all the latest info about Casey. He had followed his exploits in the news and on TV and wanted very much to meet him. "Well, Admiral, you may get your chance. He is landing on the Potomac on June 18," I told him.

I hadn't a clue if the admiral was impressed by Casey's biographical build-up. But in one long stroke of his right hand, swooping across the space in front of my face, Dunleavy said he only wanted to know one thing: What in the hell did Casey, as well as ourselves, expect from the Navy?

"Simply," I said, "all we would like is your support, if we need it. And, this help could come in many forms, but the kind of naval support we may need includes finding a suitable place for Casey to land his plane and getting refueled with 100LL avgas.

"For example, we would like to land in Keflavik, Crete, Subic Bay, and possibly Yokosuka and Misawa.

"We are not asking for special favors, but can we have points of contact in each of those sites so we can ask if Casey can land there? I have been in all these areas and know their geography. I will be able to guide Casey into each of the landing areas.

"If we run into pushback, we would only ask for your assistance as a last resort. And, if we get permission to land at those sites, we would clear all flight plans through OP-05 and not misuse any of the services offered by the navy. I promise you that."

The admiral looked at both Knight and me and said ok. "Help can come in many ways," he said. "Tell you what. I will direct my liaison officer Captain Jon Coleman (Admiral-Select) to take part in your June 18 press event. He will show the Navy Colors and tell the world that the Navy is there if Casey needs us. Godspeed."

We met with Dunleavy for less than 20 minutes. It only seemed like a lifetime.

How would our future relationship unfold? Dunleavy would have many reasons to call me in the future. Many of these conversations were not filled with hugs and kisses, but rather focused on some exploit by Casey which called for U.S. Navy involvement. The majority of these situations occurred after our pilot had landed at a naval installation. Casey would then tell everyone who would listen that Admiral Dunleavy personally had approved him to enter their establishment.

Following the Dunleavy meeting, Knight and I smiled. We had a game plan and tomorrow Casey would be on D.C.'s doorstep, where he would be given a sendoff into history.

Later that night in my hotel room, a myriad of unanswered questions were apparent. Primarily, after D.C., we didn't have a broad-based plan on where he was going. Or, where he was landing and, finally, who was in charge.

I calculated the promised assets: Pan Am said it would file his flight plans and the Air Force said it would track his movements. The Navy was on board promising to help find Casey bed and breakfast accommodations upon leaving the U.S. Most of all I wondered, Where is Casey really going? I knew the Soviets weren't on board with him flying the last leg up the Russian Eastern coastline. How in the hell then was he going to complete this journey around the world?

# Twelve

# D.C. Never Saw Anything Like This Before

Early to rise on June 18, my team was excited. Today would be a first and the whole world was going to see it.

The skies were bright blue; the Potomac River reflected calm like a sheet of glass. All the major TV stations had cameras set up to capture Casey's arrival. The media had been briefed that Casey would make a low pass down the Potomac (all cleared by Washington Control) and then make a westerly turn and land.

Casey was to line up on the Potomac, then fly over the 14th Street Bridge and land. From there, he was to follow a police patrol boat to his mooring site.

The previous night, Casey had told Knight that he was concerned about overheating his engine if the patrol boat ran at a no-wake speed. And, if his air-cooled engine overheated, something catastrophic could happen – like a blown cylinder. Knight was told by Casey, "The patrol boat must keep up with me."

Once at the reviewing stand, we waited for an engine roar. While my team had moved down to the dockside mooring site, Knight was now on the patrol boat waiting for Casey. In the distance all of us could hear the roar of the reciprocating engine. Casey swooped past the patrol boat and glided past the reviewing stand that held all the guests and media. He made a left hand turn like a soaring eagle, circled back down the river, and then lined up for his pass over the 14th Street Bridge and subsequent landing on the Potomac.

As the engine roared, his red, white, and blue Liberty II float-plane passed before the TV cameras and a crowd that had now swelled to more than several thousand spectators.

Once off the patrol boat Knight exclaimed that "I thought he was going to be shot down by the Secret Service because he was actually in the glidepath toward the White House. He was previously ordered to make a short run-up past the bridge and then return and land. The Secret Service didn't expect the grand fly-by.

"Additionally, once he landed, he tried to outpace the police patrol boat. I kept making hand motions for Casey to slow his plane down. I really believe he thought I was waving to him."

Eventually, Casey passed a few hundred feet from the review-ing stand. He then taxied to the Gangplank Marina. What an effort to have Casey follow these directions, which had come from a reluctant Secret Service. This was a first on the Potomac — no seaplane had ever landed this close to the White House.

We had all the major newspapers and aviation publications in attendance. Dignitaries included Dunleavy's staff member, Cap-tain Coleman; NOAA and the AOPA Safety Foundation; a U.S. State Department representative; many Secret Service agents; and several members of Congress. Life was good.

Casey docked his aircraft at the marina pier and sprinted up the gangway. Dressed in a white shirt and khaki pants, he proudly displayed the Phillips 66 ball cap he wore. He climbed up the stairs to the reviewing stand and podium. Out of breath and almost collaps-ing at the podium, he bellowed, "Hello Washington, D.C.; today is an epic occasion as I am the first person with a floatplane to land on the Potomac. I waved to the President and I hope he saw me. Thank you, Secret Service, for all of your support. It is so great to see everyone here today. I'm trying to prove to people how safe general aviation is. I don't see any reason this record-setting around-the-world journey shouldn't work."

He was beaming from ear to ear. His white teeth and ruddy complexion portrayed an introspective pilot on a mission. He was now in the nation's capital and his adventure was nearing reality.

You could see some skepticism in the demeanor of the media; after all, his first attempt through Russia had failed. But once Casey openly responded to questions shouted by the media, the atmosphere changed. One could feel that everyone was now on his side. Casey could be charismatic, and it was in the air that day.

*Press conference on the Potomac in Washington, D.C.*

The biggest news came from Casey's bold prediction on the longevity of the trip. He boldly told the audience, "After I left for Alaska on May 20, I became delayed from my original plans of completing this world record in about 60 days. Why? There was a mix-up from the inner workings of Russian bureaucracy." Knight and I cringed.

"But," Casey went on to say, "I have had time to restructure my flight plans and I can say without hesitation that I will now complete this west to east journey in 40 days. My timetable began on June 14, the day after I left Alaska, stopped in Seattle, and flew here."

Applause rang out and a very attractive female ABC reporter asked, "In what countries do you intend to make stopovers?"

Excited, he threw his arms in the air and tossed his head to the far right. That action caused him to not address the microphone directly. As a result, the audience only heard in a semi-muffled tone that from D.C. he was heading north, touching down in Halifax, Nova Scotia; Goose Bay, Labrador; and Narsarsuaq, Greenland before crossing over to Scotland.

He added, "I'm making an overnight pit stop in Hackensack, New Jersey to see my sister. My dad is in the hospital in New York and we are going to visit him before I head on this journey." The rest of his trip planning would come after he discussed flight plans with Pan Am in London. He also planned to fly down the Thames in London to Big Ben and to say hello to all the Brits.

We had remarks by all the dignitaries, but it was Captain Coleman's promise to Casey that the Navy would be there for him that resounded in Casey's mind and drew a smile. "My boss, Admiral Dunleavy, said if Casey had a real need, then he reinforced to me that he would try to make available all the resources of the U.S. Navy. We want everyone to know that the Navy, along with the Air Force, duly support your mission," Captain Coleman said.

While the words of encouragement that came from Captain Coleman may have been heartfelt, to Casey they meant something different. From now on, when it looked like Casey might have to seek refuge or couldn't get proper clearance to proceed into another country, Casey could invoke what would become a redundant famous saying: "Admiral Dunleavy said you were to give me all the help I need."

Of course, those very words would come to boomerang back at me during the journey. More than once, Dunleavy would become displeased as to how his name was being used and would tell me so. Memories of Navy discipline were to come back to me countless times, while Dunleavy continually chewed my butt.

Meanwhile, back at the podium finalizing the ceremony, Knight, who represented the AOPA Air Safety Foundation, said, "Speaking for my boss, Vice Admiral Donald Engen, we have a great deal of faith in Casey's flying ability. All the series of forthcoming adventures, in this general aviation pioneering saga, will become folklore and will certainly be shared with many youngsters aspiring to become aviators.

"We also know the vast amount of 'attention to detail' that has been taken by Casey to ensure the airworthiness of his aircraft. These efforts will lead to the utmost safety on this journey. I can assure you that Tom Casey knows his limitations. We feel strongly that he will complete this arduous journey."

Knight added that in order for Casey to stay on schedule and make this trip in 40 days (as he had predicted), he must fly at least ten hours a day. (Little did we know at that time that the 40 days Casey referred to was the exact time limit in which his insurance policy on the plane was due to expire.)

Following everyone's comments at the press briefing, in almost a whisper Casey confided to me that he would keep in touch by phone, and he also swore that Captain Hood at Pan Am had everything worked out flight-planning-wise. As for my services, Casey was only concerned that I keep the media alerted to his every movement.

Now for the retort that would falsely echo in my head for the following several weeks: "Hood or one of his associates will give you a daily call."

Walking to his plane, Casey loudly told everyone, "The U.S. Air Force's Military Air Command promised to furnish me navigational and communication assistance and is providing a 30-year daily history of weather on every leg of the route to supplement flight planning." I knew that Colonel Sills at Scott AFB was my contact regarding the Air Force's involvement.

(For the record, Colonel Sills didn't know where Casey was or had been until he reached the Air Force Base at Goose Bay. After Athens it was all U.S. Navy. But I'm getting ahead of myself.)

All of a sudden, Casey's eyes became fixed on someone near him dockside. His ensuing actions lived up to his almost movie star persona he planned to exhibit at each of his stops along the journey.

He walked over to the ABC reporter, a beautiful five-foot, five-inch blonde and put his arm around her waist. Then in one swift move, he gave her the longest kiss – one belonging only in the movies.

Stepping back from the stunned reporter he said, "I just wanted to say goodbye, plus I will remember those beautiful lips while flying in strange lands. Please forgive this pilot — your beauty overwhelmed me."

The stunned reporter came back at Casey and said, "Have a safe trip and give me a call sometime." Knight slammed his open palm to his forehead.

Now in his aircraft, Casey taxied east up the Potomac and in less than 20 minutes he was airborne and heading north. He headed up the coast until he turned northeast at the head of the Chesapeake Bay and landed near the town of Havre de Grace, Maryland. Tying up at the Yacht Club, he had hoped they would have an engine part he needed. They didn't. He then headed to New Jersey.

In D.C., with Casey out of our hair, we all looked forward to a quiet evening with the Knights — Margo and David.

David Knight's even-tempered manner and deep baritone voice were distinct qualities that made him clearly cut out for a run at the diplomatic corps. Yet, tonight he was utterly dumbfounded by the day's events. Margo, a lovely and very warm person, had previously been indoctrinated into the Casey legend as he had stayed in their home twice before. She just rolled her eyes and said nothing ever surprised her about Casey. "I just hope this is a success for the admiral's sake," she said.

I remained the eternal skeptic. In the end, we were all comrades-in-arms and would be bound forever together by this singular event.

Among my staff that day were two very close associates who accompanied me to the D.C. launch and would in turn become my confidants and staunch supporters as the world record trip progressed. Tim McCormack was an Irish redhead and St. Bonaventure grad who could really write. He missed many a St. Paddy's day parade as we were often on the road together. He taught me so many valuable tips about my craft. He and I, it seemed, were tied at the hip during this adventure.

Kyle MacDonald was the magician. She would make things work out when we all thought the sky was falling. She was as beautiful as she was super brainy. A Connecticut gal, she was one of three strong women in my firm.

Others working on this project included Jill Miller, Christine van Moorsel, and Ralph DeRosa, who stepped in and out on this journey. My boss, Al Hirsch, was always the pessimist. "Just don't get us fired ... and how much are they paying for this?" And, Debbie Channer, our accountant, always worked with me to ensure that the hours we had charged to date for this project matched the parameters previously set by the trip's sponsor and our client, Phillips 66.

Tim, Kyle, and I just laughed and admired the great job we had done. Each of us agreed that we didn't know what this Washington, D.C. event would lead to. We just hoped we wouldn't lose Phillips 66 as a client. Had we known just a small inkling of the events to unfold, I am sure we all would have updated our résumés.

The next day we headed back to New York. News coverage was outstanding. Casey was now a worldwide household name. *The Washington Times* had a big story and cover photo of Casey's taxiing up the channel off Hains Point and being escorted by a Washington, D.C. police launch. One quote by Casey caught my attention: "Wouldn't we all like to do something no one has ever done before?"

Other commercial news outlets covering the event included the three TV networks, Reuters, the BBC, the Associated Press, United Press International, and Cox Newspapers. AP reported that Casey did not slam into a seawall similar to what he had done when he took off from Seattle. The story focused on Casey as a pioneering pilot who had this urge to fly around the world.

"Will your exploits become a world record?" he was asked. The adventurer went on at great lengths to describe a similar flight in 1924. But in Casey's case, he was taking a greater risk to succeed since he expected to complete the journey in just one plane while using only one engine. "This feat will stand up to record holders such as Lindbergh," Casey said. He was quoted as saying "that the whole world would welcome him with open arms."

The reporter asked Casey if there was a chance he would get lost at any point during the journey. Casey supposedly smiled and said, "Are you mistaking me for someone else? Frankly, the question is stupid."

The news story gaining the greatest visibility overseas was USIA (United States Information Agency) staff writer John Holway's article alerting all the U.S. diplomats, agencies, and information outlets that Casey was coming. Holway would cover Casey's exploits through many parts of the voyage.

## Thirteen

# Up the East Coast to Greenland

Casey had flown a total of 5,570 miles from Anchorage to Washington, D.C. To get to D.C. he had landed in Seattle, San Diego, Oklahoma City, St. Augustine, and Lancaster, SC.

Casey left his Maryland stopover at gross weight as he often did after fueling. This included: 1) a 220-pound pilot; 2) maximum permissible takeoff weight; 3) 236 gallons of fuel, plus two suitcases; ten bottles of oil; four sleeping bags; 25 packs of beef jerky; and 12 six-gallon empty plastic containers to use for refueling. He further added to his overweight condition when he filled the extra space behind the left seat with mooring lines and food for in-flight quick meals.

While reviewing his strategic plan, several key items emerged. There could be some problems when normal refueling devices were unavailable. Envisioning what to do, he thought that without a standard mechanized refueling apparatus (fuel handle), there was no easy way to get fuel into a floatplane. So, it became apparent that to refuel his plane, he had to employ the same method one does when one runs out of gas in a car: Walking to a gas station and filling a plastic can to be carried back to the car.

Thus for most places he would land, Casey would need to fill his six-gallon plastic containers from fuel trucks loaded with 100 low lead avgas. Once he filled two containers, he would lug them back to the aircraft and siphon the fuel into the wings and floats.

But what happened if he could only get a supply of fuel from 55-gallon drums? Quite probable — in many developing countries, there would be no large avgas fuel trucks. For this encounter, he also invented a siphon device that could be used for pumping fuel from 55-gallon drums into his red six-gallon plastic containers. In turn, he would reverse the process and use the device to pump fuel into his aircraft.

"For right now, I am prepared for even minor problems," he thought.

Out off the Eastern coast, the beautiful beaches paralleled the left hand side of his aircraft. Straight ahead was a wide open, crystal clear panorama of deep blue shading accented with transparent gray clouds that seemed to span the horizon of the Atlantic Ocean. What a view as the aircraft's image seemed to bounce off the ocean waves. And it seemed that the sun's radiant glimmer off the waves took the appearance of Claude Monet's surreal painting *Garden at Sainte-Adresse*.

Refocusing his attention to the flight, Casey thought to himself, "To keep my original promise back in Seattle of completing this trip in 60 days and subsequent promise in D.C. of 40 days, I need to make up the time I lost while in Alaska. First step in achieving that goal will be taking only 12 days to fly from Seattle to Greenland."

Our pilot was in good spirits as he was heading towards where he grew up. His craft flew north until he reached Hackensack, New Jersey. He tied up at Little Ferry Seaplane Base. The facility was a mile east of the central business district of the Borough of Little Ferry on the Hackensack River in Bergen County, New Jersey.

Casey would be met by his sister Kathleen and they both would go into New York City to visit his father, who had been hospitalized in a diabetic coma. Later, alone with his sister, both envisioned the many possible hiccups that could befall his journey.

Not all parts of this journey would be stressful, he promised his sister. In fact, he would stop and visit their Irish relatives. Kathleen told him, "I saw you on the nightly TV news. I am the hero's sister of Hackensack." She smiled.

With family issues resolved, Casey left the next morning for Halifax. Once at full power, he hit the step and was airborne. As he

pushed his craft to gain several thousand feet of altitude, he thought
of the famous words uttered by John Glenn as he left the earth for the
first time: "Zero-Gs and I feel fine."

We never knew Casey's exact flight planning ritual. Only
later did we learn that he finally left for Halifax on June 19. He never
followed the same route he previously told to the press in D.C. Casey
often never followed the same course he predicted. For us in the early
part of this trip, we had little control on assisting in the flight planning.

Casey took about an hour to fly from Hackensack to reach the
Goodspeed Airport and Seaplane Base in East Haddam, Connecticut,
in order to pick up an engine part he needed and spent several hours
repairing the engine leads to his magnetos. From there he headed
straight to Halifax for the night. He flew some 500 miles into the
Royal Nova Scotia Yacht Squadron (RNSYS) marina, which dates
back to July 1837.

What a surprise I received a week following Casey's departure
from Halifax. I heard from the club's Commodore, who fashioned his
speech in a British Oxford type dialect. He said that Casey was vastly
entertaining with all the club members: "Your American pilot showed
off his aircraft to many members and told tales of his aviation exploits to those gathered at our bar."

The Commodore commented that Casey bragged to all the
RNSYS members that he was also an avid yachtsman and that he
had been dreaming about his next great exploit. He might take a solo
sailing journey around the globe. With his arm stretched out at full
length, plus making waving gestures, Casey went on to explain that a
sailing journey would give him a chance to revisit with all the friends
he would have made during this current Liberty II adventure.

"When word got to the members that we had an international
celebrity docked at our marina," said the Commodore, "his arrival
turned into an all-night affair. We naturally wouldn't let Casey pay for
anything (fuel, meals, booze, lodging, and mooring included).

"He made our local TV news and when he left the next mid-
morning, there were well over 200 folks at the docks waving goodbye.
We wished him Godspeed."

Leaving Halifax behind on June 20, Casey would spend some

five hours (640 miles) reaching his next destination in Goose Bay, Labrador. When I spoke with Air Force Colonel Sills he said there was a Canadian Air Force base at Goose Bay and they would welcome him stopping for fuel and a good meal. Canadian Forces Base Goose Bay was operated as a NATO tactical flight training site.

Subsequently, Casey brought the base up on his radio and, surprise of surprises, they were waiting for him. Sills had called ahead. Casey got landing directions and put his bird down at Goose (Otter Creek) Water Aerodrome, located in Terrington Basin at Lake Melville near Happy Valley, Goose Bay.

"Very tricky landing at Goose Bay," Casey told his Canadian hosts. "I had to dodge the large chunks of ice that seemed to cover the entire lake's surface. Wow, it seemed that as soon as my floats hit the surface, I immediately was forced to steer in almost a U.S. Navy ship's zigzag pattern to avoid the large chunks of ice. When I slowed enough, I could drop my float rudders and steer clear of any large pieces of ice.

"My going to this Canadian base was very exciting," he would later relate. "After landing, I was treated to a great dinner and many aviation tall tales. My most vivid memory was meeting the Exxon fuel representative for the base. He told me that all the fuel for my plane — about 110 gallons — had been donated by a Phillips 66 competitor (Exxon). He said to justify the donation, he would just explain that they had a seepage from the avgas truck and it evaporated on the tarmac.

"The Canadians were the most polite people in the world. Also, they saved me a good deal of money as the aviation fuel in Goose Bay was $8 (U.S.). I would find out the price in Greenland was $11."

Before he left for Greenland the next day, Casey read up about this destination in the Canadian Air Force library. Narsarsuaq (original spelling Narssarssuaq) was the principal city of Greenland in the times of Erik the Red, where there remain traces of an early Norse settlement.

At 0830 on June 21, Casey was faced with a 785-mile leg as he headed off to Narsarsuaq. He would land on the river adjacent to the main commercial airport. Following a brief stopover for refueling, he would then head on to Iceland.

At about 400 miles into this leg, Casey saw an SAS aircraft heading into Greenland. "Just think," he thought, "I will be with the early North American settlers and also some of the pioneers in aviation." It was his understanding that Greenland has been inhabited, though not continuously, by Arctic peoples via Canada for 4,500 to 5,000 years. And, he thought, "The airport I was heading towards was the staging point for all aircraft heading to the European theater in WWII."

His thoughts then turned to his early days in aviation and what gave him the impetus to try such a journey as this. "Not too many years ago, I was towing advertisements in my J-3 Cub. I would fly from the tip of Cape May, New Jersey to northern beaches in Wildwood. Towing ads paid me ten times as much as when I was a lifeguard in Wildwood. Life seemed good." For ten years, he towed an average of ten banners a day, at $3 a banner.

"Aviation changed my life. By 25, I had my commercial ticket plus adding seaplane, instrument, and instructor endorsements."

The roar of the engine snapped his mind back to reality. Ice was building up on the wire braces to the float. The ice-coated wires actually made a humming sound, which is why Casey knew he had taken ice on the wires.

Craning his head to take a quick glimpse of the outside of the aircraft, Casey quickly noticed he had ice on the leading edges of the wings. Abruptly, he left 9,000 feet and descended to flight level 4,000 feet. "Am I having the same luck as Lindbergh?" he thought, feeling muscle spasms in his stomach.

"Almost as soon as I flipped my nose over to descend, I lost radio contact with Greenland Control," he would later explain. "This problem was ingeniously solved when I decided to relay my mandatory position reports through a Continental commercial jetliner. Funny, they had just taken off from Paris and received my radio message. I asked if they could relay my report to the Flight Information Center in Greenland.

"Below me were glaciers, and a whole lot of icebergs. Did this mean having to land and steer around them?

"With my full attention on the icebergs, out of the corner of my eye my mind just shut down. I was blind in the sky. Why? At that precise moment, my wet compass was swinging back and forth. That meant I had no idea of my direction due to a lack of landmarks, since everything below me was ice and water.

"In order to stop the compass from swinging, I remembered I needed to turn due north. This was the only maneuver that could stop the uncontrollable gyration of the compass. Back in my flight training days, my instructor detailed that any magnetic compass will stop on true north.

"Now in order resituate my aircraft on its original track and my flight plan heading, I needed to do a standard rate turn to a compass reading of 060. This was a turn of approximately three degrees per second (in layman's language, this was a 20-second turn) to reset the directional gyro. With a sigh of relief I was back on course. Now my adjustment knob allowed me to align the adjustment indicator with a precise course direction.

"For the next 300 miles I relied on my compass heading as I was without radio contact. I maneuvered by dead reckoning. Probably the name came from some pilot who lost his way and was killed trying to figure out where he was.

"My last heading was 2 o'clock north. Factoring in my time and distance, I decided to maintain this course. My compass was working. Good thing that there was no darkness here. I also liked my aircraft's shadow on a sheet of ice and, sure enough, I was heading directly northeast.

"Greenland loomed very large and the swells looked awesome. My radio now picked up Greenland Center. I needed weather (mainly wind speed and direction) from the commercial airport's tower.

"But, they can't give wave height. I would just make a flyover and observe my possible landing area, which turned out to be a beach."

Picking up his radio mike, Casey raised Narsarsuaq Control. "This is N1990L, a Cessna 206 floatplane, Seattle registry, requesting weather and wind speed and direction."

Tower: "N1990L winds at 15 knots, northerly direction. Cleared to land on West Bay in an easterly direction. Head to beach area near the airport for docking craft."

Casey had been IFR (instrument flight) for most of the flight and now, after radio contact, went to VFR (visual flight) for the last segment.

He easily made a left turn toward the airport and then flew over the airport and circled the parameter until he was heading in an easterly direction that allowed him to make a straight-in approach on West Bay. Once on the water he had to navigate around icebergs.

Casey was not the Titanic nor was he the size of a PBY landing in the bay. The icebergs were enormous. Some were the height of a seven-story building and had a base width of what seemed to be the size of three football fields. Even scarier was the fact that there was no direct course to the beach landing site from where he was. He would pass one iceberg and another would lie directly ahead. He kept throttling back and forth to adjust power settings. He had no brakes (just flaps and rudder), but by using both he found a way to slow the aircraft and not hit an iceberg.

He just prayed that none were impassable. The beach finally loomed ahead, and the airport's lights illuminated the area. He was safe for now, until he had to take off. But for now he wasn't wet. He taxied up onto the beach.

Casey called for fuel and soon an aviation fuel truck appeared. He loaded the expensive fuel in six-gallon plastic jugs. He then asked the whereabouts of a pay phone as he wanted to call his U.S. coordinators — that is, me. His intention for the call was to ask for assistance in having the U.S. Navy let him land in Keflavik, not Reykjavik, Iceland. Why?

More than a year ago, while attempting this same record, his plane was wrecked when strong winds and gale force rain overturned his aircraft in the Reykjavik harbor. "How am I going to avoid this same fate again? I know the U.S. Navy has a large base at Keflavik, but how do I get in there?"

He never reached me. It would have to wait until Iceland.

Casey thought of his favorite quote from Helen Keller: "Life is either a daring adventure or nothing."

\* \* \*

Back in New York, I tried my best to keep Hammond and

other Phillips 66 executives abreast of Casey's whereabouts. The hardest task was telling them that all was fine and Casey was on course. I had not heard from either Casey or from Pan Am. And, Colonel Sills wouldn't answer my calls because they were having a hard time locating him, too.

Hammond as well as Admiral Engen seemed not to be concerned. Hammond assured me that I had the whole thing under control. (Was he smoking loco weed?)

Back in my office, we would have daily briefings and I would have the same response at every meeting. No, I didn't know where Casey was and I was concerned.

We were in the midst of planning for a London landing on the Thames. I had my airline ticket bought, but the dates were not yet determined.

My direct Phillips 66 report (Geiger) in Bartlesville just wanted me to know how much this whole affair was costing. I assured him we were on budget. ("What budget?" I thought.) Hammond said to get it done and he would pay for it. I was going down the rabbit hole with no support. I just knew I was going to be fired (so did Geiger). I never asked for this assignment.

My thinking was becoming skewed. I felt that if I went to London and organized this event, I could then corral the son of a bitch and get the flight back on track. At that time I felt Pan Am was a joke — so was the U.S. Air Force. Later, as Casey briefed me, I realized I was right about Pan Am but not the Air Force. The AF had been doing a splendid job of keeping abreast of weather and helping with flight plans.

I knew Casey would eventually call me as I had all the money. At the start of this journey, I had set up a bank account in his name and put funds into his account so he could draw from it as he needed. I saw some withdrawals at Hackensack and Halifax but that was it. I was also traveling a good deal and was working on a number of other Phillips 66 projects. But, even on the road, I would call my office with the same resounding phrase each night: *Where the hell is Casey?*

# Fourteen

# Iceland Ahead ... and Storms

For Casey, another 770-mile leg lay just ahead. He left Green-land at 1630 and, depending on the weather, his expectations were to arrive in Iceland on June 22 at around 2100. His stewardship of the flight meant that in only eight days he had reached Greenland from Anchorage. This was well ahead of the 12-day timeframe he predicted at the D.C. press conference.

His Iceland weather briefing from the Air Force showed calm winds and relatively little chop in the Reykjavik harbor. Casey again checked all the vitals. He was well prepared if he had to take on low-er-octane fuel and burn it with his on-board 100LL aviation gasoline.

Owing to the uncertainly of octane rating of fuel in some foreign locations, the left wing tip tank (38 gallons) on Liberty II was reserved to carry a supply of 100LL-octane fuel. This fuel was held in reserve for high-power usage, such as full-power takeoffs and climb. These high-power settings were needed in rough weather when flying through countries such as Iceland.

Changes in temperature were a constant worry, too. Getting the cold engine started in below zero weather could be difficult. Casey could preheat the engine and, with a good quality fuel, nothing should go wrong.

Casey landed in Reykjavik and refueled. The crowded harbor looked the same as it did when Liberty I was destroyed in 1989. He

asked the harbor master what the weather forecast looked like and
was told that they were forecasting high winds, especially that night.
The winds always came over the mountains and blew strong gusts
directly into the harbor.

As Casey would later explain, "I mentioned to the harbor
master at the time that I was a friend of Admiral Dunleavy at the
Pentagon and that the admiral said if there was any possible danger
that might damage my plane, I could inquire about staying at the U.S.
Navy base in Keflavik."

"I was completely ignored," Casey would tell me in a phone
call. "I immediately asked for a phone and called the Navy base. I told
the person who answered about my promise from Admiral Dunleavy
and I was put on hold. Several minutes later, a commander, who said
he was the Command Duty Officer, simply stated there was nothing he
could do. That is when I called New York and got you (reverse charges) for help."

"Coleman, I was told to tie down my plane in the harbor.
There's no protection from gale force winds," he said.

Casey's call to me was totally amusing. I had not heard from
him since his Washington, D.C. departure — not even a postcard. After listening to an emotional plea that included Dunleavy's name more
than a half dozen times, I frankly told him, "Button it."

The essence of the conversation was that I understood that
Casey's plane was in a precarious location and that he wanted help to
move his craft to the Navy base at Keflavik. I told Casey to stand by
at the harbor master's phone and to wait for a call.

To this day, I remember phoning Dunleavy and telling him
about Casey's request. No less than one minute into the call Dunleavy
said, "Admiral Tom Hall is at that location and, by the way, he is from
Bartlesville, the home of Phillips 66. Maybe you can ask one of your
buddies at Phillips to call Tom and get the help your pilot is looking
for.

"And, by the way, tell that pilot this was not an emergency. I
got a call from the Fleet Air Keflavik Command Duty Officer saying
some civilian pilot, yelling my name, was asking for asylum. I told the
CDO it was Pan Am and the Air Force's problem and their responsibility. And, if I have to, I will walk down to the Air Force's Chief of

Staff's office in the Pentagon's D Ring and piss all over this pilot's propeller. I am sure Casey will get the word then. Repeat after me: Don't indiscriminately use my name."

I was now tongue-tied after being yelled at by a Navy vice admiral. Further, Dunleavy's pitch of his voice (raspy tone) made me glad I wasn't on his staff. Although he couldn't see me, I must have looked pretty funny (at full attention and waiting to salute). "Yes Sir, Yes Sir, I will tell Casey," is all I could muster.

Hammond was the first person I called (at dinner time) after Dunleavy's learning session. It seemed that the admiral at Fleet Air Keflavik (Tom Hall) was a personal friend of Hammond. Following my plea, Hammond made a quick call to Admiral Hall and, in the next few minutes, Casey was getting a call from the CDO who said Casey was now allowed to fly his bird over to the Keflavik naval facility and stay overnight.

I also called Casey to deliver the good news, which he already had. Casey began our conversation with one of his bullshit remarks. "See Coleman, it was my using Dunleavy's name that actually turned the tide in my favor and got me permission to use the naval facility," he said.

When I heard that, my whole demeanor went into a slow burn and I let the guns fly. "You dumb asshole," I said. "Dunleavy had nothing to do with you being allowed on the base.

"In fact, he said if you use his name again — like you just did — he will personally blow your plane out of the air. He mentioned either by missiles or naval airpower. For God's sake, Casey, don't use Dunleavy's name unless it is a real emergency and you need the U.S. Navy's help. The person you need to thank is Jack Hammond, who is good friends with Admiral Hall, commander of this facility. He called and made this happen."

Casey mentioned something about those beautiful Icelandic chicks he remembered from 1989. "Hey, sorry about all the confusion, but I got it settled here," he said. Now as always, Casey's explanation was like that of a high-flying Irish bullshit salesman and one whose hearing was selective.

Prior to taking off for the Keflavik Naval Base, Casey inquired about London. Had I cleared it with the British for him to land on the Thames River? I explained that Knight (really Engen) was work-ing on it. I asked when he would be there and he paused before being forthcoming with this reply. He didn't know and would call me later. "I fully expect Pan Am to handle the whole thing," he said, and then hung up.

Following the Casey call and as a true gesture of insecurity, I called Knight and briefed him. Knight, now laughing out loud, said, "I don't know if Admiral Engen called Dunleavy or Admiral Hall. But there were sounds of laughter and good ol' boy slang coming from Engen's office during several calls he was on. All during these calls, the name Casey may have been used more than 200 times by Engen.

"The admiral is hot on obtaining a landing spot on the Thames — the first ever for a civilian float plane," he went on. "He has many friends in the U.K. Parliament and I would expect this avia-tion first to be a done deal. I think you told me that Casey was waiting on Pan Am to make the Thames landing a reality. If so, he may be waiting for hell to freeze over."

Fleet Air Keflavik (the senior U.S. Navy command in Iceland) now gave Casey landing coordinates and instructed him to tie up at the long pier. The Iceland Defense so-called "long dock" was used for offloading supplies and provided a perfect place to tie up a seaplane. Casey was met by a lieutenant who escorted him to the office of Rear Admiral Thomas F. Hall, Commander of Fleet Air Keflavik and the Iceland Defense Force.

After much discussion about the round the world journey, Hall explained that his staff was throwing a reception for Casey at 2200.

It was a gala affair. There were some 25 officers and wives at the O Club — for Casey, that meant drinks were on the house. Casey gave a 20-minute speech that embellished on the rigors of the trip so far, and then gave a forecast of the events he foresaw still to come.

Of those events, Casey explained, possibly one of the more taxing involved his engine, which would have to withstand the hot temperatures he had to face through the desert in Saudi Arabia, as well as the temperate extremes in Pakistan and India. "To safeguard my engine, I have specially designed cylinders," he explained.

"Besides the abrupt temperature swings, other potential ob-stacles may come when I hit a few typhoons. But all in all, the roughest challenges may be getting the clearances to fly across or even land in some of the Middle Eastern and Asian countries. Here, I have Pan Am and the U.S. Air Force to do my advance work."

Ah, little did he (or I) know about the obstacles ahead to get those clearances.

Naturally, he sprinkled in lots of praise about U.S. Navy support. At about midnight, Casey and a contingent of three women and one super drunk navy officer remained before calling it a night. (Casey spent a long time saying goodnight to one of those beautiful Icelandic blondes.)

Admiral Hall awakened Casey at about 0500 on June 23. The admiral was concerned that a major storm was approaching which would bring with it enormous ten- to 12-foot swells in the harbor. This could put Casey's floatplane at risk of being destroyed while taking off.

Casey would later explain, "While I appreciated all of the U.S. Navy's hospitality, I just kept tossing and turning most of the night thinking about my disastrous episode just a year ago in Reykjavik. Smooth sailing was my wish. I gathered my wits about me and sat down to eat a bite of breakfast, but not much stayed down. Afterwards, I wanted to stop by Admiral Hall's office and say goodbye."

Casey, now standing fully erect (at attention) in the doorway to the admiral's office, suddenly lurched forward and almost landed upside down on top of the officer's desk. Casey tried to recreate for the admiral the moment in 1989 when he found out his Liberty I plane had been destroyed.

The admiral fully comprehended. "We are all sure you will make it safely off this time and we all wish you good luck, Tom," said Admiral Hall. Casey looked out the windows of the admiral's office and saw a westerly build-up of clouds. Admiral Hall and his Chief of Staff — both savvy naval aviators — pointed out that a gale was on its way.

By the time Casey made it to his aircraft, it was approaching 1330. He had waited for final flight clearances to Scotland. By now, the wind had really picked up. The temperature had dropped from a mild 40 degrees Fahrenheit to almost zero. Rain was now pelting his face and those around him appeared like a crowd of Vikings waiting to board their ships.

"Everyone told me now was the time for me to head out," Casey later recalled. "My air of confidence was almost believable when I said my engine had the additional power boost to step up on any large swells. Had they known my fears, I am sure they would have wrestled me to the ground and locked me away."

The plane's interior seemed a tighter fit than normal as Casey settled in his seat, continuing to eye the swells in the harbor. He swallowed hard and let off a series of exhausted sighs. He clicked on the engine switch and then turned over the prop until all six cylinders of the engine sang out in repeated harmony. He idled the engine and pulled from the dock. Gripping the stick, he was prepared to surge power into his engine.

"The 1989 Liberty I wreck flooded my brain. As I taxied out into the harbor, I could see the swells increasing in size. I figured I had 20 to 30 minutes to get this bird into the air."

Once Casey had taxied out into the harbor, he was facing six- to eight-foot swells. "The air smelled like a storm was brewing. As I taxied away from the base I headed upwind. Out of my right hand side window, the fog and mist settled on the shoreline. The trees along the shore were bent almost in a 40-degree angle; above me, the seagulls seemed to be in a holding pattern in preparation for a landing. Can I make it — will I have enough power?

"After taxiing for more than several miles, I swung my float-plane around and into the wind. With the wind in my face, I slowly pushed the throttle forward until I was at full power and pushing my aircraft right over the swells.

"After about the length of a football field, my right wing was buried in a swell. It seemed to stay there forever, but then just popped out. Next, when I reached the airspeed that was needed to take off, I turned head-on into what I thought was a four-foot swell and then turned into the wind to get my aircraft airborne.

"It was now 1530. I actually faced the beast head-on and went directly into what appeared to be a six-foot swell. This course of action seemed like it lasted a lifetime, but in reality it was just a couple of seconds. All at once, I slammed through the water around me and was soon airborne and on my way to Scotland.

"I circled the base, and there was Admiral Hall with his staff, waving goodbye. Those sailors are really great guys."

Admiral Hall called me in New York the next day. He said Casey was a pleasure to have at his base and that they had had a reception for him. His fuel was bought by the Navy. Explained the admiral, "What a takeoff he made. Just before he took off, he seemed to have totally buried his plane in a 12-foot swell. Just think of this image: a giant whale breaking through the water's surface in the ocean — that was Casey. And Liberty II shot up from the swell and looked like it was gasping for air.

"Damn good flying. He would have made a great naval aviator."

I told the admiral that Casey had been an enlisted man in the navy. The admiral replied that someone in the navy screwed up — he should have been wearing "Wings of Gold", he said. Admiral Hall added that he was calling Hammond. I thanked him.

## Fifteen

# Repairs in Scotland; and a Tip o' the Hat to Irish Relatives

Ayr, Scotland, was now 878 miles southeast and more than four hours until landing. The tailwinds from Iceland were tremendous — some 40 miles per hour. (Tailwinds result from eating beans in the airport coffee shop, which often causes oxygen deficiency in the immediate vicinity.)

Casey was flying at 9,000 feet with an air temperature near -10 F. If he went higher, the ice would start building up on his wings and engine cowling. His flight plan was cleared for Ayr, and UK Flight Center called for him to maintain a southeasterly heading and a cruise speed of about 140 miles (or 120 knots) per hour. Casey knew at this speed and altitude, he should be in Ayr at about 2000.

For geography buffs, Ayr is a coastal town at the mouth of the River Ayr, which flows out into the Firth of Clyde. From the coast, the Isle of Arran can be seen. On a very clear day, one can even see the tip of Northern Ireland. The north side of Ayr Harbor hosts a commercial port that mainly exports coal.

Scotland loomed over the horizon and at 1930 dusk had settled over homes below. The city of Ayr was off in the distance and he now had a good view of all the small communities along the Ayrshire Coast. "As I descended toward Ayr Harbour, the landmark Two Bridges, which spanned the river — about 700 feet from the harbor's mouth — loomed very large in my windscreen," he later recalled.

"On the radio, I tried to raise my U.S. Air Force contact at

RAF Mildenhall, United Kingdom. I was now VFR."

"The Air Force master sergeant was very helpful. He lined me up on the harbor's entrance and directed where to set my bird down. He also told me about rocks in the river and advised me to land short once I passed over the Two Bridges, and to stay to the right.

"I think he said watch out for rocks, but that was crazy. He asked if I understood. I double-clicked my mic to mean I understood, but I doubt that meant anything to him. All at once below me I saw big rocks in the Ayr River — or as the Air Force dude said, 'Channel.'

"It was now 2030 and I lined up in a pattern to come in about ten feet above the 100-foot bridges. I immediately cut power and landed 50 feet past the bridges, where I was able to taxi up near several docked coal barges.

"Opening my door, I surveyed the area. I was about 800 feet from the harbor's breakwater, whereupon I made a mental note that when I had to take off I would take my aircraft downstream of the bridges, where I would actually have more than 1,000 feet for takeoff.

"Safely down, I keyed the harbor master on my radio and was told, as I taxied west on the River Ayr, to follow the 30-foot seawall up to my reserved dock space that was near the coal ships. This was a very small harbor and everything looked the same. I headed downstream to where eight ships were docked."

The attendant that met Casey said he was there to offer support. "I had no idea what he said. I realized that I was in an English-speaking country that nobody could understand. It was the Scottish accent," Casey would relate.

Once Casey tied up to a small boat for the night he inspected the aircraft. At that point he determined there was a mechanical problem. It turned out that the V-brace, located under the cowling against the fuselage's firewall, was bent. The V-brace was the main support for the left float strut.

The strut was now jammed into the plane's fuselage. This V-brace maintains rigidity and stabilizes the floats, and is enormously important in providing load-bearing strength to the floats during take-offs and landings.

Casey, with his hands behind his head, stood in disbelief. He immediately panicked and could only think his voyage was over. The bent V-brace was actually slammed into the plane's firewall, which meant no more flying on those babies (floats).

Casey later explained, "I needed to repair the damaged parts — but how? I then asked the attendant: How do we get my ship out of the water in order to make repairs?"

The Scotsman laughed and in his foreign dialect told Casey to "take a look with eyes upward." He pointed to a large crane more than 300 feet overhead.

The next day, the Liberty II was pulled from the water. Wipaire (the float supplier) in Minnesota was called and they promptly sent new V-brace supports overnight. The Scots not only put Casey up and bought him great meals, but they also donated docking and crane costs. British Aerospace (BAE) put on the new struts.

Said Casey, "I told BAE that I was sure the series of hard pounding to my floats during the long takeoff run into heavy swells in Keflavik caused the damage. The Scots agreed, I think. I would spend from June 23 to late evening on June 25 in Ayr for repairs and then it was off to Ireland for a day of fun and relatives.

"I was lucky that there were good mechanics in Ayr. I stayed at this beautiful hotel right next to the Prestwick race track. No horses running though. One day, I even could see all the way to Ireland from the seawall in downtown Prestwick. I loved the place and the people. Always had good food, too."

After his plane was repaired, Casey got his avgas from the Prestwick/Glasgow Airport. (As it turned out, managing the airport was a soon-to-be close friend of mine, Eddie Allison. He recalls the plane and fondly wished Casey good luck.)

Casey left Scotland for Foynes (close to Shannon Airport) Ireland. It was a short haul of some 277 miles. He was now somewhat behind schedule — it had been 12 days since leaving Alaska.

His favorite Irish poet came to mind. He had repeated this poem many times when trying times in life seemed to overwhelm him:

*A man may drink, and no be drunk;*
*A man may fight, and no be slain;*
*A man may kiss a bonnie lass,*
*And ay be welcome back again.*
— Robert Burns

Halfway to Ireland he was refused clearance to land. The Shannon Airport Controller told him to sit tight as there was no one minding the store. "He said that everyone was watching the 1990 FIFA World Cup in Bolivia," Casey said. "Virtually the whole country watched as Ireland beat Romania in a very tight match.

"I was over Northern Ireland when Shannon put a hold on my landing at Foynes. After about 45 minutes, the radio crackled very unexpectedly."

Shannon came up on the radio and said, "We now have beaten Romania. Who is first?"

All the pilots in the landing pattern could only assume they (Shannon Control) were asking who was first in line to land. Casey later learned they were talking about the world ranking of the teams in the World Cup.

When Casey did make contact back with Shannon, the same controller responded: "And where have you been? We expected you three days ago based on your flight plan."

The Shannon controller cleared Casey to 3,000 feet and told him to fly direct to Foynes. Then the controller asked a startled Casey a very unusual request: "Can you please fly by our tower? Many of us have not ever seen a floatplane."

Casey followed the request to the letter and Liberty II became the first floatplane to ever buzz the Shannon control tower. The controller came up on Casey's radio frequency and said, "Your aircraft took up the full view we had from our windows. Good job."

I can only imagine that Casey may have been the last to ever attempt this feat. Later Casey docked his craft at Foynes on the river at 1900 and was picked up by his cousin. That night at a bar in Limerick, he told the "buzzing story" and never paid for a pint.

All of his cousins wanted to see Liberty II. Pride busting from every pore, Casey saw the wee ones climb into his craft and become pilots. Casey had additional contraband stowed in his plane that included freshly pressed shirts his sister provided and, of course, a suit in case he met royalty or other high-level officials. But thinking ahead to the long journey, he had a new set of hip boots for those landings where there would be no seaplane dock.

Casey told all his relatives he was hoping later to land on the Thames. Pan Am was working on it.

Sitting comfortably in a lounge chair at Bobby Byrnes' pub, the atmosphere was conducive to affording Casey a chance to explain a dilemma he was facing.

The pub was quaint and cozy with an open fire, slate floor, and home-like atmosphere. Casey explained his London connection. "My insurance policy for this aircraft I'm flying was purchased from Lloyd's of London and was obtained by putting up my other plane, back in Seattle, as collateral."

Now mad as hell, Casey was almost yelling when he added that this Seattle-based aircraft was the plane Captain Bob stole while he was in Alaska and he didn't know where the aircraft was stored. "Moreover, if Lloyd's finds out that I no longer have the plane, they will cancel my insurance," he said.

"Even more worrying is that the insurance policy is only good for 60 days, and I haven't paid any premiums on it either. I was told from the broker that the premiums were donated. I never verified the truth.

"Can't tell Coleman or Phillips 66 because they will be pissed and probably dump me."

## Sixteen

# Landing on the River Thames – or, What a Bloody Mess

The day after I heard from Casey on June 22 in Keflavik, my team began to put together an extensive plan of having Liberty II land on London's River Thames. We would have media coverage from all over the world.

Besides planning for his London landing, we also had to respond to everyone in the Philips 66 camp, Pentagon officials, State Department queries, the national media, and of course all the Seattle TV stations that wanted live feeds.

Phillips 66, Dunleavy, and Engen were told by Iceland's naval commander, Admiral Hall, that Casey was close to landing in Scotland. The news reporters were told that London was within sight.

That same day, I left for Washington, D.C. (a mission that would soon become a weekly bad habit). I hooked up with David Knight and we mapped out a strategy for Casey to gain permission to land on the Thames. We projected that either June 27 or 28 would work. Our only concern was what we didn't know: Where the hell was Casey?

Knight had the great pleasure of working with the British Aviation Authority (BAA) in an attempt to gain permission for Casey to land his plane on the Thames. When Casey was previously in Washington, he told both Knight and me that Pan Am was working on getting him permission to land on the Thames and for us not to bother.

Our research showed (by checking with BAA) that Pan Am had never even tried.

But Engen, Dunleavy, and Knight were resourceful. How they did it, I don't know. So, on June 23, Casey gained approval to land on the Thames between Tower Bridge and London Bridge.

Jokingly, I presumed both admirals had talked to the Queen and probably the Prime Minister. I know Admiral Engen spoke to several influential people at BAA. Remember, Engen was the head of the FAA during Reagan's term in office. Also, Admiral Dunleavy called the British Admiralty, and I am sure that was the final touch in gaining approval to land on the Thames.

After approval was obtained, my job was to immediately determine a suitable location to hold a press briefing and have local dignitaries welcome Casey to London. I spoke with the Mayor of London's office and reps at Lloyd's of London. Later the same day we gained approval and were notified that we could hold the event on the London Bridge City Pier.

We now had only four days to finish all event planning; one day to contact all the media; one day for me to fly to London; and two days to put all planning in place.

Casey would land on the Thames at noon on June 28. London City Airport tower would direct Casey and provide the correct approach coordinates to land on the Thames (depending on wind and area congestion). Casey would then tie up at the London Bridge City Pier. On this platform, in the Thames, we would have a cadre of dignitaries and the press meeting him.

Lloyd's seemed very keen on this simple plan and even wanted to invite several members of Parliament to attend. Of course, representatives from the BAA were coming and would act as Casey's onsite unofficial air traffic controller once he landed. Monitoring on handheld radios, they would direct him to the pier. The media wanting to attend seemed like a Who's Who ranking. The total number of attendees grew and it made me question whether the pier could withstand the weight. The event was no longer simple.

Meanwhile, I must have made more than 40 attempts to reach Pan Am. Neither Captain Dan nor the contact source he provided me in case he was unreachable could be located. I also called Colonel Jim

Sills' desk and the U.S. Air Force contact was not clued into exactly where Casey was. His last flight plan had him heading to Shannon, Ireland, but nothing more.

Now, as far as we were aware (Knight and myself), no one knew where Casey really was nor how to get hold of him. Man, was I drained. Knight and I had been all over D.C., from the Pentagon to multiple embassies. Finally back in my hotel room with a cool drink in my hand and the TV blaring, I found some calm. Like all suspenseful movie plots, the mood changed almost instantaneously. As the phone rang, my senses only imagined a person running their nails across a blackboard.

On the other end was a maintenance rep at Wipaire (the float manufacturer). He informed me of a problem Casey was having with his floats and that they had sent him a new V-brace to arrive the next day, June 24, in Ayr, Scotland. I asked if they had spoken to him and they said yes.

Chuck Wiplinger, maintenance supervisor at Wipaire, gave me a phone number of where I could reach Casey. I woke myself at 0500 and called on June 24. Of course Casey was not there; I spoke to the BAE people doing the work on Casey's plane and left word for Casey to call me. I never actually reached Casey.

Later that same day, in desperation, I again left word with the BAE people, being very specific as to what we had planned for London. I even asked for the message to be repeated.

My message was short and terse: *Casey approved to land on the Thames. When: June 28. Event hosted by Lloyd's of London and British dignitaries; would be held on the London Bridge City Pier on the Thames. Casey would be the first floatplane ever allowed to land on Thames. Call Coleman ASAP.*

The BAE folks said they would deliver the message and have Casey call me back. Of course, I never heard back that day or the next. I was pissed and so were the admirals. I never told Lloyd's, as I hoped Casey somehow got the message and would arrive as planned. He had done so in the past.

On June 25, I boarded a morning Concorde flight to London. I knew this would be an event of the century. The media so far wanting to attend included: BBC, ITN (Independent Television News),

CBS, NBC, *Reuters*, AP, UPI, *The* (London) *Times, The Observer, Daily Mail, The Sun,* and *The New York Times.*

I arrived early that afternoon and immediately headed to my first London meeting with Lloyd's and the London mayor. I spent that evening (my first ever in London) looking over the press conference site — London Bridge City Pier.

Now I had to explain the cost, which was becoming significant, to Phillips 66. Prior to leaving for London, I spoke with Hammond and filled him in on the Thames landing. He wanted to attend but had other commitments. I told him we needed to have a gala reception with good food and booze. He said to go for it.

I was now making arrangements for a reception (food and top-shelf liquor) following Casey's landing. But with no word, I kept thinking: Where the hell is Casey?

The next day, I had a myriad of meetings lined up with several members of the British Parliament, the office of the mayor of London, Lloyd's, and several representatives of the BAA.

Rhetorical questions were abundant. Everyone asked what time he would arrive. Did he know how to line up his aircraft for a landing on the Thames (especially between two bridges)? Was he aware of all the special dignitaries that would be present? To all of these questions I merely answered "of course." He will be here close to noon on June 28, I continued to repeat myself. (God, I was freaked out.)

That night, I called Pan Am and the U.S. Air Force again and left word with both about the planned event. No response by either party.

Tim McCormack in New York had drafted a news story and faxed it to me. I had hired a photographer, managed to rent a pavilion for the reception that was close to the pier, and had it catered. All was set.

My frustration had reached a boiling point. I was about to embarrass Phillips 66 before the British establishment. How could I tell all those folks that my pilot won't possibly show (or, so it seemed)? The media was a problem, too. Hell, I had the interest of the most influential media in the world and all I could do was offer them a news story that made no sense if Casey didn't show.

My mind began to wander to how that news story might read: *Phillips 66 held a reception for its beleaguered pilot who never showed. Reception was full of beer, wine, tea, and cucumber sandwiches.*

Back in Ireland, while we were planning for the London event, Casey was telling well-embellished stories to his relatives at a local Limerick pub. Casey had received my message in Ayr and tried to call my office. Somehow, either his collect call was not accepted by my company's receptionist (he said a collect call to Bill Coleman from Casey) or the receptionist was not paying attention.

When I later asked my company's receptionist what happened, she said she told the international operator that Mr. Coleman was not there and please call back in a few days. (Note: Our receptionist was often on a distant planet.)

The other explanation was that the message Casey received from BAA never indicated there was an urgency to call Coleman. Casey also claimed to have called Pan Am and was told that the Thames landing was not approved and to fly over London. So, in Casey's mind, all he had to do was take off from Foynes and fly to Lake Como, Italy. Pan Am had his flight plan approved.

It was now D-Day, June 28. We had well over 100 guests on the London Bridge City Pier. Again, neither I nor my office (so I was told) or Knight had heard from Casey. All I could hope for, and hope I did, with many prayers mixed in, was that Casey got my message. At least he must have checked in with the Air Force and they would have told him. Sills was off my radar as he was not too fond of Casey at present due to the pressure relying on U.S. Air Force logistics.

**1000 Hours:** On the Pier in the Thames, we all stood. The water was very calm and it was a perfect 20 C (72 F). Most of the dignitaries (and I really hadn't been introduced to many of the attendees) were handsomely dressed in evening wear — men in tuxedos and women in very elegant and stylish attire. The media had cameras all set on tripods and the reporters all seemed to gather with each other to compare information.

**1100:** To a person, they all asked when Casey was coming. To a person, I answered very soon. All the boats had been cleared from the landing area chosen by the BAA for Casey to land on the Thames. The only stationary ship was the HMS Belfast, a WWII cruiser museum.

What a backdrop for Casey's landing. Lloyd's had also planned a special dinner that evening for Casey. It was to be a surprise. (Boy, were they surprised.)

**1140:** We now heard a northwesterly roar of a reciprocating engine in the distance and my gut said it was Casey's plane. To make matters worse, the roar was not coming from a plane that had lined up to approach Tower Bridge, on the Thames, from an easterly direction. The engine roar was definitely at a higher altitude.

I was choking as I watched the faces around me. In the next several minutes, we would all see the red, white, and blue Liberty II fly directly overhead of us. The TV crews asked if that was him and I said yes. They scrambled to get footage. I know they didn't get anything.

**1200.** The BAA tried to bring Casey up on their hand-held radios. Did I know Casey's frequency? No. They raised Shannon, which said Casey was passed along to Euro Control from them. BAA tried Euro Control who said Casey must have turned his radio off.

**1215.** I was screaming inside my head. What the fuck? How could this go so bad? I wanted to jump in the Thames and drown.

**1230.** First I blamed Pan Am. Next the folks in Ayr, Scotland. But most of all, I had a real hard-on for Casey. I and the dignitaries and media standing on the pier all agreed that we saw the plane flying at about 7,000 to 8,000 feet. But we all were sure that the plane wagged its wings at all of us below. We thought the pilot was waving to us. (Maybe he was saying "fuck you.")

**1240.** I invited everyone to join me for refreshments. And, when most of the dignitaries and media gathered in the pavilion I had rented, all seemed very polite but most kept asking me why Casey had not landed. Perhaps the most pissed off was the mayor of London who was going to present Casey with the Key to the City. Next pissed in line were the BAA and Lloyd's. The latter would come back to haunt Casey at a later date when they would attempt to revoke his aircraft's insurance.

The reception after the Thames disaster went well. I apologized so many times that I began to sound like a politician running for office. That night BBC had a 20-second news clip showing all dignitaries (glad I was not in the footage) at the pier. They explained the story and said the pilot chose not to visit London. That was it.

**1900.** I finally got hold of Pan Am and read them the riot act. They really didn't seem to care. Kind of a "so what" attitude. (No wonder they went broke.) The person on the other end of the phone call at Pan Am was a stupid bimbette who only knew that her company tried and failed to get permission for Casey to land on the Thames. She added, "We told Casey about the Thames deal."

I shut the bitch down. In an abrupt tone, I told her that I got the clearance and she screwed up. I wish I could remember her name so I could put it in this book in bold uppercase letters.

I went on to explain to her that I left detailed messages saying the Thames landing was approved. She said no message ever was given to her. I asked if she had any mental problems and she hung up the phone. Now that was how Pan Am treated me and let Casey down. I never did find out what message the folks in Ayr had communicated to Casey.

When I finally caught up to Casey in Crete on July 5, he said that Euro Control cleared him to Lake Como and he was told to maintain 9,000 feet. Had he been lower, about 3,000 feet, he thought he might have seen us below as he was glancing at the Thames. He wished he could have landed there.

I took a couple days in London to see the sights. I was staying at the Marriott Hotel Grosvenor Square, which was quite comfortable. I got invited to a number of lunches and dinners by MPs and the mayor. They all really treated me like I was Casey — even when flying back to the States, courtesy first class on Virgin.

# Seventeen

# The White Cliffs of Dover and Navigating the Alps

Casey had an easy morning on June 28 in Limerick. He said goodbye to relatives. His father had been born there as well as most of his family. He called back to New York and his father's health seemed fine (though there were still more tests to be made.)

He departed Limerick about 0800 and taxied to the Port of Foynes and took off in the large harbor area. He had not heard anything from Pan Am about flight clearances to any future destinations, nor messages of goodwill. Since Pan Am had previously said the British nixed a Thames landing, Casey was now intent on heading directly to Lake Como and then on to Greece. By 1000, he had achieved his flight clearances to fly direct to Lake Como in Italy.

He left the Port of Foynes at 1030. Once in the harbor, on a very calm day, Casey was facing a 935-mile trip that should take about seven hours to reach Lake Como, Italy.

He also had a strong impulse to pass over London and take a lingering look at the Thames. Some two months ago, Pan Am had previously promised him a landing on the Thames. ("They had told me a week prior that they couldn't get the approval. It didn't matter much now — Pan Am had never kept any promise.")

Casey's flight path was passed off from Shannon Center to Euro Control. The "cowboys," as Casey called the Euro folks, told him to climb and maintain an IFR (Instrument Flight Rules) altitude at

11,000 feet and "squawk ident" (a method by which an aircraft electronically communicates position with air traffic control via a tran-
sponder) every hour. He didn't like the altitude adjustment from his
usual 9,000 feet, as it was really cold the higher he went. He now relied
on forced air from his engine to heat the cabin. He thought maybe
the controllers wanted him to weave his way through the Alps. Casey
hastily paged through his flight manual looking for a course to follow.
What was the tallest mountain in the Alps?

When previously speaking with the U.S. Air Force representative in the U.K., Casey had made copious notes. The AF dude told him
that Lake Como was situated in a lush valley and surrounded by the
Alps. While mountains reached 6,500 feet and steep-sided valleys extended far inland, the landscape was made up of many elements that
made one marvel at the wonders of nature. "This reads like a perfect
destination," Casey thought to himself.

By 11:30, he was near the Thames. Could he have made a
landing? Would it have been safe? Why not see it firsthand? Casey
eased his stick back, cut power, and headed down towards the center
of London. "I see the Thames," he exclaimed now at about 8,000 feet.

He recognized the Tower of London and Big Ben. "Man, look
at all those people on the dock down there," he thought. "Probably
waiting for someone special."

The radio crackled. Euro Control came up and asked why he
had descended to 8,000 feet. They saw this deviation on radar and
wondered if Casey was having engine problems. Casey (lying his ass
off) acknowledged that he had not correctly monitored his fuel flow
from his tanks and his engine had lost power. All was good now; he
had made proper adjustments and was beginning to climb again. He
requested 9,000 feet and squawked his altitude at that level.

Now past the Cliffs of Dover and over the English Channel, he
mused about his place in history. "I was the one flying the plane, not
the plane flying me," he would later say. "It struck me at that moment
that I was just not a pilot but an aviation pioneer."

As he journeyed over France, the colors of the landscape
seemed brighter. The mountains ahead seemed more majestic, and the
world just looked more beautiful through the aircraft's window. He
would soon be reaching Switzerland.

Next up was the ride through the Alps, and his next contact would be with the Center at Geneva. As he squawked Geneva ATC, the radio crackled and a French accent said to climb to 14,000 feet. He thought he was still in France, forgetting that the Swiss speak French, too. "I replied back that it would take me some time to reach that altitude as I was just a single-engine plane with floats," Casey would later explain.

"Merci, floats," the Swiss controller responded. "Repeat that November 1990 Lima: *Je ne comprenais pas ce que vous entendez par flotteurs. Pouvez-vous répéter s'il vous plaît?*"

"Excuse me for the French," the controller said. "Will you repeat that you have floats? I didn't quite understand you."

Casey thought these traffic cops were just like the dudes at Shannon. What the hell was a floatplane doing in the Alps? "Maybe I should have said 'Pan Am Clipper,' he thought.

"Center, this is the floatplane," Casey responded. "Got two heavy-weight fuel tanks where the wheels should be, and that means it will take me 200 miles and about two hours to attain 14,000. Will squawk at assigned altitude. Over."

Casey pulled the stick back and slowly climbed. He reached behind the seat and grabbed an oxygen mask. He slid it over his face and began to inhale. It was getting colder as he climbed and he began asking himself, "What the hell was the Center thinking?"

He grabbed a blanket from behind the seat and wrapped it around his shoulders. With teeth chattering, he wondered how long it would be before he froze to death.

Casey grabbed his mic and shouted to air traffic control, "Oh my God, I have a real problem! I am almost out of oxygen and that means I could shortly pass into unconsciousness. I'm not thinking clearly and my console looks blurry."

He kept telling himself, "Wake up, wake up; don't fall asleep."

"Center (very urgent tone of voice), I made the 14,000, but my oxygen canister reads close to zero." He kept repeating: "I am almost out of oxygen!"

Almost in desperation, he asked the Swiss, "Hey, in an attempt to save my life and not pass out in the Alps or become a skiing accident, I need permission to descend to 9,000." (He thought the skiing accident comment was really funny.)

Center replied in a very reserved tone. "N-1990-L, you are cleared to 9,000. Watch the peaks. That was a joke, floatplane. We have you on radar. Fly the center course between the mountains and watch out for updrafts. Over."

"Have my ears on and descending to 9,000. Don't plan to ski today. Thanks for all the help," Casey replied, laughing. It took a half hour and 70 miles to descend. The mountain peaks had just enough snow on them to remind Casey of a whipped cream topping on a chocolate fudge sundae. The air was crisp and the engine's hum sounded very smooth.

For Casey, the trip was now really running perfectly. He was a bit off target, schedule-wise, regarding his boastful projection at the Washington, D.C., press conference about finishing this journey in 40 days.

He remembered Phillips 66's Hammond saying it was not the time but the endurance of completing the actual flight that people would remember about this record. Hammond speculated about any of the great flyers in history having similar thoughts.

Casey thought about what his personal heroic flyer, Charles Lindbergh, had said about his challenging flight over the Atlantic:

*"I owned the world that hour as I rode over it. Free of the earth, free of the mountains, free of the clouds, but how inseparably I was bound to them."*

His thoughts now were refocused on the excellent operating performance of his engine and how he had needed high-quality avgas plus a change of aviation oil every 40 hours to keep his baby purring. In particular, he needed an aviation oil that would enable his engine to operate in the "green" during the temperature extremes his plane was being subjected to – close to minus-20F at Iceland, Greenland, and now in the Alps.

On the other extreme, really hot temperatures of more than 120F awaited him in Saudi Arabia, Dubai, and India. For engine safeguards, he was receiving cases of Phillips 66 20W-50 X/C oil at key refueling points along the journey. In the desert, he may even change his oil every 30 hours.

Shifting mental gears, his mind again was focused on the outside environment. He was in the mountains but could see the lush open valleys below. Switzerland was a beautiful country. At 9,000 feet and with only birds to keep him company, Casey amused himself by toying with the radio to see if he could pick up commercial airline chatter. Seems the boys weren't talking much today. He did pick up a lady pilot in a twin-engine turbo talking about her brother's get-rich scheme. "Boy, I have to write her and find out if her brother got rich," he thought.

Casey soon picked up Milan Center and requested permission to land at Lake Como. Milan Approach Control said to contact Lake Como on the same frequency. A Como controller responded when contacted: "No land, no land. Go talk to Milan and land there." Casey replied he was a seaplane and had already filed with them. He had been cleared to Lake Como. Como answered, "No land."

Casey later recalled, "I told the Como idiot on the other end of Unicom that I had flown eight and a half hours and the tanks were running on fumes."

Como insisted: "No land. Call Milan."

Frustrated, Casey contacted Milan and the controller told him that this was a normal trick of Como approach. "They're stupido Italians. Just fly your aircraft to Lake Como and set her down directly on the lake."

Casey repeated, "Just land." Milan said, "Yes."

So without hesitation, Casey lined up between the mountains on either side and landed on the lake. The landing was picture perfect. He headed for a docking area where there were two seaplanes docked. The birds were Pussy One and Pussy Two. The pilots were *molto belle donne piloti* ("very beautiful women pilots"). They were about to leave so Casey waited for them to depart and then docked his craft.

That night he spent a quiet evening at a very nice bed and breakfast. Casey would spend the next two days waiting for his clearance to fly to Athens, Greece. The U.S. Air Force was working on all the details and making arrangements with a local yacht club in Athens for Casey to moor the aircraft.

What gave him the greatest pleasure during this brief stopover was telling young children about the thrill of being a pilot and the overall beauty of flying a seaplane. The kids would climb all over Casey's plane. "I remember the look in the children's eyes when they sat in the cockpit seat. You could almost feel their excitement," he would later relate.

The beauty of his surroundings left a lasting impression. The crystal clear water of the lake and the beauty of the mountain backdrop swept Casey's mind and body to a mystical island. To him, it could have been Nirvana.

He left for Athens on June 30. The events that would follow would only make Knight and myself (plus Phillips 66 and the media) just throw up our arms in the air in utter disbelief.

# Eighteen

# A Greek Repast; then Exit Right to the U.S. Navy in Crete

Authorization to enter and exit a country en route remained one of Casey's single greatest hurdles. For this leg, from Lake Como to Athens, he flew over Milan and headed out to the Adriatic Sea. From there, he headed south and overflew Split, Yugoslavia (now Croatia). Continuing southward, he was cleared to take a straight path through Albania.

After crossing the Albanian-Greek border, he flew to Piraeus, Greece, about 30 miles southwest of Athens. He would dock at the Yacht Club of Greece at Piraeus. Casey had flown through nasty headwinds most of this leg for nearly 930 miles in eight and a half hours (averaging about 120 miles an hour) and was dogged tired.

Subsequently, he radioed the Hellenikon Air Base in Athens and notified the controller that he had tied up at the Yacht Club at which he had previously been instructed to dock his plane. The sergeant on duty at the 7206th Air Base Group remained the primary USAF unit at the Athens airport. He instructed Casey to sit tight and that one of his airmen would be down to pick him up.

"The airman arrived and drove me to the Marriott in Athens," Casey said.

Casey would later convey all the particulars to me of his trek from Ireland to Athens during a long-awaited phone call after July 4 from his new home on the island of Crete. He said that he didn't want to stay at the Air Force Base as he wanted some freedom. He was really bushed and all he wanted was a hot meal and a bottle of Scotch. He got both, plus he found two lovely TWA flight attendants staying at the hotel. No worries till the morrow, he thought. "Lots of time tonight to tell the stories all the 'stews' like to hear."

The following day, our pilot contacted Pan Am representatives and was moved over to the Pan Am Hotel. Located in the city center of Athens, the hotel was within walking distance of the Metropolis Greek Orthodox Cathedral, the Old Parliament House, and the Hellenic Parliament. Also nearby were Syntagma Square and the Ancient Agora.

He later conveyed to me that he began using Pan Am Athens' offices to try and gain clearances through Egypt. The communiqués between Casey and Egyptian aviation authorities seemed rather dubious. It seems the Egyptian aviation folks had never seen a seaplane before and wondered where he could land safely to obtain fuel. He was having no luck at all.

"My next three days in Athens proved interestingly confusing," he later explained. "More important, not a single word back from the Egyptians. Pan Am was no help."

Back at his hotel, Casey interfaced with the Air Force and continued to try and get clearance to fly to Alexandria and beyond. His game plan was to fly to Alexandria, refuel, and proceed the same day to Jeddah, Saudi Arabia. But he was not getting anywhere with Alexandria.

All his Air Force contacts, both back at Scott AFB in the U.S. and in Greece, couldn't help. On the night of July 3, the plot thickened and with the help of his co-conspirators — the TWA flight attendants — they planned an Independence Day get-together that would go down in the annals of Athens folklore.

Meanwhile, Air Force Colonel Sills at Scott Air Force Base called me with a report on July 3. Casey popped up on their radar on July 2 and had made it to Athens. Not much else was talked about.

Now the diplomatic curse began. On July 4 at 2100, my phone roused me away from a great TV show at home in New York. Every detail of the July 4th soirée in Athens was told to me by the U.S. Consulate Econ (Economics) Officer in Athens where it was 0400 on July

5. He asked that his name never be revealed due to his own security considerations.

(Let's examine my attitude at this point. I was really pissed as I had not heard from our wayward traveler since Keflavik, Iceland. I had tried Pan Am, but they had totally washed their hands of him, or never really kept their word. I don't think they ever had done squat.)

This U.S. "deep throat" diplomat used lots of "he did this and he did that", all leading to the eventual climax: "We want your pilot thrown out of Athens and ask that he never comes back."

The Econ officer added, "This proclamation was made directly by our ambassador. He told me to call you immediately to make sure this gets to that pilot of yours. So get his ass out of Athens or we will pursue civil action by the Greek military or local police."

I asked how he got my name and number. He said he had spoken with the British Consulate coincidentally after he had read about our pilot pissing off the British by not landing on the Thames. "Your name came up as the organizer of the trip," he said. "Do I have this right, Coleman?"

I said yes and thanked the gentleman. What I didn't care for was the insinuation that the U.S. Ambassador might call Secretary of State James Baker regarding this matter. Phillips 66 would (rightly) have had a shit-fit.

As much of what the Econ officer told me was "hearsay" and could not be proven in any court of law, I hesitate to recount all the details. Here is just a quick recap.

I understood that Casey and the gals found Ouzo, the potent elixir of the Greeks. Casey also learned the Sirtaki, a popular dance of Greek origin shown in the 1964 film "Zorba the Greek." Everyone dances in a line or circle with hands extended on a neighbor's shoulders.

Somehow the party made it back to the Yacht Club and subsequently grew in intensity. The Consulate's Econ officer said mostly everyone was singing and dancing and the noise was deafening. Complaints then poured into Yacht Club officials from all the boat owners who were living on their yachts. They in turn called the American Consulate.

To quell the disturbance, Greek naval police were dispatched and arrived at Casey's mooring along with Yacht Club security guards. All the forces descended onto the scene at about 0100 and the party came to an abrupt end.

The Econ officer said that the "American Consulate was called and I got involved. We understand that your pilot was too embarrassed to return to the Pan Am Hotel, so he slept in his plane."

While July 4th was raucous, the next day turned infamous.

Before the rooster crowed at "O-Dark Early," I received another nasty call from the U.S. Consulate in Athens. Now the same caller from the day before was back again at 0100 (or 0800 in Greece). I had hoped things had blown over; they hadn't.

His first words accentuated the alarm in his voice: "Hey Coleman, remember me? I called about seven hours earlier. This is your friendly Econ officer in the American Consulate in Athens."

He reiterated what the U.S. Ambassador earlier had said: "Get that seaplane pilot out of Greece."

I told the Econ Officer that I couldn't locate Casey. He countered by saying, "That pilot of yours has caused an international incident here in Greece."

My brain shook. The call and remarks were coming from a U.S. diplomat in Greece. I had been in Greece before and loved the place. How could this situation be happening on my watch? I gained a quick lesson in how U.S. diplomats cover their ass.

I was speaking to this dude whom I never met nor probably would ever want to have lunch with. His tale of woe made me think we might be going to war with Greece. Had Casey fucked up diplomatic relations so bad that even Aristotle would have cried foul? And, why wasn't Casey calling me? I could only imagine something worse had happened. Maybe his plane had been sabotaged.

(This worldly experience would come to equal other embassy dealings as Casey later would make his way through the Middle East, India, and the Far East. Both Knight and I learned from this incident. Later on in Casey's journey it seemed we were constantly being interrogated by State Department officials and other countries' U.S. Consulate officials. We learned to articulate our responses more professionally.)

My wandering mind quickly refocused on my Athens buddy.

"Last time we spoke," he said, "I reiterated that we got the Greek naval police involved. Casey told an officer in the Greek Navy that they needed to call either you or Admiral Dunleavy, the Chief of Naval Operations. Since I'm not wired into the U.S. Navy nor do I want to buck the military establishment, I was determined to call you again.

"This incident was very close to having Casey locked up with the key thrown away," said the Consulate official, his voice reaching a soprano pitch. "Now, we want him out of here immediately. It is our understanding that your pilot kept telling the Greek naval official that he only wanted permission to fly to Alexandria on his way around the world.

"Mr. Coleman, if your pilot doesn't get his plane removed from his slip at the Greek Yacht Club in the next several hours, the Greek Navy has been instructed to blow his plane out of the water, and then they will lock him up and throw away the key. Do you copy?"

I told the gentleman that I would immediately call Admiral Dunleavy's office and we would definitely make arrangements for Casey to moor his aircraft in another location that was overseen by the U.S. Navy. Crete was a viable option. I promised to spell out all the details to him after talking to Dunleavy.

About the time I hung up the phone, I got a call from the Duty Officer in Dunleavy's office. The person on the other end identified himself as Lieutenant Commander Foster. He addressed me in a rather clipped tone. He adroitly said that "OP-05 had made arrangements for my pilot (Casey) to find safe harbor on Crete. There is a Naval Support Activity at Souda Bay and Casey can take refuge there. And, they are expecting him right away," Foster said.

To this day, Dunleavy has never disclosed how he knew about the planned expulsion of Casey. My demeanor lightened. This problem/solution action left me speechless — Dunleavy made all these arrangements even before I could call him.

I called the U.S. Consulate back immediately and the Econ Officer actually sighed when I told him the news. He immediately passed on the positive news to his ambassador, who was assured that Casey would not reenter Athens ever again. The Econ Officer added, "This does mean forever."

Casey would be locked down in Crete until he exited the Greek

Isles for Alexandria. Further, the ambassador genuinely hoped that the negative atmosphere would quiet down.

The Econ Officer also actually thanked me and said if there was anything he could do for me, like sink Casey's plane, he would be glad to help. I passed along my apologies and hoped Greece and the Yacht Club would return to being American-friendly. At the end of our conversation he actually further wished Casey fair winds and success for the rest of his journey. "No hard feelings," he said with his tongue in cheek.

At about 0930 on July 5 Casey was given the word to exit Athens by a cadre of people, including several Greek Naval Officers, the Yacht Club Commodore, the harbor master, and the American Consulate. He was told to immediately vacate his slip and head for Crete.

Casey acted a bit puzzled. He had not been told that the ambassador's aide had called me. Casey was told nothing, and he earnestly believed he was just moving on to a friendlier environment. He assumed he had done nothing wrong.

He stood his ground on the dock and started to complain about how he was being treated. He said he wanted to talk to the ambassador as well as to that rude person (the Econ Officer) he just spoke with from the U.S. Consulate. Casey was told that the U.S. Navy had made arrangements for him to stay at the naval facility at Souda Bay.

Finally on July 5, after not hearing from or talking to Casey since Iceland or more than 12 days prior, he phoned me. Casey asked me what the hell was happening. I told him his welcome in Athens and the mainland of Greece had run its course and that that he should shut up and take off immediately for Crete. As it was close to 0230 my time, I was going to bed and I would talk to him once he got settled on Crete. I hung up. At 1030, Casey left Athens.

At 0330 I received a call from the Greek Yacht Club accounting office stating that Casey had never paid his mooring charges incurred over a three-day period. There were also other charges such as avgas, water, and other incidentals (whatever they were — probably Scotch) .The bill came to more than $3,800 and I gave them my American Express card number.

Alas, it was at this exact time, during Casey's departure flight from Athens, that the U.S. Air Force backed off from providing further assistance. It would not be until Casey's journey made it to the Aleutian Islands that the Air Force would re-engage. We were now all alone in getting Casey's future flight clearances. Phillips 66 was now his only friend.

Casey launched from Piraeus, at the tip of Athens, where all ferries originate and all the yachts are moored. His white-polished plane reflected off the beautiful aquamarine water of the Aegean Sea. His plane stepped up on the calm waters and had the appearance of a majestic eagle.

His Irish humor came running through his veins as he took off from Athens. He pulled the aircraft's nose up and climbed upward to about 1,500 feet. He then swung the bird around to the north and in the direction of Athens. He had every intention to buzz the Acropolis and, if at all possible, the U.S. Consulate.

Later on that day the Econ Officer called me again and said Casey had left but seemed to f——- around with the naval authorities. He explained that Captain Pavlos on the HS Hormi had tried to communicate with Casey's radio. The Econ Officer explained that the Greek Navy Captain had ordered Casey to turn his aircraft around and head for Crete. "If you do not follow this order, we will be forced to shoot you down," he said, according to the Econ Officer.

Casey turned abruptly and headed to Crete. Virtually underneath his aircraft were two large Greek naval vessels. Casey was to contact the Naval Air Station on its frequency and then get landing instructions for Souda Bay harbor.

He kept an altitude of about 1,500 feet. His radio crackled again and it was the Ops officer at the U.S. Naval Air Station. He gave Casey landing instructions: "Several yards offshore please put your anchor out." This was in the waters off the naval base in Souda Bay harbor. The Ops Officer also gave wind direction and wave height. "We welcome you to our island," he said. "Admiral Dunleavy and Greek Navy Captain Pavlos send their best."

Casey would actually anchor about 100 feet from the shore and would be picked up by a navy launch and then be met by Lieutenant Holmes, a representative for the naval facility.

Souda Bay is a natural harbor near the town of Souda, on the northwest coast of the Greek island of Crete. The bay is overlooked on both sides by hills, with a relatively low and narrow isthmus in the west.

The United States Naval Support Activity (NSA) Souda Bay is strategically located on the northwest coast. NSA carries out its vital mission of extending Joint and Fleet War fighting capability through Operational Support to U.S., allied, and coalition forces. NSA also acts as a Naval Air Station and Naval Weapons Facility.

Our pilot was now safe. Dunleavy's Pentagon office called me on July 6 to say Casey had landed in Crete. Later the same day, Casey and I finally touched base. His merry vocal tones gave the appearance that "all was right with the world." He even wanted to claim that he had obtained approval to land in Crete once he mentioned Admiral Dunleavy's name.

I abruptly told him the truth. Dunleavy's office had heard of his problems in Athens – how, I didn't know — and had arranged behind the scenes to open the doors for him to stay at the Naval Support Facility at Souda Bay in Crete, after which his aide had contacted me in New York. It was not because Casey had thrown around Dunleavy's name.

Also, I told him about the American Consulate calling me in the middle of the night in a very heated state and about him being escorted out of Athens by the Greek Navy. Casey said he never saw a navy ship following him and just couldn't believe he had done anything wrong to merit his expulsion.

After my full explanation of all the sordid details, his only response was to ask if we had gotten clearance for him to fly on to Alexandria. In all earnestness, it was all of our fervent desire that he stay a couple of weeks in Crete while we file flight plans and gain approvals for him to fly to Alexandria and then on to Jeddah, Saudi Arabia.

Now here is where the story really takes a flyer. He emphasized that he was going back to the American Consulate in the next several days. Stunned, I yelled empathically not to go back to Athens. But then again, Casey never listened to anything I ever said. "Seriously," I told him, "When you head to Athens and go back to the Consulate, be prepared to go to jail."

Casey thought I was kidding. I wasn't.

After hanging up the phone, I kept thinking what the Econ Officer had told me: "For your pilot friend, it's either leave Athens or go to jail. Good day, Mr. Coleman, and please don't give me a reason to contact you or the U.S. Secretary of State ever again."

But at the present Casey seemed to be steering a rudderless ship. If only he followed what he preached: to become a goodwill ambassador for aviation. His most pressing problem was that he had never taken any diplomatic courses. Which leads to the very next day ...

His mind was set on going back to the Consulate and demanding they help him get clearance to fly into Egypt. Filing new and amended flight plans were the first order of business. He was exceedingly ambitious in filing plans all the way to Japan. He was unaware that Dunleavy's group wanted him to stay in Crete until the diplomatic problems settled down. In fact, the State Department had discussed this with Dunleavy directly.

Further, the Ops folks at the Souda Bay Naval Air Station were getting strong pushback from Alexandria and the answer coming through channels from Egypt was that they didn't want a small floatplane landing there for fear that an accident might happen and they would be liable.

Convinced he had no other recourse and going completely against my wishes, Casey jumped aboard his plane, turned over his engine, and sped out of the harbor with great abandonment. He had the idea of going back to the American Consulate and meeting with the Marine Attaché (the closest link to the U.S. Navy) in an attempt to garner support to obtain the necessary approvals to land and refuel in Alexandria.

He landed at the Greece Yacht Club and tied up to the aft-end of a large yacht. The owner was an acquaintance he had made during his previous stay. No authorities (police, Greek Navy, nor American diplomats) knew he was back in Athens. But Casey was totally oblivious that he was breaking the law, as he never really accepted he had been thrown out of Athens.

Upon his return to Athens, he headed for the U.S. Consulate. He was forced to wait for more than six hours to see the Marine Attaché. Finally, after nearly a seven-hour wait, a Consulate employee called Casey to her desk. The woman, according to Casey, was Anne Cusack. She proceeded to ask Casey why he was there and how did he get into Greece without proper papers? Also, where was he going? Did he have approval to go there? When was he leaving?

Frustrated and very flustered, our pilot explained he was not a tourist, but a pilot setting a world record and that the U.S. Air Force, which had supported the trip, had cleared him to Greece.

She explained that there was commercial significance attached to Casey's unauthorized visit to Greece, which was compounded by him bringing his plane into Greece. She explained that to those in the Consulate it appeared as if Casey was trying to sell U.S.-manufactured seaplanes in Greece without the necessary import/export documents.

His face was beet red by now. Horribly frustrated since no one was listening to him, Casey said that all he wanted was approval from Cusack to be in-country and also to see the Marine Attaché to help with his flight planning.

Smiling, she agreed and stamped Casey's passport "GOOD". Casey asked what that meant. She explained that if any official in this country or other countries saw this stamp, it meant, "You are a good person," she said, smiling. "Thank you for coming down to the embassy and have a good trip to wherever you are going."

Had Casey previously listened to me, he would have realized that to the U.S. Consulate and Greek Government, he was considered persona non grata. That is why the Marine Attaché never wanted to see him. But Casey just blamed the woman. He was lucky he was not thrown in jail for reentering Athens.

Casey was madder than a teased grizzly bear. He called his acquaintances at the Athens U.S. Air Force Base but was told that they could no longer help him and he was in the hands of the U.S. Navy now.

The end result was that Casey would spend the next 23 days in Crete. I would get reports on a regular basis from Navy Captain Stevenson, head of the Naval Facility. Casey would spend time with the Commanding Officer in his home and at the base. Early on, Casey stayed in a local hotel in the town of Chaniá, about 10 kilometers from the naval base. Later, from July 12 on, the CO invited him to stay in the officers' quarters at the Naval Air Station.

Casey spent his time giving flying lessons. He even formed an aircraft flying club. Casey was proud that he taught more than 20 Navy personnel how to fly.

He also tried to get clearances, to no avail. Knight and I would get updates on Casey's whereabouts from Dunleavy's office. During this time period, Knight and I were spending our time duplicating efforts in an attempt to get Casey clearances to fly to Alexandria and beyond. The Washington grind now would begin in earnest.

# Nineteen

# Options: Where Does Casey Go Next?

*"If you are going through hell, keep going."*
— Winston Churchill

With Casey safely tucked away in Crete, thanks to my U.S. Navy friends, a lightning bolt of reality hit both David Knight and myself at the same time: What had we gotten ourselves into? That harsh reality was that we were now totally responsible for Casey making it around the world. We had unknowingly assumed the role as his flight planners and, laughably, the executioners.

On July 8, Knight and I sat down for breakfast at the 14th street JW Marriott hotel in D.C. Almost without any hesitation and even before I could sip my first ounce of freshly brewed coffee, Knight rushed to judgment. "We probably aren't going to know for several weeks what countries will let Casey land, refuel, or even overfly. I have written to the Egyptian Embassy and asked for special favors for Casey," he said.

"I have also implored our Aircraft Owners and Pilots Association (AOPA) Safety Foundation members here and in the Middle East to provide us any kind of leverage to gain an open dialogue with the Egyptian Embassy in the U.S. and/or the Egyptian Ministry of Civil Aviation. Nothing has caused either to budge. Right now, my sources tell me that Egypt has refused to offer any diplomatic support for this record flight. I think our only hope is having the U.S. State Department run interference for us."

I reviewed our very few options left to help execute Casey's flight plan. We spread the world map out on the restaurant table. Side by side, we unfolded several flight planning aeronautical charts to gain a perspective regarding the best route for Casey to follow. We explored: What were our alternatives?

The most direct route was going through Alexandria to Jeddah. Casey could then fly across Saudi Arabia to Bahrain, then on to Dubai. After that he could fly to Karachi and on to India.

The longer option — and one fraught with a lack of landing sites (lakes, rivers) — was to go through Turkey, then Kuwait, down to Dubai, and finally Karachi. The last option was Israel to Kuwait and finally to Karachi.

But getting the Israelis to buy into this plan brought thoughts of Jim Carrey in the movie "Dumb & Dumber" when he asked the woman if he had a romantic chance with her. She responded, "One-in-a-million." And Carrey said, "Wow," as though he thought he still had a chance.

"Each of these options," said Knight, "Requires getting diplomatic clearances to enter and exit (take off from water) each of those countries, many of which are suspicious of any outsiders from the United States. And, if we pursue the Israel option, consider that most Middle Eastern countries do not have diplomatic relations with the Israelis.

"Saudi Arabia — our oil partner — is our best choice for crossing this section of the world. Maybe we will get lucky."

Knight remembered what Engen had proudly proclaimed about this record-setting event: "Liberty II sends a message to other countries that they too can enjoy the fruits of aviation. After seeing and touching Liberty II, most developing countries can look to owning piston-powered aircraft."

My buddy Knight had very broad football shoulders but his mannerisms (those of a shrewd and pensive thinker) portrayed the image of a Washington politician. He never seemed flustered. He had both hands outstretched on our table top. By now, I had expected him to show signs of anger or frustration. He held his course.

We had intentionally found a booth near the rear of the restaurant as we didn't want eavesdroppers. While not wanting to raise our voices, it was becoming clear that my frustration level was poised to explode. I wanted to yell and curse at this whole frustrating world record ego trip.

Knight remained calm. He pursed his lips and in his deep baritone voice said, "We can do this. We are not going to let these bastards outwit us. So far, our strategy to gain him clearance to enter Alexandria has failed. But let's look at other choices we can make.

"Remember, the Egyptians don't know anything about seaplanes, nor do they especially understand my explanation that Casey's plane is a single-engine plane with pontoons (floats).

"I tried to describe this concept to the Egyptian Consul General at their D.C. Embassy and was left with a blank stare. I thought perhaps it was the translator. Then I realized the Consul General was really not even listening. I left and subsequently wrote a letter. It was ultimately answered with, "Sorry, can't help you." I suggested that perhaps a photo of Casey's plane would have helped.

We pursued several alternative directions during the remainder of the day. We spoke with the Saudi Embassy hoping they might intercede for us with Egypt. But no one was willing to do so. We also drafted a letter and dropped it by the Egyptian Embassy. We sat for three hours in their luxurious waiting room and the only reply was, "Come back tomorrow."

David's wife Margo, who worked at the Smithsonian, was the very vocal one in the Knight family and often when we had dinner together might say Casey was his own worst enemy. Yet, she really appreciated what Casey was trying to do and wished him well. That evening at dinner it was Margo who said, "David, go back and knock on the Egyptian Embassy's door and don't leave until you have them give you the clearance."

The next day, Margo's direction only ended in her husband again sitting in the embassy's waiting room for five hours and not receiving any response.

Several days passed with no results. On July 11, we had a date with destiny.

Knight agreed that we had only one option left. We needed to gain the support of our State Department. After cutting through red tape, we were able to set up a meeting with Dick Eason, State's head of aviation.

Both Knight and I understood the turmoil and drawbacks that faced us. We would have to rekindle our efforts in trying to convince our government that the Casey adventure was a "Red, white, and blue" cause. We needed State to support this effort, but knew from previous attempts that we would be facing an audience of naysayers.

The first goal was to convince State to use backchannels to encourage the Egyptian government to allow Casey to land and refuel in Alexandria.

The State Department building is awesome, with a beautiful facade and granite steps leading to large cast iron doors. One steps into a large portico where there are large security scanners, similar to the ones at an airport. Prior to going through security, we were asked who we wanted to visit. Once a call was made to our appointment, we waited for an escort to Dick Eason's office.

Eason's office was very large and bland with military gray walls and three secretaries sitting at military solid steel desks. He sat behind his mahogany desk like a head of state. Eason was fair-skinned and wore glasses; had curly hair; and stood about six feet high. He looked across the desk at both Knight and me and asked what he could do for us. As this was our first face-to-face meeting, we brought along ample background materials, which he scanned and again asked what he could do for us.

With my eyes staring at the ceiling, all I could sarcastically think was that this conversation wasn't going well. Was I being too pushy? I nudged Knight and he took over the sell. "Casey is and will become an asset to America's image," he said.

Our message to Eason was that Casey's purported record-setting flight would capture the world's attention and thus make all the principals involved magnanimous participants. Anyway, that was the spin being offered. "We need State to help get us flight clearance to land at Alexandria," I said.

It seemed I needed more ammunition to gain Eason's attention. I looked him straight in the eyes, which were beady and tilted skyward. We cautioned Eason that if Casey didn't get State Department's support, he could crash and burn. And who gets the bad press? Phillips 66 and the U.S. Government. Why? Because I will be telling the press how you were instrumental in his failure since you didn't support his mission.

To back up these claims, I said that we needed help to secure the shortest option — namely, the Egyptian/Saudi route — for Casey to fly. Emphasis was conveyed that carrying pontoons instead of wheels puts extra stress on the engine. Therefore, the shortest distance between landing sites would benefit the overall performance of the aircraft.

Finally, this suggested route would allow him to land on the Red Sea and tie up in Jeddah. My reasoning for Jeddah was that was where I could work with Saudi Arabian Airlines' maintenance division in order to take a good look at the engine. Casey would be halfway around the world and I wanted assurances that he would finish. The Saudis, with American flight crews and maintenance staff, could give the engine a once-over.

Eason seemed to understand. Almost like the Red Sea parting, Eason quickly acknowledged by nodding his head and indicating he understood what we needed from him. He already knew we had tried to go through the Egyptian Consul General and even the fact that Knight had written letters, all failing to gain clearance. But he wasn't going to play his hand until we looked like flaming fools.

Eason scratched his shoulder, swiveled his head, and then very abruptly said he couldn't help us. We were left with the dutiful task of putting all of our literature back in our briefcases and humbly leaving his office.

"What a fucking dick-head," I screamed at Knight. David had the same opinion but in rather less expletive terms. Knight said he would have to rely on AOPA, and he had some secret friends he could call. He said he would find a friend for us in the Egyptian embassy.

Moving on to July 12, we intended to just visit with the aides at both the U.S. Air Force and Navy offices at the Pentagon. But that wasn't what happened. We had come to beg.

The day was beautiful for July. The sky was covered with a fine layer of cirrus clouds and the air was a brisk 78F. We had grabbed a coffee earlier but managed to recall that the coffee we had the previous day in Eason's office really sucked.

Knight explained how the night before he had sent new letters to the Egyptian embassy as well as the Saudi embassy in D.C. He had used the names of the government officials his friends had suggested. The letters were sent by messenger and we could only hope a phone call back to Knight's office would ensue.

Knight drove faster than usual today. He kept cursing at the fact that we had been left to act as nursemaids to Casey. Our wheels spun over the 14th Street Bridge on the way to the Pentagon. Knight just continued to murmur under his breath that his whole waking hours lately had been wrapped up with Casey. I thought to myself, was this the same clear-minded, self-controlled man I sat with in the coffee shop back on the 8th?

He also often mirrored the self-discipline characteristics of Admiral Engen. "If he (Engen) wasn't involved, I would have asked the Navy to have blown his plane out of the water long ago," Knight said.

The Pentagon loomed closer and Knight was still ranting. Today would become a test case as to how much the U.S. Navy would be our friend. We also later had an appointment with the Air Force, which promised to be interesting, too.

We both wondered what avenues lay ahead of us at the Pentagon. I told Knight that the Air Force had basically washed its hands of Casey (after Athens), but the Navy stepped up. I added, maybe we might get a chance to actually visit with Dunleavy.

The result of our meetings was that we found total support from the Navy. Captain Jon Coleman met with us and said the admiral had our backs and we could count on the Navy's support — but please, no surprises.

Captain Coleman said we would need to use official channels (Military Attaché) through the respective countries' embassies we intended to visit, and also directly with the countries themselves. Knight smiled and said, "We had already tired of banging on Egypt's door here in the U.S. and abroad and to date nothing."

Captain Coleman advised us to contact the Marine Attaché in Cairo and get his help. "Mention Dunleavy's name and you will get some action."

At the Air Force's Military Airlift Command Office, we only got to visit with a sergeant. No officer would consider spending time with us. We mentioned General Duane Cassidy and Colonel Sills, but we got a blank stare from the receptionist. I know they knew who both men were, but to us it seemed the Air Force was not acknowledging any support for Casey. It was as if all hands had been told that "Casey was a liability, so neither acknowledge any of his requests nor speak of him casually."

We did get a couple of "maybes" where we would get Air Force support — catastrophes such as if Casey crashed or if he was held captive by terrorists. Or, if he ran into a flock of U.S. Air Force jets, they would come to his rescue.

At dinner following our Pentagon visit, David and Margo discussed the many alternatives ahead of us. David commented that he would call the Marine Attaché in Cairo and that I should start drafting flight plans.

My mind raced. I realized that I hadn't put together a flight plan, much less an international flight plan, since naval aviation training in the late 1960s. Where do I go? The library? My only recourse was to call the navy.

A Chief Petty Officer at OP-05 sent me samples in the mail. Once I finished the first plan requesting clearances from Crete to Alexandria and then Jeddah, I faxed it to the chief and, once he approved, I then faxed it to the respective Marine Attachés in Cairo and Riyadh and also to each country's respective aviation authorities. We officially had now embarked on the second half of the journey.

The following day, we contacted the Marine Attaché in Cairo. He had received our flight plan request and his help would prove invaluable. I left for New York the next day.

Along this journey we had learned a valuable lesson. Diplomacy had no fast pace button. It grinds very slowly. As a result, to gain access to Alexandria and beyond, it would take another eleven days before we actually hit a home run.

Also during this waiting period, Knight had not been sitting on his hands. He had contacted the Saudi Embassy and even had an audience with a representative of Bandar bin Sultan, a member of the

House of Saud and Saudi Arabia's Ambassador to the United States. The Saudis were more than happy to provide clearance for Casey and were very excited about the event.

Knight pushed on through clearances. He had help from the Marine Attaché and this pushed the Egyptian Embassy in D.C. to tell its Consul in Alexandria to allow Casey passage into their country. Alexandria was now the next stop after Casey's takeoff from Souda Bay on July 28.

All Casey knew in Crete was that he got clearance on July 27. He never knew how he got it. He thought either Dunleavy or people at the Naval Air Station in Souda Bay had worked wonders.

# Twenty

# The 'Mystery' Seaplane – Confusion in Egypt, Saudi Arabia

"No one in Egypt has ever seen a seaplane, let alone known what to do with one," was the reaction of the U.S. Embassy Marine Attaché acting as a liaison with the Egyptian government. "If the Egyptians agree, Casey can land; we will make sure he has all the support we can provide."

Casey bade farewell to his friends in Crete. Captain Stevenson had been a good friend and had opened his home and family to Casey. Our pilot had started an Aero Club there, teaching the art of flying in their Cessna 150 trainer aircraft. He gave many of the base sailors free flying lessons and he will be especially remembered for starting a flight school for the U.S. Navy enlisted personnel.

On July 28, the 45th day of his new journey that started back on June 14, Casey boarded his aircraft and headed south. The next leg would be 435 miles to Alexandria, Egypt. He had a mid-morning launch and expected to be in Alexandria close to noon.

The Naval Air Station tower cleared Casey on a direct route to Egypt. Now at 4,000 feet, our pilot could look down and see the azure blue and green waters of the Mediterranean. He saw a herd of sperm whales passing underneath him. His senses also focused on the hundreds of beautiful yachts sailing with full-blown sheets. Life was good and it was splendid getting back in the air. Casey had no idea what experiences lay ahead of him.

Likewise, the Egyptians had never befriended nor seen a pontoon plane and they voiced their skepticism to the U.S. Consul in Alexandria. They just didn't know what to expect. What was his size? What fuel did he need? And, where would they dock him? Knight had tried unsuccessfully several times to communicate and answer these vexing questions to the Egyptians. He never got a reply.

In retrospect, all Casey wanted was to keep his experience in Alexandria a very simple event. He was only focusing on organizing some locals and having them help obtain avgas and load it into his aircraft.

Casey turned his radio setting to bring in Egyptian air traffic control. He broke through the Arabic chatter to ask in English for a true course heading to Alexandria and where to land. In a broken English response, he was told to head to the harbor area. Casey was told to look for a long dock that was about 200 yards inside the harbor's entrance. ATC then passed Casey to Alexandria's Flight Center.

He quickly keyed his mic and asked Alexandria for an exact landing area in the harbor. The reply bewildered Casey. Again, in broken English, he was now told completely opposite instructions. They commanded Casey not to land in the harbor but rather to land on a patch of dirt, outside the harbor near the extended freight and cargo pier.

Casey exploded at the Center's request. To himself, he yelled out loud: "I have never been here before and the stupid Egyptians don't want me landing in a safe haven. So where else is there any water to land on? Are they telling me to put down on land? What the hell do I do?" Over the horizon Casey saw a beautiful harbor area and many yachts. He made a pass around the harbor trying to locate the pier.

Alexandria is the main port in Egypt. It dates to 1900 B.C. when the pharaohs established a port west of Pharos Island. The physical area of the port is about 2,300 meters (7,550 feet) long and 300 meters (984 feet) wide and it has more than 1,000 docks at different depths. There are two harbors (east and west) with a T-shaped peninsula separating them. The city is considered to be the second most important city in Egypt and the western port is where more than three quarters of Egypt's foreign trade passes. The western harbor is protected by marine rocks and two breakwaters. Casey was told to head to this location and tie up at a dock outside the harbor break-water.

"I was so concerned that the breakwaters outside the harbor might present a problem as there seemed to be large waves cresting," Casey later recalled. "I again asked Alexandria tower if I could land inside the calmer eastern harbor. They said no as I might damage some of the costly yachts tied up in the harbor."

Just outside the western harbor area there was a large pier and on the pier there were several people waving their arms and motion-ing for Casey to land. Casey was now being controlled by a bunch of Egyptians, whether he liked it or not.

"For a moment I actually slid over the cresting waves. Water smeared my windscreen. Even though I had no permission to land in the harbor, I landed nearly in front of those directing me where to land.

"Upon landing, I heard a horn and stretched my head out the side window opening to see several Egyptians frantically waving to me. My eyes spotted the pier. There were at least 20 people about 50 feet away waving at me. Maybe I would have some help getting fuel after all.

"I tossed my line to the outstretched arms of several young men at the pier. An elderly gentleman, who I presumed was the of-ficial Egyptian welcoming committee, actually came to attention and saluted me as if I were docking a destroyer. He was Abdul Hassan, the official emissary for the Egyptian Consul in Alexandria. Two Ameri-cans from the American Consul were there, too. I asked the Americans why I had to land outside the harbor and also why I couldn't land on the beach. Each just shrugged and neither one had an answer."

He took a look at the pier where they wanted him to tie up. There were large spikes protruding from the docking area exactly where he would have to secure the aircraft floats. If he tied up at the pier, the two-foot long spikes would most certainly have punctured the floats. All he could do was ask the young Egyptian boys to keep the lines very taut and prevent the aircraft from hitting the spikes. And, to ensure added safety to the floats, he asked several other boys to use their feet to push out the floats, in case the lines became slack.

"Knowing that fuel was the most pressing issue, I asked directions to the nearest fuel farm or truck to purchase avgas. Abdul said I had caused much confusion since no one had ever seen a plane like mine and said they thought it might take jet fuel."

But now Abdul told all the others at the dock that Casey really needed avgas. In a hurried manner he called someone on his hand-held radio. Minutes passed very slowly, but finally he nodded. They had avgas but it was a far distance away. Seems many of the motorboats used marine fuel and it had the same octane as avgas, or so the Egyptian experts said. So, Casey was left to take it or leave it.

To obtain the fuel, Abdul made arrangements with a group of young men. They assured Casey that it was the same as avgas. Before heading off on their task to fetch the fuel, the young men wanted to touch the funny looking plane. "They all called me Captain Casey and each one saluted me. It was Abdul who told them my name and presumed rank," he remarked.

Several hours passed, and 'Captain Casey' spent the time cleaning his windscreen and polishing the prop. Then, almost as if Aladdin had rubbed his magic lamp, the crew of Egyptian fuel haulers came down the pier carrying ten six-gallon containers.

As Casey later related, "Now came the hard work. I had to climb up from the floats onto the wing and have the boys physically hand me each of the 35-pound fuel containers. One at a time, the Egyptian boys handed me each container and I poured the lifeblood back into my dual overhead wing tanks. I grabbed each one and almost had to painstakingly balance and pull each container up onto my shoulder and then pour in the fuel."

Lugging these monsters up to where he was sitting on the aircraft's wing and pouring the fuel really took its toll. In fact, this heavy labor almost ended the world record event.

"With the very last container, I felt a strong shooting pain in my lower back. The pain was excruciating and I knew right away that I was in serious trouble. I had either pulled a shoulder blade muscle or tendon. Actually I had done much worse. The later verdict was that I had done some bad damage to my vertebrae in the lower back. In pain, I finished loading and now had ample fuel to make the trip to Jeddah.

"Abdul approached me and said he had just received permission for me to take off. He told me to contact the Alexandria airport tower and that they would hand me over to Saudi ATC. Maybe I would see all the pyramids. I didn't know.

"I physically was unable to climb into my bird. Abdul and several lads had to almost position me on their shoulders and then push me into the plane. The pain was enormous. But I kept repeating to myself that I only had a muscle tear and everything would be fine once I got to Jeddah. At 1300, I departed Alexandria for an 890-mile leg to Jeddah.

"The tower cleared me to Jeddah. My course would be over the Suez Canal, and then I would fly a straight line with the Nile on my right and the Rea Sea on my left."

After flying almost 450 miles, Casey, now at 9,000 feet, made a left turn about 150 miles before the Sudanese border and flew the rest of the way to Jeddah with the Red Sea below.

His back was frozen in place — he couldn't move. During the last several hours of the journey, he was afraid of blacking out and didn't know if he would make Jeddah. "I had no pain pills but I hung in there for the next 270 miles," he later recalled. "My only regret was not seeing the pyramids. There was a humongous sandstorm below and it looked like it stretched for hundreds of miles. Here I was in the cradle of civilization and all I saw was sand. Go figure."

Casey was now running down the Red Sea and was flying a direct vector to Jeddah. He picked up the radio beacon at Jeddah and his direction finder verified his course heading. He later explained, "It was really dark down there by the time I reached Jeddah. Now at 1950, I turned on my running lights on the wings to make out some type of a landmark, maybe a building or a camel caravan. I wanted to see a port structure that indicated I was closing in on Jeddah. My course speed and distance indicated I was about ten miles away from Jeddah proper. But I wasn't sure.

"At about the time I calculated I was maybe one mile out, I could see lots of people standing on the shoreline below. Jeddah Approach confirmed my position and said to land in the Red Sea near the docks.

"But wait – I was being blinded by powerful lights, super large floodlights. Hell, the British had used them during World War II to track German aircraft over London. Next, I saw those same search lights aimed below me and the stream of light pointed directly at the Red Sea. Were they trying to give me landing directions? Were they pointing to a particular spot? I had to go down and find out.

"I flew past the crowd of people. But the absolute darkness past the lights on the Red Sea made it seem like I was flying into a black hole in space. As I turned left and made my way back toward the search lights, I saw this large destroyer positioned right in my path, exactly where the previous light source had indicated where I should land.

"I pulled the stick up hard and cleared the top mast of the destroyer by what seemed like five feet. Once over the destroyer, there were two other large vessels directly in my path. Where did they come from? I was now really out of sorts.

"In the next moment, one of the large ships turned on its search light. The light was directed straight at me and flooded the interior of my cabin. The Saudis had used three large Coast Guard ships (the size of an American destroyer escort) to outline a landing path and site."

Casey would later tell his Saudi hosts, "I was blinded and I told Air Traffic Control that they needed to turn those lights off before I landed.

"Anxiously, I strained to find a place to put my 206 down. All of sudden, off to the right I saw these large reefs — water was cresting over them. I had to land behind the reefs because that was where the calmer waters were. As I was about to line up for a landing near the reefs, flood lights on shore seemed to lay a new suggested landing path in between the three Coast Guard ships.

"My gut immediately told me I needed to put down away from those ships. I made my decision on where I was going to put this bird in less than ten seconds. Pulling back the power, I made a hard right-hand turn and this lined up Liberty II over the reefs into calm waters. This maneuver allowed me to make a very short landing that positioned me close to a large yacht which was docked adjacent to a huge Jeddah estate near the main docks. The landing was textbook."

Once safely down, Casey was then able to sail his aircraft back toward the welcoming committee onshore. One of the Saudis (using a loudspeaker) told Casey to sail up to one of the three Coast Guard vessels and tie his craft to its aft section. Casey tried to climb out from the plane onto the Saudi vessel but had to be helped by several of his new Arab friends. In severe pain, he saluted the crowd.

Then turning to outstretched arms of what appeared to be a Saudi emissary, Casey exclaimed, "I almost crashed into one of your destroyers and missed several large reefs coming inches away from flipping my plane over. Your search lights blinded me." The Saudi gentleman, first to meet Casey, said they had expected a much larger plane, maybe one the size of a 747.

The emissary then transported him to the safety of the main executive offices at the Jeddah port, which had an excellent location in the middle of the international shipping routes on the western shores of Saudi Arabia.

Meanwhile Casey, displaying his bone-crushing diplomatic approach, began bellowing about all the dangers he had faced. But in mid-sentence he was stopped dead by a very impressive looking figure who had a soothing and soft-toned voice. He typified the stature of an Arab dignitary.

"We thought you would be the size of the old "Yankee Clipper," which is why we had all those ships on the Red Sea," said Prince Sultan bin Abdul Aziz, Minister of Defense for Saudi Arabia.

"When your engine noise was heard in the distance and then your plane was spotted by the search lights, we thought you were a scout plane for the Yankee Clipper. Our control center knew you were aloft and you responded to our radio directions. But locating your plane was another matter. And, when you almost hit those reefs, we knew it must be you looking for a place to land. Please accept our warmest apologies. We know you are very tired. Tomorrow we have planned a special event in your honor."

Casey rested well that night. He was living in luxury in one of the finest hotels in Jeddah. In his new digs, paid for by the Saudis, he had a chance for a nice dinner, a bottle of Scotch (smuggled from Greece), and a hot shower. Casey would learn to appreciate Saudi hospitality in the coming days.

The following day, the Saudis pulled Casey's plane from the water and put it safely in Saudi Arabian Airlines' maintenance hangar. Back at Jeddah's U.S. Consulate, there was somber relief that the American pilot had made it safely to Jeddah. "Apparently the Liberty II was the first seaplane to land on the Red Sea since World War II," said Phillip J. Griffin, U.S. Consul General to Saudi Arabia.

Casey would later tell me in a phone call that he felt it was his past experience in seaplane flying that brought him to a safe landing on the Red Sea.

# Twenty-one

# The Hero Is Decorated; Then His Back Alters the Plan

The day after Casey landed in Jeddah, Knight heard that Casey had become a national hero in Saudi Arabia. They had presented the dude a medal. For us back home, confusion reigned. We had made sure he got to Jeddah, but where do we go from here?

We had not expected Casey to put in so many requests for clearances; it led to confusion with Egypt and many other countries. Most countries wanted to know, "Who was actually in charge?" For that matter, confusion on flight times and dates almost jeopardized the overall schedule and operating flexibility. In the latter cases, such as flying between Greece and Egypt and on to Saudi Arabia, a schedule change could create permit revisions for all subsequent countries. We had used all of our diplomatic chips to gain approvals for Egypt.

An overriding question was: What had we learned to date?

Once overflights and landing permits had been secured, it was important that we were somewhat cautious in terms of revisions, particularly with countries such as India and Japan. Permit revisions were not always straightforward. Actually, we found that most countries didn't give a damn that Casey was trying to fly around the world. When planning permits on your own without a third-party service provider, caution is advised as permits may be rejected if all required documentation is not provided.

One thing was clear: We needed to clarify who was running this show. We had control of his purse strings, but he was just doing his own thing as if he didn't know we were now actually the only ones with enough leverage with the State Department to gain all the country clearances for his flight.

It was time for a "Come to Jesus meeting." But we had no idea how to contact him. We knew he left Alexandria because the Marine Attaché in Cairo at the American Embassy had called and informed me about his refueling stop. We also knew he made Jeddah but had no idea where he was in Jeddah. That was all about to change.

At the State Department's request, Knight and I headed back to Eason's office in D.C. We had no idea why anyone there wanted to see us. Maybe Casey was the new Moses and had again parted the Red Sea.

We cleared security and again found ourselves in the homely decorated office of Dick Eason, head of the aviation department. He mentioned receiving an internal State Department memo that said Casey had landed in Jeddah. U.S. Ambassador Chad Freeman had called Secretary James Baker and told Baker that Casey had had a big ceremonial dinner with the Saudis earlier that day (the evening of July 29).

Eason smugly told us, "Seems to me you've done the best for this pilot. Why? Because you have been contacting all the right people. The Secretary wants to be kept informed. So I will be your conduit. Ambassador Freeman may be calling either of you. That's it. Have a good day."

Wow, I thought. Was this a reprimand or compliment? What gives?

Knight and I left State still wondering exactly where Casey was in Jeddah. What was to be our next plan? Knight again wondered if we could find some way to impress upon Casey the need to communicate directly with us. We were currently getting all current information from the American Embassy in Riyadh.

Knight reminded me that he was getting numerous calls from the media. At the top of the list was John B. Holway at the USIA (United States Information Agency). He had already sent out a news story on July 16 that said Casey was expected to land in Alexandria on July 18. Now he wanted to contact Casey in Jeddah, since he was planning on running another story that corrected his first story and also filled in his readers on our pilot's future plans.

We knew that Eason and Secretary Baker had prompted Holway to draft the first piece. Hell, maybe Holway's efforts could help us get flight clearances into other countries on Casey's flight plan agenda.

Knight would fill in Holway. We never found out whether Holway had contacted Casey. Nor did we ever get a copy of his second story.

I made sure everyone at Phillips 66 knew about Holway's first story. I hoped that after reading it that Hammond could now hold his head high. Hammond was also briefed about Casey becoming a national hero in Saudi Arabia and that he was now halfway around the world.

Equally important, Holway's story was the catalyst that would alert all the U.S. embassies that there would be flight clearance requests to their respective countries where they were stationed.

Knight also had *The Washington Post* calling. He told the *Post* that the Saudis had presented Casey with a medal for fortitude as an aviation pioneer. After speaking with the *Post*, Knight secretly exclaimed, "We could have the U.S. Navy shoot the bastard out of the sky and then we could have him awarded a Distinguished Flying Cross. That is the least we could do for all the shit he has caused us so far and he is only halfway around." We both laughed and went our separate ways.

That afternoon I visited the Navy at the Pentagon. I stuck my head in on Admiral Dunleavy. He had such a commanding presence and his stare could cut right through you. With his arms stretched toward the ceiling in clear defiance, he asked how our "boy" was doing.

Not totally capable of stringing a complete sentence together, all I could say was "Jeddah". I then thanked him for all his help in Crete. Dunleavy said Casey had a long stretch ahead of him and asked if we had all the clearances. I said no. Dunleavy reassured me that the U.S. Navy would give us all the help we needed. I also visited with Captain Tutterville (my flight school classmate) and we laughed at all the events so far in the saga of Casey.

I had a great dinner with Knight and his wife Margo that

night. We made no plans as we had not heard from Casey. What new twist to this adventure would surface on the horizon? When would Casey leave for his next destination and where?

But then again …

The next day, no more than 20 minutes after stepping back into my office in New York, I had the U.S. Consulate in Jeddah on my phone. I was now speaking with David Rundell, Economics Officer for the Consulate General in Jeddah. "Mr. Coleman, I have some good news and some bad news," he said. "First, yesterday (July 29) your pilot Mr. Tom Casey was awarded the top Civilian Aviation medal by the Saudis. The bad news is that Casey will be delayed. He needs some very serious back surgery."

I asked Rundell the whereabouts of Casey. He responded, "Today, Casey was admitted to the King Fahd Military Hospital. He was really fortunate that the Saudis were willing to put him in the military hospital."

I asked Rundell how he got involved. He told me that all the flight clearances for Casey had come through to the embassy in Riyadh and that the ambassador had called Secretary of State James Baker in Washington to alert him that Casey was in the country. Then he wired Rundell in Jeddah.

"We were proud that the Saudis honored an American and, frankly, we all took the whole matter of his flight as routine," Rundell explained. "But now, it looks like your pilot has caused somewhat of a diplomatic stir, both here in Saudi Arabia and in Washington, D.C. Frankly, you have to understand that it's not a normal practice for an American to be admitted to a Saudi military hospital, especially when his surgery is elective.

"Your boy could have gone back to the States to have his surgery, which would have stopped his record-setting attempt." (I swore under my breath that this American diplomat sure sounded very British. I could only assume that next he would refer to Casey as Chap, Good Ole Boy, or Barmy (crazy).

I abruptly asked Rundell what the hell he meant. "Well, he may be moved out of the Fahd Hospital and then have to pay for his own care," he answered. "Or, we may just have to ship him home at our taxpayers' expense."

"What?" I said.

Rundell repeated the shipped home scenario and I just froze on the phone. "What about his plane?" I asked. "Well, that stays here until Casey can get it back to Seattle," was the response.

"Mr. Rundell, will you let me know what the Saudis decide, or will this decision be made by the U.S. Ambassador?"

All Rundell would say was, "We will get back to you."

I then half-heartily thanked him for his help and hoped everything would turn out for the better. What else could I say?

Upon hanging up from Rundell, I immediately called the King Fahd Military Hospital. It took the international operator considerable time as I was calling person to person. After what seemed like more than one hour, I finally got Casey on the phone. New York was seven hours behind Jeddah, which meant it was 1800 there. He sounded tired and somewhat in pain.

Casey quickly explained. "By the time I got to Jeddah on July 28, I could hardly walk. Then I found out I was to be the guest of the Saudi Defense Minister, at a Saudi Coast Guard dinner. The Minister, Prince Aziz, was to honor me for my flight around the world. What an elegant event. Everyone was sporting white flowing headdresses or shemaghs along with stately white robes. The climax of the evening for the Saudis was to present to me a plaque and a medal. (Casey never had these returned to him from the U.S. Consulate).

"The Saudis literally rolled out the red carpet, but during dinner I turned to Mr. Aziz and told him I was in too much pain to continue this flight," Casey said.

"I was immediately put in the King Fahd Military Hospital, where I am now. The hospital administrator agreed to admit me even though I had no health insurance. After multiple X-rays, they diagnosed my condition. The disc in my back had blown out and would require a major operation.

"I phoned the U.S. Consulate to alert them of my condition and ask for their help. I assume the person who answered the phone at the Consulate took my message to the big guy as later that afternoon a man called and introduced himself as David Rundell at the U.S. Consulate. And Coleman, that is all I know at the present."

I made Casey aware of my conversation with Rundell (who

also took credit for getting Casey into the hospital). I then hammered Casey. In the ensuing heated conversation, I explained that if I had not heard from Rundell, we would have never known the location of our favorite seaplane pilot.

Again, I repeated to Casey the importance of keeping in touch with me. Why? Because without keeping me aware of where he was or what he was doing, he would be cut off from any or all of the logistical support from the U.S. Navy, Air Force, State Department, and any monetary support from Phillips 66 and the rest of mankind.

It was at that moment that I told Casey I had assumed full responsibility for his journey. The Navy only took orders from me. He would have never made it out of Souda Bay and to Alexandria without the efforts of Knight or myself.

I would write the remainder of flight clearance requests. We (Knight and me) would talk to every ambassador in the countries he intended to fly into as well as their respective ambassadors in D.C. "Casey, we heard from the State Department that you were awarded a medal by the Saudis. That is only how we knew you made Jeddah," I said.

I told Casey that just this morning, when I was asked by Phillips 66 and yesterday by Dunleavy, "Where is Casey?" my response to everyone was, "We have him in our sights and I expect to hear from him very soon." On hearing this, Casey immediately made some lame half-ass excuse about not being able to find a phone and a lack of money.

To both excuses, I told him that I knew he had called his sister in New York the previous day and about his expiring Lloyd's insurance policy. And as to money, I had already topped off his credit card with $5,000, which he knew because he had just used the credit card to buy fuel in Alexandria.

I told Casey that the trip has been postponed for the time being and that I would let him know what the future held.

God, I could really feel for him at that moment. We talked a bit longer — just small talk about the landing and how he was being given excellent treatment in Saudi Arabia versus how badly the "stupid" Egyptians abused him. I told Casey that I would let him know of any news as soon I received it.

Before hanging up, Casey said, "I will not give up and I plan to finish this mission."

After the call, I immediately called the National Aeronautic Association in Washington, D.C. They are the keepers of aviation flight records such as Charles Lindbergh's Atlantic flight crossing. "Since this is a world record never attempted before, there is no time limit," said Everett Langworthy, head of the NAA, responding to the delay of the Liberty II round-the-world-flight caused by Casey's back problem.

I also called the Federation Aeronautique Internationale in Switzerland and explained Casey's plight. They were very understanding and asked that I keep them alerted.

It was now 47 days since Casey turned his aircraft around and decided to leave Seattle again and fly his world record from west to east.

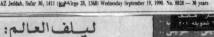

منوعات

# الاسبوعية

● السنة الثلاثون ● العدد ٨٨١٢ الاثنين ١٤ صفر ١٤١١ هـ ــ (١٢ السنبلة/الحمل ١٣٦٨ هـ ش) الموافق ٣ سبتمبر ١٩٩٠ م ●

OKAZ Jeddah, Safar 30, 1411 (Virgo 28, 1368) Wednesday September 19, 1990. No. 8828 — 30 years

## ليـف العالم:

## "كيس" يصمم

# طائرة صغيرة!

الكابتن كيس .. ا

■ الدوران حول العالم كان حلمه الذى ظل يراوده ويتردد على مخيلته منذ كان على مقاعد الدراسة الابتدائية . وكبر معه هذا الحلم . وكبرت معه هوايته . رافقت طفولته وصباه وشبابه ولانه درس الطيران .. واصبح طيارا . فقد احس بان الامل في تحقيق حلمه القديم بات قاب قوسين او ادنى منه . وفعلا . شرع في تصميم طائرة صغيرة اسمها « سيلندى - ٢ » وجهزها على ان تتحمل كافة الظروف والاحوال الجوية . وبدأ رحلته محلقا بين السماء والارض ومجاورا « كثبان ، السحب .

منطلقا من سياتل ومارا بالساحل الشمالى للولايات المتحدة مع عبور المحيط الاطلسى عبر جرينلند وايسلندا .. وتوقفت في اسكتلندا وايرلندا وفرنسا وايطاليا واليونان ومصر ووصلت الى جده قادما من الاسكندرية .

وغواية الرحلات .. هواية محببة ومشوقة جدا .. ولكنها تحتاج الى توفر قدر كبير من روح المغامرة والجرأة .. ومن المؤكد ان هاتين الصفتين توفرتا لدى الكابتن كيس الذى لم أضاف .

لم أواجه مشكلات رئيسية في رحلتى عدا المعاناة من سوء الاحوال الجوية في بعض الاحيان مثل ماحدث لي في ايسلندا حيث اضطررت الى التحليق على ارتفاع منخفض بسبب الضباب والغيوم والبرودة الشديدة والثلوج اضافة الى انقطاع الاتصال تماما وانا بين مطارى الاسكندرية وجدة !

الكابتن توماس بتريك كيس الامريكى الجنسية والذى اصبح طيارا عام ١٩٦١م ... ولكن بداية .. بقول

استعداده لحلم العمر لم يبدأ الا قبل عدة شهور في مدينة سياتل الامريكية ..

يترجل من طائرته ..

بهذه الطائرة طفت العالم !

*Casey was a high-profile figure in the Saudi media.*

## Twenty-two

# August 2 — Iraq Invades Kuwait

*"More than 100,000 Iraqi soldiers backed up by 700 tanks invaded the Gulf state of Kuwait in the early hours of this morning. Iraqi forces have established a provisional government and their leader Saddam Hussein has threatened to turn Kuwait City into a 'graveyard' if any other country dares to challenge the 'takeover by force'."*

— BBC News
August 2, 1990

This day was not like any other. Stunned, I called Knight immediately. "David, here we have a pilot in Saudi Arabia (waiting for an operation) and the Middle East may be on the threshold of war." My friend David's attitude was steeped in verbiage of a true Washingtonian. He waxed on about how the Arabs always fight amongst themselves and we had nothing to worry about.

I reminded David of the previous Iraq-Iran war where hundreds of thousands died. But he countered with a cynical analysis that it (the invasion) was just a local conflict or tribal religious feud. The U.S. would never take a side on this one.

Knight was well aware of Casey's predicament. I asked if he wanted to seek Engen's advice or should we run this latest Casey scenario through Secretary of State Baker's office or the Navy? David said no in such an emphatic tone that I silently thought he wasn't telling me the whole story. Did he know more?

As it turned out, he knew from Admiral Engen that the U.S. was on a war footing but he couldn't say a word to me. Over the next week, Washington frankly shut down. Streets were noticeably not crowded. Restaurants at night were vacant and most apparent was that all the bars from 16th Street to the Capitol were packed full. That fact alone said we were headed for a major conflict.

My next phone conversation that morning would be the hardest. Hammond was calling and I had to brief him on Casey's medical disposition. I recall hedging the whole truth but actually feeling a sense of abandonment toward Casey. During my conversation with Hammond, another Phillips 66 manager came on line. He ran the promotions department and had budgetary control over most projects which Phillips 66 paid my company to execute.

His questions focused on how much this Casey adventure was costing. How did they (Phillips) get into this mess of sponsoring a pilot that pissed off a lot of U.S. ambassadors plus the U.S. State Department? Hammond interrupted and said he got Phillips 66 involved — not Coleman.

Again the manager attacked me. How did the Navy get involved? I said the Navy contacts were either friends of mine or those of Admiral Engen.

The promotions department manager couldn't blame Hammond because he was head of the Aviation Business Group. But hell, he did everything in his power to blame me. But then, he was paying all our invoices. And, I was amassing many bills such as the cost for the London press briefing that went very badly.

My neck was on the line. I didn't mention the fact that Casey was in the hospital waiting for an operation. Nonetheless, Phillips 66 was sponsoring a plane in Saudi Arabia with a major Middle East war just on the horizon, a fact that didn't get lost on the promotions manager.

I finally got Hammond alone on the phone and told him about the latest Casey news. "Holy shit," he said. "Back operation or go home and a war on the horizon? If he does have the operation, how in the hell will you get him through the Middle East?"

"I don't have the faintest idea," I responded, but jokingly added, "I will think about it." Hammond just grunted and said for me to call him when I had an answer.

About this time I wanted to look for another line of work. All my crew — Tim, Kyle, and Christine — were on my side and trying to bolster my spirits. "What's next, Boss?" Tim asked, adding, "Let's find out what Geiger (our direct report at Phillips 66) says."

As I picked up the phone to make the call, another thought occurred to me: What if some enterprising Associated Press journalist in the Middle East hears about Casey, his adventure, and about his plight of needing a back operation? I already knew that Aziz, the Saudi Defense Minister, had called his local Arab press buddies about giving Casey an award. But did he mention the back operation? Logic told me that the Arab media would probably alert their buddies in the international press and then it would take about one-point-zero seconds before the AP was all over it.

A story that is laced with empathy for a man seeking a world record but is hospitalized awaiting a back operation reeked world news exposure. I could envision the headline: "Lone Seaplane Pilot Seeking World Record Delayed; Awaits Back Surgery in Saudi Hospital."

The story would bring tears to one's eyes. Sadly, much of the copy might make it seem as if the U.S. had abandoned him as well as his sponsor, Phillips 66. The reader could come away with the thought that only the persevering desire of Casey would get him through these obstacles to continue his flight.

Well, good thing I called Geiger, because no more than one hour later the AP broke the story:

> *Casey Stuck in Saudi Arabia*
> *AR RIYAD, SAUDIA ARABIA (AP)—Se-*
> *attle pilot Tom Casey's global-circling seaplane flight*
> *underwent another setback when he injured his back in*
> *late July, while loading fuel in Cairo, Egypt, for a flight*
> *to Jeddah, Saudi Arabia, just two days before the inva-*
> *sion of Kuwait by Iraq.*
> *Casey said in a telephone interview, "I am det-*

*ermined to finish this flight." He is attempting to set a
record as the first pilot to circumnavigate the globe landing
only on water.*

    *Despite his injury, Casey attended a state dinner
given in his honor where he received the highest civil aviation medal from the Saudi Defense Minister.*

They had picked up the story from the July issue of the Saudi
monthly magazine, *Civil Aviation*. Geiger was neither amused nor
angry; he just wanted the whole mess to go away. He reiterated that
he had initially said no to the Casey flight but was overruled by Hammond.

    Geiger asked me how long I foresaw Casey being laid up in Jed-
dah. Was the Iraq invasion going to have an adverse impact on Casey's
trip (as seen from the eyes of the U.S. Navy and State Department)?
To the latter question I said to Geiger that I thought he gave me far
more credit than I could possibly ever deserve to be able to discern an
opinion from either of the two parties.

    I told Geiger that my guess was that the U.S. would get
involved in the conflict and hell was about to break loose. And as of
right now, Casey didn't have a doctor and stood the possibility of
being thrown out of the Saudi military hospital. I told Geiger what
Rundell had fed to me — that the U.S. Embassy wanted Casey to go
home. What I told Geiger next took him totally by surprise.

    "Whether Casey gets operated on at a military hospital or
some other facility, or whether the embassy gets its way, will depend
solely on the wishes of the Sultan of Saudi Arabia." I explained that
the Saudis, at the highest levels, considered Casey a guest of their
country and they were not going to send him packing.

    Casey was a hero and probably would get his operation. When
and where that operation would take place was still to be decided. I
was worried about Geiger's boss, the promotions manager. He could
fire you for just coming to work.

    Geiger passed on the story to his boss. Red-faced and with a
heart monitor reading well over 250, his boss called me. Holding the
phone at a lengthy distance away from my ear, this manic depressive
began reading me the riot act. "How dare you bring shame to Phillips

66? How dare you do this to me? You are lucky you are not here today as I would slam my fist down your throat."

He again reminded me that this whole project had been run badly from the very beginning and that I was going to pay for this in the near future. As far as he was concerned, Casey could rot in hell.

While this asshole was venting his spleen, I reminded him that I was not the one who initiated this project. I said he might recall what Hammond told him earlier that morning. I added that when I spoke to Hammond after he got off the conference call, I explained how pissed you were at me and how you wanted to fire me. Hammond reassured me that would never happen.

Upon hearing this, the manager backed down but warned me if anything else went wrong, he would pull the plug on the whole project. I asked if I should repeat this threat to Hammond. With that said, he just hung up the phone.

I got back on the phone to Hammond. He seemed reasonable about the AP story and was amused at some of the content. He told me to get my body to Bartlesville so we all could map out the future. I said I would be on the next plane.

The following afternoon, before I left for the airport, Hammond again called and said management had seen the AP story and wanted more info. So Hammond told me to stay put in New York for the time being and find out all the details about Casey's operation; where his plane was; condition of his engine; reaction from the State Department; reaction from the Navy; and other assorted facts. He wanted me to be in Bartlesville the following week to brief whomever wanted to be briefed. I called Geiger to let him know.

Now it was time to hold my own staff meeting. Everyone at the conference table, including my boss, had their mouths hanging wide open. Disbelief, puzzlement ... and what the hell are we going to do now? Such thoughts were the order of the day.

# Twenty-three

# Help! We Need a Back Surgeon

*"It is the greatest shot of adrenaline to be doing what you
have wanted to do so badly. You almost feel like you could
fly without the plane."*

— **Charles Lindbergh**

Following the staff meeting in New York, I headed to Bartlesville. Not much to do; maybe play some golf. I left my staff in utter
disarray. No word on whether Casey could stay in Saudi Arabia.

While I was in Bartlesville, Casey was busy trying to
schmooze the Swedish nurses while waiting for an operation (while
I, too, awaited an operation of my own at Phillips 66). Casey lay in
bed wondering what would be happening to him, a position he would
endure for more than 20 days.

Frustrated by hearing nothing from either the Saudis or Americans, he let it all hang out to AP reporter Laurie Lande.

"Six days ago, when I was admitted to the King Fahd hospital, they told me that my disc in my lower back was blown. As soon as
I could get to a phone I called the American Consulate in Jeddah and
asked for help. I spoke with this dude Rundell, who said he would look
into it. But I never heard from anyone again because four days later

Iraq invaded Kuwait. Everyone on the U.S. side was now preoccupied and nothing was happening to me," Casey painfully told the reporter.

"The Saudis didn't forget me. I was awarded a civil medal by the Saudi Civil Aviation authorities in the hospital. I got a plaque at a special dinner.

"I knew I was in trouble in the hospital when after five days of sponge baths, I decided to go into the shower and take a long-awaited scrub down. I was washing myself when my legs gave out. Luckily, I slid down the tiles closest to my back and deposited myself flat out on the shower floor. All I could do was yell for help. It seemed like an eternity, but after about 40 minutes two beautiful blondes — very well-endowed nurses — were grabbing both my arms and picking me up from the floor.

"They held me tight but it seemed like they were dragging me to bed. At my hospital bedside, they lifted my now 210-pound frame onto the bed. In their beautiful ABBA voices, they emphatically explained that they were the only ones to give me baths — not me. I was told that I had very little use of my legs and that a serious operation was being discussed by the surgeons. From then on, they would take special care to bathe me all over.

"And each time they would tell me what a brave pilot I was and that someday they wished that I could come to Sweden and meet their families. I think I was being proposed to. Or maybe that was in my dreams."

The AP reporter was so interested in Casey she didn't file a story until after Casey had actually left Saudi Arabia. But for now she would visit Casey often and monitor his progress.

"As each day passed, while lying in this hospital without an operation, I knew my right leg, which had been immobilized by the disintegrating disc, was now becoming deader by the day." he said.

Casey told the reporter that he had tried reaching Rundell several times at his house and left some pretty heated messages. Casey wanted to know how Rundell could push the Saudis to get his operation. He knew his condition was getting worse and hoped to use Rundell as leverage.

Meanwhile, Rundell was rather pissed off that Casey called on the weekend and left these irate messages that his family could hear.

He called Casey and explained that the Saudis were planning to give Casey the operation in the military hospital but had not scheduled it yet. Rundell said he would try to clarify an exact date, and then added that right now the Saudis were increasingly involved with planning for a possible military conflict.

The reporter could see that Casey's health was not the major focus of the Saudi government. She told Casey she would make some calls as well.

The mood in the country was becoming grim. On August 7, Dick Cheney arrived in Saudi Arabia and met with King Fahd and Prince Bandar bin Sultan. Life in the military hospital changed. The whole staff was preparing for war, which led to the facility's reconfiguration into a triage.

The drums of war beat harder on August 8 when Iraq annexed Kuwait. By August 14 an untold event, not related to the Iraq invasion, drastically heightened the tensions in Casey's ward. The staff wheeled into Casey's room a new bed partner. Casey didn't recognize him at first but got the picture that he was someone of importance since there were seven armed guards at the door and at the new patient's bedside.

"Everyone was talking in Arabic so I thought I would welcome the gentlemen in my room. I said, hello, how are you? He was very gracious and said hello to me. He asked who I was and I told him I was an American pilot that was waiting for a back operation. He smiled and said he was also a pilot but was very sick.

"One of the Swedish nurses came close to me with her lips touching my ear. Her perfume and just general lovely scent dizzied my thinking. She said the man in next bed to me was Idi Amin Dada, formerly the third president of Uganda, who was now in exile in Saudi Arabia. He was here for a possible diagnosis of cancer.

"Almost out of nowhere, this giant of a man had positioned himself right next to my head. He cheerfully said, 'Hello, and you must be the famous pilot everyone is talking about. I am President Amin and it is a pleasure to meet with you.'

"His bodyguards stood motionless near the door of our room. Amin said he was here in the hospital to find out why he had his latest round of discomforting pains in his back. 'The doctors think I am very ill, but I am not sick and I will live forever,' he said."

Casey couldn't get over the fact that he was lying next to a man who had seized power in a military coup in 1971 and committed many atrocities. Casey remembered reading an article in a recent issue of *The New York Times* that Amin's rule was characterized by human rights abuses. The number of people killed as a result of his regime was estimated by international observers and human rights groups to range from 100,000 to 500,000.

Then there was the Air France jet that was hijacked and forced to land in Uganda in 1976. Many of the passengers were let go except for 83 Jews and Israeli citizens, as well as 20 others who refused to abandon them, among whom were the captain and crew of the hijacked jet. The Israelis rescued the passengers in a great raid on Entebbe Airport. In 1979, Uganda rebelled against Amin and he subsequently sought exile in Libya. He later came to Jeddah, Saudi Arabia.

Casey only met Amin that one time but well remembers his awesome presence.

Over the next several days Casey tried to reach his family in New York and New Jersey, but the international phone lines were all dedicated to the war build-up. On August 15 Casey met his newest trusted ally, Captain John King of Saudi Arabian Airlines. Lucky for Casey, this inquisitive American pilot based in the Kingdom wanted to seek out this new national hero of Saudi Arabia.

In fact, King happened to be the appointed caretaker for Casey's plane. Defense Minister Aziz made sure of that. "Our first meeting seemed almost magical," Casey would later tell me. King, who headed up the maintenance department for Saudi Arabian Airlines, stood almost at attention at Casey's bedside. "I came here to shake the hand of the world's newest aviation hero. And, by the way, I have your plane in my hangar," he said to Casey.

King had received the aviation oil for Casey's plane from Phillips 66 and promised to inspect the aircraft's engine and make sure the Cessna 206 was hunkered away from any curiosity seekers. Casey said it would be good to touch base with Coleman in New York and told him I was working for Phillips 66.

King reached me that week and related that he had just finished a lengthy conversation with Casey. "He seems pissed off at the world. Guess I would be too. But I kept telling him everything will come together and he would be on his way in no time," King explained. Over the next several months he and I would become close confidants. (King died several years ago and we miss him.)

King added, "That gentleman is a full-fledged Irishman — you know, the type that can talk the hind legs off a donkey. He told me about the severe pain coming from the bad disc in his back, but the Saudis plan to operate soon.

"Bill, the most interesting bit of blarney to slip from his lips was that he guaranteed that almost immediately after the operation he was going to continue his journey. 'Have it gassed up and ready to go,' the tall Irishman directed. 'War or no war, I am off to Bahrain.'"

King mentioned that Casey also asked him if he could help with flight clearances, which he agreed to do. "By the way Bill, how is that coming and are there any curve balls I need to worry about?" he asked.

My response: "John, believe me, I don't know what lies ahead."

Over the next several weeks I would work closely with King and I even relied on him to write some of the international flight requests for clearances (Bahrain, Abu Dhabi, Karachi). But it also turned out that I would have to draft requests for formal (diplomatic) entry to most of the countries' officials where King was seeking clearance to land.

And, I had to make special pleas to the U.S. embassies in Pakistan, India, Thailand, and the Philippines. At the advice of our State Department, I took this action so as to have each of our U.S. Consulates act as go-betweens with each country's aviation minister. Often the request for Casey to enter a country went right to their respective prime minister or even the country's monarch.

I also explained to King that we needed him to really do a close maintenance check of the engine as a new technology was being used to protect the inner workings of the engine. I explained the complexities of the Cermichrome process being used, and King was amazed. He promised to fulfill my requests. Over the next week, King's crew performed compression checks on all of the cylinders but they never borescoped the inner guts of the aircraft's engine. (That eventually would prove Casey's undoing.)

The following day, I called Casey to brief him on my latest calls from Rundell and John King. Casey was not in a good mood as he was getting sicker by the day.

On August 19 Rundell reached out to me again. Stoically, he acknowledged that Casey was being moved out of the military hospital because all the wards were being turned into a Simple Triage and Rapid Treatment area for possible war wounded. Immediately I thought this sounded pretty fishy as war hadn't been declared against Iraq.

Then again, the news media had the Arab alliance all but blowing up Baghdad, so I guessed we could be assured we would soon be fighting Saddam Hussein.

Rundell further explained that Charles W. Freeman, Jr., the U.S. Ambassador to Saudi Arabia, had become very annoyed and impatient with Casey. Why? Because Casey was calling the U.S. Consulate in Jeddah (where Rundell was stationed) on a daily basis as well as the ambassador in Riyadh on several occasions.

Rundell seemed very frustrated and said, "We have had about all the Casey phone calls we can take. Coleman, everyone in Saudi Arabia knows he's sick but right now all we want to do is kick his ass back to Seattle."

Now came the surprise twist to this tale of woe. I was very aware the Americans wanted Casey out of their hair; but the Saudis didn't. Here it comes, I thought.

Rundell's voice quivered, "Ok, so he has friends in very high places in the Saudi government. Minister Aziz has come to his aid and he is being transferred to the King Fahd General Hospital. The minister has also requested that top-level specialists do a thorough examination and prep his ass for surgery. Bill, I am sorry, but the U.S. is preparing for front-line action here and Casey is frankly in our way.

"If we never see or hear from him again, so be it," Rundell added.

Slowly putting down the phone receiver, after hearing the singular buzzing noise in my ear from the disconnected international call, I realized that all I could do was to try and swallow as I actually couldn't breathe. Let's see, the whole fucking world was up in arms, including our own troops, and Casey was in a hospital bed waiting for a back operation. There I sat in the middle of it all, diplomatically speaking. You can't make this shit up.

Yet, thinking back to the previous week when I was in Bartlesville, I remembered feeling then that nothing could compare to that scene. There I got my ass chewed out by the promotions manager. Following that episode, I frankly wanted to hide under my bed and never come out. Who knew then that one week later I'd have all the American diplomats screaming at me too?

Even my boss at G+A Communications (my employer) was losing faith in my decision-making. He told me so. At this point, my only continuing support came from Hammond at Phillips 66. Guess that's all I needed right now, I surmised.

Later that afternoon another phone call came from Dick Eason, the aviation head in the State Department. He wanted me in D.C. the next day for a 9 a.m. meeting. "Would the Secretary of State be there?" I asked. That comment was met with silence from Eason. "See you and Knight tomorrow," was all he said. (I wondered if this was like the Chinese making you pay for your bullet when they plan to execute you.)

I immediately called David Knight and filled him in on Eason's call as well as Rundell's diatribe. We planned to meet for breakfast. "And Dunleavy in the afternoon?" I queried. "You will have to go that one alone," David remarked.

On August 20, President George Bush authorized the call-up of U.S. reservists. Back at the military hospital where Casey had been for 22 days, he was in the process of being transferred to the King Fahd General Hospital.

While the Saudi doctors deliberated concerning Casey's predicament, another doctor, Mohammad Assad, a close relative of a Saudi Coast Guard top brass, heard about Casey's illness and wanted the opportunity to examine the patient himself.

First, Assad wanted to move Casey again to a private hospital with special imaging equipment where he could make an accurate evaluation of Casey's condition. The next day, Casey was moved into Al-Hamra Hospital, which was owned by Assad.

Immediately that afternoon on August 21, the operation

on Casey's back took place. Assad had brought in a leading Jeddah neurosurgeon (also identified as King Fahd's personal physician) to operate on Casey's herniated back. A total of three surgeons worked on Casey; seven hours later, he was in recovery. The operation was a success. (Assad later told Casey that he would have lost his right leg if the operation had been delayed another 24 hours.)

Upon recovery from the operation, a smiling Casey asked about how long he had been under. Those at his bedside told him about the length of the operation and how long recovery took — in all, one whole day.

"King Fahd sends you his best, Captain Casey," the neurosurgeon said in the recovery room after the operation.

Casey later remarked that the doctors got him walking about an hour after he fully woke up. "I thanked everyone. I was so overjoyed that I offered to pay them (Phillips 66 money, of course). The Saudi doctors wouldn't take a single riyal from me," he said.

Two days after the operation, Casey called me back in the U.S. and asked about country flight clearances; he also told me to notify everyone that he "was well and walking." He said that he would be resuming his trip in maybe three weeks.

I emphasized to him that his future itinerary was dependent on two people – John King and myself – and that he should avoid bringing (or harassing) other people into the discussion regarding the logistics. At that point Casey, in a rather groveling voice but also sounding very tired, wanted to talk insurance and his aircraft.

Apparently, his associate Cindy told him that Susan Gerk, manager of general aviation for Forbes Westar (an underwriter for Lloyd's of London) "wrote a letter to me on May 18 and subsequently left a phone message for me. In both the letter and message, Gerk said that I owed $19,000 for my aircraft's insurance policy and that if I failed to pay this amount by August 14 the policy would be null and void.

"Bill, she also said that Gerk wrote a letter to Phillips 66 on July 13 requesting that they pay this amount as they were the sponsors. I never knew anything about this until now. I don't have that kind of money. Lloyd's of London promised me that they would pay the premium as part of their sponsorship agreement for this trip."

I reminded Casey that he had flown right over the Lloyd's ceremony. "We had arranged through the British Aviation Authority and key members of Parliament for your aircraft to land on the Thames and dock near London Bridge," I said. "By not taking part in this rather regal ceremony, where all of the world's media was present, you embarrassed Lloyd's and the British government. Frankly, they are pissed at you."

I wished Casey good luck and said I might call him later. I added (very sarcastically) that I had damage control to do, while all he needed to focus on was bitching (to anyone who would listen) about the embassy for letting him sit in the hospital so long.

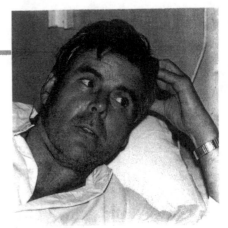

المغامر الامريكي وجدت في المملكة كل عناية وترحيب

التي يشعر بها وبادرني سائلاً
« أين أجد في هذا العالم مثل هذه الرعاية والاهتمام البالغ » .

● بادرته سائلاً كيف بدأت فكرة الرحلة ؟

■■ فكرة الرحلة بدأت في رغبتي بأن اكون اول طيار في العالم يتجول بطائرة سيسنا ٢٠٦ بمفردي وبطائرة صغيرة تستطيع الاقلاع والهبوط على سطح الماء وقد كان هذا الحلم يراودني لاعادة مجد الطيران الفردي القديم والقيام برحلة مشابهة لرحلة شارلي لاندبرج الذي كان اول طيار عبر المحيط الاطلسي بمفرده عام ١٩٢٧م ولكن طائرتي تختلف عن طائرة لاندبرج بأنها مجهزة بالتقنية الحديثة .

والمغامرة للمغامر لاندبرج .

● وماهي المواصفات الفنية للطائرة ؟

■■ كما ذكرت فالطائرة تستطيع الاقلاع والهبوط على سطح الماء ويمكنها النزول بالصحراء ايضا وطائرتي « ليبرتي ٢ ،طائرة من طراز سيسنا ٢٠٦ بمحرك واحدة ، وطولها ٨ أمتار وربها محرك ذوست اسطونات بقوة ٣٠٠ حصان وتنطلق بسرعة ١٢٥ عقدة ٥ ١٤٤ ميل في الساعة ، وتستطيع التحليق لمسافة ١٩٠٠ ميل ولفترة ١٢ ساعة اذا استطاع الطيار تحمل ذلك ، ونظراً للظروف الجوية وما تتطلب عملية الطيران فوق المحيطات والمناطق الاستوائية والصحراوية من استهلاك اكبر

حينما علمت من احد المسئولين برئاسة الطيران المدني بان طيارا امريكيا مغامرا يدعى توماس باتريك كيس يقوم بجولة حول العالم بطائرة صغيرة تقلع من الماء وتهبط على سطح الماء وانه قد وصل الى جدة يوم الاحد ١٤١١/١/٧هـ مساءاً في الساعة ٩,٣٥ دقيقة وهبط في منطقة شرم ابحر شدني هذا الموضوع لاجراء مقابلة صحفية مع هذا الطيار المغامر والذي يتلقى بعض الفحوصات الطبية في مستشفى الملك فهد العسكري بجدة وبادرت بإخبار العميد علي حسن عبدالغني نائب مدير مشاريع المطارات الدولية المساعد للعلاقات العامة والامن والمطبوعات ورئيس هيئة تحرير مجلة الطيران المدني برغبتي في إجراء مقابلة صحفية مع المغامر الامريكي حيث رحب بالفكرة وقام بتزويدي بمصور وبميدالية تذكارية لمطار الملك عبدالعزيز الدولي وبعض الكتيبات الاعلامية التي تعكس التطور الذي تعيشه صناعة النقل الجوي بالمملكة . واتجهت فوراً الى المستشفى العسكري بجدة حيث اجريت هذا اللقاء .

في البداية قمت بتعريفه بنفسي ونقلت له تحيات المسئولين في

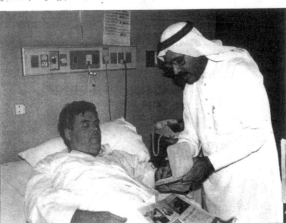

فؤاد حلبي يقدم ميدالية مطار الملك عبدالعزيز الدولي التذكارية للمغامر الامريكي

للوقود من المعدل العادي فقد قمت باضافة خزانات اضافية في العرامات لاستيعاب كمية اكبر من الوقود حيث وصلت القدرة الاستيعابية للوقود الى ٢٠٦ جالون .

● متى وأين بدأت الرحلة وأين ستنتهى وماهو خط سيرها ؟

■■ بدأت الرحلة في ٢٠ مايو الماضي من مدينة سياتل بواشنطن على

التي استطيع من خلالها الاتصال المباشر بالاقمار الصناعية للادارة الاهلية الامريكية للمحيطات والاجواء ، في حالة الطوارىء حيث يمكن لفرق الانقاذ تحديد المكان الموجود به الطائرة في اي موقع من العالم ورغم فارق السن بيني وبين لاندبرج حيث انني ابلغ من العمر ٥٣ سنة الا انني املك نفس روح الحماس

الطيران المدني بالمملكة وعرضت عليه رغبتي في إجراء مقابلة صحفية معه ستنشر في مجلة الطيران المدني وقت بإهدائه الميدالية التذكارية لمطار الملك عبدالعزيز الدولي وبعض الكتب الاعلامية حيث اعرب عن شكره وفرحه بهذا الاهتمام الذي وجده بالمملكة والذي خفف عليه من الآلام

# مغامر أمريكى يطوف العالم بطائرة صغيرة

طائرة سيسنا ٢٠٦ اثناء تحليقها فوق مدينة واشنطن سياتل فى بداية الرحلة

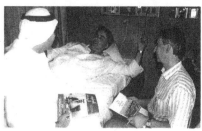

محررا مجلة الطيران المدنى مع المغامر الامريكى وهو على السرير الابيض

تعادل ٦٠٪ من طول الرحلة واطول مسافة قطعتها كانت تسع ساعات بين تلك مافاناز فى ارزونا وبين برتس بال فى اكلاهوما .

● ساهم المدة التى ستقضيها فى المملكة ؟

■ فى الحقيقة كنت اتوقع ان اتوقف فى المملكة للتزود بالوقود واخذ قسطا من الراحة ليوم او يومين ولكن التهابى الم شديد فى ظهرى فتم تحويلى الى المستشفى العسكرى بجدة ووجدت ان هناك انزلاقا غضروفيا فى فقرتين من العمود الفقرى وفى حالة عدم فائدة العلاج الطبيعى سيتم اجراء عملية جراحية بالالم الذى سيؤدى الى مكوثى فى المستشفى لفترة قد تصل لشهر وهذا الامر سيؤدى الى تعطيل الرحلة ولم يكن هذا الالم ناتجا عن الاجهاد بسبب قيادة الطائرة لفترة طويلة ولكن كان هذا الالم ينتابنى احيانا .

● ماهو الانطباع الذى خرجت به من خلال زيارتك للمملكة ؟

■ فى البداية اتقدم بالشكر لخادم الحرمين الشريفين على كرم الضيافة الذى وجدته فى المملكة كذلك وجدت كل عون ومساعدة من قبل صاحب السمو الملكى الامير بندر بن سلطان بن عبدالعزيز سفير المملكة فى الولايات المتحدة الامريكية من اجل تهيئة السبل والسماح لى بالمرور والنزول بالمملكة العربية السعودية كذلك لقيت اهتماما وترحيبا من رئاسة الطيران المدنى والتى كانت دائمة الاتصال بى منذ دخولى الاجواء السعودية عن طريق المراقبة الجوية والاقتراب الآلى الذى ساقوم بايقاف الطائرة فيه لكى تأمين عبورى بسلام من خلال خطوط الطيران بالمملكة كذلك اتقدم بالشكر لخفر السواحل بالمنطقة الغربية الذى يقوم بحراسة طائرتى كذلك اشكر وزارة الدفاع والطيران على العناية التى قدمتها لى وعلى المستوى المميز للخدمات الطبية والعلاجية التى اجده فى هذا المستشفى وما اجده من عناية فائقة من الفريق الطبى .

● ماهى الصعوبات التى واجهتك اثناء الرحلة ؟

■ لم تواجهنى صعوبات تذكر انما الشىء المهم انه فى حالة لزوم اجراء عملية جراحية فيسؤدى هذا الامر الى مكوثى لفترة فى المملكة قد تصل الى نهاية شهر اكتوبر وبالطبع سيؤدى هذا الامر الى صعوبة هبوط الطائرة فوق الماء لوجود الجليد الطاف فى المحيط الباسفيكى ولكن لدى هذا الامر خطة بديلة لذلك .

● كيف تم تمويل الرحلة ؟

■ قامت شركة فيليبس ٦٦ بالولايات المتحدة والتى تنتج زيت الطائرات بتمويل قيمة تكلفة الوقود كذلك قامت شركة اكسبريس كومبونانش - بتكساس بطلاء اسطوانات المحرك بطلاء خاص لخفض استهلاك الزيت وتقليل حرارة المحرك للالم حرارة الاجواء الاستوائية اما باقى تكاليف الرحلة فقد قمت برهن كافة ممتلكاتى لتوفير المبالغ اللازمة لنجاح الرحلة .

● ماهو اول عمل ستقوم به بعد عودتك للولايات المتحدة الامريكية بعد نجاح الرحلة ؟

■ بعد نهاية الرحلة ووصولى الى الولايات المتحدة ساقوم بتأليف كتاب عن هذه الرحلة وعن تجربتى بالتجوال حول العالم كاول طيار يتجول حول العالم بطائرة تقلع وتهبط على سطح الماء .

وفى نهاية هذا الحديث ودعنا المغامر الامريكى توماس كيس متمنين له الشفاء العاجل وان يقوم بتكملة مغامرته للوصول الى لقب اول طيار يتجول حول العالم بطائرة تقلع وتهبط على سطح الماء .

● البطاقة الشخصية :
- توماس باتكن كيس - امريكى الجنسية .
- يبلغ من العمر ٥٣ سنة .
- متزوج وله ولد واحد يبلغ من العمر ٢١ سنة .
- يعمل مدرس طيران فى مدينة ايفرت بالولايات المتحدة الامريكية .
- قطع ١٠٠٠٠ ساعة طيران خلال ٣٠ سنة .
- تخرج من الجامعة كمدرب رياضى وعمل بعدة نوادى رياضية .

الحركة الجوية بالطيران المدنى بالمملكة منذ دخولى الاجواء السعودية وحتى وصلت فوق مدينة جدة حيث تلقيت تعليمات عن طريق جهاز اللاسلكى باتباع اضواء اربعة زوارق خاصة بخفر السواحل السعودية تقف فى انتظارى لمرافقتى وارشادى للمكان الذى ساقوم بايقاف الطائرة فيه لكى اتجنب الاستطدام بالصخور وهناك نقطة احب ان انوه عنها وهى المنظر الرائع لمدينة جدة ليلا من الجو والتخطيط المميز لهذه المدينة .

● بعد مغادرتك المملكة الى اين ستتجه وكم قطعت من رحلتك حتى الان ؟

■ بعد مغادرتى المملكة سأتجه الى البحرين ومنها الى كراتشى فبانكوك ثم مرورى باليابان وبقية دول شرق آسيا مع التزود بالوقود ثم سأطير عبر المحيط الباسفيكى الى الاسكا واما بالنسبة للمسافة التى قطعتها حتى الان فهى

الساحل الغربى من الولايات المتحدة الامريكية واتوقع ان تنتهى فى بداية شهر اغسطس القادم . وبعد اقلاعى من مدينة سياتل توجهت بمحاذاة كاليفورنيا ثم فلوريدا على الساحل الشرقى للولايات المتحدة ثم وصلت للعاصمة ( واشنطن دى سى ) حيث عقدت مؤتمرا صحفيا هناك بعدها طرت فوق بحرات كندا الشرقية ثم جرينلاند ثم عبرت الجزء الشمالى للمحيط الاطلنطى الى ايسلندا فبريطانيا وكان معى فى هذه المرحلة ابنى البالغ من العمر ٢١ سنة ثم توجهت بمفردى الى ايطاليا ثم ذهبت الى اليونان عبر البحر الابيض المتوسط حيث مكثت بها ٢٨ يوما ثم قمت بالاتجاه الى الشرق الاوسط حيث مررت بمدينة الاسكندرية بمصر وتزودت بالوقود ثم توجهت الى المملكة العربية السعودية الى مدينة جدة مستعينا فى ذلك بارشادات مراقبة

# Twenty-four

# Insurance? Who Needs Insurance?

As I had not heard from the folks at Phillips 66 regarding the insurance problem, I presumed they were going to "let sleeping dogs lie." But that was about to change.

Sipping my coffee at 1000 (1900 in Jeddah) on August 24, after I had just hung up the phone with Casey, I was totally shocked when I looked up from my ponderings of Casey's drama to see my ace lieutenant, Tim McCormack, standing in front of me waving several sheets of paper.

Tim stood 5-foot-9 inches and had shock red hair. He had an Irish appearance and was a handsome young man in his 20s. Tim was efficient and a scary excellent writer. (He is an English professor today at City College in New York City.)

"Just a bit of light reading boss," McCormack blurted out. "Guess Geiger and maybe some others at Phillips 66 are out to throw a hanging rope over a tree limb and string you up." His words evoked an instant reaction — panic and bewilderment.

"Casey has had no insurance (effective August 14, it turns out) and it looks like his flight may be at a dead end," McCormack added.

I read Geiger's memo, which read like an obituary. His memos always came right to the point ...

"We are well aware that Casey is still in Saudi Arabia. We estimate that after his recent back surgery that it will be at least four

weeks before he can fly again. The attached insurance contract from
his insurance provider, Forbes Westar, states that his insurance ran out
at noon August 14. The insurance was gratis from Lloyd's of London
and the actual coverage date was from May 14 to August 14; Casey
would need to pay a substantial premium to reinstate this policy.
Looks like the renewal fee is about $20,000.

"It is my understanding that Wipaire Inc. of St. Paul, MN has
a lien on the aircraft for $40,000.

"Nobody at Phillips 66 has talked to the insurance people.
Bill Coleman at G+A has informed them how to try getting a hold
of Casey. He also told them about Wipaire. Since Casey can't fly now
anyway, it gives the insurance company a month to work this out with
Casey and/or Wipaire.

"A copy of the Phillips 66 agreement signed by Casey is attached."

The most noteworthy part of the memo followed ...

"As part of the consideration for this agreement, Casey agrees
to release, defend, indemnify, and hold Phillips 66 harmless from and
against any and all claims, expenses (including attorney's fees), li-
abilities, loss, obligations, and cause of action for injury to or death of
any or all persons (including Casey), or for damage to or destruction
of any property, arising out of or resulting from the aforementioned
flight or activities in connection therewith."

Geiger added: "I see no reason for Phillips 66 to get involved
with this (insurance policy). We are not acting as an agent. Our situation is only that of a sponsor."

After reading that note from Geiger, I immediately called
Wipaire. After a lengthy discussion about how we needed to get his
plane back in one piece (as Wip had so much money already invested),
I just grabbed my balls in anticipation of what I was about to request.

Could they (Wipaire) possibly be willing to pledge to Forbes
Westar that they would be responsible for the cost of Casey's insur-
ance? I was sure an arrangement could be reached that would allow
Wipaire to only initially pay a percentage of the past due premium.

My reasoning for the exorbitant request from Wipaire was
that once Casey finished the trip there was the potential for a book,

movie, and endorsements for personal appearances. Casey would then have more than enough money to repay all he owed.

Wipaire's owner Wiplinger said he wouldn't promise the whole amount of $20,000. What he would do was pledge to pay one-half the premium in the amount of $10,000 to Forbes Westar, if they in turn agreed that the insurance would remain binding until Casey returned to Seattle. I called Susan Gerk at Forbes and presented the monetary pledge by Wipaire. She talked to the owners and they agreed to extend the insurance in principle.

It took several days to finalize all of this with Lloyd's of London. Finally, in the end, we had the insurance restored. Casey could fly with no problem. Yet, one problem still existed. Casey needed to buy war insurance in order to fly in a war zone. That would cost $2,000.

*ITEM: August 25 — the United Nations authorizes military interdiction against Iraq.*

The war footing was at its highest and the Saudis were allowing U.N. aircraft to operate from their bases. Meanwhile, Casey was now in rehab and walking without the support of a walker. He had a cane for support.

Five days after Casey's operation, he was befriended by the Director General of Airports Engineering, Ministry of Civil Aviation, Abdullah A. Mejallid. He invited Casey to be a guest in his home during his recuperation. During the next six days, while he healed somewhat, all he did was worry about whether there would be a Middle Eastern war soon.

With his massive girth now trimmed by 60 pounds due to his lengthy hospital stay, Casey's usual loud mannerism was now somewhat muffled. During a special dinner party he discussed his plight with several of the minister's friends. "I am worried about the health of my father," he told them. "Equally, the impending monsoon season could truly affect my journey as that weather condition would most certainly jeopardize my planned schedule to arrive in Japan. Why? I need to be there before the beginning of the Russian winter.

"I planned to leave by September 8 or 9 but don't have any clearance to Bahrain, Abu Dhabi, or Karachi, Pakistan. My handler,

Bill Coleman, told me several days ago that he was working on the clearances and said we needed each country's approval, and that the only way to get these approvals was to go through the American Embassy in each country I planned to visit.

"But my friend Mejallid has another idea. He is sure he can get me approvals to exit Saudi Arabia and take me all the way to Karachi, Pakistan. Mejallid also promised to work with John King of Saudi Arabian Airlines to expedite obtaining clearances to Bahrain and Abu Dhabi."

Casey went on to explain, his arms waving in the air as if he were actually the aircraft flying to its destination, "So as not to add to the confusion of who is doing what for me, let me add that yesterday John King briefed me as to his conversation with Mejallid and added that he (King) was the master at filing flight plans."

The subject of the insurance policy never surfaced during the party's conversation. Casey indeed needed to talk with me, but for now he was the master of ceremony. His being able to get flight clearances would remain the topic of the evening.

Knight and I agreed that we now needed to alert Casey about the turmoil regarding his insurance policy and the reaction from Phillips 66 and the embassy. After about six calls with several disconnects from the Al-Hamra Hospital, the staff there informed me that Casey was now an official state guest in the home of Director Mejallid.

When I finally got hold of Casey, I briefed him on how his Lloyd's insurance policy had only been good for a certain time period — 40 days. The policy lapsed on August 14. We elevated his stress by telling him I had arranged for Wiplinger to pay one-half of what was owed on the policy. Again, Wip was paying $10,000.

For background, Casey had never even attempted to make one installment payment. If Casey had bothered to read the small print (which I am sure he did not) he would have realized that he had to make monthly payments.

Lloyd's had discounted the policy by promising a 40 percent rebate upon finishing the trip with no damage to the aircraft. I explained to Casey that his rebuke of Lloyd's for attempting to cancel his policy was unwarranted. In a sarcastic tone, I told him that maybe even the British Prime Minister would come to the U.S. on Casey's return and personally offer congratulations.

There was no answer on Casey's end.

As this went on, McCormack just stood there in my office doorway and laughed.

Casey heard all the ins and outs of my getting Wip's guarantee to pay the $10,000. I was pissed off because he didn't even thank me for helping out. I also told him he would not be able to leave Jeddah unless he had war insurance. Casey had the balls to order me to obtain this insurance for him. I said he himself had to make those arrangements and pay for the war insurance. The whole insurance mess was now in his court. Later, Casey had his sister pay Forbes Westar $2,000 for war insurance.

During this latest phone call, Casey blasted the U.S. Consulate in Jeddah and Rundell for not taking proper medical care of him. "The U.S. forgot me and let me lie in the hospital. Hell, even you didn't care," he ranted. "Thank God for the Saudis."

Enough. "Shut your fuckin' mouth about the U.S. Embassy staff," I exploded. "Call me names if you wish, but without my help your ass would have been sent home by the U.S. Embassy. They had a plane ticket ready for you. Rundell interceded with the Saudis and behind the scenes helped you get the operation. And don't forget the war footing."

Casey seemed to dismiss me as one might dismiss a servant. "From now on I will rely on the Saudis for help," he said. "Oh, I need some money. Can you put about $3,000 on my card?" Then he hung up.

# Twenty-five

# The Calm before the Storm

*"The four elements: earth, air, water, and fire. Of these, I call your attention to two: air and fire. As pilots we live in the air, but we die by fire."*
— **Major Sherman Joy, Tuskegee Airmen**

From August 26 to September 3, Casey rested at the home of Director Mejallid. He sat silently for several days just conjuring up what needed to be done to continue with his trip. To him, there seemed like endless tasks. The problem was that others had to get them completed. He felt out of control. He wanted back in the game but at the same time he needed to rest. The doctors had given him a wrap-around back brace that would serve him when lifting things (like fuel jugs) and help his posture on long flight legs of more than 10 hours.

Meanwhile, Casey was in constant contact with John King regarding the health of his engine and aircraft. Almost six feet in stature, King was in his late 50s and as crusty as John Wayne in "The High and the Mighty". His military style haircut was always covered by a New York Yankees baseball cap. The tone of his voice always commanded attention. Not loud, perhaps, but very strong, like an officer leading his troops over the top.

King had well over 30,000 hours in both turbine and reciprocating engine aircraft. He had worked for Saudi Arabian Airlines
for ten years without an incident from either his flight department or
maintenance division. He actually walked a bit like Peter O'Toole in
*Lawrence of Arabia.* King gave his crew marching orders to make sure
Casey's aircraft and engine were in perfect working order.

Deep within the recesses of a Saudi Arabian Airlines hangar
was Liberty II. All 16 airline mechanics therein stood enamored of the
single-engine floatplane.

Each man mulled about compression checks, valve adjustments, integrity of fuel bladders, verifying all power settings. The
aircraft looked tiny, resting in a hangar built to accommodate 747s.

King heard constantly from Casey about the necessary clearances for the remainder of his projected destination points. "John, explain to the countries I'm on my way. I am the Goodwill Ambassador
for Aviation. They should know that. Just tell 'em that, John." Such
was Casey's plea.

King took his usual deep breath and sighed. "I've got to tell
Coleman his pilot needs to shut up," King told Ernie Conners, his
right-hand man. "He may be on a mission, but hell he's really getting
on my nerves. Frankly, Ernie, I like the guy and he is a great pilot,"
King said to Conners, as both checked off maintenance items performed on Casey's aircraft.

As chief mechanic for Saudi Arabian Airlines, Conners super-
vised all maintenance activities. "Cleanest engine I've ever seen, especially after running the time and distance — at extreme temperature
changes — Casey has subjected this bird to so far," said Conners.

After inspecting Casey's aircraft during an engine compression
cylinder check and oil change, Conners put down that exact evaluation in writing on the maintenance ticket. Further, Conners sent off
the oil analysis sample back to Hammond at Phillips 66.

Casey's bird would soon be ready to fly again.

Yet, by September 3, the whole of the Middle East was in
turmoil. By now the Saudis had agreed to let NATO forces build up
their air arms and use Saudi bases. Concurrently, the Soviet Union's
Mikhail Gorbachev was enacting his perestroika ("restructuring") of

the Soviet political and economic system.

And, the Soviets remained the principal weapons supplier to Iraq. Despite Gorbachev's overtures of peace, he offered no support to the United Nations' goal of the ouster of Iraq from Kuwait.

China, too, wanted no part of the U.N. plan. China was experiencing a growing wave of public protests, particularly in rural areas. With China's rapid economic development, the gap between rural and urban income was widening. Contrary to this phenomenon was the economic fallacy that layoffs from state-owned enterprises were causing hardships for urban laborers. Unrest was taking hold in both social climates in China.

But war was in the air, and Casey now saw himself positioned between a rock and a hard place. "Hell," he thought, "I will never get out of here. I will never get clearances because the powers that be in all the countries I intend on landing in don't give a damn about me."

Anxiety prompted him to spend the next several days preparing to "get out of Dodge" and leave Jeddah. Casey and members of Saudi Arabian Airlines got Liberty II out of the large hangar and back to an easily accessible dock site on the Jeddah port.

He also spent time with Conners and reviewed all the maintenance checks that were performed on his aircraft. Casey had never asked Ernie to borescope the engine. That was one critical maintenance step, as it would turn out, that would have prevented Casey's worst eventual nightmare, still to come.

Casey eyed with intense interest all the shipping traffic on the Red Sea. Right across from Jeddah was the country of Sudan. He marveled at all the smaller vessels competing for space with the larger tankers. He strategized on how he would need to avoid the shipping lanes when taking off.

Casey also took in the sites of Jeddah. His back was well enough for him to take in some of the history of his host city where he had been for the past 38 days. Historically, Jeddah was well known for its legendary money changers and it was the principal entry point to Mecca, Islam's holiest city. It has the largest seaport on the Red Sea.

As his cab rolled through the streets of Jeddah, Casey recalled the days waiting in the hospital and the many phone calls to the American consulate. He remembered his not so warm reception in

Alexandria but quite the contrary in Jeddah, which was almost like a warm family reunion. Whatever happens in the war, if there is one, Casey thought, he hoped the U.S. would protect his newfound friends.

Back in Washington, D.C., during this same period, I was keeping a very low profile. As far as Phillips 66 was concerned (after the insurance debacle), Casey was holed up in some prince's palace. I did little to change that impression.

I was helping King draft international flight plans and Knight was working on getting the diplomatic approvals for Casey to fly into Pakistan, India, and Thailand. Admiral Engen had several lengthy phone conversations with Secretary of State Baker, but Knight and I never knew the context or any other details. (We considered that maybe our executions were being plotted.)

The Casey epic was now in a holding pattern with my staff. McCormack went off to a Borger, Texas refinery to develop a story on avgas. Kyle MacDonald was busy sending out thank you letters to everyone who had supported us so far. She was also trying to get more publicity for Casey's adventure. Kyle stood about five-foot tall and was a young woman (20s) who exuded self-confidence and high self-esteem.

By this point in time, Knight and I felt beat up and chose not to call each other until the next disaster. As fortune would have it, that fate was about to come calling.

George Bukota, in Seattle, was almost daily responding to queries from the Seattle media. He provided general updates (which we gave him). After Casey's successful back operation, the media even interrupted local programming to highlight the event. Casey had become a hometown hero.

Around this time Knight and I found ourselves again entering the hallowed grounds of the U.S. State Department. Seated in Dick Eason's office, we awaited another dose of gloom and doom. Both Knight and I remarked that it seemed strange for the head of aviation at State to not have one picture on his gray walls or any memorabilia on his desk. You would think he might have some models of planes or even large photos of aircraft. All he had was a mahogany government desk and two personal items (calendar and memo pad with his name) on his desk. Eason had to be over 40 and appeared to be the typical government working stiff.

That type of person does not neatly dress in a pinstripe suit but rather wears boorish casual wrinkled attire. He lacked passion and decisiveness. He sat stiff in his office chair and doodled on his memo pad as we discussed Casey's plight.

Eason, in a low monotone, said to us that the Secretary had passed along his comments about "your boy Casey." Eason made every effort to repeat Baker's words verbatim: "How does Casey expect to fly over 150,000 troops, cross over military airways, and land safely in Bahrain? And then the cowboy wants to land in Dubai and then cross over our carrier fleet in the Gulf of Oman and land in Karachi? Finally, he has the balls to ask for an immediate flight clearance to execute a direct airway course to Bombay? I don't think so."

Eason also asked if we knew what Phillip Griffin, the U.S. Consul General of Saudi Arabia, had told the Associated Press yesterday. Eason said both he and the Secretary wondered if Griffin was smoking something funny. We told Eason we had not seen his comment.

"Well," said Eason, "Griffin acknowledged Casey was a hero in Saudi Arabia. His exact quote was, "He (Casey) is the greatest goodwill ambassador ever to come to Saudi Arabia."

"But even with Griffin's supposed comment, that still doesn't mean we at State endorse this so-called adventure," added Eason. Rather pissed that some D.C. civil servant could talk to us like that only heightened our disdain for trying to work with our country's finest bureaucrats.

We politely thanked Eason and sarcastically said we hoped the Secretary recovered from all the good news. Our deep down hope was that Bandar bin Sultan, Saudi's U.S. Ambassador, would be very pleased with Griffin's comment. Knight and I more or less exited "left" as if we were actors in a Greek tragedy.

Eason had played his hole card. He never said Casey couldn't proceed with trying to get clearances, or that State wouldn't try and block them. Now it was up to Saudi Arabian Airlines Captain John King and Saudi Civil Aviation Director Mejallid to obtain the clearances to Bahrain, Dubai, and Karachi. In turn, we would continue efforts to gain support from these countries' embassies.

I called King that evening (early morning for him) from my hotel and briefed him on State's position. I also drafted several suggested international flight plans and faxed them to King. I mentioned this was my first attempt to draft a flight plan since my Navy years, and most important it was my first-ever international flight plan. We had not prepared flight plans for Casey's romp to Alexandria or Jeddah — the Navy and Admiral Dunleavy's office had taken care of those.

King laughed. I liked him; plus, he believed in this record flight and he thought like a true aviator. Looking back, we would have never gotten Casey out of Saudi without his help, which would soon become evident.

On September 4 at 0400, Casey stood at the dock before boarding his aircraft. He planned to launch today with or without clearances. He was taking the chance that he could safely fly over Saudi airspace without being detected. Hell, he had flown many times in the States and hadn't needed to file a flight plan. He had flown VFR hundreds of times without any FAA interference. The Saudis shouldn't care — he was a national hero. "I will stay at a low minimum altitude," he thought.

King had assured Casey that Bahrain would let him land without a clearance. "But to be on the safe side," said King, "We will have Bahrain's permission to land long before you even enter their airspace. And, Director Mejallid promised to get Dubai's OK by the time you land in Bahrain."

In essence Casey was seeking to force Bahrain's and Dubai's aviation communities (maybe even both countries' ruling parties) to allow him to land in their harbors, have fuel ready, and give him a place to eat and stay at their expense. If forced, he could pay.

Yet, above all else, Casey was about to become one again with his beautiful sleek red, white, and blue aircraft. His hand stroked the leading edges on the wings; he curled his hands around the struts leading to the floats. He gave the prop a quick turn as if he were preparing to turn over the engine in a Sopwith Camel biplane.

He mused about the aircraft being his ticket to fame and fortune, the vehicle that would allow him to be the only person to ever finish this strenuous record-breaking feat and live to tell about it. He was feeling confident and it showed. Someone remarked that Casey looked as if he were a "knight of old off on a quest."

He stepped onto the aircraft's floats and immediately felt like he was home. Adjusting himself in the left seat, he switched on the fuel pump and turned the large blue control knob to lean the fuel mixture. Next he made sure the engine throttle was shut. He scanned the seven glass display indicators, paying close attention to the artificial horizon at the upper far right. He wanted to make sure the horizon bar read straight and level. He flipped the ignition switch and, swish, contact was made with the magnetos that would fire up the engine. The propeller spun slowly at first in the dense warm air; then, in a burst of power, the propeller roared like a lion after a kill.

Casey felt good, inspired by the sweet sound of an engine purring. His eyes centered on his manifold pressure gauge. The outside temp was 130F and he knew a rich fuel mixture would corrupt the performance of the aircraft. The manifold pressure gauge is one of the best measurements to determine just how much power is being developed in the engine.

He shut the cockpit door and then saluted King. The aircraft was packed and had a full load of 200 gallons of fuel which would provide a 12-hour range to fly some 800 miles to Bahrain.

The trip, by his calculations, would take about seven hours, which would leave some fuel in reserve. Upon leaving the dock, the aircraft remained close to the edge of the Red Sea so as to be far away from the shipping channels. He slammed forward all his controls in order to obtain maximum takeoff power.

The aircraft shuttered and jumped forward in the water. He needed to skip the aircraft off the water like a boy trying to skip a flat rock on the surface of the water. This is called stepping an aircraft. That use of the water's surface was needed to throw his plane into the air.

Now, invariably, temperatures as high as 130 degrees will put heavy stress on an engine. Good oil helps lubricate it, but the stress of having to constantly keep the engine running with a lean fuel mixture and at full power can place a heavy toll on any aircraft's engine. Normally, water takeoffs require lengthy taxi times to build up speed. This type of takeoff normally could be executed in the length of several football fields. Today, Casey would need nearly twice that distance.

As it turned out, the fully loaded aircraft could not take off –
it was too hot and there was no wind. Casey had to lighten his load.

He had to return to the dock three times that morning, finally
dumping more than 60 gallons of fuel. This allowed him to successfully take off at about 1000, almost six hours after he first boarded
the aircraft.

Now aloft with a slight tailwind, Casey anticipated landing in
Bahrain by 1700. After some three hours his aircraft reached the outer
aircraft control area of the capital, having flown from Jeddah direct to
Riyadh, covering some 400 miles. Riyadh was also the home base of
the Saudi Arabian Air Force and, unaware, Casey was about to enter a
new phase of his adventure.

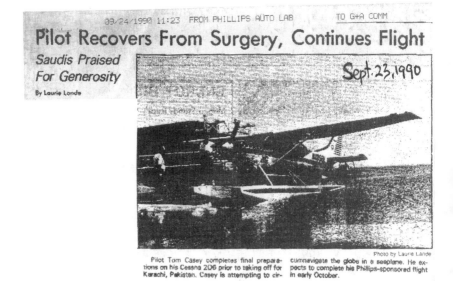

09/24/1990 11:23  FROM PHILLIPS AUTO LAB     TO G+A COMM

# Pilot Recovers From Surgery, Continues Flight

**Saudis Praised
For Generosity**

By Laurie Londe

Sept. 23, 1990

Photo by Laurie Lande

Pilot Tom Casey completes final preparations on his Cessna 206 prior to taking off for
Karachi, Pakistan. Casey is attempting to circumnavigate the globe in a seaplane. He expects to complete his Phillips-sponsored flight
in early October.

## Twenty-six

# Another Day, Another ...

Just off to Casey's left on the horizon appeared three fast moving jets. He was about to receive a fond greeting from three Saudi Air Force British-made Tornadoes. The flight leader hailed Casey on the civilian Riyadh Air Traffic Control frequency. In very excellent English, the Saudi pilot asked Casey where he thought he was heading. Smiling, with a sheepish grin, Casey grabbed and keyed his mic and replied, "To Bahrain."

The Saudi pilot came back up on Casey's frequency and harshly explained that he had not been cleared by any official Saudi agency or government official to fly over Saudi Arabia and on to Bahrain. He further explained in terse terms for this American pilot to turn around immediately and head back to Jeddah. Casey, in deep shock, mumbled that he knew the Defense Minister Aziz and Director General of Civil Aviation, Abdullah Mejallid.

The Saudi pilot seemingly tried to regain his composure while telling Casey that his orders came from Minister Aziz, and if Casey did not comply with this immediate order he would be forced to shoot him down.

More specifically, the Saudi pilot said that Aziz gave him the direct order by phone. His order was: "Tell this disoriented pilot in a single-engine plane with floats branded Liberty II to go back to where he came from. It seems he has no regard for Saudi aviation rules and regulations."

Casey could only assume that meant a return to Jeddah. But perhaps the Minister of Defense meant the United States. We will never know. Casey turned tail and went back to Jeddah; three hours later he was again landing on the Red Sea. John King met Liberty II and Casey found himself now staying with friends of King in a small Jeddah suburb called Saudi City. Casey rambled on about how he was being denied clearances because of the military build-up. He called Rundell at the U.S. Consulate and asked for help again.

Rundell would try and help but told him his hope maybe rested with "Coleman's office". Casey was alone but erroneously he now believed his only hope for clearance would come from either King or Mejallid.

I arrived at my New York office at 0730 on September 4 in an effort to catch up on all the flight clearance traffic from the night before. Our fax machine was full to the brim with messages from the Saudis and other countries. Seconds after I hung up my suit jacket in my office, the phone rang. It was Rundell. He sounded almost out of breath as he began a long diatribe.

"That ignorant pilot of yours just about got his ass shot down by three Saudi military jets," he said. "Ambassador Freeman and Consul General Griffin are thinking about hanging me out to dry. Or, maybe pushing me out a window. I want that bastard out of this country somehow. Get to Washington and talk to State. Maybe the Secretary can put the pressure on the Saudis to clear him to Bahrain and even further for all that matters. Coleman, you have to save me. Please."

After that I called Knight and then left immediately for the D.C. Shuttle. I asked if Admiral Engen could somehow intercede and call Secretary Baker to grease the skids on helping make Casey's clearances go through. I was sure the military was monitoring all the aviation traffic and when they saw Casey looking for permission to fly over the troops, the big red 'No' light came on.

Knight met me at the Lincoln Memorial (one of many clandestine meetings in the months to come). What a beautiful sight from the steps that faced the memorial pool and the Washington Monument. I kind of hoped that Lincoln could come down from his stately chair and offer to help mend some fences.

Knight appeared shortly after I got there and looked rather perplexed. He came directly from his home in Bethesda. Casey's action had resulted in Ambassador Freeman losing great face before the Saudis. It also didn't help with his relationship with General Norman Schwarzkopf. Freeman had called Baker during this whole international uproar. Engen, after speaking with the Secretary, had told Knight that the Secretary almost wanted to put up a post office 'Wanted' poster on Casey. But after talking to Engen, it was agreed that the skids would be greased and approvals would be given for Casey to leave Jeddah.

The message from State was very clear. Just put the flight requests through the respective aviation agencies, copy each country's embassy, and Casey can take off for Bahrain, Dubai, and Karachi on September 10.

Knight and I had lunch and then I went back to my hotel to ride out the storm. I had no idea where Casey was. Once again the refrain: Where the hell is Casey?

Days in Jeddah remained very hot now and high noon temps would only vary one or two degrees, averaging up to 130F. So to gain a lower temp that would not affect Casey's exit from Jeddah, the Liberty II takeoff needed to be made at about 0430, when the temp was only 95F.

Casey was on his own for the next several days. He spent time mostly in the company of the Saudi Arabian Airlines folks. The flight plans were flying from everyone — King sent out some; I sent out a number as well. Mejallid was calling his friends in Bahrain and Abu Dhabi and Karachi. No one had any idea what buttons Secretary Baker and Dick Eason had pushed to authorize the clearances. Why? Well, because no one asked.

During this period, over 20 requests for clearances went out to embassies, aviation agencies, and flight control centers in Bahrain, Abu Dhabi, Dubai, and Karachi.

Just imagine the fury and fervor put in by both King and Casey to write these messages, plus the action of having them transmitted by telefax to these outbound countries. All were doing Casey's bidding. The scene had to be very stressful for anyone in the airline's flight center. Yet there was Casey, directing by shouting.

King remained rather stoic in this maelstrom. It was in stark contrast to Casey, who looked like a person who had just made it through a back operation. But Casey had not lost his 'A' game and wanted results immediately. King kept telling Casey that a war was about to happen and he was just a flyspeck on the wall.

King was unaware that previously Casey had sent faxes to the Consul General at the Pakistani Consulate in Jeddah on September 2 and 3 to request clearance to land in Karachi on September 5. King, not Casey, received a reply from them granting flight clearance approval after September 10. The U.S. State Department had greased the skids.

**Message from Bahrain.** Finally on September 7, King got a message back from Bahrain. "Aircraft called N1990L (Liberty II) on Sept 10 stop. Permission granted landing at Bahrain stop. Operate out of Port of Sitra stop."

**Message from Abu Dhabi on September 7.** "Permission granted to land at only International Airport and (repeat) NOT IN THE SEA stop."

The latter message was a blow to Casey. Mejallid said that he would try Dubai.

**Urgent Message to Dubai on the 7th.** Finally one message got attention — sent by Saudi Arabian Airlines, the request was titled *Urgent Attention in Dubai and Karachi.* "Liberty II approval to land in Bahrain on water approved for Sept 10 and stay overnight. Request landing in Dubai on Sept 11. Will land from attitude 4000 or 3000. On landing kindly arrange for fuel upon arrival for this aircraft type 100LL stop."

**Message from Dubai on September 8.** "Permission to land at Port Rashid. Proceed to docking area. Confirm on landing and arrival stop. Operator will be provided tie-down area in Port of Rashid stop."

**Message from Karachi on September 8.** "Liberty 2 permitted to land in Karachi stop. Be advised we do not have proper facilities for sea landing at Karachi harbor stop. Neither provision of refueling at sea stop. However if you still intend to operate through Karachi you may do so at your own risk and responsibility. Dock at Port Qasim,

Karachi stop. Confirm ETA stop."

All was set, Casey could fly to Bahrain (Jeddah to Bahrain - 799 miles), stay overnight, refuel, and fly the next day to Dubai (Bahrain to Dubai - 301 miles).

In Casey's logbook he wrote: "Will take on fuel in Dubai. Final time of arrival needed to be confirmed with Karachi aviation officials in order to proceed (hopefully NLT one day). Distance to be flown (Dubai to Karachi - 741 miles)."

Now all he needed to do was to receive confirmation from Karachi (or proceed at his own peril) and make arrangements for parking his plane, fuel, hotel, and meals.

On Day 87 (September 8) in the Casey round the world saga, he felt a need to call our New York office to share and relate all the events that had transpired over the last several days. He desperately wanted to tell how approvals had been given for him to fly and make multiple stops on his way to Karachi. He wanted to boast that he, King, and Mejallid had done all the work.

After extolling the merits of all his cadre of friends, Casey briefly asked something about the State Department and the war. He never mentioned the Saudi military jets. He never brought up how pissed off Rundell had been.

I interrupted him and said Ambassador Freeman had put out a "contract" on him. There was no reaction from Casey. And, he never even questioned how much help we may have been in the States to get him out of Saudi Arabia. No, it was all about him.

I asked if he had enough money to buy fuel and food and lodging. How much did he think he needed? Quick to provide an impulse response, he said "$30,000." I countered with topping his credit card with $8,000. I also asked if he realized how badly he had pissed off the U.S. government and military with his crazy antics. I mentioned that those jets over Riyadh could have shot him down. He responded, "What jets?"

He then went on a long diatribe about how we needed to thank both King and Mejallid because without them he would never have gotten clearances. While my anger was building, Casey's emotions blustered. He stated emphatically, "I got the clearance to leave on September 10!"

Immediately, I clearly pointed out that we knew all about
his September 10 clearances because we had done it for him. We just
didn't know how to get in touch with him about the State Department's positive intervention. We told him to ask King about it all. (I
have no idea if he ever even brought the subject up to King.)

Casey rebutted me by saying, "The only reason I got clearances was because of Mejallid and King."

Again, I repeated to Casey, "Believe what you want, but that
wasn't how it went down. State had talked to the U.S. Consulates in all
the countries. Subsequently, Eason had contacted the Saudi Military,
U.S. Military (General Norman Schwarzkopf's staff), embassies in
Saudi Arabia, United Arab Emirates, and Pakistan, and subsequently
all parties that supported providing you clearances. The end-game
paperwork just was perfunctory."

I sat back and conjured up a nuclear explosion. Hell, he could
think whatever he wanted. I repeated to him, "Let me know when
you want to get clearances to fly through India." Then I hung up the
phone.

For all I cared at that moment, Casey could cool his heels in
Karachi for more than ten days before I would even lift a finger. And
I knew King would try and help, but if State wasn't going to let him
into India, Casey didn't stand a chance. I told King that exact thing
and he said he would work with me. I thanked King for all the help
so far. We both agreed that our pilot was a bit too pompous to believe
we in the U.S. had anything to do with getting his ass out of Saudi
Arabia. King said Casey was so focused on the trip he forgot about us.

I asked McCormack if he could draft a news story saying
Casey was back on his adventure again. Our news story told the world
that Casey would be traveling to Bahrain, Dubai, Karachi, Bombay,
Calcutta, and then Bangkok. From there our flight planning could
take multiple directions. Our end game was to get him to Japan, and
then up through the Russia Kamchatka Peninsula and over to Nome,
Alaska.

In the subsequent news story Jack Hammond, head of Phillips 66 Aviation, said, "We greatly appreciate the help Tom has been
provided. Phillips 66 would like to personally thank the U.S. Embassy,
its Ambassador, Consulate General and their staffs, Saudi Arabia Air-

lines, as well as the government and the people of Saudi Arabia who have gone out of their way to assist and support this record attempt." The rest of the story provided a timeline regarding Casey's expected stops and flyovers.

Casey's flight plan, in reality, truly only had approvals to enter Dubai. Karachi was speculative, although they said Casey could come at his own risk in their September 8 telex. But we needed to provide the Pakistanis final flight coordinates, timing, and where we intended to put the aircraft down, to gain entry approval. We knew the target was their harbor in Karachi.

Right now, with the U.S. having one giant foot poised to jump into a war with Iraq, no one at the U.S. Navy and Air Force departments or embassies wanted to talk to us. But one force remained on our side and that was the State Department, which assured us that the American Embassy in Pakistan had forged ahead with approvals. Casey would probably be allowed in country on September 13. A flight advisory would be sent to John King at Saudi Arabian Airlines.

Leaving for Bahrain was now old hat for Casey. He knew how much fuel he needed plus the exact coordinates for his flight path. Standing on the dock in Jeddah, with one foot on the aircraft's float, he paused to make a short speech. Winston Churchill would have been proud of his bravado.

"I would like to personally thank Prince Sultan Bin Aziz, Minister of Defense; the Saudi Arabian government; U.S. Ambassador Charles W. Freeman, Jr.; Abdulla A. Mejallid, Saudi Director General of Civil Aviation; John King and Ernie Conners with Saudi Arabian Airlines; and my doctors for the excellent care and attention."

Although he had had no contact with American soldiers or any other nation's troops, he commented that he would also like to offer words of encouragement. "I'm very proud of my country and what they are doing. The Saudis are a beautiful people and I personally don't like the threats Saddam has made against the Saudis, so he has to be stopped. I hope my adventure will be a morale boost to all the world's troops. I know many newspapers and magazines are covering my journey, and I hope these publications will print that I am totally behind any war effort the United Nations proposes against Saddam.

"I have flown all over the U.S. and the world, too. I am just glad I had this medical problem (back operation) here and not anywhere else," Casey added.

He stood for a moment reflecting on his words and then slowly climbed into his chair at the wheel of the Cessna 206. Sliding back slowly into the cockpit's left seat, he slid open the side window next to him and began waving to all those admiring friends standing on the dock and awaiting his 0620 takeoff.

In a flash, his bird was gliding down the Red Sea, then stepping up on the water and finally, like a fulcrum, being thrown into the air. He was a pilot again. He circled the pier area, again waving to the cheering crowd. At last, Casey was on his way to Bahrain.

Once well over the desert, Casey strained his eyes for troops below. About 450 miles south of Riyadh there were armored trucks and tanks doing maneuvers in the desert. The sand clouds could be seen for miles, and Casey just stared at the miles upon miles of columns of tanks and support vehicles. America was getting ready for war, he thought.

He was glad he got clearance to get out of Saudi Arabia when he did. Any later and he would have become a permanent citizen. As he later related, "Air traffic controllers had me deviating from a straight or direct course to Bahrain. Normally, the flying distance to Bahrain is about 800 miles. But, due to the military buildup, my flight plan had many deviations and I added more than 150 miles to the flying distance to reach Bahrain. So my trip was an uneventful 950 actual miles."

The trip took some eight hours and got him into Bahrain about 1430. Based on information from Bahrain's Air Traffic Control operators, he dialed in his radios to the correct frequency for landing. He lined up with the entrance to the Port of Sitra. He was directed to a docking area — more like a large boating slip.

"The harbor master came alongside my aircraft and said they would direct me to an area to purchase 100LL once I had secured my aircraft," explained Casey. "A young lad came to my plane and said he would help me get fuel. He ran away and then in about 20 minutes a truck showed up, and there was my fuel in drums.

"Equally exciting was the stranger who appeared dockside

during the refueling. The stranger turned out to be Sheikh Hamad bin Isa Al Khalifa, the son of the Emir of Bahrain. The Sheikh exited from a beautiful white Rolls Royce. He commented that he had read about me in the Saudi Arabian *Civil Aviation* magazine and knew from the Saudi Arabian Embassy here in Bahrain that I would be landing here today.

"He asked if I had enough fuel (for which he paid the bill) and was the docking area for my aircraft suitable? Then he asked if I would be his guest for dinner." Casey was elated.

The Sheikh directed Casey to a nice hotel, where he later picked him up for dinner at the twin towers in Bahrain. The unique building's sail-shaped towers channel the strong onshore winds directly onto the three 29m-diameter turbine blades, which are expected to provide 11-15 percent of the building's power.

Explained Casey, "We were the only ones at the Causeway Restaurant (later to be renamed the King Fahd Restaurant) at the very top of the twin towers. Imagine me, having dinner with the Sheikh of Bahrain; he treated me like a hero.

"I was really taken aback. The highlight of the evening was having pitchers of beer brought to my table by this cute blonde. This was the first alcohol I had had since a few U.K. Scotches early on at Aziz's home."

Casey and the Sheikh left the restaurant about 2000 and the Sheikh gave Casey a great tour of the city. By the time he reached his hotel at 2300, he was very tired. Bahrain was magnificent — tall buildings and bright lights; but Casey needed to rest. He was in bed by midnight with the knowledge that his flight tomorrow would be a very short two-hour leg to Dubai.

As an aside, he had a personal mission of finding the U.S. carrier America in the Gulf of Oman. That was the boat Admiral Engen once commanded and now supposedly was the same ship his eldest son was aboard. Tomorrow or the next day, he wanted to fly over the carrier fleet and salute the crew below.

Upon awakening, he set out on the next 260-mile leg of his journey. When he reached Dubai he was met by the harbor master's boat and directed to the Dubai Creek. The harbor master told Casey to navigate up Dubai Creek about a mile and a half and look for a landing area near the water ski takeoff and landing area. He couldn't miss it.

The Dubai Creek is the lifeline and pulse of the city; it separates the city from Deira to the north and Bur Dubai to the south. Once at the mouth of the creek, the harbor boat departed. Casey found this body of water to be only one-half mile wide and about three miles long. Dubai International Airport was off to the left. Casey maneuvered up the creek until he could park his aircraft at a water ski dock. He could tie up and then try and locate a fuel supply and hotel.

As luck turned out, Casey found fuel at the airport and a truck that would deliver. He also found a place to stay. Before heading to the hotel, Casey had the pickup truck, loaded with fuel, brought up to his docking site. He had brought the Liberty II partially up — only half the length of the floats — onto the concrete ramp. This was the same ramp used by water skiers as a takeoff area and now acted as a staging point for refueling Casey's aircraft.

To refuel the aircraft, he used the device he had invented to siphon avgas

*Casey and his device.*

from the fuel drums on the truck and into his various fuel storage tanks — wing tips, pontoons, and aircraft belly. He could control the rate of flow and make a precise measurement of the uploaded fuel to each tank.

Casey assessed that he could handle the weight of having his aircraft take on a 70 percent fuel load. He reasoned that he had ample takeoff space and the temperatures were far lower than those experienced while trying to get off the Red Sea.

Concerned not to put any undue strain on his newly repaired back during refueling, Casey was timid about having to haul the plastic containers of fuel up onto his wings. Fortune smiled on him this day and precisely as he was about to begin the refueling exercise, a young U.S. Navy sailor asked if he could help. By coincidence, this young lad, stationed on a U.S. Navy ship that was tied up directly in front of Casey's aircraft, had actually gone to school with his son in Portland during the mid-1980s.

Previously, Cathay Pacific Airlines had been wired by John King at Saudi Arabian Airlines and the carrier had arranged for Casey to stay in a Dubai shared house owned by the airline. "A chap named John Brunner was my host and we ate dinner together both nights I was there. Great drinking partner, too," Casey would later relate.

The next day was spent trying to get clearances filed to Karachi. "I went to the American Embassy and waited for about three hours and in the end no one could see me or help me. I was told the whole staff was either in closed door meetings or were just plain unavailable. The possibility of a pending war and briefings from Washington were the reasons given. I was asked to come back the next day," Casey said.

What Casey didn't know was that the State Department had already gotten him a time slot to fly to Karachi the next day, September 13. He would be told this eventually. "Brunner made me the main speaker at an X-Patriot Dubai Business Men's lunch. That event was really enjoyable, as I told them about the adventure to date and what I had to look forward to still to come. I received many hale and hearty pats on my back plus an ample supply of good Scotch," Casey said.

Final clearance came through from Pakistan. The Sheikh's office in Bahrain called to say that all was a go and to offer a fond wish of good luck. To clarify, Casey was also told by the Sheikh's office that he was cleared to land in Port Qasim.

Casey had the Pakistan clearance telex faxed to his hotel. The Pakistani telex message from Karachi was further detailed by the Flight Servicer Center:

"Taxi N1990L to entrance of Port Qasim stop. Meet Harbor Master's Launch and tie up to launch stop. Launch will take aircraft to the upper Northerly edge of Port Qasim stop. Launch to continue to second inlet stop. Enter Phitti Creek (lettering earmarking the various creeks is in Arabic) stop. Launch to proceed in Phitti Creek to very end and that is the Port Qasim Industrial Sector Area stop. Launch to help aircraft locate dock area and tie-up stop. Harbor Master may want aircraft also to tie up to buoy stop. Squawk after tie-down stop. N1990L Pilot will wait and be met by the Tourist Bureau stop. Good luck stop."

Before proceeding to Karachi, Casey could only think of executing his patriot act. This would mean exploring the Gulf of Oman and locating the American fleet. He had been told in Dubai that the fleet was 100 miles west from the tip of the Emirates. Casey was determined to find the U.S. Navy and say hello.

# Twenty-seven

# Recon with the U.S. Fleet, and then Karachi

*"There are no extraordinary men ... just extraordinary circumstances that ordinary men are forced to deal with."*
— Admiral William 'Bull' Halsey

These were the days of no laptop computers or any other technological gadget to assist Casey in locating the U.S. naval fleet, so he decided that the only way of finding the carrier task force was to cross over the edge of the Emirates and take a GPS heading southeast. He felt sure that once he spotted the USS America he would locate Admiral Engen's oldest son, Charlie, who was supposed to have command of that ship. This was based on information he had obtained from a source he had met in Dubai.

Casey's fuel state was good — Karachi was only five hours from Dubai. He kept playing with the dials of his radio, hoping to catch traffic from any of the American commercial passenger aircraft or naval carrier task force. Suddenly, over the horizon, Casey spotted an enormous congregation of warships. But whose?

He needed to take a closer look. So almost as if he was on final to land on the carrier deck, Casey, now about ten miles from the fleet, brought his aircraft to about five miles aft of the carrier. He began closing in at 3,000 feet on the super structure when he executed a swooping pattern (about four miles out) so that all aboard the USS Independence CV-62 (alas, not the America) could see his red, white, and blue markings.

As Casey got a bit closer he could see men scurrying to their posts on the deck. Almost like a lightning bolt to the brain, Casey had a brilliant but logical thought: His flying close to the carrier might be perceived as stupid and reckless, since the United States was in the midst of Desert Shield (the preliminary step to Desert Storm). So, he pulled his nose up, took a sharp right hand turn away from the Independence, and accelerated upwards. He waved his wings in the hope that all aboard would also see his American flag.

The carrier's Air Group Commander yelled into what he thought was Casey's radio frequency: "Get the fuck out of my aircraft's flight path!" (Casey later said he never heard him.)

In fact, Casey felt proud of himself. As he flew towards Karachi he recalled some lines from his favorite Irish poem: *An Irish Airman Foresees His Death*, by Yeats:

> *"I know that I shall meet my fate*
> *Somewhere among the clouds above;*
> *Those that I fight I do not hate*
> *Those that I guard I do not love*
> *....A waste of breath the years behind"*

The USS Independence's Captain Robert Lee Ellis, Jr. was now measuring his disdain to that of the Irish pilot. Casey's aircraft had been getting in the way of his carrier's operations in the landing pattern. He immediately got on the horn and told his communications officers to send OP-05- Admiral Dunleavy a "Speed Cat" message (top secret, priority traffic, and for Dunleavy's eyes only).

Back in New York on that day, September 13, just as I was about to head out for lunch, a call came in from Admiral Dunleavy. Thinking back on the call, I now imagined that Dunleavy had just gotten the message from Captain Ellis and I just happened to be on Dunleavy's speed dial.

I remember him sarcastically asking me if I recalled knowing anything about a single-engine red, white, and blue aircraft with tail number N1900L. Also, did my memory serve me as to how carrier flight operations are handled? And did I still remember that props don't mix with jets in the landing pattern? I acknowledged, "Yes, sir," to all his questions.

"Good, you are not a mental midget and maybe you heard something constructive when you were a navy lieutenant." Dunleavy was shouting now, or maybe it was sputtering. His gravelly voice always did command respect, but today I stood up at my desk and went to attention. I responded to Dunleavy: "Casey did what? No, really? That type of action seems impossible. And the captain said what? And CAG said what? Oh my God, Admiral, I am very sorry."

Dunleavy used more expletives than usual — he had developed a way of expressing himself when the name Casey came up in conversation. The next utterance made me cringe and a streak of fear went up my spine.

He said something about not ever darkening his doorstep again. Secretly inside myself, I knew that would be impossible. I just wouldn't call in the next several weeks. Hell, I was just relieved that the only task that lay before both Knight and I was only to kiss some ambassador's ass the following week and not meet with anyone at the Pentagon. We had the weekend coming and knew Casey wasn't moving from Karachi for at least two weeks.

I called Knight and all he did was laugh. He told Engen and the admiral didn't laugh. He also didn't believe that Captain Ellis or Admiral Unruh (Fleet Commander, Carrier Group) would ever invite Casey to muck up the carrier's operation. Engen called Dunleavy.

Casey was unaware he had caused any trouble. He was just trying to boost the morale of the sailors.

Let me explain this incident further. When discussing this situation with Casey in Karachi, he firmly reiterated that he had been delivered an invitation to fly over the carrier USS Independence in the Gulf of Oman by an Air Force colonel whom he had previously met the night before in a Dubai bar. They discussed Casey's desire to seek out Engen's son.

The colonel said he regularly visits the carrier on station and it was the USS Independence, not the America. Casey caught up with

the colonel the following day, just after the latter had returned from
being aboard the Independence.

While on the ship, he had asked the captain if it was OK if
Casey could fly over the carrier and wing-wave to the men aboard.
Casey wanted to send a patriotic message since his plane was painted
red, white, and blue. Supposedly, the ship's captain said OK and the
colonel relayed this message.

Casey couldn't remember if the colonel spoke to an admiral of
the carrier group or maybe it was a captain. But he had permission to
fly by the Independence and wave at the troops. When told the admiral's name — Rear Admiral Jerry Unruh — and the captain's name,
Casey couldn't recall either nor even the name of the carrier. Casey
then said it must have been the captain who told him to fly by his carrier.

He also said he only wanted to find Engen's son who was commanding the America. I explained to Casey that the America hadn't
entered the Persian Gulf. Casey said he got the wrong info from the
Navy (from whom, we don't know). Anyway, Casey said he only desired to fly by and wave to the sailors.

What concerned me about his approach to the carrier was that
the normal landing cycle and flight pattern for recovering aircraft or
lining up for a Carrier Controlled Approach starts about ten miles out.
Casey said he made visual contact with the carrier about ten miles
out, but came within five miles before being told to leave the area.
Whether he had an invite or not, Casey was in err of disrupting the
landing cycle and could have been shot down or possibly have hit one
of the jet aircraft on final.

Getting back to the flight of Liberty II, Karachi ATC was
now coming up on Casey's radio. Ahead in Karachi awaited a long
20-day rest. Why so long? The pending war, plus money negations
with the Indian Aviation Minister in Bombay had become stumbling
blocks.

For Casey, flying across the Gulf Of Oman was like a rite of
passage. He was entering the true second phase of his trip. He wondered what Pakistan and India would be like. He had seen many
television shows and movies but to actually be on their soil would be
quite exciting. Mentally, he brushed up on polite greetings he would

use with the harbor master in Karachi and with other dignitaries that might meet his plane.

"Hello" in Arabic is *as-salam alaykum*. Other sayings would have to be left to an interpreter, if one was needed. He was excited now as the lower half of the Asian continent came into view. ATC squawked the radio frequencies. He was directed to line up with the Pakistan coast line and was nearing the long barrier of land that protected the main Karachi port entrance.

At 2,000 feet he could see the harbor entrance. He called Karachi Tower and asked for instructions to land. He was told to proceed north of the main port entrance and then land. He wanted to land in the calm waters of Phitti Creek that led to Port Qasim.

"I followed the tower's directions exactly," Casey recalled. "I lined up my bird with the Phitti Creek entrance that would eventually open onto the Port Qasim Industrial Park. The Port Muhammad Bin Qasim, also known as Port Qasim, is a deepwater port in Karachi. The port is located in an old channel about 21 miles east of the city center. I don't know if I ever got to the Industrial Park. My bird must have taxied several hundred yards before I was met by a Pakistani naval cutter. The craft was about the size of a World War II PT boat. Maybe it was a PT boat."

The craft came alongside Casey's plane and a gentleman dressed in blue military khakis and donning a fore-and-aft cap with Eagle Wings (captain insignia) addressed him in broken English. He requested that Casey follow his craft.

"I steered my aircraft behind their boat as we made our way east another 100 yards until we reached an enormous 20-foot-tall blue buoy in the middle of Phitti Creek. The Pakistani boat stopped right next to the buoy. Using his arms to provide directions, the captain told me to tie up to the buoy. What concerned me was that I could clearly see a far safer docking area just about 50 yards ahead.

By safer I meant that there were T-shaped docks with the 'T' facing me. "Both the captain's boat and my aircraft were now sitting stationary in the water. I pleaded with the captain about not forcing me to tie up my plane to this buoy.

"Now shouting over the din of the boat's motor, I yelled out that if I were forced to leave my aircraft tied to the buoy in the middle of the creek, it would be a foregone conclusion that my aircraft would either be swamped or clipped by passing large cargo ships that ferry in and out of Port Qasim.

"I finally convinced the captain to let me dock my craft at the T-docks. After much consulting with whom I presumed were junior officers, he agreed, but with one condition. He wanted to be in command of the docking process and demanded that I tie up to the cleats at the aft of his boat. He would then tow my plane to the dock. We had only about 50 yards to go. Now the fun began.

"After proceeding no more than 20 yards, he tried to make a turn to the left and swing my aircraft towards the dock. But since his boat only had one screw, all we did was flounder, meaning that my aircraft never actually turned towards the dock, and instead took direct aim at slamming into the left side of his boat. At that moment, I was yelling, "You are about to smash into my plane."

"Envisioning my floats piercing a hole into the side of the Pakistani PT boat, I literally jumped from my open pilot's left-hand door onto the pontoon below. I untied all the ropes that were tethering my aircraft to his boat.

"But as luck would have it, my left leg slipped off the float and slammed on the float's sharp aluminum edges, lacerating my leg. That uncoordinated action left me with a nine-inch gash and blood spattering everywhere."

Casey had made his grand entrance into Karachi. He was told he would be taken to the hospital. Before going to the hospital, all Casey wanted to do was safely dock his plane.

Now with no attachment to the Pakistani boat, Casey had full command of his aircraft. The creek's current was pushing his plane in a westerly direction towards the mouth of the creek. But, by using his rudder and flaps, he was able to actually steer the aircraft, turning it to a northeasterly heading. Casey was actually "sailing" the plane straight towards the dock. About 20 yards out, he cranked it up and in one easy motion, the aircraft slid into the dock. He could safely tie up.

The captain of the Pakistani boat saw the blood and almost fainted. It was at this very moment that a statuesque gentleman, dressed in a starched white uniform, appeared on deck of the Pakistani boat. In perfect English he asked if Casey was hurt. Our adventurist pilot just nodded, plus added a scowl to show off his agitation. He told the Pakistani admiral (stars on his collar) that all he wanted to do was just land at this 'T' dock.

Moreover, he explained that he could have done without the help of this idiot captain who almost wrecked the Liberty II aircraft. Explaining further, Casey told the admiral that the captain's actions actually led to his leg being lacerated. "Why was the captain being so difficult?" Casey asked.

Rear Admiral Akbar Khan explained that he was in command of the Pakistan Defense Flotilla and also Chairman of the Port. He explained that this boat's captain worked for him. "Today, he wanted to impress me, but all he did was earn a glorious seat at an empty desk at the back of our offices here in Karachi," commented the rear admiral. "We are deeply sorry for any infraction to your beautiful aircraft. And, one of our drivers will take you to the hospital and then your hotel. Godspeed on your journey."

While Iraqi forces stormed a number of diplomatic missions in Kuwait City on September 14, Casey was nursing his wounds and watching Pakistani television. He sat through 22 episodes of "The Andy Griffith Show" and 32 of "Gunsmoke".

John King called me this day to say Casey was tucked away in a Karachi hotel but had revisited the hospital. I thought, oh no, not again. At least we had Casey safely situated in Karachi, albeit with 20 stitches to his leg. He was resting his head in the Holiday Inn.

Now for the real news: The State Department didn't want him continuing his trip or any other movement until the Arab countries could figure out who would side with the United Nations and what was going to be the action plan against Iraq.

Each of the Arab nations, except Jordan, was allied with the U.S.-led coalition. Jordan's decision troubled our Defense Department as it bordered Israel. Saddam Hussein had promised to destroy Israel if his country was invaded.

During this hiatus, we wanted to tie up all the loose ends in Saudi Arabia. We personally sent thank you letters to the U.S. Ambassador and his Economics Officer, Dave Rundell. Equally important was Rundell's recommendation that Philips 66 send thank you letters to Prince Sultan Bin Abdul Aziz, Minister of Defense, and Prince

Bandar Bin Sultan Aziz, Saudi Arabia's Ambassador to the United States.

Regarding the letters, Jack Hammond, the Phillips 66 Aviation head, wrote to Prince Bandar the following:

> *September 14, 1990*
> *Dear Ambassador:*
> *On behalf of the Phillips 66 Company and Tom Casey, we would like to take this opportunity to formally thank you for the assistance you provided to the Flight of Liberty II.*
>
> *Specifically, we would like to express our gratitude for the flight plan approval you helped attain, the health care you were able to provide to Mr. Casey, and the honors you presented to him, including the civil aviation medal. We feel the medal is symbolic of the goodwill and mutual friendship between our governments and people.*
>
> *We hope there will be a time when we will be able to return the kindness and support that you have so graciously provided. You have reflected the spirit and goodwill that the Flight of Liberty II was designed to generate between all people.*
>
> *Cordially,*
> *Mr. Jack Hammond*

Hammond's letter to his Royal Highness Aziz included a sincere 'thank you' for taking care of Casey in the hospital and his home. Equally, his letter to Director Mejallid expressed Phillips 66's gratitude in helping with flight clearances.

Dave Knight was the author of these great letters. He of course was schooled in the language of Washington, D.C. These letters also made the State Department (Baker and Eason, in particular) very pleased. They sincerely hoped the best for Casey's trip and also wished that it would be uneventful.

Little did they know ...

By September 15, gaining Russian Clearance (up the Eastern Peninsula) was also on our minds. We had not received any responses from any of Knight's requests made to the Russian Embassy in D.C. Knight had even taken the time to walk over to the embassy, looking for someone with authority to discuss the matter. He walked back empty-handed. That left us with a simpler approach: We made a phone call to the U.S. Embassy in Moscow. We spoke with John Blaney, Head Economics Section. He asked that we send him a formal telex regarding our request. We sent the telex, brief and to the point:

> *ATTN: John Blaney, Head Economics Section*
> *Request: Need assistance to gain clearance for*
> *flight of Liberty II through USSR in October. Dates to be*
> *confirmed stop. Since June 22, we repeatedly applied for*
> *permission from the Ministry of Civil Aviation for clear-*
> *ance of the flight of Liberty II stop. We have received no*
> *response stop. The following was resubmitted on Septem-*
> *ber 13 stop. At the strong recommendation of Dick Eason*
> *EB/TA/AVP and Rebecca Joyce UR/SOV, I am asking*
> *for your assistance to gain clearance stop.*
>
> *We have received full cooperation from 14 nations*
> *in assisting this flight stop. The pilot, Phillips Petroleum*
> *Company, and others have some $500,000 invested in*
> *this effort to prove the versatility of aviation and many*
> *technical advancements this flight will prove stop. With-*
> *out Soviet cooperation this pilot will face a very danger-*
> *ous flight over the North Pacific Ocean to the Aleutian*
> *Islands to avoid the USSR stop.*
>
> *The flight plan has been developed to minimize*
> *our requested landings in the Soviet Union. We request*
> *any/all assistance in gaining their permission. As dis-*
> *cussed, we await your response stop.*
>
> *BC/Flight Controller*

We also drafted a four-page document to the U.S.S.R. titled "Resubmission of Request to the USSR-Ministry of Civil Aviation for Overflight and Landing Permission for Liberty II." Information included all specs on the plane, sponsors in the U.S., and a complete detailed itinerary for Casey's flight. We also included banking information and key U.S. contacts.

We never received any response.

We also needed to firm up Casey's flight segment to Bombay. We wanted to make sure he had permission to enter India's airspace. We called the U.S. Embassy in Delhi and were put in contact with Pushpa Sapru in the Economics Section. He said we needed to coordinate with the Aviation Ministry in Bombay.

Getting hold of the Aviation Minister was next to impossible. We did talk to his assistant, who said to call back when the minister was there. I asked when. He didn't know, but asked me to call back anyway. This was only the beginning.

Then came another surprise: a letter from Secretary of State Baker to the head of Phillips Petroleum, to wit:

*September 17, 1990*
*Mr. C.J. Silas*
*Chairman & Chief Executive Officer*
*Phillips Petroleum Company*

*Dear Mr. Silas:*
*Word has reached us about a project that Phillips Petroleum is sponsoring that positively contributed to our relationship with Saudi Arabia, particularly two important representatives of their government.*

*The friendship between the Phillips Petroleum sponsored flight of the Liberty II pilot with the Ministry of Defense and Saudi Ambassador to the U.S. demonstrates how much can be accomplished by international cooperation.*

*Building bridges between nations is not just the responsibility of government. It takes people in both the public*

*sector and the private sector working together to success-*
*fully achieve and sustain these ends.*

*I commend you and the work of Jack Hammond and*
*your aviation division for the warm relationship that has*
*been developed between Phillips and the people of Saudi*
*Arabia through the flight of Liberty II.*
> *Sincerely,*
> *James Baker*
> *Secretary of State*

Thinking beyond India, we further decided to directly call the
U.S. Embassy in Bangkok. We were told to telex our request to Mr.
Tom Cadogan, Econ Officer. Surprisingly, we received a warm reply
and approval to enter their airspace. But the next piece of information was even more startling.

Her Royal Highness, a daughter of His Royal Highness, the
Crown Prince of Thailand, wanted to meet Captain Tom Casey. The
telex message from Thailand's representative, Mr. Songkram Somboon, follows:

*Attention Mr. Coleman and Mr. Maccormac (Thailand's*
*Aviation Ministry)*

*(1) HRH Pah, a daughter of HRH Crown Prince, is*
*interested in your historic flight. Her presence at the land-*
*ing place will involve many organizations. So please keep*
*informing your updated flight plans to Mr. Tom Cado-*
*gan, U.S. Embassy.*

*(2) Definite landing date/time should be confirmed at*
*least 2 days earlier for a sufficient time to inform all par-*
*ties concerned, i.e., Aviation, RTN, PTT, irrigation,*
*customs, immigration, etc.*

*(3) Landing on Friday October 14 is preferable. HRH*
*Pah might receive your audience on Sat. 15. Press an-*

*nouncement will be made the same day at a hotel on Pat-*
*taya Beach. You are advised to stay 2 nights and take off*
*on Sunday morning.*

*(4) "Bang Phra Reservoir" is arranged for your landing.*
*It is located about 110 KM east of Bangkok not far from*
*Pattaya Beach.*

Meanwhile Casey, resting in Karachi, spent several days at
the airport and was successful in negotiating an excellent price for
two large 55-gallon drums of 100LL avgas (almost 110 gallons) for his
aircraft. He was able to barter a deal with several airport employees to
drive the barrels to his aircraft. Casey would tell the Pakistanis when
to deliver the fuel, based on when he could get clearance to fly to Bombay.

Later that evening he met four U.S. Navy personnel, two
officers and two first class petty officers, who were there to help the
Pakistani Navy re-commission a U.S. naval destroyer purchased from
the U.S. mothball fleet. The four invited Casey to eat with them at the
U.S. Consulate.

Seems that the U.S. Marines attached to the consulate were
providing meals to the Navy guys, so why not Casey? Not a bad idea,
since the previous night one of the hotel guests had died from pto-
maine poising. Casey now ate all his meals at the consulate.

Casey would wake up each day and try a variety of efforts to
gain clearance to Bombay. He never tried to call me but did try calling
Dunleavy's office.

Commander Mathews in Dunleavy's office said he would look
into it. Casey also asked for Captain Jon Coleman, but he been transferred to NAS Jacksonville to head up a P-3 squadron.

On September 17, Casey thought he had a firm appointment
with the U.S. Consulate. He waited more than five hours and saw no
one. Why? He was being stonewalled.

And, the same day, Casey called India's Civil Aviation Directorate and was told he would have to wait three more days for an
answer. When he called three days later, Casey was told that no one at
the Directorate had ever heard of him. He even tried the Port Qasim

Port Authority Director to see if that office could make contact with the Bombay Port Authority. Casey was running down a blind alley and no one had a positive direction for him.

Casey had hoped he would get permission to leave Karachi by September 20. That was not in the cards as Casey had no clout. He thought he called everyone who mattered. John King at Saudi Arabian Airlines was trying his best as well, but the doors to India were shut tight. There was no rhyme or reason.

There was also the question of paying for his way through India. Casey called Universal Flight, an aviation service provider, to seek its assistance. When Universal International Trip Support (service provider for business aviation aircraft) provided a quote to handle all the requirements to get Casey into Bombay, the sticker-shock sent chills right up his spine. Casey balked. He didn't have that much money.

Why Casey never called his handler (me) or Knight was one of the great mysteries. It was like he didn't believe that either of us could do anything for him. Had he called, Casey would have been told that State put a hold on opening any countries to him until the alliances were forged for the war with Iraq. Dunleavy, as well, was planning for war and where the U.S. Navy would be deployed. No one wanted to hear about a stranded pilot in Karachi.

Both Knight and I had been told that the State Department had put the word out to all its embassies that Casey was to cool his heels in Karachi. And they were vehement in their decision that the time period would be about 20 days and they meant it. Why?

Operation Desert Shield was gaining traction and the current U.S. military deployment of manpower and equipment had the highest priority to defend Saudi Arabia. Staging of troops, machines, and aircraft grew rapidly, becoming the largest American military deployment since the Southeast Asia conflict.

The Gulf region was within the U.S. Central Command's (CENTCOM) area of responsibility. Eventually, 30 nations joined the military coalition arrayed against Iraq, with a further 18 countries supplying economic, humanitarian, or other types of assistance.

# Twenty-eight

# Long Stay of Introspection in Karachi

After several calls with John King, we finally found out that Casey was at the same hotel he had been since landing. We had previously thought he had moved several times in the last week but that was because the Pakistani operator couldn't understand English. During this time we continually asked each other: Where the hell is Casey?

I finally reached him at the Holiday Inn on September 21, Knight's birthday, which was Day 100 of the adventure. All Casey could immediately bring to my attention and equally try to impart high drama to was the fact that he had spent more than $1,800 on phone calls. Why so many calls? Was he bored? Or maybe he wanted to enlist? So, I asked him why.

He responded to my sarcasms by explaining his calls were pleas for help. He was just trying to get assistance in obtaining a flight clearance to fly into India. Calls went out to the Navy, Air Force, Pan Am, the U.S. Embassy in India, the Indian Aviation Ministry, Universal, and Saudi Arabian Airlines. He may have called the Pope, too, for all I knew.

Summarily, John King had previously briefed me about Casey's phone fetish so we made a $1 bet that he would call almost anyone who would listen to him. Further, King said Casey had written "tons" of flight requests to enter India and all were either turned down or no response was given. King won the bet.

Now it was my turn to tell Casey I had been in contact with King and all the other parties he called (except the Pope, of course). I told Casey the hard cold facts of life about the State Department and U.S. Navy. Both parties were steadfast in not allowing Casey to move anywhere. All international agencies had been alerted that Flight N1990L Liberty II was requested to remain in Karachi for 20 days (ETD Oct. 3). He would have known that if he had called me. There was no response from his end.

His purgatory was almost over. He would be given the OK to depart October 2, for takeoff on October 3. We were working with Universal Flight Services and the Indian Civil Aviation Authority, but it was going to cost a lot of money to gain the clearance. We were very sure that Casey would be able to fly into Bombay, but the wheels needed to be greased. Hopefully, he knew what I meant. He would either hear directly from King or Universal saying he had clearance to go to Bombay. Most likely he would get a telex from Universal.

I told Casey we had set up interviews for him with the *Karachi Daily News* and the *Dawn* newspapers. He would hear directly from both publications to schedule interview times.

After further explanation, Casey was made aware in the clearest terms possible that we had not fully worked out all the details for the needed approvals to enter Bombay and beyond. We still needed to go through State and I mentioned that the Indian government may want him to fly straight to Calcutta from Bombay.

Hopefully, fuel would be available in Bombay, but if not Casey assured me his aircraft had the range to make the extended journey without needing fuel in Bombay. He was also made aware of the State Department's embargo of his flying over Burma to Bangkok.

Knight and I had previously been given strict instructions by Dick Eason that we would be in a world of hurt if we allowed Casey to fly over Burma. "We have no diplomatic relations with Burma and they are a military junta. The Secretary is emphatic about this request," Eason had said. And Knight and I had just nodded.

We were still working on that detail.

I emphasized to Casey that at this time all he should do is just relax for the next several days. His ass would be out of there by October 3. The conversation was short but packed with information. One major stipulation Casey was sworn to uphold was the promise to call me once he got to India. Wow, the best laid plans of mice and men. Also, at his request, we put another $8,000 in his account.

Regarding an interview with the *Karachi Daily News*, it was a direct result of our drafting and releasing a news story about Casey leaving Saudi Arabia and reaching Karachi. The Associated Press took our news story and expanded upon its content. The end result was an International AP story detailing Casey's adventures. That story positioned Casey as arriving in Karachi and now looking to get a clearance to fly to Bombay. Both Karachi newspapers got the AP story and held interviews with Casey. A synopsis ...

> *New York-borne Tom Casey said that "everybody wanted to do something in life. Nobody has ever done this before and that is why I wanted to set a new world record in the history of aviation. I want to fly around the world on floats, because it's never been done before."*

Casey went on to talk about going forward to Bombay and other destinations. Then he recounted where he started this journey. He said he had now flown nearly 15,000 miles. He said he needed 24,960 miles to set the world record and by the time he arrived back in the States he would have flown more than 27,000.

Casey told the reporter that his plane had successfully met many challenges placing many stresses to the engine, especially at different air temperature changes from -20 to 130F over a few days. The news story continued on to recap his trip to date. He took the reporter through his many problems and health issues. Casey also spelled out all the research and safety devices he had on board, including his GPS and other supporting navigational aids.

How Casey was financing the trip was extremely scary. Under the subhead 'Expenses' in the news story, Casey said that the flight was being accomplished "purely on his own expenses, and the whole project would cost him nearly $500,000 including fuel amounting to $50,000." He said the cost of the plane was around $200,000 to $250,000.

He said that during this trip so far the biggest problem had been getting clearances for landing in some countries, which was costing him heavily like staying in hotels and making constant phone calls.

The story went on further as to explore aspects about Casey's personal life and his impressions of Karachi. Regarding his personal life, he said that 14 years ago he divorced his wife and had only a son who was 21. To a question about marrying again he said, "I wouldn't hesitate to marry; if I find the right woman who could take interest in my affairs and share my responsibilities."

He further said, "I liked most of the people in Karachi. After completing this flight around the world, I would like to come back and lecture to the students at Karachi University."

He praised the Chairman, Port Qasim Authority Rear Admiral Akbar H. Khan, for providing him all the necessary facilities he required during his stay in Karachi. Casey recalled that the admiral was the same one "who applauded Casey's docking of his aircraft at the Port."

The story broke all over the world. Casey was now a hero again and one recognized for his exploits. The folks at Phillips 66 read everything that had to do with Casey. Remember there was no Internet so the most authoritative information came from the *Tulsa World* back in Bartlesville, Oklahoma, where Phillips was based.

Prior to this Karachi AP story making news, previously on September 27, Laurie Lande's article appeared in the *Tulsa World* and extolled the adventures of Casey. In her story, Phillips 66 was given significant coverage and everyone was happy with the report. Hammond called to thank me. Good day for my team.

But two days later echoes of anger in Bartlesville could be heard all the way back to my office in New York City. Hammond called me about 1000 and said the Karachi AP story on Casey in today's *Tulsa World* was causing great distress with management. He dare not leave his office for fear he might lose his job.

"Jack", I asked, "What the hell did the story say?"

He replied, "Casey said that the flight was being accomplished purely on his own expenses and the whole project would cost him nearly $500,000, including fuel amounting to $50,000. He said the cost of the plane was around $200,000 to $250,000.

"He gave no credit to Phillips 66 and really knocked the State department, both in the U.S. and Saudi Arabia. As far as he was concerned, it was his show and his show alone.

"I am tempted to pull the plug, but I can't because we are in too deep. Bill, control his mouth. I don't care if you have to go there yourself and be his mouthpiece. But tell him to stop the bad press."

I told Jack I would take care of it. After hanging up with Hammond, I sat there wondering just how I chose not to go to Karachi. I called Casey before his next interview and explained how Hammond had taken his last story in the *Karachi Daily News*.

I told Casey that Hammond almost pulled the plug. Why? He just can't keep saying Phillips 66 was not a help financially or logistically. And stop knocking the State Department.

Casey apologized, albeit half-heartedly. He gave no answer to why he was such a butt-head. "Hell, I didn't know those Arabs sent their stories back to the States. Laurie's story was great. Hey, can you get me a copy of the newspaper? Just send it to King and he will put it on his plane. Also, I am ready to leave; and thank God for King in getting me clearance."

Again, I told Casey 'no' to the paper and 'no' regarding his comment on King. Yes, King helped, but it was our State Department as well as Knight and I doing the heavy lifting to gain his clearance to Bombay.

Casey just ignored me as he was now Saudi Flight #2, or so King told him.

Casey had another interview with the newspaper *DAWN:*

*US pilot who lands on water*
*by Nafisa Hoodbhoy*

*When his Liberty II plane landed on floats at Port Qasim, he was pleasantly surprised to see a hundred volunteers waiting to help. The curiosity was evident on their faces. Even though it was totally different, the pilot found it beautiful to see.*

*The authorities at Port Qasim were no less enthusiastic.*

*As Public Relations Officer, Mumtaz Hussain said: "We had only seen it (the float plane) in films, but for the first time, we saw it here." he said. Even the Chairman, Port Qasim, Rear Admiral Akbar Khan, stayed back to watch the plane land on water," he added.*

*Mr. Casey was hurt in the shoulder (really leg) when he landed at Port Qasim. The workers therefore provided him first aid without requiring him to complete immigration formalities. The immigration woke up only a week after the flier had been here to grant him a 72-hour visa.*

*Flying around the world, the 53-year old pilot says, "The engine did better than I did." Sponsored by Phillips 66 oil company using multiviscosity aviation oil, Mr. Casey says the engine has successfully withstood the stress of many takeoffs and landings in water. In addition, the plane has battled frequent and sharp temperature changes in air temperatures.*

*A grueling flight of 11,000 miles to Jeddah caused Mr. Casey's back problems to worsen to the point that he had to be admitted to a hospital on July 30. "At the Al Hamra Hospital, they told me if I had come in one-and-one-half hours later, I would have been paralyzed for life," he pointed out.*

*Lying ahead of him is another 11,000-mile journey through Bombay, Calcutta, Bangkok, and over the Far Eastern countries to Japan. Some delays have been caused by his illness and now Mr. Casey is worried about flying over the Soviet Union in winter "when the rivers are frozen."*

*His plane can land on grass in emergencies but can't "take off unless there is a very long runway (water)."*

*Walking through Karachi, the American has enjoyed the free and congested traffic "where there is total disrespect for the law. It's a race to get nowhere," he says of the motorists, adding "my driver would be totally lost if he didn't have a horn to blow." He was also surprised to find out that Karachi was such a sprawling city with simplicity.*

*After returning to the U.S. Mr. Casey says he plans to tour the country and to lecture young people on what he has seen and experienced.*

*"My advice to them is to seize opportunities while they are young," was his simple and straightforward recommendation.*

I had the reporter fax to me a copy of his story and then I sent a copy to Hammond at Phillips 66. There was no comment from anyone. Casey was now ready to launch to Bombay.

## Twenty-nine

# $12,000? For What, May I Ask?

Hanging up from our call at 0630 (ten-hour difference) he felt it necessary to explain his frustration at having to wait for the War Lords to make up their minds on whose side they would fight. Casey roared out to an acquaintance who was seated across from him at breakfast at the Holiday Inn. This fine gentleman had now been listening to Casey's diatribe for the past week and often would look for another table to sit at. But today, his luck ran out and he got the full brunt of Casey's ire. "Let's Hope Coleman/Knight and the U.S. State Department can perform better during the rest of my trip. The dude in New York who is working for Phillips 66 even said I was to meet the Crown Princess of Thailand. What a bunch of rubbish."

Casey's interview the previous day went well and he was pleased with both the Karachi news articles. Now it seemed like his stay in Karachi had been a total success. He rested as he'd been directed and waited patiently for the clearance to come on October 1 or 2.

I subsequently heard from John King and his was a tale of woe. "Clearance and flight plans for Liberty II are still in process for the flight from Karachi to Bombay and beyond. We are following the progress of these requests through our SITA communications network (which offers airlines the ability to talk to each other) and working

with the concerned Saudi stations along the intended flight path of
Liberty II.

"We have been discussing that Tom is having a difficult time
getting airborne in the hot climates he is currently encountering,"
related King. "He definitely needs the high octane avgas for his future
planned flight legs. Conversely, we have been looking at alternate rout-
ings that can be flown with shorter legs which will give him greater
safety and reserves after he arrives in Calcutta. We recommend: Bangkok; Kuala Lumpur; Kuching, Brunei, and Zamboanga, Philippines."

As we talked, I rushed to my maps and flight charts. "John,
you are brilliant. We will seek the appropriate approvals for all." And
that is what we did.

My time now spent on the phone attempting to obtain Casey's
approvals to enter certain countries seemed endless. I had tried several
times to gain assistance from the U.S. Embassy in Delhi. My note to
Pushpa Sapru, Economics Section, was to no avail. We later called
him several times and when we finally made direct contact with
Pushpa we implored the gentleman to provide us the name of someone who can give us clearance and tell us what else we needed to do.
During these several phone calls to him, he finally pointed us directly
toward the Civil Aviation Authority in Bombay. In response, we
tersely explained to Pushpa that our several previous calls to the aviation ministers in both Bombay and Calcutta led us to believe that they
were only interested in us paying an exorbitant fee to gain clearance
approval. Now there was only silence on the other end with Pushpa. I
said goodbye and he said 'cheers.'

David Knight in the meantime was trying to use his skills
in D.C. to get Indian clearance. He had all the capabilities of easing
strained relations, in particular when immersed in heated or stale-
mated political situations. He was the master of calling a high official
in any nation's embassy and finding the right person to answer his
request.

Case in point: We needed India's Civil Aviation agency to allow Casey to fly from Karachi and land in Bombay harbor. He would
later travel to Calcutta where he would then take the most expeditious
flight routing to Bangkok.

What a pleasure it was sitting next to Knight as he called different departments in India's Embassy in D.C. Later that same day, we even met with several officials at the embassy and were greeted with grace and kindness.

The outcome from all our efforts over a three-day period was very simple: Please call India's Civil Aviation Authority in Bombay and Calcutta directly and tell them that you spoke to officials in India's embassy in Washington, D.C. Explain what you need. These same Indian officials assured us that we would get prompt action by just calling and asking to speak with the Civil Aviation Minister.

Now I know why everything runs very slowly in India. No one can or wants to make a decision. But in the case of India's Civil Aviation Minister, our course of action would be clearly defined. It seemed that only money talked.

At the stroke of 2400, we again made a call to the Bombay Aviation Minister on September 28. It was during this call that he curtly explained that obtaining flight clearances for Casey, having the harbor master guide him to a docking area in Bombay's harbor, and providing security for his plane would be a costly expense for his poorly funded Aviation Ministry. But if the pilot was willing to help defray these costs, he was sure that clearance could be obtained.

When Knight asked what the cost might be, the minister indicated that $12,000 American dollars would suffice. The money could be wired to a special account. After a brief discussion, I immediately told Knight we would send the money, but it would take several days for the actual funds to transfer between our New York bank and their special account. We would anticipate that he would have the money by October 1. We clearly outlined the funds process to the minister and noted when the monies would arrive.

We asked, "Once you receive the monies, would we get an immediate telex that the flight clearance to Bombay was approved?" The Aviation Minister repeated our timetable for the receipt of the money being sent to him by October 1. He said that upon receipt of the money, he would send the flight clearance for Bombay.

His response was difficult to understand because of his broken English. He repeated himself again and this time he definitely asserted that the official notification would be sent to Universal, which assisted in flight handling. "Was that Ok?" he asked. We told the minister that would be fine. We asked if Calcutta was also included and he said no. We would have to call the Civil Aviation Minister in Calcutta. He gave his name and number.

We provided the minister with all the information on Casey's aircraft. Casey would now get his clearance through Universal. This service provider would provide Casey all the flight information he needed to land at Bombay. Payment to coordinate the flight planning would also need to be paid to Universal for their services. That would be worked out after Universal got the clearance documentation.

We contacted Lex Denherder at Universal and repeated everything the Aviation Minister told us. Lex said we would be working with the Red Team. He also needed to know our plans for Calcutta and Burma. He would bill us after Casey reached Bangkok. Universal was super at handling all the particulars and well worth using their services.

Knight and I left the Hyatt Hotel and took a limo over to the State Department. We were pleased with ourselves. Hell, it only cost $12,000 plus Universal's costs to get Casey out of limbo.

We met with Dick Eason at State and told him we had abided by their Casey shutdown request for Karachi, and we were now in the process of getting ready to move him again. We told Eason that India would clear his flight October 1 from Karachi to Bombay. We still had not formalized the planning for his flight to and out of Calcutta and beyond. Our goal was to fly him across the Sea of Bengal to Bangkok. (This really was not our game plan, but it had to suffice for now.)

Eason was very straightforward, commenting, "Don't you dare fly over Burma. That country is considered a no-fly zone for American aircraft (the U.S. did not recognize Burma's military regime) and by flying over them you could cause an international incident.

"If you dare to fly over Burma that means you would greatly embarrass the United States. If you even try to make contact with Burma that would be considered a severe violation of our trust in you. And, I am sure you don't want to piss off the State Department. Do you understand?" Eason furrowed his brow and tried to give us a steely stare. His facial expression reminded me of Freddy from "Friday the 13th".

Now assuming we had no wiggle room based on the latest breaking news from State, I wondered how the hell we would get him to Bangkok. After all, the Crown Princess was waiting.

Eason continued. "I don't know what are the various options available for your pilot to reach Bangkok from India, but it seems to me that his only choice is to take a direct flight path over the Bay of Bengal to Bangkok. I hope he has the range. Temperatures are in the 100s Fahrenheit."

We replied, "Yes". (What a flaming idiot, I thought. But he had helped us in the past.)

Now we were screwed. How the hell do we get him out of Calcutta to Bangkok? I immediately called John King at Saudi Arabian Airlines and gave him the good and bad news. King said he may have an answer. "We could rename the Liberty II the Saudi Special Flight #2. That way, he becomes connected to Saudi Arabia and not the U.S. Then there would be no prohibition on Casey flying over Burma." I immediately praised him as a true genius.

I told him to convey this plan to Casey, because if it came from my mouth there would be hell to pay at State. King would tell Casey. (Casey never believed me that I knew the whole time about the special name for Liberty II from King. In fact, Casey never knew we paid off the Indian ministers. He thought all approvals came from King's work.)

John King asked about how we got the Indian clearances. We told him it was the use of diplomatic incentives — money. John laughed and pointed out that he had no luck with the Indian authorities in gaining clearances for Casey. But we all agreed that the renaming of the plane for a flight over Burma was "True Grit".

King explained, "I kept getting passed around to a different authority each time I called. And, forget about sending requests for flight approvals — the requests were never answered.

"Casey told me that the Karachi people never ever saw a floatplane before and I am sure that holds true with the Indian authorities.

"Thanks, Bill, and please tell the Indian Civil Aviation folks to send a copy of the flight clearance information to me as well as Universal. I promise to get hold of Casey and fill him in on all the particulars."

I told King that the Indians were crooks. They knew what was happening regarding Casey's flight because they read the newspaper stories. It was no mystery that Casey had to pay to get into Bombay, and that the same would surely hold true for Calcutta.

I asked King for another favor: Tell Casey to call me. King laughed. "Bill, I rubbed the same genie bottle as you did. We need to meet someday. Casey is like a sandstorm in the desert. Everything and everybody definitely knows he is there, but when asked where he is going and when or how, he never seems to answer what you asked or do what he says he is going to do. And that means calling or sending even a postcard."

I responded, "John, my response has always been: *Where the hell is Casey?*"

King laughed loudly. "Someday you should write a book and call it 'Where the hell is Casey?' Hey, I am sending you copies of the *Karachi Daily News* and *Dawn*. Casey was featured, along with a photo, in both newspapers. I am sending them ASAP. Some of the things Casey said I am sure will piss off Phillips 66, like saying he is getting no outside financial support nor has he been offered any."

I told King that Phillips 66 already saw the *Karachi Daily News* story as it went out on AP. "They were mildly pissed, John, but I still have my job," I said, to which King laughed.

Casey called me after he had just received flight approval information from both King and Universal. He wondered why he couldn't leave until October 3rd. I explained the State Department's position. Casey said the State Department had nothing to do with anything. It was all King and Universal.

At that point, I called Casey a stupid asshole. I told him to ask King who got him approvals. I said that Philips 66 was paying his way to India to the tune of $24,000 plus fees to Universal. These payments got the clearance to Bombay and Calcutta.

I also opened another wound. Again I queried Casey why he told the *Karachi Daily News* that he was financing the whole record flight. He said it would cost him about $500,000.

Casey responded that he told only the *Karachi Daily News* that story in an attempt to have people feel sorry for him and maybe help him get free services the rest of the trip. "Hopefully it will work here in Karachi," he said. Casey told me that he had spent close to $3,500 in Karachi. I told him for the hundredth time that he was using monies we had put on his credit card, "So stop bitching."

I finally asked what he did at night. He recounted that he spent many nights either talking to his new friends at the Holiday Inn or walking around Karachi. The city was teeming with people at night. Many of the sidewalk vendors had been selling their goods for more than 13 straight hours. He liked to talk to the people and learn more about how they lived, along with their likes and dislikes.

He explained that most afternoons he would go to the dock to check on the security of his aircraft. It was in safe hands (because of about ten young Pakistani boys he paid), but Casey wanted to make sure.

He also related that the majority of conversations he had with anyone in Karachi were about the impending war with Iraq. Once they learned that he was from the United States, they were eager to find out when the war would start. They also wanted to know if Casey thought the war would spread to Pakistan.

Casey would spend hours talking about the great military the U.S. had. He would brag about his friends in Saudi Arabia and how American ships were in the Red Sea and Gulf of Oman. Some of the Pakistanis would tell how they had seen the American aircraft carriers in the Gulf and the planes flying from their decks.

The Karachi newspapers and evening TV newscasts all focused on the impending conflict. Aerial film footage showed a significant buildup of multinational forces, their equipment, and aircraft both in Saudi Arabia and Dubai. Several of the TV stations sent out boats with camera crews to film the U.S. carrier activities. Other ships in the Gulf came from Great Britain, France, and Canada. By now the whole Middle East was expecting a war, but there had not been any pronounced date when such action might take place.

Now as the self-appointed official U.S. orator, Casey assured people that Pakistan was safe from this war against Iraq. But in the recesses of his mind, Casey wasn't so sure. Suppose Pakistan comes in on the side of Saddam Hussein? What if the U.S. has to fight a war on two fronts? All he could hope for was that by October 3 the war with Iraq had not happened and that he would be more than halfway to

Bombay.

On the evening of October 1 Casey was making a physical exterior preflight of his aircraft. During the exterior inspection, Casey found that barnacles had attached themselves to the bottom of his aircraft's floats. This presented a problem, especially when trying to take off. What could he do?

Casey queried the harbor master about the barnacle problem. Did he know of anyone he could recommend for this arduous task? The harbor master said he knew of an elderly gentleman who was an expert in barnacle removal. This gentleman was actually there right then at dockside.

Casey gave the approval to hire the elderly gentleman. The old man was probably about 70, but he couldn't tell the age of any of the elderly Pakistanis. He was slim and a bit bent-over, and spoke no English.

The elderly man was handed a large block of wood to scrape the barnacles off the floats. Casey watched as the man jumped in the extremely filthy water and dove under the right float. All Casey could see was the man's hand, scrapping the barnacles off the float. Once he had finished that float he stopped for the day; he would work on the right one the next day.

After completing the task, Casey gave the man $10 (U.S. dollars) which the harbor master said was way too much. "You can feed a family of four for a week on that much money. You have just destroyed the local economy," he said. Casey didn't care. The man had done a splendid job that took more than seven hours and took until midday on October 2 to complete. Now Casey waited for October 3 and leaving for Bombay.

Meanwhile, as Casey was preparing to leave for Bombay, I was trying to gain future approvals from countries like the Philippines, Taiwan, Japan, and our dear friends in the U.S.S.R. for Casey to land in their waters.

Before leaving for Bartlesville on October 2, I did contact an old friend of mine in Kuala Lumpur. He owned a large fishing operation and had dock space for Casey to tie up on the island of Penang. My friend was the same person I had as a key contact during the Vietnam conflict. We had worked together on several clandestine operations. It was good to renew the connection.

I also knew Casey would be happy with Pattaya Beach in Thailand. During Vietnam, it was an R&R location for American troops. I imagined that by now it had become more popular than when I was there in 1970-71. Then, dried squid cost one Baht. Our U.S. currency was strong then and an American nickel was worth one Baht.

Also, later that morning, I talked to Dorothy Aron in the Commercial Department at the U.S. Embassy in Brunei. She was very pleasant and explained that we needed to send her a complete dossier on Casey and his adventure. Again, we had to explain what Casey's plane looked like. Most embassies or consulates we approached had never seen a floatplane before. All they were familiar with was the Pan Am Clipper, a much larger aircraft and one requiring more landing and docking space.

Finally, I got calls off to the U.S. Embassies in the Philippines, Japan, and Russia. Additional information would need to be sent to all who were called.

We needed Casey to fully understand all aspects of our future game plan. Most important was his total buy-in. We approached the U.S. Embassies in the respective countries where they were located to gain approval for him to enter each. We drafted flight plans to gain flight clearances.

Now we made it imperative that Casey study each and every document, plus execute and comply with all facets of our plan. Most important, we expected no deviations or surprises. He was now under our thumb, so to speak. If not, I was prepared to fly to the Philippines and, well, you can assume what I would do.

We sent Casey all this documentation on October 2 for early delivery on October 3 to the Taj Mahal Hotel in Bombay. The package was meant to be opened when he arrived there. Fingers crossed, we expected his reply.

With Casey's planning out of the way, I headed to the airport. My thoughts turned to what I was going to tell everyone at Phillips 66. As I had direct responsibility on the outlay of funds, the people I reported to at Phillips would want to know how much money I had actually spent on Casey. At present, only Hammond knew I had just spent $12,000 to get Casey to Bombay and was sure that I would need to pay another $12,000 to get him through Calcutta.

I flew out of JFK to Tulsa that night. From there it was a one-hour rent-a-car ride to B'ville, as we called this Oklahoma oasis. I had all the numbers with me. But to divulge all the actual costs would mean death by firing squad. I would tell Hammond and Geiger alone.

You have to understand Hammond. He lived and breathed aviation and his heritage prompted him to be a very proud and aggressive businessman. Remember his father worked for Jimmy Doolittle, who was on the board of Shell Oil, and headed the Aviation Department at Shell. Also his father was a pioneer of the fixed base operation, the type of facility that services business aircraft at airports.

I will always remember sitting in Hammond's office directly under a framed picture of a Doolittle Raider's B-25 bomber that was personally signed by Jimmy Doolittle. I remember asking Jack one day the significance of that photo. He related that at an early age (I think he was 6 or 7) he met Doolittle. As it turned out, this picture was passed onto Hammond by his father. More importantly, Hammond's father was considered 'the father of general aviation' by some.

Jack, as head of Phillips 66 Aviation, only wanted success from any endeavor he pursued. He was an accomplished pilot, and Casey's seemingly impossible "Walter Mitty" tales only induced deep belly laughter. Hammond and I typically would spend a good three hours at lunch recounting Casey's latest exploits.

Now back in Jack's office, the time came to tell him how much I had to pay for Casey to land in Bombay. "I hope that money isn't coming out your pocket, Coleman," he said. I assured Hammond that it wasn't. I explained that I was going to tell Geiger and explain we would bury the cost in other projects. Hammond agreed to keep this between the three of us.

Hammond also wanted to know if there was any ambassador in the world that wasn't out to shoot me. I answered that my name was becoming somewhat of a household swearword to many countries' Econ Officers, Marine Attachés, plus actual ambassadors. How did that happen? Well, the U.S. Saudi Ambassador, Mr. Freeman, had informed his fellow colleagues in countries where I would be attempting to gain flight approvals that Casey's adventure (or road show) would soon be coming to their neighborhood. I understand his description of this impending event was not favorably endorsed. On the bright side, I told Hammond that both Admirals Engen and Dunleavy still loved me — at least for now.

Hammond asked how long Casey's journey would take. I said I didn't know, but I was sure that the Russians would not allow him to fly into Russian airspace. "Premier Gorbachev is on thin ice with the Soviet Politburo after his recent visit with Bush in D.C. and he has Yeltsin knocking at his door. Gorbachev doesn't need a pilot in a seaplane to worry about," I surmised.

Hammond and I went over Casey's anticipated next stops and tried to project his arrival back in Seattle. I estimated it would take another 30 days depending on how cooperative the countries were in providing either overflight clearances or permission to land.

I asked Hammond about the oil analysis samples Casey was sending back to him. He said he only received two samples and those samples were for oil changes before Saudi Arabia. He had not received any samples from Saudi Arabian Airlines yet or from anyone else after leaving that country. I explained to Hammond that we had used Federal Express to send cases of oil to Casey in Jeddah and Karachi. And just this week, we made sure Casey would have oil waiting for him in Subic Bay in the Philippines. Additionally, at every stop where we had arranged landing clearances (after Greece) we made sure that avgas was available.

Hammond acknowledged that the analysis of the oil samples to date showed Casey's engine was running smoothly. "Curiously, Dennis Boggs (technical director for Phillips Lubricants) asked me if I had received any more oil analysis kits," he explained. "Lubricants does the evaluation." I said not to date.

"So far, Dennis has said we have not seen any metal particles in the oil or other suspicious byproducts in the oil, thus meaning all the internal parts, such as pistons, gears, and cylinders in the engine were functioning perfectly."

I also mentioned to Hammond that John King and his mechanic at Saudi Arabian Airlines had checked Casey's engine. "Jack, I got a favorable report from Ernie Conners, the airline's chief mechanic. And, he told me he had sent the oil analysis sample back to

you. I am sure you will have it in several days and you can provide it
to Dennis Boggs."

Hammond asked, "Are you planning a big arrival event? And,
what about after he makes it back and establishes the record? Do we
have him on the speaking circuit? Do we have him at our booth at
the big aviation conferences to tout our aviation oil? What are your
thoughts?"

I explained that all those were possibilities, but first we needed
to make sure he was going to actually arrive back in Seattle. "Jack,"
I cautioned, "Casey has some very large hurdles to overcome. First,
if Russia turns him down, then he will have to fly across the Northern Pacific from Japan to Attu in the Aleutians. That will take some
great airmanship, luck, and balls. Second, we have to get him into all
the rest of these countries before even considering Russia: Thailand,
Brunei, Philippines, Japan.

"We have our work cut out for us. Moreover, I know Bernie
Coleman at Engine Components wants to promote the Cermichrome
cylinder coatings and the same equally holds true for Wipaire and
its floats. Casey will be a hot commodity once he makes it around
the world. But, first, let's get him on U.S. soil and welcome him back
home. We are in contact with the White House and I have received
a promise that President Bush will write a congratulatory letter to
Casey upon his return to Seattle."

Hammond told me to do what I had to do. "And, for God's
sake don't listen to that promotions manager; he would spoil good
sex," he added.

Tom Geiger (again, my direct report at Phillips 66) and I
had lunch. Geiger had told me to see Hammond first, which I did.
I told Geiger all about my conversation with Hammond and about
the monies I had spent. To date, we had spent almost $200,000, but
had invoiced some of those costs to other existing aviation projects. I
needed to tell Geiger the truth, as all our billing came through him for
approval. His boss (the promotions manager) never saw our billing —
only a monthly tally of what we had billed for each individual project.

I met with the promotions manager the next day. We went
over Casey's events to date. He kept shaking his head and repeating
in a condescending way, "How did you get Phillips 66 involved in this

mess?"

I countered by explaining that this was a project Hammond wanted our agency to execute and that I had briefed Hammond the previous day regarding Casey's activities to date. "Hammond was extremely pleased and encouraged me to continue the excellent efforts."

The manager reminded me that I worked for him and not Hammond. He explained that if he wanted to pull the plug he could do it. He pressed both hands directly down on top of his desk and leaned forward toward me. "If you didn't know previously, I have the ear of top management and everyone is worried that Casey will make Phillips 66 look bad. Answer me this: What would it take to remove the Phillips 66 logo from Casey's plane?" I was unresponsive. He then addressed me with his lower lip quivering and kept repeating, "Get it done, Coleman."

And, being a wise ass I said, "Do what?"

"Get the fuck out of my office," the manager said. "And he better finish this trip soon or your life won't be safe. I may even fire both you and Geiger for having the audacity of getting us involved in this never-ending story."

Geiger stuck his head into his boss's office and emphatically slam-dunked this comment: "I was against this Casey sponsorship from the beginning and I have written proof that you penned the opposite —your approval — right on top left of my 'no go' recommendation," he said. "That means you endorsed the sponsorship. And, if you threaten to fire me because of Casey, my written proof goes right to our lawyers and Hammond." Geiger calmly turned his back and walked away.

At that precise moment the whole Business Promotions floor in Phillips 66's Adams Building seemed to explode. The promotions manager was in a rage. His face was flaming red and his arms were vigorously thrashing over his head as he stormed off the floor.

What a day. Luckily for me, that was my last encounter with him until much later in Casey's saga. I stayed a few days later, played golf with Gary Schoonveld and had lunch with Hammond several times. His only instructions were to not let Casey's adventure fail, as any negativity could seriously affect the company's stock price.

I left on October 5 for New York. Our pilot had already

reached Bombay. I realized that Casey would be some ten and one-half hours ahead of me when I got to New York City.

# Thirty

# I Never Liked Curry

Casey remembers the message he received from the Aviation Ministry just prior to his taking off for Bombay. "You can come tomorrow, but maybe not, because that is a holiday. In fact, our holiday is for one week. Please call back later." "Should I take off?" he wondered. He had gotten approval from Universal to land in Bombay harbor. And, he had been told by me that the minister had been paid off. "I'm leaving and landing in Bombay. If I have to, I will go to the minister's office and ask for a refund," he decided.

Casey now realized why obtaining permission to land in Bombay had been so difficult. He would soon learn that landing in Bombay would certainly be out of the ordinary. At that moment, Casey remembered the similarity to Charles Lindbergh's emotional comment to his well-wishers:

> *"It's the greatest shot of adrenaline to be doing what you have wanted to do so badly. You almost feel like you could fly without a plane."*

That day he was an early riser at 0500 and went to the consulate for breakfast with his Marine buddies. He said goodbye to all hands. There were no political officers from the consulate to bid a farewell to as they never ate with the enlisted men.

Reflecting on his continued hard luck during this adventure, our pilot thought of himself as resembling the lead character in the great book by Ernest Gann, *Fate is the Hunter*.

After breakfast and many hugs, Casey made his way, by a honking taxi, to the docking area at Port Qasim. At the large dock area, there must have been more than 1,000 cheering onlookers. He was told that most had started gathering before 0400 as by now everyone had heard of the famous pilot flying around the world. The local news articles sparked the attention. The smile on Casey's face radiated the pride he felt, being the catalyst of this historic adventure.

Casey wanted to make a speech but he found that most of the older spectators, cheering for him, didn't understand any English. Conversely, most all of the children spoke excellent English. Casey concluded that this attribute to fluently speak English was directly related to their survival mechanism. Why? To make money for their families, most of the children ran errands or performed tasks for the English-speaking tourists.

It was time to go. The harbor master's large craft, with its engine running, swayed about one-half mile from the aircraft's dock. No admiral of the Pakistan fleet this time. Casey did a cursory preflight inspection and then jumped on the left float and opened the left hand door. Now seated firmly in the captain's command chair, he found himself regaining his positive attitude. He was going to India.

He primed the engine and flicked the starter switch. The engine's propeller slowly rotated and then with a loud burst came to life. He was now ready to taxi out and tie onto the harbor master's boat. He would then begin his long trek towards the mouth of Port Qasim.

Once in the breakwater, he pushed the Liberty II's throttle to full power and made a long five-mile run and lifted off. Once airborne he headed directly out toward the Arabian Sea. Now on October 3, he set off on his 552-mile jaunt to Bombay. Casey had departed at 0800 and expected to be in Bombay about 1200.

Casey was totally amazed by the congested shipping traffic below in the Arabian Sea. It all seemed to stretch for miles. There were large oil tankers and cargo container ships, plus smaller craft with single large sails. The sea was alive with humanity. There were no military ships in sight, but that was to be expected as most were in the Persian Gulf and off the Emirates. Casey had been cleared by Karachi ATC to maintain 9,000 feet, where he would enjoy smooth air. Some commercial aviation traffic appeared to his left as they were going into Karachi's airport. Other traffic was well above him and headed to places unknown.

As he later related, "It was time to scrutinize the maps and see where I would be landing. The only clue I had was that I was supposed to land in Bombay harbor, which is immense. I was supposed to be met by the harbor master. That is what the Aviation Ministry verified in its telex."

The land off to the right side of his aircraft was very green, as the Monsoon season had ended earlier the week before. Monsoon season usually lasts from June to September and during Casey's stay it rained almost every day in Karachi. He wondered if Bombay would still be flooded or perhaps most of the flooding had receded.

The next barrier that stood in his way beyond Bombay was getting approval to land in Calcutta. Casey knew that after Calcutta there was the tricky run to Bangkok. A lot of ifs, he thought. But that is how it had been from the start. And, Casey wondered about the U.S.S.R., too, as winter was closely approaching Eastern Siberia. He remembered that I had promised to have a fax (special documents) awaiting for him at the Taj Majal Hotel in Bombay.

As his aircraft approached the outer boundary area of Bombay, Air Traffic Control Bombay wanted to hand off Casey to Bombay's Harbor Control frequency. Someone in ATC was heard saying, "Where are we going to put this massive seaplane?" Casey heard the comment on his radio and answered back by providing the aircraft's details: length, wing span, one-engine, two floats and one pilot.

None of that information made any difference (English-speaking traffic managers were not too prevalent) to what would happen next. A so-to-speak 'official' came up on the harbor master's radio frequency and in broken English denied Casey permission to land in Bombay Harbor. He was given orders to touch down outside the harbor in the Arabian Sea. Casey now wondered what kind of clearance the Indians had agreed to.

The landing at 1215 was rough and his Liberty II aircraft

slammed into four-foot swells. Yanking the yoke (controls) back, Casey applied as much forearm strength as he could just to keep the aircraft's nose upright and steer the aircraft into the wind, but at the same time keep the aircraft straight and level. Now that was flying, he smugly thought to himself.

Momentarily, he was afraid the floats would slam into high swells (and damage his struts like in Iceland), much like what a surfer experiences when paddling out through big waves. He feared that his plane could flip over or he imagined his plane could shutter and break apart, possibly breaching and going under the seas. Casey yelled over the radio that unless he could come into calmer waters, his plane would possibly sink. Maybe it was the Indian Hindu God or some other act of providence, but the harbor master gave Casey approval to enter the harbor. It was now 1330.

The harbor master again threw no lifeline to Casey. In fact, he wanted Casey to drop his anchor in the middle of the shipping lanes. Casey thought, "Does the flaming Indian asshole think I am a PBY?" By staying in the middle of the harbor, not only would Casey's aircraft be threatened by freighters and tankers but by what seemed like hundreds of passenger ferries as well. The ferries were the water taxis for Indians and their appearance mimicked their decorated motor Jitneys used to navigate the roads in Bombay.

What options did Casey have? None. So he decided to sleep in his plane until he could work it out (factually arrange with the harbor master finding a suitable mooring or anchorage for his aircraft; but waiting out the harbor master meant he had to sleep in his plane all night or even beyond until a dock space could be arranged).

That same night there were two-foot swells and heavy winds in the harbor. He would crank up his engine and run the aircraft into the wind for about two miles. Then he would turn off the engine and actually coast or "sail" his aircraft back in the opposite direction. His wings and flaps acted as the sails and the rudders on each float acted as his steering mechanism.

Casey stayed in his aircraft all through October 3, and he remained there almost all day on October 4. He repeatedly called the harbor master and asked for help. He contacted ATC — they could not do anything, either.

At about 1600 that day the harbor master's official boat came alongside Casey's aircraft and boldly informed him that his aircraft was in a dangerous position in the harbor and he would need to follow the boat in order to provide a safe area to tie down the plane.

Tied safely to the aft end of the harbor master's boat, they passed a large landmass on the leeward side. Now, Casey's plane finally was directed into a calm area with many docks. Liberty II had at last found anchorage in Victoria Dock.

"At about 1800, I finally got the aircraft where I could tie up to the dock and was told this was a very secure area," Casey recounted. No more than 15 minutes later, after Casey had fully tied up his aircraft safely to the new mooring, the Minister of Aviation for Bombay regally appeared with an entourage of 20 Indian assistants.

Dressed in a British Officer's Dress White Uniform with an array of ribbons, he came down the stairs to Casey's slip at the Victoria Docks. He was a tall stately individual and he politely asked Casey to call him Colonel Samir.

"We discussed how I was to obtain fuel, where I was staying, and the cost for docking," Casey remembered. Colonel Samir said he had been following Casey's exploits in the newspapers. Further, several Bombay TV stations had evening news reports highlighting Casey's adventure that culminated in his landing outside Bombay Harbor. The colonel reiterated that he had discussed Casey's requirements with Casey's handler in New York and that all arrangements had been made. Casey was to get fuel from the airport and he would be staying at the Taj Mahal Hotel.

The serenity of this pleasant welcoming soon came to an abrupt end. Casey's jaw dropped when the colonel said Casey must immediately take a commercial flight that evening and fly to Calcutta. Why? The Calcutta Aviation Minister had asked the Bombay Aviation Authority to find out where Casey intended on landing in Calcutta. "What the hell did that mean? Was I cleared to land in Calcutta?" Casey asked the colonel. "Not yet," the colonel said.

At that moment a famous quote by astronaut John Glenn came to mind: "As I hurtled through space, one thought kept crossing my mind: Every part of this rocket was supplied by the lowest bidder."

"Now run to Calcutta? Do I need to pay more money? What the hell was happening?" Casey didn't have the faintest idea where his floatplane could safely land in Calcutta. Casey had expected the authorities in Calcutta to provide that information. At that point in time all Casey could tell Colonel Samir was that he hadn't finalized his flight plan.

Based on that answer, the Bombay Minister emphatically told Casey that he needed to identify where he intended on landing and taking off. Confirmation must be made to both the Calcutta Aviation Minister and harbor master. "By when?" asked Casey. Samir responded, "Tonight."

First Casey needed to check into the Taj and then later, at almost midnight, fly to Calcutta. The colonel said he had a limo (of sorts) waiting to take Casey to the Taj Mahal hotel and later to the airport. Distance-wise, the hotel was only three miles away; time-wise that meant maybe an hour's drive.

The colonel asked Casey if he had ever heard of Kipling. Casey said he thought he had. "Well," the colonel went on to explain, "Rudyard Kipling, the poet, was born in Bombay, India, where his father was an arts and crafts teacher. His mother was a sister-in-law of the painter Edward Burne-Jones. India was at that time ruled by the British."

"Very impressive," said Casey. In all honesty, Casey wondered why Samir even brought up Kipling's name. "I shall always remember that fact and when I get back to Seattle I will tell all my friends." Casey thought he was impressing the colonel. In fact, the colonel thought Casey was making fun of him. In short order, word of this incident would find its way back to our New York office. (Samir called the consulate and relayed this story about the horse's ass he had met. And, several days later, the Marine Attaché at the Bombay Consulate told the same story to Dick Eason at State. Eason then called me.)

Meanwhile in Bombay, thrust into the middle of horrendous traffic, Casey marveled at how the street was designed to handle four cars across, but tonight there were eight cars across and no one was moving. Most small cars were either stopped or were taking the outer access road that led to the traffic circle. Where they were headed was anyone's guess. Honking was a key weapon as no one listened to the yelling coming from each of the cars.

Bombay sidewalks were also crowded and everyone was either walking, talking, or buying from local street vendors. The smells were over-powering. A stench was coming from somewhere. Casey asked his driver, who replied that some pungent odors came from decaying animals while other smells were from the garbage strewn over the landscape that had accumulated during the monsoon season.

It seemed that when the heavy rains caused the harbor to overflow, garbage floated to the top of the water. "Now that the waters had receded, the beaches, streets, and even the tops of houses are covered with decaying garbage," the driver explained. Finally the majestic Taj Mahal Palace Hotel loomed into view. Casey left the limo and was escorted inside.

The history of Bombay and the Taj Mahal Palace are dramatically intertwined. The hotel was Bombay's first harbor landmark. For more than a century, the Taj hosted dignitaries and eminent personalities from across the globe.

Much to his surprise, Casey was escorted to a beautiful junior executive suite that was larger than his home in Seattle. Fresh flowers adorned his room and on the serving bar were two bottles of Johnny Walker Red Label for his personal consumption. Not one to stand on ceremony, Casey immediately broke the cap on one and downed about one-third of the bottle.

It was close to 2200 hours and Casey needed to be at the Bombay Airport for a 2400 plane to Calcutta. The limo driver who had taken him to the Taj had waited in the lobby for him. The colonel had made arrangements for Casey to be driven to the airport.

Again tons of cars, but now all of them seemed to be going in the right direction. The airport was 15 miles away and they made the trip in less than 45 minutes. Casey tipped the driver $20 (U.S.) to which the driver bowed to Casey as if he were a Regal Potentate. "Hell, it's only Coleman's money," he thought.

Casey had time for dinner plus a bottle of wine, and then boarded the plane for a two-hour flight to Calcutta. The plane left Bombay at 0100 and plane landed around 0330. "Now what to do?" he thought.

Early on the morning of October 5, Casey made his way to

the Hooghly River (the suggested landing site by Colonel Samir) and looked around to see how much room his aircraft would have to land and take off. Lights from surrounding buildings made it easy for Casey to make a judgment call. The river was as wide as the Hudson River or the Mississippi — at least a mile across in many areas.

Hooghly is the most westerly of the Ganges channels and is a well-used route for transporting goods. The Hooghly (or Hugli) River stretches more than 120 miles from Calcutta to the Bay of Bengal. Navigation remains often treacherous because of the constantly shifting sandbars. Casey needed to be highly observant to avoid the hazards when landing and taking off. He would need to rely on the harbor master to provide him with clear directions.

Following his early morning expedition, he found a hotel and enjoyed a British style breakfast buffet. While at the hotel, he asked for directions to the harbor master's quarters. At about 0800, he grabbed a cab and went to the Calcutta Port Trust office to speak with the harbor master and hopefully the aviation minister.

The River Port of Calcutta is the oldest operating port in India, having originally been constructed by the British East India Company. The Port Trust headquarters, located on a tributary of the Hooghly River, was a sizeable building and had the appearance of a typical three-story London office building, painted white with black shutters.

Casey climbed the stairs to the third floor where the Port Trust was located. Once inside their offices, Casey was introduced to Dr. Ray Pir, the harbor master. Pir wore a military olive drab uniform, but contrary to his outward appearance he had a gentle demeanor.

"We need to get in touch with Colonel La La Arud, the Aviation Minister," Pir said. After a brief call, Pir set down the phone and asked Casey the proverbial British response to any occasion: "Would you like a nice cup of tea?" He also briefly explained that Aviation Minister Colonel Arud would be at the Trust in about two hours.

"Thank you; I will have a cup of tea," Casey said. But in the deep recesses of his brain, he shouted loudly to himself, "Another fuckin' colonel!"

While waiting for the latest colonel, the two men reviewed the river's topographical maps. They discussed suitable locations for Casey to take off and land his aircraft. Dr. Pir recommended that all activity by Casey should occur between the two major bridges — the Howrah and New Bridges — extending over the Hooghly River. This area was normally free of barges and other river traffic. Also, the river's waters were the calmest there. Casey should have at least ten to 15 safe miles, free of sandbars, to land and take off. After two hours of talking, poring over maps, and drinking lots of tea, Pir signed off and approved Casey's flight for both his arrival and departure.

Yet, upon the aviation minister's majestic entrance through the office doors of the Port Trust, with a six-man entourage, the discussion quickly became moot as the colonel immediately said 'no' to Casey landing in Calcutta. The colonel explained that his ministry could not handle a plane of this enormous size. Again, the Indian's mentality harked back to a familiar 100-year old British response to any questionable dilemma: "If we have not heard of you, then we have not heard of you."

Casey almost dropped to his knees in disbelief. What was happening? He went on to explain that his plane only had a 39-foot wingspan and the length was 12.5 feet. Casey then went on the offensive and attempted to play to the minister's ego: "You will be featured in stories all over the world in both newspapers and magazines. You will be featured on TV news."

Casey later told me that he just kept getting the runaround from the colonel in the mind-blowing one-hour meeting. "Arud seemed to waver when I mentioned worldwide recognition, but to no avail — the answer was still a flat no," Casey explained.

"On leaving the Trust, the colonel left the approval option slightly ajar. He asked me to wait in the Port Trust office for an hour or so, as he wanted to make another important phone call related to my clearance into Calcutta. I had no idea what that meant.

"Here is the real kicker: After about two hours of waiting, the phone rang and it was for the harbor master. Pir was told to politely tell me to call Arud tomorrow morning once I got back to Bombay."

Almost in a state of hysteria, Casey's voice stammered as he said to Pir, "I am totally in the dark. Do I have a chance for clearance or not? What is happening?" Pir just shrugged his shoulders and repeated Arud's request.

He was back at the Calcutta airport by 1700, but now he faced even more confusion. His frustration was compounded by all kinds of problems getting a return flight to Bombay. Finally, he was ticketed to leave at 2030 but that flight was postponed and later cancelled. He was then transferred to a 2400 flight that didn't arrive in Bombay until 0300 on October 6.

By this time Casey was mentally spent. So at 1900 he just left the airport and stayed at the nearby transient hotel. He would leave in the morning. Before retiring, he spent about three hours trying to get all his flight plans approved. He was unable to do that as the Calcutta portion was still in limbo. (Casey was unaware that $12,000 had been paid to clear him to Calcutta.)

The thought occurred to him that he might have to fly the length of India to the city of Colombo in Sri Lanka. From there he would need to fly 1070 miles to Banda Aceh, Indonesia. He could resume his regular planned path from there. But a new flight plan would be a great inconvenience as he would have to deal with harbor masters at each new destination. Plus, he would need to have our New York office contact all the embassies in these countries.

Casey arose early October 6 and booked a flight on Air India. It left at 0930 and arrived at 1230. He arrived back in Bombay very disheartened. He was really tired and just wanted to take the day off. Back at the Taj, he sat before his TV. About 1500, he saw a thin paper envelope off to one side adjacent to his room door. He must have pushed it there when entering the room. Casey energetically opened the envelope and inside found a long telex from New York. It was more like a memo, but the contents made his day:

**Memo to Captain Tom Casey**
**October 5, 1990**
Dear Tom and salutations from all of us here in the
States cheering you on.

By now, you are back in Bombay and a bit depressed
I am sure. Let's start off with the good news. You are
approved to immediately take off for Calcutta. Both
the Aviation Ministry and Harbor Master have ap-

proved your flight plan.

Gaining Colonel Arud's approval was rather difficult but how that was achieved is a matter to be discussed at a later date. Arud is a rather persuasive person who genuinely had many concerns about how to accommodate your large craft on the Hooghly River. We assured him you were the greatest pilot in the world and as such you could land any size aircraft onto the Hooghly. We know you have all the particulars for landing in Calcutta.

You can file your IFR Flight Plan from your room. The Indian Flight Service Center is awaiting your official paperwork. All technicalities for this leg to Calcutta have been arranged for; i.e., docking, fuel, and hotel, by all parties (Indian Foreign Ministry and U.S. State Department).

The following is a list of key contacts (phone numbers) for the remainder of your trip. You should keep these for reference. In addition, attached is a proposed Flight Plan and a proposed Clearance document to be filed with Japanese authorities. We still need to gain official clearance with Japan as we need to meet all the parameters of the U.S. Status of Forces Agreement (SOFA), of which I am very knowledgeable as I lived there for many years.

Here are the next stops on your journey:
1. Burma. Universal has arranged clearance. You will need to contact the U.S. Consulate in Calcutta and explain you will be overflying Burma. As you recall, the State Department did not want us to fly over Burma. But we are now having you designated as Saudi Special Flight #2 which will circumvent this restriction.

2. Bangkok. Attached is all the flight clearance information plus landing information for this leg of your journey. Just file your flight plan with the Service Center.

Go direct from Burma to Bangkok ATC. Your Embassy contact is Tom Cadogan, Diplomatic and Consular Affairs Officer (DCA).

Pattaya Beach is your destination (110 miles South of Bangkok). I will contact the U.S. Embassy when the date is set for your takeoff from Calcutta. Please call or telex me the time and date. Once I know your ETD from Calcutta, we can set plans in motion for HRH Pah's visit with you—hopefully on October 15. As the Princess has a significant entourage, we will need precise planning for this event.

3. Penang. Clearance has been obtained by the Civil Aviation Department at the U.S. Embassy for you to land in Georgetown, capital of Penang, on or about Oct. 15 or 16. Person to give you clearance was Karim Ali, DCA Kula Lumpur. 603-757-6666 or 1141.

All flight requirements were coordinated with Donald Cooke, Aviation Officer. Cooke has been working with Captain Jones (DSAO/Navy) in Georgetown to secure a place to land. At Georgetown, we have hired Mr. Soon, c/o Syraikat Soon Trading, to arrange port clearances, refueling, and tie-down (604-626-028I). I have spoken with him and he is able to supply avgas in barrels. I worked with Soon when I was in Southeast Asia. He is a personal friend and has gotten me through many scrapes. Please know he will do everything he can for you, but don't take advantage.

NOTE: Here is the dilemma in your Flight Plan. I

know that the distance from Georgetown to Brunei is about 910 miles. I don't know if you can make it that far (mainly worried about takeoffs in very hot weather). Do you want to land in Kuching? If so, you need to tell Capt. Jones this on arrival or in your flight plans. Also, I have told Soon that you may want to stay overnight.

You need to file a flight plan out of Bangkok (by phone at Pataya) to Penang and state route and time. Also, in-bound to Georgetown radio Port Authority and Penang Airport. Please verify your ETA and flight path to land.

4. Brunei. Clearance has been obtained through Dorothy Aron, Commercial Department, U.S. Embassy, Dorothy also has indicated that Hassanal Bolkiah, the Sultan of Brunei, will meet with you personally upon landing. The Embassy has blocked out a landing area for you at the Royal Brunei Yacht Club. Again ATC will provide instructions.

5. Subic Bay. The U.S. Philippine Embassy has been contacted and it appears there is no problem with clearance. Navy has been contacted (as I am back on good terms with Admiral Dunleavy). The Naval establishment is ComNavForces, Philippines. The PAO is Lt. Commander K. Murki and Chief J. Jones. I spoke with Jones and he alerted the Philippine Aviation Department. The U.S. Embassy has all the flight plan clearance info and all PR materials.

They will also have a case of oil and oil analysis kit. The Admiral at the base is Tom Mercer and he is a personal friend of Adm. Jon Coleman. Phone number is 63-4738-43451.

6. Taipei. Shows as stopover on your flight plan. Spoke with U.S. Embassy and they said there is a lagoon near the Taipei airport (end of runway). Source of avgas near airport. Have not officially requested clearance from them but will once we determine your exact routing.

7. Japan. One stop shopping. The Navy has been great in offering support. We plan for you to go to Taipei and then onto Sasebo Naval Station. From there to Yokosuka and finally onto Misawa. The Seventh Fleet Admiral at Yokosuka is Jesse Hernandez. Right now they are at a high level of alert due to the Iraq situation.

So is the Air Force in Yokota. The Yokosuka PA folks have all the info materials. Contact Lt. Jeff Gradeck, 81-468261-911.

8. Russia. Neither Knight nor I have heard from the Russians. We have pushed both the FAA and State and they have not gotten a response. Eason at State plans another correspondence. I will be calling Ambassador Jack F. Matlock, Jr., in the next several weeks. It is very hard to get through on the phone.

9. The Pan Am Affair. On another matter, Dan Hood, your friendly Pan Am liar, called Cindy. She called me and relayed this information. Hood says he hasn't heard from you. He is planning to go to the Pan Am offices in NYC and tell the executives about all the wonderful things he has done for Pan Am and you. He also wants you to send a personal letter to the Pan Am brass at the NYC headquarters saying what a wonderful job Mr. Hood has done for you.

I tried to control my anger. I curtly told Cindy that

Hood can call me. I then screamed at her at the top of my voice: "Where the hell has Hood been for the last three months?"

Cindy had no reply. I guess he's not been banging her anymore. Cindy was also informed that Phillips 66 has spent considerable funds on fuel, lodging, and gaining clearances.

Cindy countered my angry comment by telling me that poor Hood had a $200 phone bill trying to track you (Casey) down. I rebutted by saying we incurred the same cost the first day Casey left my office in New York City.

Here is the best part. This bit of garbage will go down in history. After Cindy hung up with me, she must have called Hood. This prompted Hood to call Knight. Hood complains to Knight that Coleman has taken over the whole show away from him and Pan Am by getting Casey clearances.

Knight exploded and told Hood (in polite terms) to stick it up his ass. Hood retorted by saying he wanted the praise because he had originally put up a very large sum of money and time to get Casey on this journey. Hood wanted to know if Phillips 66 would reimburse him for his time and money. Knight called Hood a fuckin' gold digger and said if Hood persisted in his claims then we would take legal action and sue him. Knight then hung up on the stupid idiot.

Hood also called Universal and spoke with my contact Lex Denherder (Red Team) and said Pan Am could have gotten Indian clearances and wouldn't have had to bother Universal. He really pissed off Universal.

Hood also claims to Universal that he could get Russian Clearance and would complete this task by October 4. He was to call Knight with the info. Universal called Knight, and Lex and David had a big laugh. Why? Hood never called on October 4.

Knight and I thought that a brief bit of levity for your flight to Calcutta would cheer you up to no end. A little British humor for the ride home.

Lastly, another bit of info. I will be leaving for Hawaii October 12 and stay until October 22. While I am there, I want to determine if there is a need for me to go to Japan in order to help you gain clearances through Japan and possibly Russia. I will make that determination once you reach the Philippines. Call me collect at the Waikola Beach on the Big Island @ 808-886-6789.
**Good luck.**
**Bill**

* * *

It was not until he read the lengthy memo and also later talked with King that his demeanor totally changed. He had been approved to go to Calcutta. Tomorrow the world would again see that Casey was on his way around the world.

Casey attempted to take off on October 7 at 0930 but couldn't get airborne. "I was only drawing 27 inches of manifold pressure and that was not enough power," he later recalled. (For the uneducated, manifold pressure is a measure of power. If the throttle is opened, allowing more air into the cylinders, manifold pressure rises.) "In my case, it wasn't a problem with throttle, but rather the hot ambient temperature of 103F that thwarted my gaining power. Also, I felt my floats were not totally cleaned from the barnacles. Had to get those inspected again," he explained.

"Now October 8 and I tried to get airborne by 0730. Three times I ran my craft for more than eight miles each time and had no success of getting up on the step as I was still drawing only 27 inches of manifold pressure. Further, the humidity was so strong that you could cut it with a knife. This major setback by nature had a direct impact on my getting off the water as it lessened the power of the engine.

"My bad luck that morning continued as Bombay's Center radar cancelled my IFR clearance to Calcutta since I missed my window to take off.

"Tried again the next day. Had my takeoff clearance again, but now I was faced with 30 knot headwinds and three-foot large swells in the Bombay harbor. I also was concerned about the amount of fuel I thought I could actually have on board that would allow me to safely take off. As such, I took on less fuel to lessen the load for takeoff. Also, I would be arriving at dark in Calcutta and quickly determined that would not be a good idea. So, I had to cancel current plans and I hoped like hell that tomorrow would be in my favor and also that the Taj held my room.

"Finally on October 10, I made it off Bombay's waters by 0715. To make sure I could beat the heat and increase my chances of success, I was at the dock by 0500. But, by the time I got my weather briefings complete and took care of other incidentals, I finally was able to maneuver up the channel to where I could safely begin my run-up and take off. During my lengthy takeoff run I now drew about 29 inches of pressure as the temperature had dropped and I also leaned my mixture," he said.

The distance to Calcutta was about 1,040 miles and should have taken him about eight hours cruising at 120 knots per hour. Actually it took a bit more than eight and one-half hours. He later explained, "My journey was beautiful. There were large cumulonimbus clouds (squall line of heavy thunderstorms) off my right wing on the whole leg to Calcutta. The whole trip was in IFR mode, but below me at 9,000 feet was Highway 40, jammed with trucks, which was the main route from Bombay to Calcutta. I passed over the Kanhan River. I could not get over the green landscapes below and in the distance.

"The engine seemed to hum perfectly. I had changed my oil in

Bombay and told the front desk at the Taj to send the package with the oil sample to Hammond. I hope they did. (The only oil samples to date had come from the U.S. Navy in Iceland and then from Jeddah through Saudi Arabian Airlines).

"I had difficulty coming down into Calcutta. Calcutta tower vectored me towards the river, but actually I was in a massive cloud buildup and by the time I realized my actual position, I was actually right over the dock site where I was supposed to tie up."

Casey's landing occurred between the Howrah and New Bridges extending over the Hooghly River. The clouds parted like the Red Sea and Casey, not knowing exactly where he was, burst through the clouds exactly over his docking area. He chopped power and came straight down. This maneuver allowed him to land within 20 feet of his assigned Khidirpur dock. "Believe me, I landed so close that people were running and jumping off the dock," he said.

Casey remembered that the harbor master Pir told him people sometimes hung their clothes across the river where the widest part was only 50 feet across. And there were fishermen he had to worry about, too.

Casey laughed to himself as he remembered Pir explaining to him that he and the colonel previously imagined Casey would actually be flying a 747 with floats. Maybe the people who had never seen a seaplane before thought the same thing. Or, perhaps no seaplane had ever landed there before. He turned off the Calcutta tower frequency and turned his radio frequency so as to speak directly to the harbor master's boat. Again, he had to tie onto the boat and be towed into the dock.

"Once tied up at the dock," Casey later related, "I got out and saw five uniformed officers approaching me. I had a warm all over feeling since I presumed they were there to welcome me to Calcutta. I was totally wrong. These dudes were there to arrest me. They explained (each with his hand on a holstered revolver) in broken English that they were Customs and Immigration Officers who wanted me to accompany them somewhere, though they never said where. This was almost as if I now had a military escort to the Calcutta airport."

In a tiny all-metal room, no larger than 10x10 feet, Casey was told to take a seat and shut up. Then in the next five hours he was continually questioned about why he was in India; what were his intentions here; who did he know; whom did he work for; and what was his name — over and over again. He was being driven nuts.

"Their complaint was simple," said Casey. "I had no approval to be in India. At that juncture, I explained my dealings with the aviation ministers and harbor masters in Bombay and Calcutta. I begged them to call them and verify my story.

"I had been led to believe that I had official clearance to be in India; almost as a last resort, they finally read all my documentation.

"The senior Customs agent (he had more gold braid hanging from his shoulder than the others) said he could not get hold of either aviation minister or harbor master, so I should get a good night's rest and they would visit with me tomorrow. They asked what hotel I was staying at and I said I didn't know as I just got there. They recommended the Taj Bengal as I had stayed in the Taj in Bombay. They called and got me a room and drove me to the hotel. By the time I got to bed it was almost midnight."

Taj Bengal was a city landmark in downtown Calcutta and the nearest hotel to the government offices and consulates. That worked for Casey, as he had to personally drop off his flight plans to the U.S. Marine Attaché. The Taj had spacious rooms that featured inspiring Indian décor interspersed with impressive traditional accents such as Bengal tigers and elephants. The lavish stone and marble atrium soared skyward for five stories. The building stood apart from others in the surrounding area with its elegant façade and modern architecture.

The following day, October 11, he was delayed again getting to Bangkok. Supposedly, he hadn't yet cleared Customs and Immigration. Finally at 1900, he was given a two-day window to leave Calcutta airspace and could depart the next day.

Reality struck when he realized that leaving on the 12th was untenable. Why? He had no fuel. How to get fuel? Casey called the Aviation Minister La La Arud's office and was told to go to the airport and inquire about obtaining fuel.

He later explained, "Naturally, I went over to the airport and after asking at least 50 military-dressed security guards, who didn't have the faintest idea what I meant by buying fuel, I finally

met this lovely or should I say beautiful Indian lady whose English
was straight out of the movie "Gandhi". She explained to me that I
needed to take a golf cart over to the airline's fueling station. She arranged for the cart and called ahead for me. I politely bowed, as is the
custom, and she in turn shook my hand. God, I could have married
her on the spot.

"The cart deposited me at a large British corrugated aluminum Quonset hut. I asked for the manager, who said all he could sell
me was auto fuel. Owing to the uncertainty of octane ratings of the
fuel in some foreign locations or not being able to obtain avgas, the
left wing main tip tank (38 gallons) was reserved to carry a supply of
100-octane low lead avgas.

"The conditions under which this agreement was executed will
always remain truly comical. First of all, the airport did not have any
avgas so I had to buy auto fuel, which I found hard to believe. Second,
I had rented a pickup lorry and got an official escort from the airport
security force to drive me to the airport's boundary fence. Third, the
airport's fueling operation sent one of its fuel trucks (loaded with auto
fuel) to the airport's boundary fence where I was located. As I was not
allowed on airport grounds to get this fuel, the fuel truck driver had to
slide a fuel hose through the chain-link boundary fence so that I could
take the hose and fill each of 12 plastic containers.

"I had my lorry with the fuel containers driven back to my
docking area. As my load of fuel was considered, under Indian law, a
liquid bomb, we were escorted by seven police vehicles with flashing
lights and sirens wailing the whole way. Waiting patiently at the dock
were three lads who could carry the fuel to my plane and then help me
upload it.

"My chores done and flight clearance given, I planned to wait
until the early morning of October 13 to head on to Bangkok. But
when I returned to my room that evening, I had a message to call the
U.S. Embassy in Calcutta. I returned the call and was immediately
transferred over to the Marine Attaché. He told me I was not to fly
into Burma. That meant when I left Calcutta and entered the Bay
of Bengal I was not to traverse Burma to eventually land in Pattaya
Beach, Thailand.

"I told him that my aircraft did not have the distance capability in hot weather to make Bangkok other than by crossing over Burma. He said that if I did fly over Burma it would cause an international incident since I was an American citizen. He explained that the State Department had placed a restriction on Americans entering or leaving Burma. This regulation was much the same as the restriction of not being able to enter Cuba as an American."

Casey explained that John King and I had told him to tell the U.S. Embassy that his aircraft was cleared through Burma as Saudi Special Flight #2. Therefore, it would not be entering Burma as a U.S.-registered aircraft. That was met with complete silence on the other end of the phone. The Attaché put him on hold for a few minutes to verify the story and then came on the line and told Casey to have a good flight. After hanging up, it became very apparent that he had clearance from Calcutta control as well as Universal all the way to Bangkok.

Later that morning, Casey met a gal who was flying around the world in a Beech Baron but had gotten hung up in Calcutta by the U.S. order not to allow any U.S. aircraft flight clearance out of India. "I directed her to use my handle, Saudi Special Flight #2," he later related. "Hell, I think she made her flight #3 and was able to leave India."

### Thirty-one

# Burma to Captain Tom Casey: 'Good Luck'

"The temperature was a beast," Casey later told me about his Calcutta departure. "I had 20 miles in which to take off. Must watch for the clotheslines and avoid scaring the fishermen. I've reduced the rich mixture and leaned it some so as to promote more power to the engine. I've taken on auto fuel, but still have an emergency supply of avgas in one of the tip tanks. I should have no trouble making the 1,000-mile leg to Bangkok.

"The weather briefing said temperatures would range from 100F to 105F depending on which leg I stand on — that's a joke, boy. Also, typhoon season was now on all the weather charts and the isobars distinctly showed activity along the Malaysian coast."

Because of the heat, he kept monitoring his cylinder head temperatures (CHT). Engine temperature can have a dramatic impact on engine performance. The CHT gauge is an electrical device that feeds back to the pilot the engine temperature in all types of weather. He had been fortunate that the engine temperatures had remained constantly in the green to this point.

This morning would prove eventful for Casey (go figure). He ran the aircraft ten miles and couldn't get off the water. He taxied back to the dock and checked all engine instruments. Everything looked perfect to the eye. Out he went again and this time he went 15 miles with no luck. Again, back to the dock.

It became evident that he needed to lighten his load. So in haste he unloaded the oxygen bottles and mobile tanks, lightening the load by 200 pounds. Next, he stripped out his high frequency radio, and gave that to Pir with the understanding he would store it temporarily and later that month ship it to John King on a Saudi Arabian Airlines flight. The radio never showed up and it probably was sold on the black market for big bucks. The radio belonged to the U.S. Air Force and Casey would later say he gave it to the harbor master as a gift for his help.

Our pilot now took only seven miles to get aloft of the Hooghly River. It was close to 1030 on October 13 when he finally got off, but he was only able to maintain a cruise speed of 125 miles per hour at 9,000 feet. That meant an eight-hour leg ahead of him; it would be almost dark in Bangkok when he arrived. It took about an hour to reach the coast and now he was free as a bird in the Bay of Bengal. Next stop Burma, and then Thailand.

There were many military ships in the bay, probably based in the Andaman Islands. Casey now had time to reflect on his past several days. Why, he thought, was his luck running so poorly? All he wanted to do was finish this trip, but it seemed that everyone in his path was out to thwart the journey. On the bright side, he had heard his dad was doing better and that his sister was keeping a close watch on him.

Casey was playing mental football when suddenly land appeared just off the horizon on the Bengal Sea. At that moment he was focused on what would be his future flight path after Pattaya Beach, Thailand, recognizing that he was somewhat flying blind after departing Thailand. My memo to him had said Kuala Lumpur, then Brunei, and finally the Philippines. But he had no flight clearance for the Philippines yet.

Upon arrival in Pataya, he would need to call both King and myself. He started to think about the changing time zones – when he reached Thailand, it would be 12 hours later than in New York. That meant calling at 2400 to reach me at 1200 (noon) in New York the same day. A call to John King would only be a five-hour difference.

He remembered what many international flight experts in India had counseled him: "At all costs avoid flying over Burma." Then, over the radio came a pleasant-sounding voice, with a British accent. "This is Rangoon Control and we welcome you to Burma. We understand you are trying to set a world record. Over. Why don't you come down and visit us as we have never seen a seaplane. Over."

Casey sat up in his chair, almost at attention. "Yes," he replied. "How do you know about me?"

The Burmese gentleman replied, "We do have newspapers in Rangoon and even TV (said sarcastically). We have been following your adventures since Saudi Arabia and wondered if you would get caught up in the Iraqi conflict," he said.

"I asked the controller what life was like in Burma," Casey would alter relate. "I said, 'I had been told that there were many hardships in Burma.'"

He responded that everything was pretty good in Burma. "We are a very proud people and fought hard in the Second World War. We recently had a military junta takeover, but they have been very fair to the people. The previous people in power robbed and imprisoned many of us. You probably have a lot of that in your country."

Casey fell silent and tried to change the subject. "We love our democracy and that is why I am allowed to do this around the world flight," he stated. The controller said that he would love to see America and maybe they could meet someday. Casey replied, "I hope so."

They talked for another five minutes as Casey passed through Burma and over the border into Thailand. They finished by talking about sports and women. The Burmese controller added, "We welcome you over Burma, Captain Casey, and my country wishes you good luck on your long journey."

The radio crackled and Thailand's Service Center came up on Casey's radio and asked him to switch to their frequency. He said goodbye to Burma. Casey now had another 360 miles to Bangkok and then another 61 miles to Pattaya Beach. Uncertainty remained regarding a possible landing site. Meanwhile, the sun began to set, alerting Casey to the fact that he would have to make a night landing. But where?

Bangkok Control instructed him to land at Bang Phra Reservoir, though he had expected to be going to Pattaya Beach. "I was nearing Pattaya Beach and heard this voice on the radio tell me that I was over Bang Phra Reservoir and to land," he would later tell me.

"I could see the hills overlooking the reservoir, so I decided to circle the large body of water before I landed. My aim was to examine it thoroughly for obstructions such as buoys or floating debris and to note the direction of movement of any boats. I did see one boat and thought it was the one giving me directions. "Hey, come on down," they said.

"My landing at night was really quite scary. No reference lights; no anything. I turned on my landing lights and there was just some dude on a boat in the middle of the water. I couldn't detect any radio."

One immediate concern facing a night landing is when to apply flaps, and that depends upon wind speed, wind direction, airspeed, and how much water is needed to safely land. All these conditions are quite different at night, especially when you don't know your environment. This is especially true when there is no tower control or ATC to offer details. Setting the flaps too early could result in too high of an approach. Setting them too late might keep airspeed overly extreme. "I just can't use all the notches on the flaps at one time," Casey explained. "What is mystifying is that in some cases, I might land with partial or even no flaps at all.

"I landed at the slowest possible airspeed and the power-on landing was made with maximum flaps extended. Liberty II was trimmed to the manufacturer's recommended approach speed. The approach was made similar to that of a land plane, so I lined up toward the boat in the middle of the reservoir and landed.

"During my final approach, my airspeed stayed at approximately ten knots above stall speed. I landed within 20 feet of the boat — to this day I am sure everyone on the boat jumped overboard."

"Once together, we taxied to about 50 feet of shore; as we approached, I noticed flashlights and lanterns. I turned on my landing lights and to my amazement there were more than 300 children standing on shore. They all had signs welcoming Captain Casey to Thailand. In the front row of all these children was her Royal Highness, Princess Pah and her large entourage. You couldn't miss them. They were decked out in ceremonial garb similar to what the Siam monarchs wore in the movie "The King and I". What a greeting I received.

"Once I pulled my plane onto the shore, I was greeted by this young man about 12 years old. He explained he was the son of Thailand's Civil Aviation Minister. It was this same minister who visited me in the hospital in Saudi Arabia and said he would make sure my flight clearance to Thailand was approved, and would also be there to welcome me to Thailand.

"After my plane was secured, I was met by several representatives of PTT (Petroleum Authority of Thailand), who said they were special envoys of Thailand's U.S. Ambassador, Daniel Anthony O'Donohue, and the Thai government.

"PTT executives explained that a group of Thai boys would act as security guards. So, after ending a very informative conversation with the aviation minister's son (he spoke nine languages), PTT escorted me to my hotel on Pattaya Beach. They also had planned a number of special festivities, but first wanted me to see the beautiful resort I would be staying at. We drove along a beautiful ocean road full of palm trees and massive flowering scrubs. The lights surrounding the Gulf of Siam illuminated the beach areas and surrounding hills. Every sight and smell seemed to capture these beautiful surroundings. I would be staying at the Royal Cliff Beach Resort.

"Before I could check in at the resort, PTT drove around the vast acreage; it seemed the hotel had well over 2,000 rooms. The resort is located at the southern tip of Pattaya and overlooked the Royal Cliff Bay and the turquoise waters of the Gulf of Siam. The 64-acre lush tropical resort had its own distinct style and ambience, from vibrant flowers everywhere to tranquil charm that my hosts said embodied the Malaysian warmth. My room was luxurious with a wide panoramic view.

Once the bellman deposited me at my room, I no longer had a dead reckoning course back to the lobby. In fact, I lost all reference to where in the hotel I was located. Picking up the nearest hotel phone, I called the concierge desk and had someone meet me — wherever I was — to escort me back to the lobby area.

"Now the best part of the story: The escort was this gorgeous Thai lady, whose charm I immediately fell in love with. She spoke perfect British English and asked if I was that famous pilot from America who was flying around the world. In turn I reached out and hugged her. She never moved and we hugged for the longest time. Her name was Sha Sha Leu and she had been educated in Bangkok. I told her when I returned here after my journey that maybe we could date. She accepted my invitation. I was now in love. Reality set in as I was now in the lobby and waving to my hosts."

The PTT executives held a special banquet in Casey's honor that night, with more than 20 guests attending. Several embassy staff attended as well as four or five representatives of Thailand's Aviation Ministry. The meal featured platters of food passed around amongst the guests, including shrimp cooked in perhaps 20 different ways. In all, a sumptuous feast.

"Later that night I strolled the beach and gazed up at the beautiful constellations acting as an umbrella to the Gulf of Siam," Casey later recalled. "The hotel overlooked the beach and was situated on a wide semicircle adjacent to the gulf. The waves lapped at my bare feet and since it was high tide there was little room left to walk on the sand."

A grand media day was held the following day on October 14 at the hotel. Sonkram Somboon from the U.S. Embassy was making all the arrangements – he and I had talked several times over the past two months and he had been following Casey's progress through the newspapers and communications from my office. Sonkram was very knowledgeable of the media's wants and told me that all Casey had to do was tell the truth. I assured him that Casey was a good interview.

Sonkram telexed me the same day and said that he had never seen so many reporters show up for an event. The press conference included TV, newspapers, and wire services. From later accounts that day from the embassy, Casey started his remarks by saying, "Let me provide you a rather lengthy summary of the trip so far. I also want to include some details of a few tough encounters that I had faced along the way."

The embassy related that he stated how he wanted to especially thank all the ministers of aviation in each of the countries he had visited. "These officials alone," he said, "were the primary reason for me getting to where I am at present."

He further explained that he didn't have much good to say about the U.S. State Department nor his sponsor, Phillips 66. "They have let me down and forced me to stay in countries for lengthy periods." He pounded his fist on the table where he was seated.

He told the reporters that he was heading next to George Town, Penang and then on to Brunei. The leg to Brunei would be about the same in length as flying from Pattaya Beach to Penang — some 800 miles. His biggest concern was possibly having to fly near or around Tropical Storm Lola, which was now building in strength in the middle of the South China Sea.

When asked about his impressions of Thailand, he excitedly expounded on its beauty and the wonderful nature of all the people.

(As an aside, Casey later confided to me that looking back on his press conference remarks, which the wire services wanted to carry worldwide until I intervened, he should have been more gracious about the efforts afforded him by both State and Phillips 66. He said he had tried calling my New York office early in the morning of the press conference, but the lines back to the U.S. were not working. He also couldn't get hold of King. Now he said he understands why both of us continued to ask, "Where the hell is Casey?")

Following the press event, Casey spent the rest of the day dining on the local cuisine and getting measured for and buying two suits. He wanted something special to wear at his homecoming in Seattle.

"It was a Malaysian tradition to have toast slathered with kaya (coconut-egg jam) for breakfast, washed down with thick, black coffee," he recounted. "Wow, that was quite a tradition and from that experience, I have to say, I just like eggs and bacon for breakfast.

"Both my lunch and dinner that day were superior; as well was the company kept with my hosts, the PTT oil company. They had arranged for me to refuel my aircraft at the local airport, which was only about 700 yards from the Bang Phra Reservoir."

At dinner, one of the embassy officers handed him a telex. It was from New York:

**TO: Captain Tom Casey**
**From: Bill Coleman - flight handler**
**c/o Bangkok U.S. Embassy**

*Tom: RE: Update on flight path*

*Singapore clearance denied. They are unaccustomed to
handling seaplanes. Even with lots of our explaining,
they were resolute in denying you clearance. Now, here is
the dilemma. I know that George Town to Brunei is about
910 miles. I don't know if you can make it that distance
in such high temperatures you are encountering. Do you
want to land in Kuching in Borneo (about halfway to
Brunei)? If so, you need to tell Capt. Jones once you arrive in Penang. Also, I have told Soon you may want to
stay overnight.*

*I have to imagine that can be cleared up once he hears
from you. In any event, you need to file flight plans out
of Pattaya Beach (Bangkok) to George Town and state
route and time. I have covered fuel requirements with
Soon. Also, inbound George Town, radio Port Authority
and Penang Airport your ETA and flight path to land.*

*Soon called this morning and said the weather is deterio-
rating and Kuching may now not be a stopover option.
He said it is better to fly directly to Brunei. Tropical
Storm Lola from Japan is moving across the South China
Sea. Soon said you may be vectored around below Singapore and head to Brunei from a southerly direction. That
may increase the distance to Brunei by several hundred
miles.*

*Also, two other messages of concern:
1. Judy from Wipaire called on October 13 for an update
on your progress. Said they presumed you made Thailand
and finally out of India. She said she was a bit concerned
for you. When I asked why, she said that your insurance
premium hadn't been paid yet. The floats (collateral)
were not assembled and in good condition like they were
supposed to be and are not worth the $12,000 they could
have been sold for. Therefore, Wip has not paid anything*

*on your insurance policy. I told her I didn't understand what the hell she was talking about and to take it up with you once you make it back to the States.*

*2. John Scott called and said he had retired and was now in Anchorage. Said he still can refuel you gratis. Also, mentioned that the Lions would like to see you when you pass through Anchorage on your way home. Said he could probably arrange media and lodging.*

**Have a great trip to Malaysia.**
**Bill**

Casey's facial expressions seemed to give away his disappointment to others at dinner while he was reading the telex. He expected to be denied clearance to Singapore, but the typhoon situation was something he was not happy about. Casey looked at his dinner companions and said, "I don't want my aircraft to have to navigate through or around a serious typhoon."

Yet, tomorrow, he would be on track again and heading to Penang.

# Thirty-two

# Stop the Presses!

The ringing in my ears seemed to get louder and louder. What the hell? I thought. It then occurred to me that my hotel room phone was ringing off the hook. What time was it? What day was it? Turns out, it was 0100 on October 14. Still lying on my stomach, I grabbed for the phone and put the receiver to my left ear. I remember only hearing an angry and highly agitated voice.

"Bill, this is Tom Cadogan, DCA, U.S. Embassy in Thailand. Ambassador O'Donohue asked me to call you. You may recall, we have communicated several times before to make sure your pilot met with Thailand's Royal Princess; ensure that the PTT oil company executives would meet and host your pilot in Pattaya Beach; and that Mr. Songkram Somboon would arrange for the media conference," he said.

"Yes, Tom, how can I help you?" I answered. "Excuse me, what time and day are you in? More correctly put, what time is it there?"

"It's 1800 here, on October 14," Cadogan responded.

"Same day here too," I said.

While he paused for a moment this adverse sensation came over me and I could feel a big lump in my throat. "I called your New York office," he went on, "And the person answering said you were in Hawaii. By the way, how are things there?" Trying to remain cordial,

I told Tom that all was lush and beautiful here and I am waiting to see
if my presence is warranted in the Philippines or Japan to help run
interference with government officials, and be of assistance in bringing
Casey home.

"Very noble thoughts and positive gestures," he said. "But I
am calling because we have an immediate action situation or perhaps
it is really a major problem here at the embassy, and we need to discuss a solution.

"Just to update you, earlier today Casey was the main at-
traction at a major news conference at Pattaya Beach. All the majors
covered it. But take note, Bill, it is what he said during the conference
that has Secretary of State Baker hopping mad. Equally, it has my
boss pissed. And, if and when Phillips 66 reads the AP story, they
most likely will fire your ass." His voice was firm, but yet it seemed
thoughtful of my feelings.

"Where the hell does this smug aviator come from that he can
claim that the State Department and Phillips 66 had no significant
part in getting him this far?"

Cadogan further tried to rationalize some of Casey's grandiose
comments. Most were confusing, Cadogan explained. "Let me offer
my rebuttal to a few of his mistruths such as: The State Department
wouldn't let him leave Karachi when he wanted; State also didn't offer
assistance to gain clearances in India; and lastly, forbade him from
flying over Burma. The latter may be true but Saudi Arabian Airlines
helped him then.

"The State Department has bent over backwards for your stupid pilot. State had to hold him in Karachi because they needed time
to find out which Arab countries would choose to support the U.S. and
Saudi alliance in the event of war with Iraq. India was his own problem, and we know what that cost you.

"Casey also said all his support came from the ministers of
aviation that resided in the various countries where he landed. And as
far as Phillips, he said he is broke and has never gotten anything from
his sponsor. He hasn't had an oil change in some time as the oil never
arrived. He is hoping it will be there in the Philippines."

I told him the reason for that is that we didn't know where he
was and we couldn't send oil to a P.O. Box. "Tom, tell the ambassador

that we share your pain," I said.

"Bill, all those pieces of dogshit from Casey gave us a black eye," he responded. "As far as the Secretary is concerned, we may just pull the plug on the Philippines and Japan."

Now stunned, I fumbled with my pen I was using to take notes. Casey just fucked the U.S. diplomatic corps and now I am catching shit again.

I offered, "Tom, I have a plan if you give me the OK to proceed. I will call my close friend at the Associated Press in New York after speaking with you. Can I quote you on the ways in which your embassy as well as other embassies have favorably treated Casey? I will explain that, overall, the treatment he has received is a reflection of our State Department's efforts to support our pilot's journey. I will also emphasize how the U.S. Navy has provided untold services and further reiterate the support Phillips 66 has given."

"Wow, Bill," Tom said. He must have thanked me several times for this forward-thinking plan. He wondered if I could also call the two area (Pattaya Beach) TV stations plus local newspapers and relay the same info. I copied down the reporters' names and phone numbers in Thailand. I further pointed out to Tom that I would telex him the results of my efforts once I reached all parties. But of first and most immediate concern, I wanted to call and blunt this AP story.

Five hours later, I had reached all parties. My AP friend in New York was extremely happy to hear that I had a runaway pilot who wanted nothing more than to embarrass the people who were taking care of his needs. He just continued to say that this was another Coleman adventure gone bad. He promised to cut out all references to the lack of support by the State Department and Phillips.

The Pattay Beach press did the same. I finally got back to Tom Cadogan by phone and telex and gave him the good news. He later wired back to me one word: THANKS.

Now that another major disaster had been averted and no one at Phillips 66 would ever know anything about it, I called Knight in D.C. and rattled his cage just as he was about to take a sip of his favorite martini. I could hear Margo in the background: "This is not another Casey disaster, is it?" she asked.

Knight and I tried to envision where Casey might be. I knew

he had landed in Pattaya Beach, as the embassy in Bangkok confirmed that fact. Most important, we didn't know the mechanical state
of his aircraft. We had not received an engine oil analysis sample since
Saudi Arabia and wondered why.

I filled in Knight about the whole press conference debacle
and sprinkled the story with the comments made by Cadogan. Knight
would later tell me that Engen called Dunleavy and everyone had a
tremendous laugh. If nothing else, Casey was keeping us all in stitches
wondering what other great political debacle lay ahead. (God, if we
only knew then.)

Knight was told that if Casey was on schedule (a great as-
sumption on our part), he should be in Penang under the care of my
good friend Soon. If so, Casey would now be 18 hours ahead of me
here in Hawaii and there was little chance of hearing from him until
perhaps after he had touched down at the Naval Air Station in the
Philippines. I did relate (based on intelligence from Cadogan) that
Casey had read my plan on the path he would take to the Philippines.

Knight asked about our next move. I said we needed to confirm with Dorothy Aron at the U.S. Embassy's Commercial Service
when Brunei expects Casey to land. Also, we needed to make sure that
our embassy in Manila was fully briefed that Casey would soon be on
their doorstep. His previous flight clearance requests, along with the
ones we had filed, had the wrong dates and times meaning they were
all screwed up. Most important, we needed to alert them that he could
land within the next several days.

I assured Knight that I would be calling both parties that
evening. If I called Penang at 0100 it would be 1700 there October 15.
The only problem was that he would have already taken off for Penang.

Knight just laughed and said that was my problem, but
wished me luck. He also was gracious to ask if there was anything
right now he could do. I told David he needed to follow up with his
Russian contacts. As far as Japan was concerned, we still had no clearances to enter their country. I thought maybe Eason at State could
help. Knight laughed again. At that hour all I wanted was a cup of
coffee and a hot shower.

By the next day (the 15th), Casey's story had come out and it was good. Mainly, it was all about his wonderful trip. Seems they got most of the material from the news release sent out by my assistant, Tim McCormack.

Back at Pattaya Beach, Casey had a leisurely breakfast and said goodbye to all the hotel staff. He took three soft Egyptian cotton towels as souvenirs. He would take off on October 15 for Penang and its capital George Town. His host told him that all the kids who met him at the reservoir, as well as many residents of Pattaya Beach, wanted to know if he could buzz both the airport and reservoir upon his departure.

Casey later recalled, "When I got to my plane, where my trusty security guards had been making sure it was safe, my mouth literally dropped open. My plane had been washed and polished all over and it glistened in the morning sun.

"Naturally, I couldn't let my welcome wagon or any of the area citizens down. That meant giving them a real show. After takeoff near the spot where I had landed, I flew low and back towards the hills near the airport.

"Making a full arch, I came back around over the hills, buzzed the crowd at the airport, and then rocked my wings to another group as I passed over the reservoir. I repeated this gesture twice. Both times, my window side vent was open and I could hear all the loud cheers. I estimate there must have been more than 2,000 people below."

It was more than 775 miles to George Town. Once his aircraft returned to the Andaman Sea, he headed straight for Penang. He bade farewell over the radio to his friends at the airport and those on the boat in the Bang Phra Reservoir.

He marveled at the magnificent blue sky that was painted with cirrus cloud formations that looked like giant pillows. High hills were to the east and large areas of rice fields lay adjacent to the ocean-front in the west. Many people were working in the fields and large water buffalo were pulling carts and wagons of various sizes.

Now over Malaysia, the scenery below was made up of vast clumps of palm trees and tall grasses. Flying further, he came upon areas of undergrowth in what appeared to be a dense jungle canopy. He recognized that this area would not be a friendly environment in which to have aircraft engine problems.

To pass the time, he began monitoring commercial radio frequencies and listened to traffic going into Singapore and Bangkok. "I could hear lots of chatter on Kuala Lumpur's frequency," he would later relate. "I squawked my position several times to let ATC know where I was. My GPS had Penang locked in and my moving map display was programmed to electronically indicate my exact route and final destination point. I had further set in the coordinates for George Town harbor and was now well within 50 miles."

He radioed the Penang airport tower frequency, but had no response. There were several estuaries leading into George Town so he set his aircraft down in what appeared to be the North Channel that was clearly identified on his map and was somewhat north of George Town. He taxied one-and-a-half hours down the channel until it opened into a vast harbor area where he saw multiple fishing boats and other craft.

"A voice with a definite Asian accent came up on my radio and sure enough it was Soon," explained Casey. "Mr. Soon must have arranged port clearances, fueling, and a tie-down area. He waved his arms frantically from the dock space where I was to tie up. I was now in Penang. My more than six-hour flight ended about 1600. A short day — tomorrow would be much longer.

"Once I left the plane, Soon said he had a hotel room for me and would have the avgas in barrels delivered to the dock the next morning. He asked that I call him with the exact time I needed the fuel.

"Soon said I had to go through Immigration. After nearly two hours of stupid questions, I was let go to have dinner and kick back a bit at the hotel. Mr. Soon had given great directions to my hotel and I walked slowly, trying to take in every sound and smell of George Town. Later that night, I walked through the city."

George Town is the capital of Penang, which is an island of roughly triangular shape, with two of its sides jutting out into the Strait of Malacca. The port city had an extensive waterfront and beach area. The island is connected with the Malaysian mainland by the Penang Bridge, one of the longest in Asia.

"The streets were full of many vendors," Casey related. "Fresh fruit, flowers, and assorted items to wear were for sale everywhere. People milled about in the middle of the road and traffic just seemed to go around them in every direction. Previously while tying up my aircraft, I had watched as many of the fishing boats unloaded their daily catch. People were now lined up at the fishmongers to buy their dinner that came off the boats.

"My hotel was nondescript but comfortable. A nice bottle of Scotch was on my bedside end table (compliments of Soon). After a shower and meal in the hotel dining room, I went to bed. Tomorrow would be a long day and the weather forecast warned of the approaching tropical storm and a possible typhoon."

Meanwhile, on the Big Island of Hawaii, my hotel phone was ringing again. It was 0300 on October 15 — I really hadn't slept in days because of late night calls and early morning explanations. Picking up the phone, I heard Kyle McDonald's sweet voice; she had just gotten to the office in New York where there was a fax from Dorothy Aron in Brunei.

Said Kyle, "Dorothy was quite adamant that Casey can't land there, as they believe he would need aerodrome facilities. What is that, Bill?" I explained that Dorothy, like so many others, believed Casey's plane was the size of a large seaplane, like a PBY or perhaps even a 747. An aerodrome is a large hangar to store a seaplane. I also assumed that the officials at the Royal Yacht Club were scared that Casey might crash into some of their expensive yachts.

Kyle added that the embassy was concerned about their fueling capability at the Yacht Club and their lack of ability to supply avgas. On the other hand, Kyle explained, "Dorothy was worried that Hassanal Bolkiah, the Sultan of Brunei, would be disappointed if Casey didn't come to Brunei. She inquired if we could convince Casey to land outside the harbor in the breakwater."

I explained to Kyle that the breakwater to the harbor was the ocean and I doubted Casey could attempt that feat safely. I told Kyle it was now 2100 in Brunei and I would call Dorothy. The fax had been originated at 2000 in Brunei, so one could assume she was still awake. Kyle asked if I had heard from Casey and I said no, shrugging my shoulders. As far as I knew, Casey was expected to leave George Town tomorrow and head to Brunei.

Just as I was about to hang up, Kyle said that Tim needed to speak with me. He had just gotten off the phone with Dorothy while I was speaking with Kyle. Dorothy mentioned the fax she had sent, but was very excited and asked what had happened to Casey. When did the accident occur? Tim told Dorothy that we knew nothing of a crash. "What is behind the question?" he asked. She explained that The Brunei Times (Bandar Seri Begawan) had reported in a front page headline and subsequent article: "Famous Pilot's Aircraft Missing and Presumed Down on Way to Brunei." This was from the embassy's early morning copy for October 16.

I emphasized to Tim that I would call Dorothy ASAP. Further, if any other media called, tell them Casey is alive and well. He was still in Penang and would be taking off in several hours and flying to Brunei. He should cover a distance of 900 miles in about seven hours, but it may be several hours longer since he has to fly around Tropical Storm Lola.

Dorothy told Tim that the Brunei news agency near the embassy had assured her that Casey had crashed. "I asked their source and their reply was priceless: A man in a fishing boat saw him crash off Singapore."

Dorothy further added, "I asked if there was an explosion and the news agency editor said he didn't know. He only talked to the man in the boat about four minutes as he was calling long distance."

Tim explained, "I told Dorothy that the Coast Guard or local navy in that area would have alerted us if there had been an incident. Casey was on ATC radar. The reason for his late arrival in Brunei was that he stayed an extra day in Pattaya Beach. I assured her you would be calling her tonight."

When I later called Dorothy, she was awake and waiting for my call. "He will be there," I told her, "And please tell His Excellency that piece of information. He never crashed and his plane is in good condition."

I added that my friend in Penang who was taking care of Casey said his aircraft was in perfect condition and our pilot planned to leave in the early a.m. on October 16. If there are any more delays, it might be caused by the storms in the area. My representative in Penang told me that Tropical Storm Lola was in the area so he may have to divert.

Dorothy said that Tropical Storm Lola had nearly passed through that area. She wished Casey the best. She would report this information about Casey to the Sultan as well as to the Brunei news agency. Dorothy was also told that Casey's plane was not the size of a PBY and that he needed to land in the harbor and not the ocean as such a landing may damage the floatplane.

I decided to spend the rest of the day playing golf and lying by the pool. I figured not much else could go wrong as Casey would be taking off soon. Meanwhile, hurdles were still ahead: the Philippines, Japan, possibly Russia — or maybe direct to Attu.

# Thirty-three

# Navigating Weather and Rainforests on the Way to Brunei, the Philippines

The next morning, Casey had a hearty breakfast, after which he contacted Soon and had his fuel delivered. As he later recounted, "Soon was a very pleasant gentleman and when I asked about costs, he said it was already taken care of. We pumped the avgas into my aircraft and made sure I was fully loaded. Total usable fuel was more than 200 gallons, providing a 12-hour range.

"As I preflighted the bird, I knew my precise engine monitoring system would allow me to measure exhaust gas temperatures and cylinder head temperatures on each individual cylinder while in flight. But then again, the CHTs on number 6 cylinder had fluctuated some while I was attempting to take off in Calcutta. So far today, I had not noticed any anomalies.

"Prior to my leaving Penang, Soon took his time to point out some key landmarks. I would be traveling the entire length of Malaysia. His main interest was in identifying and showing me some of the renowned National Wildlife Parks that I would be flying over.

"For me these areas all seemed to be nothing more than jungles and rainforests. But to Soon, they were sacred areas where almost-extinct animals lived — the Bengal tiger, the Sumatran rhino, among others. He expected me to repeat back everything; but again, I was thinking only about the weather and landing safely in Brunei. Weather forecasts that morning were not promising."

Shortly after, Soon stood waving as Liberty II headed out to the main channel. There was enough room for Casey to build up speed and take off after about three miles. It was now about 0900 and ahead of him was a planned flight of some seven hours.

Once aloft, Casey left the control area of Penang Center and was turned over to the control of Malaysia ATC. He had fully expected to be vectored onto an airway allowing him to cross over central Malaysia, and then on a direct path to Indonesia (Borneo) and then onto Brunei. That was not to be ATC's plan this day.

In fact, he would add more than two hours to his flight plan — ATC would not allow him to deviate. Hell, he thought, he was headed directly to Singapore, the country that refused him landing rights.

Now at 9,000 feet and some 200 miles from Penang, Casey took in the landscape below, which was breathtaking. Yet, on the right side of the aircraft the clouds were building and he knew before long he would be close to the edge of Tropical Storm Lola.

The jungles and rainforests were immense and pretty much appeared just as Soon had described. Soon had also told of the phenomena brought about by these forces of nature in producing the thick canopies he was flying over. Strict government measures have ensured that the Malay jungles and rainforests remain as virgin as they were a couple million years ago. After seeing firsthand this vast ecosystem of nature, Casey concluded that it was no wonder that Malaysia enjoyed undisputed recognition as a land of rare fauna and flora.

He regained his focus on flying as Malaysia ATC handed him over to Singapore control. He was directed to fly over the harbor and then take an easterly path towards Indonesia. As Casey later described, "There seemed to be thousands of anchored ships in Singapore's harbor, from super-sized tankers to smaller cargo vessels. The harbor's edge seemed to form a giant circle around the city of Singapore. At the water's edge of the city sat the famously magnificent World Trade Center.

"I was still keeping Tropical Storm Lola to the left side of the aircraft. Lola looked enormous, with gigantic cumulonimbus clouds and lightning in the far distance. The cells must have risen to heights of more than 50,000 feet. I estimated that some 100 miles northeast of my position the rain from the tropical storm must be torrential. On the right side of the aircraft was the tropical storm, which built up on the horizon and was situated over the jungles of Malaysia. I averted that weather problem altogether. When I saw possible problems ahead, I had the flexibility of flying around the disturbance."

By the time he left Singapore airspace, Casey was over the Java Sea; from there it was almost a straight run to the northwestern edge of Indonesia. He was now under the control of Indonesian ATC, which directed him onto an airway direct to Borneo, the third largest island in the world and one which also featured one of earth's oldest rainforests.

As Casey recounted, "I looked down on Borneo and wondered if there were still headhunters lurking in the rainforests. I read somewhere in a history of World War II that during that time period, when the Japanese occupied Borneo, the local natives fighting for their country in the underground resorted to headhunting measures to scare the Japs. And, from what I could read, it really did petrify them.

"Once clearing Borneo airspace, I was passed over to Malaysia Control. I spent the next several hours winging my way to Brunei.

"What I had planned to be a seven-hour leg now turned into a nine-hour flight. It was 1800 when I finally picked up Brunei's International Airport tower frequency. I had passed over flat coastal plains that rose up to the mountains in the east. To the west were hilly lower lands which seemed to be used for agriculture."

Brunei Control soon came up on his radio and passed him over to a person with a handheld radio stationed on a Brunei Coast Guard patrol boat. This radio beacon (Casey's guidepost) was situated on a boat that was stationed very near to the Royal Brunei Yacht Club.

There was so much background chatter coming from the handheld radio on the boat that he had a hard time gaining landing instructions. He finally made clear contact with the person on the radio and immediately found out that the person on the other end was U.S. Ambassador Christopher Phillips.

"He was an extremely nice person and very politely gave me directions to his location," Casey later recalled. "He advised me that I would be seeing a very large body of water off the left side of my plane. That was the Anson Passage. I was directed to make a left turn and then head down the passage in a westerly direction, and go past the island of Pulau Muara Besar on my left.

"From there, I was to drop down and head directly towards the long strip of land jutting out maybe four miles from the mainland. That was called Serasa Beach. I presumed that my landing area was almost directly in front of this strip of land."

The ambassador soon changed that thought process: "Our embassy has blocked out a landing area on the Serasa Beach for you at the Royal Brunei Yacht Club," he said. "Once you see me waving to you from the boat, we want you to land about five miles south of my boat."

Casey responded, "I don't see the advantage — why can't I just land near the Yacht Club basin?"

The ambassador answered, "Your aircraft is too big to land near the Yacht Club. We had been expecting a plane the size of a 747 and we were afraid your aircraft might damage some of the really expensive yachts."

Casey said, "I am landing near the large strip of land, and once given permission by you I will then taxi to your position outside the yacht club basin."

There were hundreds of sailboats out in the waters off Serasa Beach. To Casey, it looked much like the regattas he used to watch on the bay in Wildwood, New Jersey, when he was a young man. He estimated that there were at least 600 sailing craft below him, ranging in size from one to three masts.

Upon landing, he kept circling around in about a one-mile radius, about a mile from the ambassador's boat. As instructed, he waited until permission was given for him to taxi up close to the ambassador's boat. Once there, the crew helped tie Casey's aircraft onto the bow.

The ambassador remarked that he was surprised at the overall size of Casey's aircraft: "Coleman, your handler spoke to our Dorothy Aron and he told her that you would be small compared to commercial aircraft, but my staff just didn't believe her. Captain Casey, who would think that an aircraft of your size could actually complete the long flights you've endured over oceans as well as from country to country — all the way around the world?"

Then, somewhat abruptly, the ambassador added, "We can't go anyplace until we observe a Royal Yacht Club tradition." He then brought out a magnum of champagne and said they had to drink a toast before he went ashore. Once the full bottle was consumed, the next major event became clearing Immigration and Customs.

Casey later recounted, "As my luck with this group had been rough in the past, this time I was amazed. The Customs agents came alongside my plane and the ambassador's boat and smiled. 'You are cleared,' they said. The formalities and ceremony taken care of, we docked my aircraft on Serasa Beach right in front of the Yacht Club."

The ambassador explained that the yacht club's boating activity really came alive on weekends and holidays. The club featured an informal outdoor restaurant along with an open-air swimming pool. The club's garden was magnificent. The facility had opened in 1980 and had almost doubled in size within ten years. It also featured a private beach area.

The president of the Brunei Yacht Club made Casey a lifetime member. "I have a plaque for that honor and I can now go into any yacht club worldwide and be welcomed," he related.

At this auspicious ceremony, Casey thought he would enlighten the 300 or more well-wishers with a quote by Albert Einstein on what he said about life: "When you are courting a nice girl, an hour seems like a second. When you sit on a red-hot cinder, a second seems like an hour. That's relativity." The crowd clapped and the music resounded and the drinks flowed from then on.

Casey finally made it to his hotel, close to the yacht club, and was in bed by about 0200. Tomorrow, October 17, he would have a six-hour flight ahead of him to the Philippines.

Dawn came early for Casey on the next day. The club had made sure there was an airport fuel truck from the international airport standing by near Casey's plane. Strangely enough, the Brunei airport had avgas. After a great breakfast and much discussion about the journey ahead, Casey boarded his plane at 0800. One regret: He had not met with Sultan Hassanal Bolkiah, who he was told was away on business.

After preflighting his aircraft and shaking more than 100 hands and signing autographs for many of the younger set, Casey turned over his engine and proceeded to make his way into the passage. After about a three-mile run he swooped up into the air, wagged his wings, and headed northeast to the Philippines.

He projected the distance from Brunei to Naval Air Station Cubi Point in the Philippines to be 1293 kilometers, or 803 miles. His estimated time to make that distance was about six hours – if the good weather held.

After leaving Brunei, Casey found himself back over the South China Sea. The skies had a layer of cirrus clouds, and the sea below reflected the image of his aircraft some 6,000 feet above. Shortly after, Malaysian ATC handed him over to Philippines Control. He would rely heavily on his moving map display, the complete brains of the aircraft's avionics that tied together all navigation and communication information.

After about two hours, he approached the tip of Palawan, one of the first outer islands of the Philippines. He thought he could spend the next four hours on a direct course to Cubi Point, until he started seeing large weather cells building to his left. He nudged the aircraft more toward the coast. He then decided because of the need to run in and out of the cells that he would remain over land up to Cubi Point.

Casey safely touched down at Cubi Point at 1430. "Wow, from the air Cubi Point looks just like a large carrier deck," he would later say. "I would have loved to do a fly-by of the control tower, but that probably would have put me before the admiral at Subic Bay."

# Thirty-four

# Old Home Week in the Philippines

Hawaii was beautiful this time of year. I had played golf on the volcano course the previous day and had lost about 20 balls in the volcanic rock. Since I was about 18 hours behind Casey, I had been receiving most of my phone calls early in the morning, so now it had become a joke when I showed up for breakfast in the dining room at 0600. We knew Casey was safe in Brunei but I awaited confirmation from Ms. Aron at the U.S. Embassy.

The phone in my hotel room rang at least 150 times (OK, perhaps a bit less) and wearily at 0500 on October 16, I raised the receiver. On the other end was the cheery voice of Dorothy Aron from the U.S. Embassy. It was 2300 in Brunei, and she chirped that Casey had arrived safely and was still at a reception that had been thrown in his honor.

"Bill, Ambassador Christopher Phillips acted as his flight controller and gave all the landing instructions to Casey while actually in a Brunei Coast Guard boat in the large basin out front of the Royal Yacht Club," she said, quite excited. "From his position on the boat, the ambassador directed Casey to land and taxi his aircraft up onto the Yacht Club beach. Greeting Casey were more than several hundred members of the club and embassy staff. It seemed that immediately upon exiting his aircraft he was whisked away to a splendid gala at the Royal Brunei Yacht Club."

"Here is some more good news that I wanted to share with you before it becomes public tomorrow on October 17. My editor friend at the *Bandar Seri Begawan Brunei News* sent me an advanced copy of tomorrow's newspaper. You will love the headline: "Missing Plane Found". The news story, with accompanying photos of Casey and his plane, speaks to his adventures so far. Also, the ambassador was extremely pleased because Casey praised all the help he had gotten from the Brunei Embassy, the ambassador, myself, and the members of the Royal Brunei Yacht Club. He also talked about Phillips 66 and even mentioned you, Bill.

"I know the ambassador called Secretary Baker and I hope you will do the same and call your contacts at Phillips."

I asked if she could send several copies of the newspaper to my New York office and she agreed. Also, I pleaded with Dorothy to have Casey call me before he left for the Philippines. I needed to go over a number of critical issues with him as well as to provide the U.S. Navy at Cubi Point with his projected ETA. Dorothy was a sweetheart and I promised that someday we would have an opportunity to meet.

No more than ten minutes after I'd gotten off the phone with Dorothy, I received a call from my associate Kyle MacDonald in New York. We exchanged pleasantries and I briefed her on the positive news story about Casey in Brunei. She said we had a small matter to clear up. It concerned Soon in Penang. Kyle said that Soon had not been paid for his services he provided Casey, which included his agency fee; preparatory boat services; avgas; transport; hotel; and watchman. All told, the invoice was MR5,245, or $1,945.

I instructed Kyle to pay it from my American Express account and then I asked: What was Soon's impression of meeting Casey? Kyle told me that Soon said his experience would have been more fruitful if I had been there. Soon did note that Casey would have possibly gotten himself killed if he had been a part of the Soon/Coleman covert team back in the '70s. "Tell Bill I am glad he only flies a single-engine plane and does not carry a gun. Also, when will Bill come back here so we can have fun?" Kyle asked what trouble did Soon and I get into? I said someday I might tell her. Kyle continued, saying that she thanked him very much for all his help and said maybe Bill might visit him someday. In the same breath, Kyle asked if I was going to Japan to help Casey. I told her that depended on the calls I planned to have later that day with Casey and Captain Smith in the Philippines.

After hanging up with Kyle, I ordered breakfast in my room and then called Knight. He was pleasantly surprised I was still breathing as he had not heard from me in two days. We talked at great length on a myriad of subjects: clearances, diplomats, Russia, and Japan.

We both wondered what our next game plan would be. I would call U.S. Ambassador Jack F. Matlock's office in Moscow and David was going over to the Soviet Embassy in D.C. Regarding Japan, I was told by the U.S. Navy Seventh Fleet headquarters in Yokosuka that I might obtain help from the FAA station in Tokyo. I was given the name and phone number of Dennis Warth at the FAA.

I also mentioned the good news coverage in Brunei and that made David happy. He would tell Engen who, I was sure, would call Baker and Dunleavy. Not much else to do at that point, as I was just waiting for Casey to call. I told David I would keep him informed. So, I went to the pool and looked at all the beautiful female bodies through my sunglasses. But not for long — I was rudely interrupted by a bellman who said I had a long distance call. Back to my room and on the phone at 1400.

It was my man Casey; it was still October 16 in Hawaii, but for Casey it was now 0800, October 17, in Brunei. He said he was set to launch for the Philippines.

Casey was his usual overpowering self and told me all the great things he had done and wondered how everyone was at home. Was I still in Hawaii? Was I coming to Japan? I told Casey about the bad repercussions from the Pattaya Beach press conference and how he almost got shut down if not for David Knight and Engen begging the Secretary of State not to punish him. I also said I killed his story at the AP.

"Why?" Casey asked. There was no answer on my part.

Casey said his remarks were all a mistake on his part and he really meant to give credit to both Phillips and State. He just forgot. I then blinked because he abruptly changed his position and commented that it didn't appear to him, or any one of the many co-conspirators he befriended on this arduous journey, that State or Phillips had done much to help his cause.

Smoking from ear to ear, I blew up and told the SOB that every clearance, every bill he hadn't paid, and every diplomatic approval he had received were initiated and accomplished through our efforts. State had supported his ass. Ambassador Phillips' positive comments to Secretary Baker ensured that he could fly another day.

"Casey, if not for our close working relationships with all the embassies, you would still be sitting in Karachi," I told him. "It is time to wake up and smell the roses. We appreciated your favorable comments in the Brunei media, but that was because the ambassador told you what to say. I know because I asked him to do so.

"The Philippines are all set and Captain Harry Smith will be waiting to meet you. U.S. Ambassador Nicholas Platt is on board and all should go fine. The State Department gave the green light for your visit. We still have not obtained clearance for you to enter Japan, plus the Soviets are dragging their feet and Knight and I are still waiting to hear from U.S. Ambassador Jack Matlock in Russia."

We had paid Soon's bill. Casey explained that Soon had told him that I would pay it, so he didn't offer to reimburse him.

Also, Casey needed to change his oil in the Philippines. I presumed that it had been over 40 hours since his last change of oil in Saudi Arabia. He said the Bangkok embassy had given him the Phillips 66 oil and he had changed the oil in Pattaya Beach. PTT was supposed to have sent the sample to Hammond.

I reiterated that once he changed oil at Subic Bay, Philippines, he needed to make sure he sent the oil analysis kit to Hammond at Phillips. I asked how the plane was running and he said he had some problems taking off in Calcutta because it was so hot, but had had no problems since. Casey said that he expected to be in Cubi in the Philippines at "about 1430 today."

After he hung up, I called Hammond and passed along the good news that Casey was heading to the Philippines tomorrow, the 17th. But it was already the 17th in Brunei and Casey would be taking off shortly for the Philippines. He should be there about 1500.

Hammond then asked me if oil had been sent to the Philippine Embassy. "Yes," I said.

Added Hammond, "Bill, we have no evidence (oil analysis) he had changed oil other than in Saudi Arabia. Did you send oil to the other countries where he landed?" Again, I answered positively. But then again, I explained to Hammond we had sent oil to Karachi but Casey said he never got it. Also, we sent oil to Bangkok and the Econ Officer Tom Cadogan at the embassy had said it was taken to Pattaya Beach by the PTT executives. He was told that Casey had changed his oil. PTT never mentioned anything about an oil sample.

"Jack," I said, "Casey did promise me that he would change it at the Subic Bay U.S. Navy base and send a sample back to Bartles-ville."

Hammond also inquired about the approvals for Casey to enter Japan. I told him that that rested with the U.S. Navy and how they could cut through the red tape. Getting foreign private aircraft permission to fly in and out of Japan was difficult. "Coleman, I don't care if you have to go to Japan and hold hands with the Japanese Em-peror," Hammond responded. "You lived there and know the country and its politics. And money is no object. Just be sure it happens. Same holds true for the Soviet Union. Tell them that Phillips 66 believes in perestroika. We can't take any chances on having the whole flight coming to end in either Japan or Russia." Hammond was now chuff-ing like a Bengal tiger.

I said, "Jack, Casey said his engine was running smoothly. He vaguely remembers changing his oil in Bangkok."

"What the hell does he know? Is he a mechanic?" was Ham-mond's response. I then briefed Hammond on the front page, highly positive news story in the latest edition of the *Brunei News*. A copy was being sent to his office.

Hammond emphasized that I needed to speak with Dennis Boggs at Phillips about the oil Casey was running, and subsequently transferred the call over to Boggs. He was the technical director for lubricants at Phillips 66 and a technical guru who literally wrote the book on how good aviation engine oil would handle the multiple stresses which occur in an aircraft engine. He also was in charge of automotive and truck lubes. Frankly, he was a genius.

He stood about six feet, wore glasses, and looked the part of a real research engineer. He had a reserved but very pleasant demeanor.

Most importantly, he commanded respect — one immediately knew never to cross or lie to him. Boggs thought his XC Aviation Oil was the best in the industry.

Boggs felt Casey didn't have the same respect for Phillips 66 XC Oil as he did. As such, Boggs never quite trusted Casey and thought of him as just a blowhard Irishman. To him, Casey was just another user of his aviation oil and one who had little knowledge of the true benefits offered by this product.

"I've not gotten one oil sample from him since Jeddah," he said. "Have you been sending the oil to him?" I confirmed with Dennis what I had told Hammond, that we had sent oil to both Karachi and Bangkok, and that Casey thought he might have changed oil in Bangkok.

I admitted to Boggs that we had had a hard time keeping track of exactly where Casey was much of the time, as he really never reached out to me by phone or fax. Most of the time I obtained all my info from the econ officers at the U.S. Embassies. I was very candid and explained that maybe the oil was never given to Casey in Karachi.

"I know the Bangkok Embassy had been pissed at me as well as Casey because of what he said at the Pattaya Beach press conference. I settled that issue," I said. "We will have a controlled environment at the navy base in Subic Bay. The oil change would certainly be a key gauge as to the health of his aircraft's engine."

Just then, I had to hang up with Boggs as a call was coming in from Casey in Brunei. I mentioned I had spoken to him earlier. "I'll call you back, Dennis," I told him.

Casey just wanted me to know that Ambassador Phillips had acknowledged what a great thing his flight meant to America. Casey hoped that this would smooth over any hard feelings I had about him. "Fly safe," I said.

When I called Boggs back, I said I had a bit of good news. Casey said he did change oil in Pattay Beach after logging about 30 hours. He had given the oil sample to the PTT oil executives and they promised to send it to Hammond. There was a loud silence on the other end of the phone.

"Coleman," he said, "If that engine fails due to lack of proper lubrication caused by not adhering to timely oil changes, then we all will hang. I will let you know what the Philippines sample conveys. Maybe we will receive the Pattaya Beach sample, too. Have a good trip back to New York. Are you stopping in Bartlesville?"

"No!" I belted out. "There is a gentleman there who wants to hang me — you know of whom I speak — and I am not going to let that bastard get me." Dennis laughed and said goodbye.

At that moment, the bellman knocked on the door and handed me a fax — a letter Kyle drafted in New York for my signature. The letter was going to be faxed to Captain Harry Smith, Commander, Naval Forces Philippines, Subic Bay. In the letter, I told Harry that Casey would arrive between 2:30-3:30 p.m. local time on October 17.

Smith likely already knew this fact, as we had touched base earlier with Bruce Beardsley, Consul General, and John Lyle, Embassy Econ department, to gain flight clearances. We also had sent a case of oil in order for Casey to change his oil.

I also wanted Smith to understand that we still didn't have a clearance for Japan as there were Status of Forces Agreement (SOFA) issues because Casey was entering Japan in a civilian aircraft. And, Russia was not calling me back. We begged for the Soviet Union to help us and had hoped that once Casey left Japan he could fly over the Kuril Islands and then proceed northerly up the Kamchatka Peninsula, from where he could cross over to Nome, Alaska.

My last paragraph in the letter conveyed that Casey will need money and that we needed to make a deposit in Smith's bank so it could be transferred to Casey. The letter also said that I would call later to finalize any future planning. I waited until 0100 on October 17 to call Harry Smith. It was now 1900 his time the same day. We exchanged hellos.

Smith explained, "We figure the safest place for Casey to land is at Cubi. We will control his approach by having the Cubi Point Control Tower assign him a landing location and safe means to approach his docking area. Plus, at the same time, he wouldn't be interfering with any of the big navy ships. We also earmarked a docking area for him for later at Subic Bay, but first we want to bring him safely down at Cubi. Maybe tomorrow we will give him a patrol boat escort over to the reserved dock at Subic Bay."

Harry inquired about my background and my role in Casey's

journey. We discovered that Harry had been in flight school in Pensacola two years after me. Even scarier, we actually grew up in the same South Jersey area, about 15 miles apart. He lived in Ocean City, New Jersey and I grew up in nearby Sea Isle City. We were neighbors of sorts – a toll bridge apart on the Ocean Drive highway.

He went to Ocean City High School and was captain of the football team. I went to Wildwood Catholic High School where I was captain of the basketball team. His aunt owned the Chatter Box in Ocean City and Harry was the sandwich man there. The Chatter Box to me was where we used to go and pick up girls for the nightly beach parties. Since Ocean City was dry (no booze), everyone either headed to Sea Isle or Somers Point.

Equally scary, Harry offered the revelation that he also knew Casey. "Every time I went back to Ocean City in the summer from college, there was Casey. I was captain of the lifeguards and Casey was a lifeguard in Wildwood. We used to see each other every summer during the Lifeguard Boat Races in Ocean City. Tell me that the world is that small," Harry said.

Regarding his military background, prior to his appointment as the Political Military Officer at Subic Bay, he was attached to the Philippines U.S. Embassy as a representative from the Commander-in-Chief Pacific Fleet (CINCPACFLEET), Pearl Harbor.

I asked Harry how he got involved in this whole aviation record feat. Said Smith, "One afternoon a U.S. State Department representative called me. He explained Casey's flight and wanted us at Subic Bay to support it. He was very helpful and said that the Secretary of State was very interested in this around the world flight. The embassy individual added that this American pilot was coming in and wanted gas, lodging, and help in obtaining clearances to Japan and Russia."

I then asked, "Did Ambassador Platt want this to happen, too? Did the Navy want this to happen as well?" He answered yes to each of these inquiries.

Subsequently, Harry called me late in the day on October 17 and said Casey had landed safely. "You know what Cubi looks like, Bill?" he began. "That is where the carriers tie up. Well, my wife Carol and the kids were at Cubi and when Tom landed we had the 55-gallon drums of avgas waiting. We tied him up at a small docking area where small boats tie up and we got him into the BOQ."

Over the ensuing days Casey found refuge at the BOQ, talking about his exploits to various officers at a small bar there. He also spent considerable time with Harry Smith, who recalled, "We spent a good deal of time mapping out his next steps. He was going to fly one-way to Taiwan and beyond. We made several calls to the Japanese aviation ministry and seemed to get the runaround.

"We needed outside help and we hoped you would pull a rabbit from your hat. My opinion is that Casey needed to just fly direct

to Japan and forget Taiwan. I still thought Russia was a long shot but Casey remained the eternal optimist. (Smith's candor would prove to be spot-on.) "Interestingly, my wife was involved in a teaching capacity with the local high school. When Tom heard about her involvement, he volunteered to talk to the

*Casey talks to students at a school in the Philippines.*

students about aviation. He went there numerous times. All the kids liked him. I saved the many letters they sent to Tom thanking him for the wealth of knowledge he conveyed about the joys of aviation."

Back in Hawaii, I was making plans to fly home the next day. But first, I needed to make important calls to both Japan and the U.S.S.R.

It was now 0200 in Hawaii; in Tokyo the time was 2100 (same day). Japan was 19 hours ahead of Hawaii. After several loud clicks on long distance to Japan, I was greeted with "Moshi Moshi" (standard phone hello in Japanese). In broken Japanese, I asked to be patched through to Dennis Warth of the FAA at the U.S. Embassy. He was my go-between with the Japanese Civil Aviation Bureau (JCAB) at the Ministry of Transport.

I had written to Dennis several weeks earlier requesting assistance in gaining Casey's entry into Japan. He had replied to me last week that the JCAB was not responding and wanted more extraneous information on Casey. My phone call today was made for one reason and one reason alone: How the hell do we get Casey through Japan without the JCAB approval?

The plot thickened. Dennis suggested that we fly out of the Philippines and land in Kadena, Okinawa. Theoretically, Casey would be a member of a sanctioned flying club in Okinawa which already has all the necessary approved documents to operate their aircraft within Japan's territorial limits. In essence, we would be stretching the truth as we didn't actually have formal JCAB approvals for Casey to enter the country.

I asked Dennis, "How do we pull this off without going to jail?"

His response: "Casey pretends that he is affiliated with the Kadena Flying Club. The club is made up of military officers and enlisted personnel. As Casey, at present, is a guest of the U.S. Navy, he would be offered the same courtesy from the navy at Kadena.

"Logically, that way he can successfully enter Okinawa, the island gateway to Japan's mainland. Once in Okinawa, Casey can then petition the JCAB to allow him to continue his journey through the mainland.

"Once Casey requests clearance while in Okinawa, the Japanese will immediately realize that Casey has entered their country without JCAB approval. The odds are in our favor that JCAB will most certainly allow him to continue on his way. If not, they will shoot me and have the American officials extradite you back to Japan to stand trial. Neat, huh?

"I'm so positive we can pull this off, I have already set the wheels in motion to help support Casey while in Japan. I and my assistant Larry Arima have contacted three aviation support operators to assist Casey with obtaining fuel and lodging at lake sites where he can land safely.

"Bill, this scheme is very risky as you may surmise, but the Japanese have strongly indicated that checking all the paperwork would take several weeks. They are acutely aware of the urgency of

Casey's plight. He needs to fly through Japan in the next several days to avoid the purported inclement weather conditions in the U.S.S.R. I believe this is the best route at present for Casey.

"We at the embassy really want this pilot to succeed. We have read a lot about him in the papers and, hell, if we can help in some small way, we'll take the chance."

I told Dennis that I had already called the Kadena Flying Club's President Mick Timkin who was most enthusiastic about Casey proceeding to Kadena. He said that Sunday, October 21, would be the best day to fly into Kadena, as they would be having an Aero Club pancake breakfast along with other activities.

Dennis was also made aware that I wanted to speak with the Tokyo Aero Club president to verify the support services at each destination where Casey was targeting to land on the Japanese mainland. "Bill, we are making arrangements and there is no need to speak with them," Dennis said.

I told him that I knew Casey had previously spoken to his assistant Larry Arima and had confirmed a shopping list of all the additional paperwork that was required to obtain formal JCAB approval. He said he had already sent off all pertinent flight clearance information to Atsushi Yasukawa, Director, Airworthiness Division, JCAB. Hopefully, that show of good faith would help in getting Casey cleared through mainland Japan.

I explained to Warth that I planned to call Casey that day to go over what he needed to do in order to fly into Kadena. Dennis and I reviewed the potential flight path that his office had mapped out previously. And again, in a show of good faith to the Japanese, I told Dennis that I intended to send off a fax to Yasukawa-san on October 21. My message would outline the route for which we were requesting permission for clearance. By that time he and the rest of the Japanese nation would know Casey was already in Kadena.

Here was the proposed plan:

- Subic Bay DCT Kadena (water landing as defined by the aero club)
- Kadena to Biwa Lake

- Biwa Lake to Kasumigaura Bay
- Kasumigaura DCT Misawa (site adjacent to U.S. Air Force Base)
- Misawa to Lake Memanbetsu (upper Hokkaido)
- Lake Memanbetsu to U.S.S.R.?

Dennis said he applauded my tenacity but said I was fighting an uphill battle in trying to gain clearance approval from the Japanese. "Remember," he said, "It is easier to be forgiven by entering Japanese territorial boundaries through Kadena than to have JCAB flatly tell you no at the outset. In other words, it's better to beg forgiveness than to ask for permission."

I reiterated that I would also send a fax letter to Jiro Hanyu, Director, International Air Transport Division, on October 21, begging forgiveness for the lack of notice to JCAB, but would ask if at all possible to now expedite a formal in-country flight clearance regarding safety of the aircraft due to impending bad weather in the U.S.S.R. We both hoped that these measures would afford us a good chance to obtain clearance.

Warth took on a positive tone and commented that the one overriding factor in our favor was that Casey had all the right credentials, such as the sacred airworthiness certificate plus added aircraft safety features. Those key factors should assure the Japanese that this whole flight was on the up-and-up

I asked Dennis if he stood to be reprimanded. He said, "I don't work for the Japanese government and our whole diplomatic corps in our government wants Casey to succeed. Bill, just make sure you don't come back to Japan in the next century. They may throw you in jail and throw away the key." His deep belly laughter echoed through the phone's receiver.

"Dennis, you realize that I had previously been reprimanded by the Japanese government," I told him.

I explained that back in 1971 I was ordered by the U.S. Defense Department to set up a flight demonstration at NAS Atsugi of the new OV-10A Bronco aircraft before the Japanese self-defense forces. The day of the event, three busloads of Japanese military descended on the navy base along with a cadre of reporters. The aircraft had

flown in from Okinawa and proceeded to present a two-hour demo.
News headlines in the Japanese press the next day said it all. It seems
that my demo of the OV-10A broke the Status of Forces Agreement
(SOFA) the U.S. had with Japan.

SOFA is intended to clarify the terms under which the foreign
military is allowed to operate. And, showing off U.S. military aircraft
to the Japanese military on a U.S. military base is not kosher. The
largest headline was in the *Mainichi Shimbun:* "U.S. Navy Lt. Coleman Advocates Japan to Arm."

This episode in my military career saw me brought back to
D.C. to testify before Congress. Thank God for Senator J. William
Fulbright (head of the Armed Services Committee) — he really stuck
up for me. But in the short term, I had to make formal apologies
*(moushiwake gozaimasen)* to several high-ranking Japanese ministers.
I just hoped this Casey episode wouldn't find me again on the front
page of the *Mainichi Shimbun* while also seeing my head roll before at
least a dozen JCAB ministers.

I called Captain Smith a few hours after talking to Warth and
filled him in on all the nefarious plans. First, we would have Warth
check with the JCAB to determine if they planned to give Casey
clearance. Second, if the Japanese continued to drag their feet and it
seemed likely there was no firm commitment to grant a clearance, we
would have no other choice than to send Casey into Kadena, under
the auspices that he was affiliated with the aero club. Then my faxes
would go out to JCAB and we would take our lumps and knocks from
there.

I was departing the next day and I thanked Harry for everything. Casey was in his command. I would be heading home to New
York as there was no need for me to go to Japan. I called Hammond
and told him the whole backstory. He agreed we were taking positive
steps. I said the oil was there and Casey would make an oil change.
Jack wished me well. I went to play golf one final time.

*Thirty-five*

# Sayonara, Subic and Konnichiwa, Japan

Casey takes over the narrative at this point ...

"Naval Air Station Cubi Point was very helpful in guiding me into a safe landing area just off the main dock where the aircraft carriers tie up. As I touched down in Subic Bay on Day 126, the Cubi Point control tower advised me to taxi over to a very long dock which was adjacent to the Naval Air Station's runway. As it turned out, this was the only dock at Cubi Point. As I taxied near to the long dock, there seemed to be a very large gathering of people and several were waving their arms frantically as if I might go somewhere else.

"My aircraft was tied up with the help of several navy personnel. First to greet me was Captain Harry Smith along with his wife Carol and their children. Captain Smith said I hadn't changed since the last time he saw me at the Lifeguard Boat Races in Ocean City, New Jersey.

"My memory went blank. What did he mean, boat races? Captain Smith allowed me long enough to regain my composure and take that dumbfounded look off my face. In a seemingly split second, I totally recalled my many meetings with Harry Smith, the lifeguard on the Jersey shore in the late '60s. At that time in our lives, we had been competitors in the races when I represented Wildwood and Harry

Smith was the captain of the lifeguards in Ocean City. This couldn't be happening. How on earth do two people meet some 25 years later, halfway around the world?

"'Harry, it is indeed a pleasure to see you again. Are you the big honcho here?' 'Not quite,' Captain Smith said. 'I am the Political Military Officer here at Subic Bay. And, you are a guest of the U.S. Embassy and the U.S. Navy.'"

At this point, Casey was safely aboard the U.S. Naval Air Station on October 17. All he wanted was to take a shower, catch a nap, and then have something to eat. Harry had told him that the Navy planned to move his aircraft the next day to a pier located in a more secure area in Subic Bay proper. It was where all the big ships tied up.

Casey's plane would be safe that night and Harry said he had secured about 200 gallons of avgas which Casey could pump into his aircraft once it was safely secured at a Subic Bay dock.

Casey's room at the BOQ was comfortable and the shower refreshing. His back had been hurting some, but he had been wearing his fabric girdle that provided support to his back during long flights and especially when refueling the aircraft.

That night, an extraordinary gala event was held. Smith had organized a reception at the Officers' Club and everyone was in their officers' white uniforms; spouses were dressed in elegant evening attire. Casey waxed story after story to anyone who cared to listen. Most important, he found that everyone wanted to buy him a drink. (The nice part about the offer was the fact that a shot of Glenlivet Scotch cost only 50 cents.)

The next day was mostly spent trying to figure out how he was going to obtain clearance into Japan. Harry mentioned that Phillips 66's New York office was coordinating with the FAA in Tokyo and felt it had the clearance puzzle with the Japanese almost solved. Yet, that fact didn't seem to grab Casey's attention. He felt he needed to do something, anything, but had no idea what.

Poring over flight planning aeronautical charts, Captain Smith and Casey determined that a direct route should be flown from Subic to Kadena. This would be a 1,020-mile journey 'as the crow flies.' They drafted up the proposed route and then filed the flight plan with both the U.S. Navy and Air Force.

Related Casey, "Meanwhile, in the interim, I had an excellent meeting with Admiral Tom Mercer, Commander, Naval Forces. We talked about the trip and what lay ahead. He said he had talked with Admiral Dunleavy and the U.S. Navy would do anything it could to help me complete my mission.

"It seemed that everyone – the U.S. Navy brass and the American Embassy included — were waiting for the Japanese to grant my petition to fly into Japan. The only problem with this picture was that there was no one in the JCAB who would even discuss with the FAA in Tokyo or U.S. Navy in Yokosuka whether a clearance would be issued or not.

"Later that afternoon, a patrol boat escorted me from Cubi Point into the U. S. Navy base at Subic Bay. Once there, I was tied up at one of the navy piers strategically located at the back end of the bay and nearest to land. This area offered the most protection to my aircraft from any high winds, often experienced during typhoons.

"Interestingly, to my left was a large amphibious warfare ship. This type of U.S. Navy ship is a warship employed to land and support ground forces, such as Marines, on enemy territory during an amphibious assault. Captain Smith said it was taking on cargo and would soon be deployed to the Gulf of Oman.

"That night I had dinner with Captain Smith and his wife Carol at the Officers' Club. Carol promised me that tomorrow we would visit the students at the Thomas Dewey High School on base."

Visiting the high school on October 19 proved to be a very exciting one for the students. More than 40 students listened to a summary of Casey's trip to date. "After my short lecture, I visited with seven students who wanted to learn more about aviation and the rigors of seaplane flying. My hope was that many would be pilots someday," explained Casey. He later wrote personal letters to each of those students and Captain Smith promised to deliver them after he left.

Later on that day, Captain Smith offered up a brilliant idea to Casey: "Why not find a way to display on the aircraft all the flags of the countries you had or will visit?" On further discussion with Casey, Smith mentioned there were several excellent Philippine artists on base and, "Why don't we hire one of them to paint all the countries' flags?" Casey was quickly sold on the idea.

As a result, an artist painted each flag directly on the red stripe that encircled the entire aircraft's fuselage. While the artist worked on his plane, Casey changed the oil and filled the oil analysis half-pint bottle which would be sent back to Jack Hammond at Phillips 66. Smith said he would take care of sending the sample to Hammond.

The following day was somewhat uneventful. As Casey was getting his aircraft ready to launch on October 21 for Kadena, he called New York and I explained to him about posing as a member of the Kadena Flying Club. Once in Okinawa I would seek to gain him a further clearance to enter mainland Japan. He really had no idea what we were planning, but I told him the FAA was behind the whole plan and that Captain Smith had thought it was an ingenious idea.

Later that day, he tried on a new flight suit. It featured an array of patches that had been sewn on it and he proudly showed them off when he arrived for a sort-of farewell dinner at Captain Smith's house. At Casey's request, Captain Smith gave a brief recap of his own military career. After flight training, Smith went to a P-3 Orion squadron and worked his way up to become on-board tactical commander in charge of the aircraft's mission. He later went to Scotland and flew with the British Early Warning Air Command. Back in the States, he worked for Admiral Dunleavy and then went on to embassy duty in the Philippines.

Casey was amazed at how fast Smith had advanced to his present rank of Captain. Smith commented that he was very fortunate to have known and worked with the best and brightest in the U.S. Navy. "Oh, let's not forget my brief time on diesel submarines," Smith added.

Dawn came early for Casey on October 21 as he left for Kadena at 0655. Captain Smith; wife Carol; sons Stephen and H.l. Smith; daughter Kelly; an aide to Admiral Mercer; and a U.S. Embassy representative were at the dock to wave goodbye.

Prior to his departure, Casey received a weather briefing from the meteorologist at the Naval Air Station. While Tropical Storm Lola was waning, a new storm, Typhoon Kyle, was building strength in the South China Sea. It was shaping up to become a Class 5 storm with winds of more than 90 to 150 mph.

The other factor about this storm that bothered Casey was that the storm encompassed a several hundred mile wide area and it was also very slow moving. In fact, it almost seemed somewhat stationary over most parts of the South China Sea. With that in mind, the weather people advised him to keep the Philippines on his left and go up to Japan through the Philippine Sea.

This leg of his journey would be long and tedious. He took on almost 150 gallons and felt that this amount of fuel would give him added protection if he needed to stay aloft longer, or if he had to divert away from the tentacles of the cyclone. With a storm that big, he was fully aware that he would feel its effects even if he were several hundred miles from the center.

Casey later related his departure from the Philippines: "It took me about two miles before I got airborne and then I wagged my wings to all those well-wishers who had gathered to say goodbye. Captain Smith had been a wonderful host. Just before I left, he gave me a letter from a student from the George Dewey High School I had visited. 'To my dearest friend, Tom: Good luck on your trip and good luck in your future,' it said.

"I followed the Philippine coastline and, almost as if the navy weathermen were seated beside me, I saw an enormously wide band of weather cells off to my left. I could feel the effects of both the downdrafts and updrafts. About 200 miles from the Philippines, I made an immediate sharp right-hand turn and headed out into the Philippine Sea. I was now running from the storm and had to go at least 100 miles further off course to try and attain calmer air.

"The weather pattern seemed to follow me and the sky darkened almost entirely around me, and it now became apparent that Typhoon Kyle had me in its sights. My aircraft shook like holy hell and the strong winds, maybe 60-mile per hour crosswinds, buffeted me continuously. The sky to my left, maybe 50,000 feet to the deck (top of the water) was totally black. Off to my right, maybe ten miles, the sky was bright blue.

"Almost four hours into the flight, I hit a really hellacious downdraft that slapped my aircraft from 9,000 feet almost to 1,000 feet off the deck. I finally regained control and leveled out at 500 feet off the water. Now I was looking for any visibility, as the rain was pounding on my windscreen so heavy that I almost wanted to stick my head out the window to gain my bearings.

"For the next several hours, it was as if I was on the roller coaster at Six Flags Over Texas. I would rise back to 9,000 feet and then hit another downdraft plus heavy turbulence, and I would ride the coaster back to 1,000 feet.

"After three such episodes, I maintained a close proximity to the water where I finally leveled off at about 200 feet and was only really able to maintain about 50 miles per hour. I headed a straight northerly course at this altitude for about 250 miles; I had unobstructed visibility. About 200 miles out of Kadena, I came into clear weather and went back to 9,000 feet. I could only presume that I had entered the eye or maybe the tail end of the typhoon, but I didn't much care.

"What surprised me was that about 50 miles from Kadena it seemed like I encountered another typhoon, or maybe this was actually the back end of the storm and it had caught up with me. This second time I was spanked again with torrents of rain and hail.

"In fact, I came out of the tail end of the typhoon, a fact later to be confirmed by the U.S. Air Force meteorologist, just about the time I landed near the U.S. Air Force Base at Kadena. Looking back on this leg, I determined that once I had left Philippines Control, I was flying without any reference points or checkpoint. I felt almost blind. Had I wanted to regain contact with any ATC within my flight path, I would have had to climb to 15,000 feet. But that was impossible due to weather conditions.

"I finally picked up voice communications when I was five or ten miles away from my final destination. It was the Kadena Air Force Base tower control. I was given directions to land in the East China Sea and I responded back to the tower that such a procedure would be unacceptable. Why? Because the water was too rough for me to land. I reiterated that this area had just been through the back end of a Class 5 typhoon and as such the seas were cresting to about three feet.

"The tower agreed with me and immediately directed me to fly over the Kadena Air Base and head in a northerly direction for about two miles until I saw the mouth of a river. On sighting, I was to make right-hand turn and land about 200 yards upstream from the river's mouth."

Further, Casey was told to taxi and go around a bend in the river; on the right would be the Kadena Boat Harbor. The harbor was jammed full of sailboats and was difficult to navigate. Several U.S. Navy personnel were to be waiting at one of the small boat docks to tie up Liberty II. From there, Casey would be escorted to the base and provided quarters.

The landing was smooth and Casey was met at the Kadena boat dock. Once driven back at the main base, he was escorted to the BOQ. He was met by Mike Timkin, president of the Kadena Flying Club. Timkin told Casey an interesting story about a C-130 aircraft which had passed very close to Typhoon Kyle.

The pilot described for him how the intense severity of the turbulence generated by Kyle had shaken the nerves of his crew. To verify this experience they were able to take some fascinating photos while skirting its edge. Casey immediately identified with the C-130 pilot's story and told Timkin that the pilot's description was exactly like the intensity of the cyclone he had experienced.

Casey later remarked, "The one comment I found intriguing from the pilot of the C-130 was that there was no such thing as a ceiling with this storm. And they also experienced marginal use of their instruments, similar to what I had experienced."

About two hours after he landed, Casey was escorted to the Commanding Officer's headquarters. A surprise was in store for him. Waiting to meet him at the CO's office was Mr. Arima, FAA Civil Aviation Assistant, U.S. Embassy. He was very forthright and pompous, and in a really high-pitched (girl squeaky) voice said, "You are not cleared to be in Japan."

Casey smiled and told Arima, "I am already here." He further told the FAA dude that everyone (the U.S. Air Force, Navy, and Tokyo Embassy) understood he had permission to enter Japan.

Abruptly turning 180 degrees, Mr. Arima left Casey with his mouth hanging open and then he found a phone to call his boss, Dennis Warth, in Tokyo. Arima began the conversation by stating that Casey was standing in front of him and was already in Japan. Warth abruptly cut him short and said he already alerted Mr. Akira Oono, Minister of Transport at JCAB, that Casey had landed several hours ago in Okinawa.

Unknown to Arima, Warth had previously planned this clandestine step. Also, according to Warth, Oono had been dragging his feet as he had all the right clearance information on Casey including a FAA Special Flight Permit. Now the fun was about to begin.

Casey returned to the BOQ and slept.

On October 22, Casey visited with the Air Force Base commander and U.S. Navy commanding officer, Captain Richardson. Casey wanted both the U.S. Air Force and Navy commands to know the special care he had taken to successfully come through all the unforeseen obstacles so far on this journey.

Briefly the CO iterated for Casey just a few of the key episodes he had been made privy to: There was his back operation; his trying to land on the carrier USS Independence; and his battles with several ambassadors and State Department officials. Richardson seemed much kinder than the Air Force CO and in a very earnest tone told Casey he had followed his flight through the news as well as from message traffic that came from OP-05 (Dunleavy's office) and other U.S. Navy establishments where Casey had visited. Richardson remarked that Casey had left a lasting impression on everyone he had met.

But most important, he and others at the base all believed that Casey was a damn good pilot and should be congratulated for his feat. "I don't think you will be on the same page as Amelia Earhart, but then again you haven't crashed yet," said Richardson laughing loudly. He added that he was kidding.

Casey, almost expressionless, seemed to exhibit a rather demure attitude and just gave Richardson his typical Irish smile. "I've have had a lot of hiccups on this journey but I've made it this far," he said.

During this visit, both men asked Casey how he had managed to get through Japan's Air Defense Identification Zone (ADIZ) without notifying Japan's ATC. For background, ADIZ is the airspace over land or water that, once entered by a civilian aircraft, the identification and location of the civilian aircraft must be declared. This boundary extends beyond Japan's airspace to give the country more time to respond to foreign and possibly hostile aircraft.

Explained Casey, "I never squawked on their frequency and

only used the U.S. Air Force designated frequencies. Those were my marching orders by the Navy and Air Force in Subic Bay when I filed my flight plan. They gave me the military frequencies to use, as my aircraft was officially designated as being a member of the Kadena Flying Club. Believe me, I had been briefed that the only way I could enter Japan was being part of the Kadena Flying Club and I executed this plan according to orders from New York and the FAA in Tokyo.

"There had been designated airways I was supposed to follow into Kadena, but to avoid the full impact of the typhoon I often deviated 60 to 100 miles off the course spelled out in my flight plan. I used my GPS as a guide to head in the direction of Kadena. Finally about ten miles from the outer boundaries of the Kadena air base, I picked up the tower's chatter and was able to make contact for landing instructions."

Casey said he needed to alert Dennis Warth at FAA that he was in Kadena. He asked if he could use the phone to call Tokyo. He asked the embassy operator to connect him to Warth. After being welcomed to Japan, Warth advised Casey that his associate Arima had already alerted him that he was in Kadena. Warth told Casey to just sit tight and everything would work out.

Warth said he had mapped out all the arrangements (landing site, fuel, and lodging) and in the next day or so he would provide Casey all the details. Casey inquired as to why he would not tell him right now and Warth, rather testy, said he needed time for the Japanese to finalize his formal clearance to fly through the mainland. The conversation was over. Casey went back to the dock and worked on his aircraft engine and had the plugs cleaned, engine oil screen cleaned, and the air vacuum filter changed.

Later at 2200 that night, Casey called me in New York. It was only 0800 the same day, October 22. Casey wanted to relate to me what a horrendous trip it had been to Kadena. "The rain was pelting my aircraft and almost beat me to the ocean floor. The winds almost flipped me over several times. Actually, the floats acted as counterweights. I made it safely but that was quite an ordeal," he recounted.

We reviewed Casey's recent conversation with Warth and I told him to expect clearance the next morning from JCAB. Warth had told me the day before that he had a plan that wouldn't fail. Casey stammered a bit but accepted that we had the Japanese situation under control. He then asked about Russia. I told him that by the time he gets to Misawa, I should know one way or another.

Thus, I mapped out his flight plan through Japan:

- October 23 — Arrive Lake Biwa (refuel and proceed to Kasumigaura Bay)
- October 23 — Arrive Kasumigaura Bay (60 miles northeast of Toyko)
- October 24 — Arrive in Misawa (contact Air Force tower for landing instructions)
- October 26-30 — Arrive at Lake Memanbetsu
- Homeward bound – via Russia or Attu

We went over all the details and I updated Casey on all the backchannel efforts by Warth that were being pursued by FAA to obtain his approval to fly through Japan. As to Warth being a bit testy with him, well, it was because he couldn't disclose all the behind the scenes efforts being made since he was immersed in a chess game with the JCAB.

Warth assured me that we now had all the approvals required by JCAB. Russia, on the other hand, was another story. I proceeded to give Casey a quick political science lesson regarding the U.S.S.R., Gorbachev, the Russia/Afghanistan War, and the desire by the Russian people to live in a free society. All factors were coming into play, I told Casey. "Believe me," I stressed, "When I say Gorbachev is not thinking at all about a seaplane pilot and his possible world record."

I explained that I continued to be in contact with U.S. Ambassador Jack Matlock, while Knight was working with the Russian Consulate in D.C. We definitely would have a decision from the Russians shortly, but I didn't have much hope we would receive a positive response.

To reinforce this hard cold truth, I told Casey I was having a close friend in Misawa provide me a big favor. Chief Derrick Johnson would prepare for Casey a comprehensive dead-reckoning course in order to safely fly across the North Pacific Ocean. We ended our conversation with my asking Casey to call me when he got to Misawa and

again later at Lake Memanbetsu. I wished him good luck and told him
that this was one time I didn't have to worry about *Where the hell is
Casey?* He laughed and hung up.

One door closes and another opens — drama was about to
play out the rest of the day for me.

At 1500 on October 22 the phone rang and it was Dennis
Warth at FAA. He was really tired (for him it was 0500 on October
23) but he wanted to tell me the good news: Casey would receive his
formal approval early that day from the JCAB.

Warth said Mr. Oono was really a tough negotiator and strictly
a hardliner to deal with. Oono-san said, "It is our standard policy that
the intended flight plan of a non-Japanese registered aircraft, within
Japanese territory, may or may not be granted by the Japanese Government under Article 127, Civil Aeronautics Law, even if the aircraft
possesses a standard airworthiness certificate of a foreign government.

"Further, our Ministry of Transport, International Air Transport Division, (also) requires ten days before permission is granted for
a flight in Japanese airspace. Additionally, a special flight permission
must be granted to the subject aircraft under Article 11, Civil Aeronautics Law, by the Ministry of Transport, in care of the Airworthiness Division, Civil Aviation Bureau."

Warth emphatically stated to Oono-san that Casey's aircraft
should not be considered a non-Japanese registered personal aircraft
but rather an experimental aircraft and this was a demo flight that
was using Japan's airspace to transit back to the United States. JCAB
permission for this flight should only take one day.

Upon hearing this crucial piece of information, Oono-san
immediately relinquished, and said he would fax Casey his official
permission about 0700 on October 23.

"Pretty good negotiations don't you think, Bill?" Warth
asked.

I responded, "Dennis, remind me never to play poker with
you. And, thank you for all the help. We could not have accomplished
this task without your brilliant assistance."

Warth then added a bit of troubling news. It seemed Oono
cried foul to the Japanese press corps following his call to Warth. Oono
told the *Mainichi Shimbun* newspaper that Casey had entered the

country illegally but gained permission to fly through Japan's mainland based on a technicality. He also laid the fault at the feet of a Mr.
Bill Coleman in the U.S.

Warth said he had an advance copy of the Mainichi newspaper. The October 23 issue featured my name blazoned across the front
page of this publication and, apparently, on many other Japanese dai-
lies. Warth saved the best for last. He read the headline on the front
page of the *Mainichi Shimbun*, which blared: *American Pilot Breaks
Law and SOFA Agreement by Entering Japan Illegally.*

The story went on to tell about how American Tom Casey
flew into Kadena under the false pretense of being a member of the
Kadena Flying Club, and once in Okinawa forced the Japanese to
grant him approval to fly through mainland Japan on his way back
to the U.S. Handling the operation was Bill Coleman along with the
pilot's sponsor, the Phillips 66 Company.

The story also made reference to Coleman and his breaking
the SOFA agreement in 1971 at NAS Atsugi when he held a wartime
demonstration of a new U.S. military aircraft. The demo was aimed
at encouraging the JSDF to purchase this aircraft. The rest of the
story discredited me and the flight, and talked about the loss of face
the JCAB had to endure. It also said Casey would never be welcomed
again in Japan.

There never was any push-back from Phillips 66 on this story.
I think everyone breathed a sigh of relief that Casey gained clearance
to fly through mainland Japan. I promised myself that I would not
try and visit Japan for at least ten years.

Casey would depart that day, October 23. He would take a
northerly heading for a total of 1,015 miles to Lake Biwa, about 60
miles south of Tokyo, and then refuel and head due north to Kasumigaura Bay, about 60 miles north of Tokyo. (While he was flying, I
would be having a good night's sleep.)

Before leaving my office, I needed to fax a memo to Geiger
and Hammond at Phillips 66 in Bartlesville to tell them that Casey
was on his way home. Attached to the memo was our promotion plan
and budget for Casey's homecoming to Seattle, which we anticipated
would be in early November.

We advised Phillips 66 that Russia was still up in the air. We also said we would review future promotional plans for Casey with Jack Hammond once we met in Seattle upon Casey's return.

The plan was straightforward. The invitation list included a host of dignitaries: the State Department; the Washington State Governor; NOAA; the U.S. Navy Chief of Naval Operations; the Chief of Staff of the Air Force; the Saudi Arabian Ambassador; and, a long list of worldwide media representatives. The event would be held at Casey's original departure point: Lake Washington. I discussed the plans with Hammond on the phone and he was well versed in all aspects. He wanted a great speech written for him.

Back in D.C., Knight seemed pleased, and now all we needed to do was take the temperature of the Russians. Knight felt our best bet was my contact with Ambassador Matlock. Thus, I told David that once Casey got to Misawa I would call the ambassador. David said Admiral Engen couldn't do any more and the well was dry of favors from the State Department. In essence, it all came down to this: What could I arrange with the Soviets?

## Thirty-six

# Traversing Japan

*"The greatest glory in living lies not in never falling, but
in rising every time we fall."*
— **Nelson Mandela**


I got to the office early on October 24 and waiting for me was
a lengthy fax from Dennis Warth at the FAA. The contents spelled
out Casey's movements and who Warth had gotten to support Casey's
efforts. According to Warth, Casey had successfully taken off from
Kadena early on October 23. While over Japan's mainland he had
been advised by Japan ATC that he had no permission to land at Lake
Biwa, south of Tokyo, and would have to proceed to Kasumigaura
Bay. Casey had taken on a full load of fuel and, after nine hours of flying, had landed on the bay. He was at his hotel and fast asleep.

Said the fax:

*"He was scheduled today, October 24, to depart for Misa-
wa at 0930 and the flight was only 320 miles and should
take about three hours.*

*As you know, at your request, I asked Mr. Onodera,*

*president, Japan Business Jet Co., Ltd. if he would help
in the arrangements for the flight and he said he would
do what he could. As it turned out, he ended up being
the only recognized agent by the Japanese Civil Aviation
Bureau for the flight.*

*Only with his assistance would JCAB approve the flight
through Japan. Being an experimental flight also helped
gain approval. As Mr. Casey passed through Japan, Mr.
Onodera and his staff reported his position to JCAB and
the circumstances surrounding the landings and takeoffs.
He also took care of the refueling services in the Tokyo
area. The fuel was provided at no cost by another friend
of mine that I also asked to help. Mr. Onodera will also
help with the coordination in the Hokkaido area, but a
different company will be involved with the servicing cost
of refueling.*

*At the embassy we all wish Mr. Casey the best. I hope we
have a chance to talk later after he safely makes it back
home."*

**Regards, Dennis Warth**

Casey would later offer his own version of that day's events.
According to Casey, he departed Kadena at 0900 on October 23. He
faced a seven-hour trip to Lake Biwa, putting him some 60 miles south
of Tokyo.

He had filed his flight plan through the Japanese flight service
center. At about two hours into the flight, as he passed over Kyushu,
the southernmost Japanese island, with about 500 miles remaining to
Lake Biwa, Japan ATC came up on Casey's frequency and inquired
where he was headed.

Casey thought that was a bit odd as he was flying IFR (Instrument Flight Rules) and his flight plan indicated his planned
destination. "You are not cleared to land at Lake Biwa. You have no
permission to land. Continue to Kasumigura Bay," ATC told him.

Casey squawked back and asked for a heading. ATC advised Casey "to turn right 45 degrees and head out to the Japanese Sea. After crossing out over the mainland, head due north 60 miles and make a left hand turn and visually pick up and land at Kasumigura Bay." Casey acknowledged.

Onsite was Mr. Onodera's representative and he tried contacting Casey after he had landed on the bay. He was waving his arms and pointing for Casey to taxi up on a concrete amphibious ramp (for a seaplane with wheels). Casey knew where he wanted to put his aircraft, so he taxied to the right of the ramp about 50 feet and pushed his aircraft up onto the beach. There in front of his aircraft stood Mr. Toyota, who was the representative for Onodera. He had made all the arrangements for the hotel and fuel.

"That night I had time to recount what I had experienced," Casey later explained. "Imagine, I had just flown into Japan. This was my second visit to Japan as I was there in 1972 for the Winter Olympics. Visiting Japan remained a lifelong dream of mine. Now I was seeing this country again firsthand and meeting its people.

"Japan was a very beautiful country. The most magnificent site was Mt. Fuji, which was about 60 miles southwest of Tokyo. I couldn't miss that massive volcano, all white at its peak. This island country has many mountains and volcanoes and the highest is the beautiful Fuji-san at 12,388 feet.

"I saw many agricultural areas and Navy Captain Richardson in Kadena said that roughly 29 percent of Japan is covered in plains, most located along the seacoast. The Kanto Plain, which I flew directly over on central Honshu Island, is the largest, spanning about 6,500 square miles. I saw many valleys and large tracts of land dotted with rice fields. As a whole, the country was very lush and green. Below me were also many large congested highways and for a second it occurred to me that it could have been L.A.

"At 9,000 feet, I could also see many commercial aircraft lining up to land at Tokyo's main airport. I flew over many large cities surrounding Tokyo and, after leaving that giant metropolitan area, the view turned into countryside surrounded by mountains."

The next day, October 24, called for Casey to fly some 320 miles from Kasumigaura Bay to Misawa AFB. He left at 0930 and arrived about 1210. It was a rough departure from the bay but a smooth flight to Misawa. The Air Force tower at Misawa directed him to land at Lake Misawa, which looked much like a small boat harbor. There were many sailboats and other runabouts tied up at buoys in the lake. He was met by a patrol boat and Air Force personnel on board told him to tie up to a buoy.

Upon coming ashore, he was met by about 100 Air Force personnel who were stationed at Misawa. They escorted him to the BOQ. That evening the officers held a reception for him at the O' Club.

During the reception he was given some unpleasant news. The weather guru explained that a severe front from the north would come thundering down on the region by October 26. Casey would not be able to depart for Lake Memanbetsu until possibly October 30. This was a significant setback, as he had wanted to leave for upper Hokkaido by the 26th. Casey had been focused on being able to fly up the Kamchatka Peninsula on the eastern flank of the U.S.S.R. and crossing over the Bering Strait to Nome.

He spent most of October 25 with the weather folks and then clearing Customs and Immigration, which the Japanese had said had to be done prior to his leaving Japan. He was a bit unsure why this had to be done in Misawa and not at his last stop at Lake Memanbetsu. Yet, he donned his diplomatic hat and thanked them for all their hospitality. There was no verbal reply from any of the three Japanese agents.

Thought Casey at the time, "Maybe Coleman and the FAA pissed them off and they blamed me. Good thing I was carrying a message of goodwill — my flight — or I might never have been allowed to fly in their country. I must tell Coleman he needs to be a bit more like me."

As Casey waited out the weather, word came from the Air Force that it might clear up enough by Sunday, October 28, so that he could depart. Meantime, as he watched the rain from the tropical cyclone pour down in sheets on October 26, the wind began to pick up in intensity. The weather vane indicated that the winds had now reached 70 m.p.h. His plane was in the lake tied to a buoy; he could feel sweat pouring down the back of his neck as he conjured up visions of Liberty II being torn apart by the gale force winds. The image

of his first plane Liberty I being torn apart in Reykjavik Harbor in
Iceland captured his senses. The storm lasted three agonizing hours.
Once the weather dissipated on October 27, he surveyed the lake area,
anticipating there might be some damage.

The storm left a path of destruction, with many of the Air
Force-owned boats blown onto the shore. Casey desperately wanted to
see if his airplane had made it through. The aircraft was about 50 feet
offshore; as he eyed the scene, it became apparent that his airplane
was listing to the right.

Several Air Force officers who accompanied him to the lake
had been advised by radio that during the storm one of their airmen
had diligently taken it upon himself to take a concrete anchor and
attach it to a long chain and then secured that chain onto the back
of the plane. The airman did this in order to make sure the aircraft
wouldn't break away from the buoy.

By taking this action, the metal chain attached to the concrete
block wasn't taut enough so the force of the wind turned the aircraft
around about 90 degrees, whereby one of the plane's floats was now
pounding against the concrete anchor. The end result was that the rear
of the right float sustained about 50 small puncture holes.

Recalled Casey, "The only words from me were, 'oh no.'

"An Air force Colonel asked how I knew it was my right float.
Hell, I thought to myself, it's listing to the starboard, so what the hell
else could it be? But I kept my trap shut and out loud said, 'My right
float is down at least two inches below the water line.' I then took off
my shoes and waded out to the aircraft. I grabbed the right float and
felt along its full length. Near the rear, I felt these puncture holes."

Back on shore, Casey asked the colonel how in the hell was he
going to have this fixed in order to continue the journey. The colonel
replied with all the faith of a crusading minister of God that the Air
Force would repair the airplane. "We are skilled mechanics who put
damaged jets back together and make them airworthy. So, fixing your
float will be a piece of cake and no trouble," he assured Casey.

The U.S. Air Force brought a gigantic boom crane to the beach
and lifted the plane out of the water near the shoreline. This was accomplished by attaching the crane's hooks to the four lifting rings on
the top of his aircraft.

Next they brought up a large generator truck that used massive air hoses to dry the beach area. Then they laid down large grated steel mats where they finally put the aircraft. "We need a secure area to work on your aircraft, plus heat up the environment for the guys to work in," said the colonel. Casey just stood there amazed at the whole process of placing his aircraft on the metal mats. At Casey's advice they called Wipaire in Minnesota who explained how to maintain the seal of integrity on each of the floats.

On October 28, the Air Force mechanics' first step was to immediately dispatch a crew who flew to Tokyo and purchased a solid sheet of aluminum. Once back in Misawa, they cut and shaped the aluminum to fit the exact spherical shape of Liberty II's right float. They then took the aluminum sleeve and snugly slipped it over the existing float and riveted it on. By about 1900 that night, the newly resurfaced float appeared brand new. They even had it painted. The repair was finished in about a 12-hour period.

The colonel came to Casey's BOQ room on the morning of October 29 and said that the plane was ready for inspection. It seemed unbelievable that they had finished in such a short time. The completed repairs on the float made it appear as if nothing had ever been damaged. Elated, Casey jumped with joy and told the colonel that the float looked brand new. His personal gear was loaded onto the plane and he went to talk with the weather folks to get all the needed info for the next day's takeoff.

At our New York's office request, Chief Johnson from the Naval Air Station gave Casey a detailed dead reckoning course; a detailed weather outlook for the whole of the North Pacific; and detailed every possible hazard one might face during the flight.

Meanwhile, behind the scenes, much had happened. I called Casey at 2200 that night with bad news. Earlier in the day he had been turned down by the Russians and Mikhail Gorbachev frankly didn't want to play any role in Casey's record-setting trip. I was calling at 0800 his time and some of the conversation was not understood, as the phone connection was extremely poor. I kept strongly emphasizing that if he strayed into Russian airspace he would get his ass shot down. If not shot down, they would force him down and take him to jail while possibly throwing away the key.

Casey was at a loss in trying to understand the situation. Why couldn't his U.S. coordinators convince the Russians to allow him to fly through their airspace? He had the whole flight planned and would have been in Nome in two days. When he got back home he was going to file a protest against the Russians to the State Department, he thought at the time.

*Misawa AFB, at the northern end of the island of Honshu.*

# Thirty-seven

# The Soviets; Engine Problems; and a Plea To Stop the Flight ...

*"I know him well and he is just the kind of man to accomplish such an undertaking. He is apparently without fear and what he sets out to do he generally accomplishes..."*

**— Wilbur Wright**

Casey was tucked away on Misawa. From October 25 on, we frantically tried to push the Soviets to allow our record-setting pilot to pass through Eastern Russia and onto Alaska. Waiting for the Soviet bureaucracy to even acknowledge that we were alive was all we had. I had hoped Ambassador Matlock would have called me back by now. It had been well over two weeks since we last spoke and the ambassador seemed to feel that he would receive a favorable response from the Soviet Aviation Ministry. But with no contact at all and Knight not having any luck on the D.C. front, we firmly believed that the Soviet Union would just say no.

Once again, time to head down to D.C. to meet with Knight. As Casey waited to hear one way or another on Russian passage, David and I tried to strategize on the outcome. We briefed Admiral Engen on Casey's latest escapade of being snuck into Japan and both David and the admiral remarked that I might not want to ever show my face in Japan again.

They asked if Warth at FAA might lose his job and I assured them he was well protected by the ambassador. Also, State and the Navy, who safeguarded Casey in the Philippines, wanted him to succeed. It seemed everyone wanted to have a hand in making sure Casey made it home (although Casey never believed that). We had hoped he realized all the efforts made for him by the U.S. Navy, State Department, Phillips 66, and of course both David and the admiral.

Engen asked about the climate at Phillips 66 and I said Hammond was strongly supportive and on board waiting to hear weekly briefings. The last time I talked to him was when Casey was making his nefarious entry into Okinawa. Jack just laughed and said, "Way to go, Coleman."

By this point in time, we had laid out all the vast promotional plans that we deemed appropriate for Casey's homecoming. Once Casey had lifted off from Lake Memanbetsu in Japan all the individuals who had worked on this project would be coming to Seattle for his homecoming. This included Knight (maybe), Tim McCormack, George Bukota, and Phillips 66 photographer Kurt Maurer. Kyle wanted to stay behind to serve as our conduit to the media and any diplomatic folks. Admiral Engen wouldn't be able to make it, but Hammond planned to be there at least two days before our pilot arrived. (An ambitious side note: Knight was working on getting President George H. W. Bush to welcome Casey home.)

That said, we held off pursuing all our efforts for the homecoming until we definitely knew that Russia was on board to let him fly through their territory. I waited until 0400 on October 29 to call Moscow. My hand was shaking as I picked up the phone. Would the Russians allow him to fly up the Kamchatka Peninsula to Provideniya, which lies directly across the Bering Sea from Alaska? From there, he could make an easy crossing to Nome.

Officially, I was calling U.S. Russian Ambassador Jack Foust Matlock Jr. It was 1200 there. His secretary seemed to know my voice and asked me to hold while she transferred the call. There were three loud clicks (or were they clunks?). Matlock answered the phone and said, "Mr. Coleman, I am in the Premier's office. He is not a happy person."

I could hear Ambassador Matlock explaining to the Premier the reason for my call.

Then I heard Premier Mikhail Gorbachev emphatically say 'nyet' and further, in excellent English, say, "If your seaplane pilot even strays 50 feet into Russian airspace, he will be shot down."

Trying to maintain my wits about me, all I could think to say was "Thank you, Mr. Ambassador" and give him my best, and the same to the Premier. Hell, it didn't take a mental midget to figure out why Gorbachev didn't want any part of an American cowboy flying through his country in a seaplane. Right now he had massive challenges at home and he didn't need one more worry to add to a long list of upheavals going on in his country at that point in history.

One could only imagine the dialogue he must have had with Ambassador Matlock: "What if he crashed?" That scenario could play in the media with an intensity similar to that which occurred in 1983 when a Korean Air passenger jet was shot down over the Sea of Japan.

Now, after a pause from Matlock that seemed like an hour, the ambassador said, "Mr. Coleman, the Premier doesn't want any part of your pilot Casey. Good day." And with that, he abruptly hung up.

One hour later, at about 2200 on October 29th, I called Casey in Misawa with the news about Russia. His reaction might best be described as one of nonchalance, and in a matter-of-fact tone he told me he was leaving for Lake Memanbetsu in Hokkaido the next day. He would immediately refuel and then head directly on to Attu at about 1900 the same day.

I wished him good luck on the newest leg of his journey to Attu and asked if we could touch base when he arrived there. I also explained that while he was flying across the Pacific to Attu, I would be on my way to Seattle to help set the stage for his arrival.

The long, arduous journey was at last coming to an end and soon all involved in seeing this adventure through would have a moment to celebrate. Well, that's what I was thinking at the time. But reality had other plans, and instead the next day would bring with it a sea of catastrophes. It would become a day I would never forget — for all the wrong reasons.

Unknown at that point was a pending catastrophe with Casey's aircraft. The latter came to light from a subsequent phone conversation I had with Dennis Boggs, the technical guru at Phillips 66, who said, "Bill, as the technical director of lubricants at Phillips 66, I can't in good conscience let Casey fly one more mile. We have to shut him down.

"Our oil analysis tests on the oil sample he sent us from the Philippines shows he is making metal. The best thing we can do is to ground him. If we don't shut him down, the engine will seize and he will crash."

His words pierced my senses like being stabbed by a hundred knives at once. We talked further about the tests and I asked Dennis if a compression test on the aircraft's cylinders would indicate the health of the engine. Assuming I could get to Casey in time, I wanted to give him evidence that his engine was failing.

Said Boggs, "Bill, a compression test is fine but it won't tell us why he is making metal. Yes, a compression test may determine if the engine is working right now, but I can't predict what it will do over the North Pacific. He may just crash." There was little point in arguing — Dennis was one of the top authorities on aircraft engines.

I told Dennis I would do what I could and my attention now turned to getting in touch with Casey before he was airborne again. My favorite catch phrase came to mind: *Where the hell is Casey?*

I again turned to Dennis Warth in Tokyo. He said he would help me, and immediately contacted Mr. Onodera, who found out where Casey was being serviced for refueling. He provided Warth a phone number that was passed along to me, and I called the company where the aircraft was being hangared for the evening.

It was now 1500 on October 30 in Japan. No one spoke English, so I dusted off my Japanese which I had learned way back in 1968 while living in Japan. I managed to have someone find the head Japanese mechanic and I asked if he could examine the engine.

I inquired if he could take a thin white cotton cheesecloth (used for drying hands) and drain a small amount of oil from Casey's engine onto the cloth. I asked him to examine the cloth to see if there were any metal particles from the oil residue. As I held on the phone, in silence on this international call, he completed the requested procedure and came back on the phone and said there were no particles visible to the naked eye.

Of course, this didn't mean Casey's engine wasn't making metal, it just meant that there weren't any visible metal particles — at least none large enough to be seen by the naked eye. (According to Dennis Boggs, if the particles were readily evident, it meant the engine had already experienced catastrophic failure.) While this conversation was taking place, Casey just happened to stroll into the hangar. Standing next to his plane, the chief mechanic handed him the phone and said, "American on phone, Casey-san."

After briefing Casey on his aircraft's potential engine problem, at 0100 my time, he responded with an air of indignation. "You really got me worried here at Lake Memanbetsu, especially when hearing some bad news from both the Japanese and you. I'm now extremely concerned. Bill, three Japanese mechanics just approached me and said in very broken English that it appears my engine is making metal. How do they know that? They say I should cancel the flight. They have me stumped. I don't speak Japanese.

"What are we going to do? Do you know of anyone who can translate for us?" Casey asked.

I told Casey I had already spoken in Japanese with the chief mechanic and I would continue to serve as intermediary.

"I didn't know you spoke Japanese," Casey said almost defensively.

"At this point, you confirmed my worst fears." he said. 'You are trying to tell me that one of the cylinders is making metal (meaning the piston was self-destructing). And, you were alerted to this fact by Phillips 66? They are saying there is the possibility of engine failure and they wanted you to advise me to shut down? Where did this info come from? I have been watching the cylinder head temperature on number six cylinder since Saudi Arabia, and I have believed there may be a problem. I know this since I had trouble getting off the river in Calcutta."

I explained that his last engine oil sample from the Philippines was run through a battery of tests in Bartlesville. The completed analysis performed by Phillips 66 technicians showed a presence of metal particles in the oil. They advised that you shouldn't be flying this plane until it could be determined what was causing the metal particles.

"Bill, did the Japs find any metal particles? Or anything at all?" he asked. I said nothing was readily visible.

His reaction: "Since the Japanese didn't find any metal particles, we can only go on what Phillips 66 said they found. Maybe they made a mistake. So, why then are you asking the chief mechanic here to take a closer look at my engine?"

Casey seemed to be mimicking me, and quickly followed that with a tone of defiance. He told me, with disdain in his voice, that he was taking off no matter what Phillips 66 or I advised.

I was now fighting an uphill battle. I got the chief mechanic back on the phone and asked him to perform an engine compression check. If any cylinder had already suffered severe damage, it would show up – that is, the compression test would uncover if the compression of any cylinder had gone down below the engine manufacturer's specs.

I told Casey, "If there is a loss of compression, then you are totally done for the rest of this journey, at least until we can do an engine overhaul." Yet, with Casey being Casey, he remained adamant about continuing onward. From where I sat in New York, the compression test was the only way I could stop him.

The Japanese used sophisticated testing gear to measure the pressure of each cylinder. The mechanics verified the pressure reading using standard ASTM measurements. After more than five hours of testing, the mechanics gave his engine a clean bill of health. The compression checks were all in line with the engine manufacturer's (Continental) specifications.

But a compression test wasn't the total conclusive answer. If we really wanted to know the complete health of the engine, we needed to do a borescope inspection on the cylinders. A borescope would allow the technicians to see the actual condition of the valves, as well as the condition of the cylinder walls and piston. And, this inspection would allow them to see if there was excessive oil, or any corrosion in the cylinder area.

But, the Japanese shop didn't have the capability to conduct such a test. I explained to Casey that I was still queasy about his going forward. He said he was going, but wanted to share that day's experiences with me.

Casey alluded to one earlier mishap — grounding his plane on a sandbar — which he said would never make it into his logbook, and then explained, "I took off from Misawa to Lake Memanbetsu at 1300 and it was a two-hour and 17-minute flight. The landing went extremely well and the Japanese handlers sent by Mr. Onodera's Japan Business Jet Company grabbed my aircraft and parked it up on the lake's shoreline.

"I was met by a horde of TV cameras and newspaper reporters. They all asked when I was leaving and, did I like Japan? I said I would be leaving about 1900 that evening.

"Yes, I love Japan and from the air it is really a beautiful country. Everyone has been extremely kind to me. The rest of the interview had to do with the trip. I did mention Philips 66, but I said the State Department had made this trip so lengthy because I couldn't get clearances."

With that I choked — Casey's continued absurdity of making the State Department the bad guy was getting old. "Casey, I will repeat myself — you just can't say that because it isn't true," I told him. "If it wasn't for the State Department, you wouldn't have gotten this far. Who do you think Dennis Warth, your savior at the FAA, works for? The Russians? I hope when you get home you won't say that stupid comment ever again." I was pissed.

This discussion soon became a moot point. We never did see any stories from that the media at Lake Memanbetsu. Events about to occur would preclude the Japanese from even mentioning Casey's news conference in Hokkaido. But I'm getting ahead of myself.

Casey continued with the story of his day. "At 1920, I attempted to take off. Leaving at night meant a daylight approach to Attu. I was gliding along on the lake's surface for about two miles, in an attempt to step the aircraft into the air, when my floats dug into a sandbar. I stopped dead in the water which threw my back and neck out again. The Japanese never told me it was shallow in the middle of the lake." Casey managed to exit the plane and began waving to several people on the beach. He did this with a flashlight.

"Then, a small craft with a searchlight approached me. Next thing I knew, the Japanese had returned with about 12 husky men (maybe sumo wrestlers?), and lifted and pushed my aircraft off the sandbar. It sounds rather easy, but frankly it took more than four hours to get the plane off the sandbar. So, they took the aircraft into their hangar for the night."

He concluded the conversation with, "Thanks for the update on my plane's engine, but tomorrow I am leaving for Attu. I will not crash!"

After hanging up with Casey, I immediately called back Dennis Boggs and told him the whole conversation. Dennis said that a compression test was OK but didn't really tell the whole story about what was happening in the engine. I added that I had asked for a borescope test but that the Japanese shop didn't have that capability.

"I guess we will find out when he leaves," Boggs said, with a sigh of resignation, adding, "Bill, I don't think we will hear from Casey again. I am afraid he will crash." I told Dennis that I fully understood his thinking. It was now up to God. We wished each other good night and good luck.

The next day, October 31, while Casey was getting ready to fly to Attu, I was winging my way to Seattle. I arrived later that afternoon at Bellevue, Washington and immediately checked with George Bukota for an update on the homecoming event. Then it was off to sleep at 1900 — I hadn't slept in three days.

Casey was one of the last great aviation bullshitters, but he probably was the greatest pilot I've ever met. His last leg of the trip was the most harrowing. Alone, over an ocean with basically only a GPS system programmed at Lake Memanbetsu (he lost satellite contact for about 600 miles), he would fly a dead-reckoning course of almost 1,600 miles from the northern region of Japan's island of Hokkaido to Attu in Alaska's Aleutian Islands. But there were still several more small feats of daring along the way that would make this an even more unforgettable flight.

Recapping a few of his highlights to date: almost stopping carrier operations in the Gulf of Oman; nearly severing diplomatic ties with Saudi Arabia; insulting several Thailand government officials; almost convincing the U.S.S.R. to maintain Cold War relations with the U.S.; straining political relations with the Greek military; and, last but not least, forcibly pushing our State Department into possibly rewriting the U.S./Japanese Status of Forces Agreement (SOFA).

# Thirty-eight

# Russian MiGs, an Aerial Feat, then Mechanical Reality

*"With a short dash down the runway, the machine lifted
into the air and was flying. It was only a flight of
twelve seconds, and it was uncertain, wavy, creeping sort
of flight at best; but it was a real flight at last and not a
glide."*

— *Orville Wright, following his first flight*

It was now approaching midnight on October 30 in Japan.
After Casey's aircraft was refueled, his service providers escorted him
to a nice restaurant for a dinner of teriyaki steak and saké. That night
he stayed in a ryokan (a Japanese inn) and slept on a traditional Japanese bed (Shiki futon). All the time he was being waited on by several
beautiful Japanese women dressed in kimonos.

The next morning, he had a breakfast of fried eggs, sushi, and
green tea. Most of the rest of the day was spent doing odds and ends
on the aircraft. He decided to change the oil and even looked for metal
particles, but found none.

He launched that night at 1905 and got off smoothly from
Lake Memanbetsu. It took him some five miles to launch the bird.
As he later recalled, "As I had a heavy load of fuel, the long takeoff
allowed me to burn off some fuel and that fact helped get my aircraft

into the air safely." As he got airborne, Casey recalled that the last person to take off from this location and fly across the Northern Pacific was Charles Lindbergh.

The lengthy takeoff took almost 45 minutes and, as a result, he was late taking off. Explained Casey, "When airborne, I was supposed to go 30 degrees south, which brought my heading to 120 degrees south. I immediately called Tokyo Approach Control and they advised me that my flight plan had been cancelled. I said, 'What?' I mentioned how long it took to get airborne with a heavy fuel load. I repeated, 'Direct Attu.'"

Tokyo Control said, "Ok."

Casey was told to follow a dead-reckoning course that had been devised by Master Chief Derrick Johnson. Again, had the Russians allowed him to fly up the Kamchatka Peninsula to Providencya, he could have made an easy crossing to Nome.

Not content with the response of the Russians concerning his flight, he decided to test the diplomacy between the U.S. and the Soviet Union. To shave time off this long leg to Attu, Casey decided to cut a corner, so to speak. At 3,000 feet, he veered off his current course heading and flew a new course heading due north, which put his aircraft on a direct line to Petropavlovsk in the Soviet Union.

This defiant action seemed as if he was challenging the Russians and ran counter to what Premier Gorbachev had emphatically warned against. Casey actually was entering the southern edge of Russian airspace off the Kuril Islands.

A Singapore Airlines crew radioed Casey and relayed a message from the Japanese Air Self-Defense Force. The pilot told Casey to return to his previous course heading and to not attempt to cut corners and enter Russian airspace. Too late — by this point Casey had awakened the 'sleeping bear.'

Back in New York, my phone rang at home at 0600 and it was Dennis Warth at FAA. "Your boy has screwed up," he said, vocally shaken. "I have the Russian Ambassador screaming at me. Your hot dog pilot violated Russian airspace and may get shot down by the Soviets. They have launched MiGs. I understand that at this very second the Premier is calling the State Department or maybe even the President. There goes my job. Thanks, Bill."

"Dennis, I can only apologize and I will vouch for you with State that you had nothing to do with this incursion into Soviet airspace," I said. "You have really bent over backwards for me and our pilot."

Casey had made himself vulnerable to the Soviets. Two MiG-25s closed in on his aircraft from behind and then straddled each side of Casey's wings. The MiGs geared down, dropped their undercarriage and actually wing-walked Casey away from Russian airspace and directed him east towards the Northern Pacific. The Russian pilots never smiled or waved but instead kept shaking their heads as if to say, "No way, crazy American." One raised his hand towards Casey, took off his right glove, and made a finger and thumb symbol as to say, "I would have shot you down if you didn't obey our directions."

The other pilot gave Casey the international middle finger salute. Casey knew he had fucked up and now turned away from the MiGs in haste. He turned south again to a 120-degree heading.

About five minutes after turning to escape the Russians, he had reached the first time and distance checkpoint on his dead-reckoning course. He turned to a heading of 055 degrees, which sent him northeast and out to sea. He was now on a direct course for Attu. He turned off his radios.

The flight was now proceeding smoothly and the beauty of the ocean below was breathtaking. There was heavy cloud cover above him, so he stayed at 5,000 feet most of the way. Below him were what seemed like a thousand large searchlights, from fishing vessels that were scanning the ocean.

As he recalled, "After setting in the complete course into my GPS, all I had to do was fly my way across the Pacific. I positioned myself to be just ten miles off the Russian defense line. So in practicality, I flew to Attu by following the Russian coast."

He would have more than 12 hours of flight time across the Northern Pacific before reaching Attu in the Aleutians. The aircraft had a cruise speed of 125 m.p.h. and its 236-gallon fuel capacity furnished a normal range of approximately 12 hours (about 1,600 miles). He would be cutting it close on fuel.

Casey later elaborated to me some of his thoughts as he crossed the Pacific and headed to Attu: "Just eleven more hours. All my engine cylinders seemed to be running smoothly. Those Russians didn't scare me. They were really funny. Again, the U.S. government let me down. Didn't they know who I was and the record I was pursuing?

"While remaining at 5,000 feet, the moon was peeking through the overcast, and its reflection off the water seemed to light the cockpit. The instruments glowed like it was daylight. There was no horizon visible, just the waves below that tossed white caps and sprayed several hundred feet into the air."

An Amelia Earhart quote came to mind, about when she became the first woman to cross the Atlantic:

> *"After midnight the moon set and I was alone with the*
> *stars. I have often said that the lure of flying is the lure*
> *of beauty, and I need no other flight to convince me that*
> *the reason flyers fly, whether they know it or not, is the*
> *esthetic appeal of flying."*

With about nine hours left, he turned his radio back on and raised Singapore Airlines. They said they hadn't heard from him in a while and were glad to hear his voice. Responded Casey, "I related that I was a bit nervous as I couldn't transfer fuel from my left tip tank. This glitch really got my attention, as I didn't think there would be enough fuel to make Attu. Singapore Airlines said they would pass this info to Alaska ATC and wished me luck. There was nothing they could do. After that, I talked to Singapore Airlines about five or six times just to keep my wits about me. I was now getting a great tailwind, which eased my nerves somewhat.

"I remember the navy chief had told me that if his calculations were correct I would hit Attu dead center. He said all I had to do was follow his directions to the letter. My flight path would make use of the simple time and distance formula.

"That meant I would fly a 500-mile "leg" at a specific speed and match that to the time he had calculated to fly that distance. Once I reached that juncture, I would make any recommended course corrections and then begin my next leg.

"There were more than seven legs I had to fly, so I had to pay attention. The navy chief had also supplied me weather info and even the height of the waves along the route. There was about 600 miles where I had no satellite coverage for the GPS, and the chief's dead-reckoning course saved the day."

Subsequently about 1,400 miles into the flight, Casey crossed the International Date Line, so in actuality it was still the same day as when he left Japan. The sun was rising, but extensive cloud cover remained. At this point he knew he wasn't far from the Aleutians — maybe one hour. The navy chief had told him that when the sun came up over the horizon, he should be only some 130 miles from Attu. The glow of the sun and its massive size gave the appearance of covering the whole horizon. The sun's rays were warming his face. The time had come to look for the land that lay ahead. He had dropped to 3,000 feet to run in smoother air.

Maybe everyone was right, he thought — circling the globe made his record even more important. He was really going to do it — become the first person ever to fly a single-engine aircraft around the globe, landing only on water.

The clouds were increasing, and he was back flying on instruments. He had maybe 30 gallons of fuel remaining and he switched from the pontoon ferry tanks to the right-hand wing tip tank. Since he couldn't pull fuel from the left tip tank, he only had a reserve of about 15 gallons of avgas available. He would fix the electrical circuit in the left tip once he landed at Attu, he thought to himself.

He increased his altitude to 5,000 feet to make sure he could clear any mountains at Attu. He finally raised Anchorage Control and asked permission to fly through the Air Defense Identification Zone (ADIZ). This was restricted airspace and was about one-half hour outside of Attu.

After some 20 minutes and still at 5,000 feet, he decided to drop down through the clouds. To his surprise, he was directly over Attu. The harbor is protected on all sides by mountains, so all he had to do was line up on the harbor's entrance, reduce power, and set it down.

He contacted Attu: "This is Liberty II, N1990L, en route from Japan. Attu, how do you read me?"

"Liberty II, this is Coast Guard Station Attu, we read you

loud and clear. Weather ceiling at 4,000 feet with five miles scattered visibility," came the response. He was now in touch with the airport's tower, which provided directions into Casco Cove, which is the harbor adjacent to the Coast Guard station. "Liberty II, make a straight-in approach to Casco Cove. Line up on the harbor entrance. Please state your intentions upon landing," came the instructions.

Responded Casey, "Attu, Liberty II here; I would like to stretch my legs, get a shower, and grab some winks, as I have just flown over the whole Northern Pacific on mostly a dead-reckoning course. Most of all I want to call my handler in Seattle so he can alert the media and Phillips 66 that I have successfully crossed the Pacific and am now on U.S. soil and on my way home. Over."

"Liberty II, your handler has made all the arrangements. In fact, we have been in touch with him and he is on his way to Seattle. He will call you tonight. Over."

"Attu, see you on the ground. Oops, I mean water."

He had flown almost 12 hours through strong winds and over the freezing cold waters of the Bering Sea. The chief had given him a course that was demanding, but one that appeared to hit his mark dead-on. He would have to later figure out exactly how close he came to hitting his end point (Attu) dead-on. His guess was that he was not off by more than 30 seconds, if that. (This would mean that if I had thrown a baseball from Japan and aimed it at the Empire State Building in New York City, it would have directly hit the beacon atop that building.)

"Luckily, only 20 miles to go," he thought. He would take a downwind approach, allowing him to make full use of the 50-mile per hour winds across his wings for maximum lift and maybe make a smooth landing, and maybe show off a bit for the sailors.

"Flying to Attu was the most difficult leg of this journey," he would later explain. "The full moon in spots and strong tailwinds were a big help. The navigation and weather forecasting support assured the safety of the Pacific crossing. In addition, the safety equipment I had on board gave me the confidence I needed."

He wondered if there were many TV cameras awaiting his arrival. He anticipated both CBS and NBC would be there at the dock. He must comb his hair, he thought. He was wearing his new flight suit he'd gotten in the Philippines. He was ready.

"I've made it," he thought smugly to himself. He now had a full view of Attu's mountains through the mist. The harbor, adjacent to the Coast Guard airfield, appeared calm, like glass. He eased the stick back.

Below he thought he saw sailors cheering – well, actually they were just waving. Upon touching down, several Coast Guard personnel helped him pull his plane up onto the beach. It would be easy to refuel from here in the morning. There were no TV people, no reporters. "Why no crowd?" he thought. "Doesn't the world know who I am?"

His prowess at the stick had allowed him to use all his piloting skills to meet the demanding crossing of the Northern Pacific. He had not deviated more than one-half mile or 30 seconds off his intended flight course at any time from Japan to Attu. That meant he had hit his intended landing point, Attu Island, dead-on.

I heard from him later that day at 1530 at the Seattle Hyatt in Bellevue. "Hey, Bill, I made it!" he exclaimed. "I really appreciate your making all the arrangements in Attu. The trip was arduous but I am a great pilot.

"You know, I left on Wednesday, October 31 at about 1900 and guess what? It is still October 31 and it is now 1330. I actually gained a day by crossing the International Date Line. Maybe there is time to shout out to the media, the Navy, Air Force, Coast Guard, Phillips 66, and the world that I landed in Attu and I'll be home in less than four days. I want that brass band and have the President there, too."

I was overjoyed that Casey had made it in one piece and that his plane didn't ditch in the ocean. "Welcome home and get a good night's sleep," I told him. "We have already drafted a news story that you landed safely in Attu. We just wanted to hear your voice before we released it worldwide."

Casey exclaimed, "I promised myself to mention Chief Johnson's support when I talk to the media later. I'm looking forward to a good night's sleep. The Coast Guard is making me a thick steak and that's really great.

"I have only about 1,500 miles to the Alaskan mainland but will fly 600 miles to Atka tomorrow and the following day about 400 to Dutch Harbor. From there, I will head down the Alaska Coast and I will let you know more details tomorrow.

"The mountains in Attu are awesome, but the weather worries me. Winds can often reach 100 miles an hour. And the fog was intense, so getting my bearings tomorrow depends on the Coast Guard. But tonight I have a welcoming group of 20 sailors wanting to hear all my tales. They won't believe half of it."

Casey finally got to bed at 0200 after some great chow and also many hard stiff drinks accented by his many air and sea stories. Before closing his eyes, he took time to write down a few notes about his impending takeoff the next day.

In particular, he needed to pay attention to 'williwaws,' which are sudden blasts of wind which can sweep down from the mountains and can quickly reach gale proportions. They are hard to predict, even for the Coast Guard, and they can stir up columns of spray and mist that resemble high waterfalls – not a good thing for a float plane attempting a takeoff roll.

Meantime, in my own discussions with the Coast Guard I learned that Casey had drunk the island dry and had 'finally shut up' at 0200. But he was the toast of Attu. He arose at 0800 and got his pre-flight check and refueling with 100LL. As he departed Attu, Casey saluted the shore flag, slammed his power stick to full power, and was off the harbor and airborne by 1030.

"My takeoff was beautiful," he would later recall. "Liberty II had full power and stepped up to the task — we were airborne in less than ten minutes. The weather was perfect. I climbed to 5,000 feet and headed due east. The beginnings of the Aleutian Islands lay to my left as I now flew directly over the U.S. Air Force base on Shemya Island."

Then it happened — Liberty II's engine shut down. It happened about 20 miles from Kiska Island. All of a sudden there was silence, except for the wind whistling across the aircraft's wings and fuselage. He went from 5,000 to 3,000 feet and realized he had no forward thrust.

He was going to have to make an emergency landing in the ocean. His mind raced as Liberty II descended in a somewhat controlled attitude toward the water below. He tried the radio: "Anchorage, Mayday! Mayday! This is Liberty II and I am about 200 miles

east of Attu, just off of Kiska Island. I am going in. Mayday! Mayday!" All his instruments were non-responsive, which indicated no
compression.

He had no time to give course information. He was pulling on
the stick to try to regain control. He knew if he was forced to land,
the westerly wave direction would most certainly smash and crush
the plane. The wave height and direction were against him. He pulled
back on the stick and pulled the nose up and the aircraft came over
the top. Then he rotated the aircraft and went from being inverted
to an upright position – that is, he did a 90-degree left hand climbing
turn and came back upright like a kayak.

The maneuver was much like the famous chandelle — a climbing turn while maintaining a constant airspeed. He also had to push
the nose to get a proper landing attitude. He had to turn into the
wind. Interestingly, when flying a floatplane, it is almost impossible to
pull off a rollover.

He still had some hydraulics and gave it full flaps. Having regained control of the plane's descent, he was now settled in and came
down at a 45-degree angle of attack. "To this day, I am convinced
that it was the 45-knot tailwind that saved my life," he would later
explain. "As I turned into the wind, I slapped the stick to the left and
went into a 40-degree bank. It was a dead-stick landing, with the prop
windmilling."

Ocean swells from ten to 30 feet high hit the plane as it stalled
into the water. The chop was five to six feet between swells. Casey's
aircraft hit the first chop with little or no damage. The second one
seemed to pull his plane apart. The left pontoon jutted upward and
the propeller tore into it. But the plane stayed afloat and, actually,
saved his life. He described it like it was bobbing around like a cork.

Casey later reflected on the experience once he hit the water ...

"From the time the engine quit to my hitting the water was
about five short minutes. I hit the ocean with a heavy force. The
aircraft slammed into the water in a slightly nose-high attitude, and
finally the tail settled in.

"The left wing at first seemed to rest on the water's surface,
but after about 30 seconds it came back to its original position. I
wanted a quick look at my plane. I opened the copilot's right door

to assess the damage. After about two minutes, I closed the door, grabbed my preserver, put on my survival suit, and waited in the plane. My aircraft somehow stayed afloat and acted as my life raft. If I had gone into the cold water I would have only lasted a few minutes. I prayed.

"I checked my Emergency Locator Transmitter (ELT). The airplane's ELT was not working so I used NOAA's ELT to send out my emergency call. I turned on the emergency radio transmitter.

"My first thoughts after that spectacular landing were about how the plane looked. I knew the Coast Guard would pick up my distress signal and immediately send help to rescue me – or so I hoped. I still wanted to survey my plane more closely and this time I exited the left side door and stood on the pontoon to get a clear view of any possible damage. The plane looked amazing for such a hard landing. Only damage, it seemed, was the gash in the left pontoon made from my swirling prop on landing. The pontoon appeared to be holding its integrity, so I shouldn't have any problems about not remaining afloat.

"Time to wait. Time to remember. Hell, I have just completed the most demanding leg of this journey — possibly I flew a more daring leg than any living or dead pilot. I just flew from Japan to Attu. Didn't need the Russians. Hell, they didn't want me in their country anyway.

"I'm now alone. Looking around all I see is the vastness of my surrounding. No land in sight. Alone in the Pacific Ocean in really rough and cold waters. The temperature outside must have been about 10 to 20 degrees Fahrenheit and I wondered how long that engine heat in my cabin would last.

"What if no one finds me? Oh, that is absurd as my distress beacon is transmitting. But truly I'm scared as I have never been in such a fix before. What if someone comes and they refuse to take my plane? I've heard stories where the CG rescued the pilot and scuttled the boat/plane. My plane is in good shape. I need it. And, it's worth a lot of money.

"So many miles taken, step by step. All the medical pain I've endured. Who could forget the confusion with governmental red tape? And most of all the effort I've put into this flight. Who can I really tell about all I've been through? Now so near, yet so far.

"This god-awful solitude, I must shake myself to avoid a worst-case scenario. Good thing it's light. I'll just look to the horizon and see if anyone appears.

"This is the most desolate spot on earth. But at least I made it back into United States airspace, although I still have 3,000 miles to complete the record.

"After about the first 30 minutes, the most important thing I had to do was actually control my mind. Immediately, I realized that my best weapon was a pencil and paper to record every event I had faced and may probably face in the next several hours. My first exercise was to put down the 20 most important survival principles. Then I realized that many of these were not in the right order. I kept up this exercise.

"After about one hour of waiting, a Coast Guard aircraft got in contact with me on my ELT. I knew now I would be saved. The CG said they had my location pinpointed and would be on scene shortly.

"Shortly became three long hours of waiting in the cold waters. Getting a bit worried...no, I have to stay positive. Wait, I hear a roaring sound. Oh my god, it is a C-130 and it has the tail marking of the Coast Guard!"

Joy overcame him. Casey climbed out of the cabin and waved. The C-130 dipped its wings in Casey's direction. He was well aware that those three hours he awaited help were filled with apprehension.

"I'm saved. But what is next? I kept up the conversation with the C-130 on my radio for the next several hours. I guess I now have to just wait for a rescue," he recalled. "Two hours passed since the C-130 arrived overhead. How long can they stay on-station? What if they run low on fuel and have to leave?"

Those succeeding hours were spent hoping that a ship was en route to him. His plane had been afloat for five hours — how could it stay afloat given these weather conditions?

As the sixth hour approached, the swells grew larger and the wind was howling and gusting at more than 60 miles per hour. Would the weather cooperate? He was hungry, thirsty, and cold, and much of the excitement of the C-130's arrival had worn off. The sun was departing and it was becoming twilight. There were only seven and one-half hours of sunlight this time of the year.

Like a miracle, off to the southwest, the horizon lit up like an early morning sunrise. What made this so startling was that it had been turning pitch-black and now it was all lit up around him. Is it the Coast Guard or a civilian craft? As it drew near, it became obvious that it was a fishing vessel. The C-130 was leaving. Is this fishing craft his rescuer? They stopped and began launching a pram (an aluminum dingy).

Explained Casey, "My most immediate thought was that once I am aboard the fishing vessel, I will demand they bring my plane aboard, too. God, I am so lucky."

Meanwhile, an early afternoon CNN Headline News report said that the Coast Guard had pinpointed the area in which Casey's plane had crashed. His distress call was used to track him and the Coast Guard estimated it would take their C-130 several hours to spot and reach his aircraft.

About four hours later, CNN reported that the Coast Guard said, "The C-130 is hovering over Casey's plane in the Northern Pacific Ocean near Kiska Island. Our spokesperson, Lt. Susan Hargiss, said that Casey had alerted the Coast Guard Search & Rescue at Juneau shortly after 1330.

"Casey's aircraft went down about 22 miles west of Kiska Island and was spotted by the C-130, which was responding to a distress signal from Casey's emergency NOAA multinational search and rescue locating device called an EPIRB.

"The C-130 found Casey at about 1600. Hargiss told the media that Casey was unharmed and remained with the aircraft while the C-130 crew hovered above.

"Casey was very lucky and he will get help very soon. The C-130 will maintain its position until Casey is picked up either by the Coast Guard Cutter Sherman, which is 200 miles away to the east, or a fishing vessel which is within 40 miles west of his aircraft."

The Search & Rescue desk in Juneau commented again on CNN about 1730 and said, "We were alerted that some seven hours after Casey ditched in the ocean, the fishing vessel 'Judy B' appeared and rescued him. It was a 120-foot trawler out of Dutch Harbor."

CNN also reported that the ship's captain later told reporters why it took so long to reach the downed pilot. "We had to cut all our nets to be able to rescue Casey," he said.

According to press reports, a boom type device with long cables was lowered by the deck crew. They attached the cables to the aircraft's lifting rings atop the wings and actually hoisted the plane out of the water and onto the vessel's aft end.

Later, following more than 12 harrowing hours both in the water with his plane and now on the deck of the Judy B, an Associated Press reporter contacted Casey while he was still aboard the boat. In a very short conversation with the reporter on a ship to shore radio, Casey replied as to how he was by feeling: "I am exhausted but my plane saved me. The Coast Guard found me and the Judy B saved me and my plane. Just imagine the sight of my red, white, and blue, 28-foot long floatplane tethered to the aft of a fishing vessel.

"What a sight. I was saved and so was the Liberty II. My rescuer, the trawler Judy B, is heading to Shemya Island, where I will now find refuge," Casey told the world.

His life on Shemya was about to begin.

*Casey's damaged plane after being offloaded from the Judy B, between Shemya and Nizki Island.*

# Thirty-nine

# A Crash "Heard Round the World"

At around 1330 on November 1st I was peacefully sitting in a Seattle hotel room and waiting for several of my staff to arrive. Casey's homecoming required our immediate attention. My phone rang and I thought it was George Bukota, my guy in Seattle. No, it turned out to be Commander Fletcher of the United States Coast Guard.

"Mr. Coleman, I have bad news and good news," Fletcher said. "First, the seaplane pilot you have been taking around the world has crashed just off Kiska. The good news is that our C-130 aircraft has located him and he is safe. He is still aboard his plane and waiting for rescue, either by a Coast Guard Cutter or maybe a nearby fishing vessel."

My brain shut down momentarily — I was in shock. For me the flight was over – and, what an ending. But on the positive side Casey's plane was afloat and he was inside the aircraft awaiting rescue. Commander Fletcher added that a Coast Guard C-130 would maintain its position over Casey's plane until he was rescued and on board a rescue vessel. The possible rescue scenario was anticipated to be made by either the CG Cutter Sherman or a fishing trawler named the Judy B, located in the area. I was told the CG cutter was about 200 miles from him; the fishing vessel was significantly closer — only 40 miles away.

"Maritime law stipulates that when a distress call is received, the closest vessel — whether it's a fishing boat or freighter — is required to respond to the emergency," Fletcher explained. "Further, if he is put aboard the Sherman, they will probably sink his plane. That, too, is the law." Fletcher said he would call me later with any additional information. (We did not hear from the CG Commander until some two hours later.)

Immediately after hanging up the phone with the Coast Guard, I returned to watching CNN's "Headline News". Casey was the lead news item. The reporters were providing more updates, generally at hourly intervals. For Casey, myself, and my staff, all hell had broken loose.

At that point there was a loud banging on the door. There in my doorway stood my staff who quizzically asked, "Have you heard the news?" They had learned of the crash upon arriving at the Seattle airport. "What is the latest, boss?" said McCormack.

Standing there in somewhat of a haze, all I could utter was the fact that Phillips 66's lubricants expert Dennis Boggs was right. He knew Casey's engine would fail. He just didn't know when. Thank God it was near a U.S. island; but still, he had ditched in the North Pacific and I could only imagine it was freezing cold. We contacted NOAA and they said the normal water temperature near where Casey was located ranged from 35 to 42 degrees Fahrenheit.

We hoped, rather prayed, that his plane could be salvaged. It was our understanding that the Coast Guard generally saved just the person and not the craft. We all just sat quietly and fixated on CNN. Yet, all we seemed to be hearing was the same news story over and over again for more than six hours. The three Seattle network TV stations were offering a similar refrain: "*Round the world pilot ditches at sea and found by Coast Guard and is now awaiting rescue.*"

Getting a real update was seemingly taking forever. Reporters kept calling me and all I could tell them was what they already knew. I did offer that perhaps once Casey was safely on board a rescue vessel, they could talk to him by radio.

Meanwhile, inwardly, the naked truth of what had happened was quite apparent. I deduced that the cause of the accident was a burned number six piston or cylinder which had caused an uncontrolled detonation in his engine. Such a destruction of the number six cylinder likely brought about catastrophic engine failure. We knew Casey had complained about the high temperatures he had experienced during takeoffs in Jeddah, Karachi, Bombay, and Calcutta. In those instances he noted increased cylinder head temperature (CHT) of the number six cylinder. But again, he later had stressed that the engine was running smoothly in the Philippines and Japan.

My hardest calls were to Hammond and Boggs. Both had seen the TV news. (Who hadn't?) Hammond asked if this accident could have been prevented.

"Yes," I said. "Dennis Boggs wanted to shut the flight down when Casey was in Hokkaido." I related to Hammond what I had tried to accomplish at that juncture with the Japanese mechanics. Even after all those efforts, Casey was not willing to shut the flight down.

"Jack, it was Dennis' opinion that he didn't think Casey would make it across the Pacific."

"What is going to happen to Casey and the plane?" Hammond asked. I told him that I didn't know.

Hammond told me to call with any updates. "And let's hope the Coast Guard doesn't scuttle Casey's plane," he said with an undertone of exasperation.

Then Boggs got on the phone. I knew he must be wanting to shout loud and clear, "I told you so but no one listened." Yet, he was also very sympathetic to my dilemma. He sensed how much I was hurting, and also knew I was going to have hell to pay with Phillips 66 management.

"Bill, as soon as we find out where Casey is going and if they saved the plane, we need to get our hands on that engine," said Boggs. "Phillips 66's reputation is hinging on examining that engine. Let me know." And with that, he hung up.

Geiger at Phillips wasn't so sympathetic when we spoke, and said that both of us would probably get fired. He did add that he was still in possession of the document he had previously shown to the promotions manager that specifically stated that he hadn't approved the project in the first place, and that the whole effort was totally Jack Hammond's responsibility.

Then Geiger, like a true friend, added, "Bill, I wouldn't want to be in your shoes right now. But if there is anything you need call me at any hour."

Next on my call list was David Knight in D.C. Of course, I had no answer to any question he posed and I must have sounded like a drunken sailor when he asked when I would know. I had no idea on how the events were going to unfold – heck, I was having a hard time even remembering my own name at this point.

Knight laughed sympathetically and said he would call Engen regardless of the lack of information. He would later relate that Admiral Engen was in total disbelief about Casey's plight, and had hoped that Casey did not suffer from hypothermia, and that his plane hadn't sunk.

As we awaited any news, dinnertime approached and we decided to try a swanky restaurant across the street from the hotel. I remember walking up a large spiral staircase. The interior decor reminded me of an establishment in the Wild West. Starving, we seemed to order every item on the menu. The guys drank the place dry.

After signing an $800 bill, I went back to the hotel and then right to bed, but didn't sleep for long. At 0100, November 2, the phone rang loudly. This time it was Vice Admiral Richard Dunleavy, calling to tell me the latest in our saga. It turned out that Casey had been picked up by the Judy B and the fishing vessel's crew had secured his plane on the back of their ship.

"He is going to be taken to Shemya Island where he will be temporarily housed for the foreseeable future," explained Dunleavy. "I have heard from both the Coast Guard Commandant and the Air Force Chief of Staff and both are wondering, or maybe trying to figure out, what to do with him.

"General Merrill McPeak, the Air Force Chief of Staff, told me that Shemya Island is a top secret Air Force intelligence gathering facility and it is not SOP (standard operating procedure) to shelter or take care of a downed civilian seaplane pilot.

"Here is the gruesome truth, Bill: McPeak said that if it wasn't for the huge press following this world record pilot has garnered, plus the continued support by the State Department, the Coast Guard would have scuttled his aircraft and shipped your pilot's ass back to Anchorage on the U.S. Cutter Sherman."

As always, Dunleavy was very straightforward with me.

"Coleman, you must have been something when you were in the navy," he continued, laughing. "Captain Tuterville, your old classmate, said you were hell on wheels."

We talked for a while longer, focusing more on the political climate in D.C. "Lots of cuts coming," Dunleavy acknowledged.

I admired him greatly. (As an aside, in 1991 he took the fall for the supposed fiasco at the Tailhook Association Symposium in Vegas. He received a letter of censure; was demoted to rear admiral, and retired. Seems like Congress had to punish someone, but in reality they should have been minding their side of the street.)

I thanked the admiral wholeheartedly for all he had done for us. He had been my Rock of Gibraltar and had bent over backwards many times for Casey and me. "Admiral, I will call you with any significant updates. But, you may hear the news from insiders before me as news travels down the hall in the Pentagon. Goodnight, admiral."

A few hours later, about "zero-dark forty," when many people are just going to bed, Kyle MacDonald called me to say that Dennis Warth was a bit pissed at Casey for skipping out on his bills in Japan. She read me the letter:

*Dear Mr. Coleman:*

*I just received a phone call from Mr. Onodera, President, Japan Business Jet Co. He informed me that Mr. Casey departed Hokkaido without paying for the fuel service or hotel costs. I am sure there is a misunderstanding, possibly language problems, involved in the situation. In any case, the bill must be paid.*

*I am sure that Mr. Casey fully understood the magnitude of how Mr. Onodera helped him. Mr. Onodera does not expect remuneration for his total services even though his company spent many "days" helping Mr. Casey.*

*Since the Hokkaido bills were not paid, Mr. Onodera's company has lost "face" with the Hokkaido refueling*

*company who serviced Mr. Casey. I also feel bad as I was
the individual that asked Mr. Onodera to help.*

*As I recall during our conversations, you informed me
that any reasonable cost would be borne by you and/or Mr.
Casey's sponsor, while Mr. Casey was in Japan. I related
this to Mr. Onodera in good faith. Mr. Onodera indicated
that the fuel and hotel costs are close to $1,000.*

*In view of the above, please contact Mr. Onodera and
resolve this problem. I would appreciate a fax to me on the
status of action taken.*

*Regards: Dennis Warth*

Kyle agreed to draft a letter to Mr. Onodera and apologize for
the oversight. It would explain that funds would be wired immediately. A copy of the letter and an apology to Dennis Warth would also
be sent. I thanked Kyle and said that yet another major diplomatic
disaster may have been averted — I think. Kyle just sighed. She asked
how the calamity was looking and I filled her in on all the calls.

Later over breakfast on that same ugly morning of November
2, Tim McCormack recommended that we draft a news release that
formally detailed Casey's unexpected ditching in the ocean and outlined the rescue steps put into action by the Coast Guard and others.
We mentioned the Judy B fishing vessel and Coast Guard C-130 and
Cutter Sherman. This story was a natural follow-up to our October 31
news release, where we had heralded that Casey had made it across the
North Pacific from Japan and had landed at Attu.

This harrowing news story about Casey ditching his aircraft
went out by mid-morning that day. It was just our bad luck that the
Associated Press followed our story with its own version that headlined, "Round-the-world pilot ditches plane."

Based on the conflicting information we had from the Coast
Guard and the Air Force, our news story we released was somewhat inaccurate. We said the C-130 reached Casey in five minutes. In reality it
took more than four hours. Our time sequence of when Casey ditched

was off by three hours.

Meanwhile, my staff and I all had lunch together and we continued to monitor the news. We wondered if Casey had stepped foot on Shemya Island yet. Calls continued from the media and we kept telling them we had no more information.

Inwardly I wanted to hide in a closet and forget we had ever met Casey. My mind raced: How did all this happen? How did I get involved? Where the hell is Casey?

I recall having a nervousness in my gut as we were about to release our second news story. Sure enough, the final proof released to the media included the incorrect assertion that Casey had made an "unplanned water landing." I blame that inaccurate piece of information directly on the feet of my boss, Al Hirsch, as he didn't want to piss off the Phillips 66 promotions manager and possibly lose the account. Casey's engine had failed! No one, it appeared, wanted to highlight that reality.

That piece of misinformation only served to fuel the fires of mistrust from the media, which in turn led to more intense queries from the editors. In general, they now forcefully asked: What the hell happened to Casey's plane? Did the pilot crash? Did his engine fail? Why did he crash? Is he alive? Where is the Coast Guard? What will happen to him and his plane? You are Phillips 66 and now you are trying to cover up this incident. Come on, what really happened?

The Coast Guard rang me early on the afternoon on November 2 to confirm that Casey and his plane were indeed on the Judy B. The fishing vessel would probably reach Shemya later that day. After speaking with Hammond and Boggs at Phillips, we sent out an updated (third) and more accurate news release within a couple of hours.

Prior to putting this news release out (at my urging) I had my boss send Geiger a memo confirming what I had been emphatically saying all along: "Casey had told the Coast Guard that it was undetermined engine trouble that forced him to ditch in the ocean." I wanted this information in the third news story but also wanted Phillips 66 to approve this language.

In the news story, we paraphrased a very recent Coast Guard phone call report to us that acknowledged Casey was safely aboard the Judy B and was headed to Shemya Island for safekeeping. More importantly, I was not going to be viewed by the media or by our clients in Bartlesville (Phillips 66) as someone who would dare to put forth a mistruth. We had done that injustice in the wording of our second news story.

As a result, following the release of the third news story, we now talked to editors with greater authority and confidence that the information we were providing was correct. To wit: Casey had experienced engine failure and we would be conducting a full engine analysis to determine the cause of the accident. The editors had been apprised that Casey and his plane were heading to Shemya. Once he arrived there, we would arrange with the Air Force to help us remove the damaged engine and then have it shipped to an appropriate engine overhaul facility for a subsequent tear-down analysis.

Most importantly, at a later date we would advise the media when we had the complete picture of what happened with the engine.

As that situation began to settle down, I received a most stressful call in the early evening from Bernie Coleman at Engine Components International (ECI) in San Antonio. (Bernie was no relation — just a good friend.) The new engine technology which had been integrated into Casey's engine for the purpose of protecting the cylinders had come from ECI. Bernie wanted the engine right away to determine the cause of the engine failure. Beside the goal of uncovering the exact cause, he also emphasized that ECI wanted to "get ahead of any speculative reporters that might serve as a deterrent to our marketing this new technology."

Bernie explained that he was shipping out to Alaska a specially reinforced crate that would protect the damaged engine. The crate would be marked to my attention in Anchorage. Once in Anchorage, he wanted me to get the crate on a Reeve Aleutian Airways flight to Shemya. "Tell Casey to put the existing engine in it and send the crate back to me. I want you to make all the arrangements. Can you promise me that, Coleman?"

I told Bernie that as soon as I heard from Casey I would alert him regarding the arrival of the crate and for him to place the existing engine in it. I would make all arrangements with Reeve Aleutians Airways. That night, we all made it to bed by midnight with the exception of Kurt, who had left that afternoon for Bartlesville.

The next morning, November 3, was peaceful until about 1100 when I received a call from a colonel who worked for the U.S. Air Force Chief of Staff, General Merrill McPeak, at the Pentagon. I was told that Casey was being held in a secure top secret location and that the Air Force had not decided what to do with him or the plane. Had this trip not been given worldwide media and diplomatic coverage plus his political pull, I was told that Casey's aircraft would have been thrown in the Pacific Ocean.

The colonel asked me what I intended to do about Casey and his plane. Stuttering, as I hadn't the faintest idea of what to actually do with Casey other than have him stay on Shemya until his plane was fixed, I responded, "Help him finish the record." There was silence from the colonel until he abruptly said, "We'll see about that." Nothing more was added; the colonel did wish us luck.

By this time it was now early afternoon. I received a call from Captain Patrick O'Brien of the Judy B. It was a ship to shore radio call transferred through the U.S. Coast Guard frequency in Juneau. O'Brien wanted to give all the details of Casey's rescue.

O'Brien excitedly related, "It was close to midnight on November 1 when we finally got Casey and his plane aboard our vessel. We put a pram into the water and rowed it up to Casey's aircraft. He got aboard the pram and we brought him to our ship.

"The swells were about four feet high and undercurrent from the waves was so rough that the pram swamped. It took us forever to bail the tiny dinghy out.

"Casey stood on our fishing vessel's deck like Lord Nelson did overseeing the Battle of Trafalgar. Almost in tears, he said he was not leaving his aircraft for salvage. He pleaded with me to take aboard his aircraft. He explained he could direct us on how to take it aboard and said he was an experienced fisherman who some years ago did do aerial scouting for a large fishing fleet.

"We asked him how he would get his plane onto our fishing vessel. Casey explained that he would first have the plane placed onto the vessel's deck. Next, with the help of the ship's boom, he would have it secured to the aft area where the fishing nets are usually stored.

"Casey then picked up two metal cables and said they could

be attached to the plane's lifter rings atop the aircraft's wings. The other ends of the cables were bolted together and attached to the vessel's loading boom. He said that the boom could now lift the aircraft from the water, lower it to the vessel's deck, and then safely secure the aircraft to the vessel's aft. After that we could make for Shemya.

"Mr. Coleman, it almost went smoothly. But when the boom dropped the aircraft on the Judy B's deck, the strut that supported the left float and attached to the left wing had snapped. It was apparent that one end of the strut had punctured the engine's firewall.

"Now here is the crazy part of this episode. Once the plane had been secured and on the deck, Casey rubbed each part of the aircraft's body like it was his own child. My crew was amazed at the love he showed.

"After demonstrating his love for his plane, Casey explained to me that he also needed to fix the damage to the left float that had been sliced open by the prop cutting through it after ditching in the ocean. Staring at this plane — now a fixture on the aft end of my Judy B — Casey seemed resigned to his fate and went below deck and slept during the three-hour trip to Shemya.

"We reached Sheyma late afternoon on November 2," Captain O'Brien continued. "The Air Force directed us to anchor in a calm harbor on the northern side of the island. This area was directly opposite to the ocean side. Once anchored, the Air Force informed us they needed to make the beach area secure. Why? Seemed there were mines buried all over the beach. These had been laid during World War II. No one ever dug them up and no one ever used this part of the beach. But the Air Force determined this was the safest place to off-load Casey's plane, and they didn't want the mines to explode or blow up the plane.

"The Air Force actually laid down more than 30 sheets of marine grade plywood on the sand. This procedure took most of November 2 and Casey just slept aboard that night. We waited offshore until first light to extract Casey's plane from our boat. By mid-morning on November 3, the beach was cleared."

According to Captain O'Brien, the next step was to bring the aircraft ashore. The captain and crew invented an ingenious pulley system. The captain told me to think of a giant letter Y. The two shorter ends were each attached to two crank pulleys on the beach. The operators then slowly pulled the aircraft ashore from the Judy B.

Once the aircraft was on the beach, Air Force personnel brought up a giant boom truck (probably used to lift large aircraft). They lowered the crane's massive hook and attached it to Casey's plane. Once attached, the aircraft was lifted off the plywood mats and set down onto a large flatbed truck.

Said Captain O'Brien, "Believe me, this operation plus the cost of my rescue of Casey must have totaled well over $3 million in labor, lost revenues from fishing, and use of planes, boats, and machines. I think this estimate is low, but this effort at Shemya by the Air Force was the biggest military operation I have ever witnessed.

"They actually drove the aircraft up a steep road to the top of the island. The steep climb angle must have been close to 45 degrees, with at least a 300-foot uphill climb. Mr. Coleman, the sight of a white airplane almost hanging off the end of a truck driving up a volcanic mountain — to where, I don't know — looked like a movie set for some action thriller.

"My crew kept saying, 'Did you see that, Captain?' God Almighty, this must have cost Uncle Sam a fortune. Maybe they can help us recover some money we lost by cutting our nets.

"This was a show we will never forget," O'Brien continued, catching his breath. "All the crew wished Casey good luck. I figure we lost about $500,000 from cutting our nets; plus time not fishing. We hope the insurance company will pay. But we had to pick up Casey — it is the law of the seas."

I thanked the Captain of the Judy B and told him I hoped to meet him someday. He wished us well with the rest of Casey's adventure.

Casey later related that upon his arrival on Shemya he was met by a U.S. Air Force official who said this was a top secret base. "Normally, we don't take visitors, but we already had prior approval for you and your plane to be stowed here," said the official. Apparently, the head of the U.S. Air Force gave the approval, or so he was told. In fact, at least 50 Air Force personnel were watching the events unfold.

Eventually Liberty II was put in a secluded hangar away from the main base area and Casey was told that someone would meet with him later. Our marooned pilot was now on Shemya, or 'the Rock' as it was called in Air Force circles.

Casey didn't call me (at the Seattle hotel) until mid-morning November 5. Upon hearing his voice, these David Bowie song lyrics resonated through my head:

> *This is Ground Control to Major Tom*
> *You've really made the grade*
> *And the papers want to know whose shirts you wear*
> *Now it's time to leave the capsule if you dare*
>
> *This is Major Tom to Ground Control*
> *I'm stepping through the door*
> *And I'm floating in a most peculiar way*
> *And the stars look very different today …*

It was really great to hear his voice. Casey then proceeded to go through all the details of his harrowing adventure. I related that I had heard most of this same tale from Captain O'Brien, but without his embellishments.

"Oh yes, he did say he spoke with you. What really has me pissed is the base commander, Colonel — can't remember his name, but I refer to him as Colonel Klink from 'Hogan's Heroes' — well, he wants to throw me back into the sea. He said I can't stay," Casey moaned.

I told Casey not to bother with the politics as we had his back. I told him Air Force Chief of Staff McPeak was on board. I further explained that I still hadn't talked to the State Department since his final arrival on Shemya as most of his great adventures in the Pacific Ocean happened during the weekend.

Then I was able to share some good news: "Wiplinger said he would immediately provide a replacement engine so you can complete the more than 3,000 remaining miles for a world record."

Casey then turned to settling in on the island.

What happened next was yet another curveball. I spoke with U.S. representative Art Greenfield for the Washington, D.C.-based

National Aeronautic Association, one of the official aviation record sanctioning organizations. He proclaimed that Casey's flight could not be validated because his plane was grounded for repairs. I told him that Casey would get the plane fixed and then go back to Attu, and he would turn around from there and finally complete the journey.

Greenfield seemed to balk but said Casey had a good case to obtain this record if he could prove that he had flown the necessary miles (more than 24,960) and had a logbook with verifiable details of this excursion. I answered he had both. Greenfield said he thought the record was then secure and that he would present the official record to Casey once he made it back to Seattle.

I called Casey back the same day (November 5) and relayed the conversation I had with Greenfield. I also told him that we had put out a news release telling the public about his forced landing and engine problem. I explained that in the next week or so there would be a very large crate arriving and to please put the damaged engine into the crate. He would then need to secure it and take it back to an awaiting Reeve Aleutian Airways aircraft, which would bring it back to Anchorage.

I told Casey that I knew the base colonel would bitch about the crate, but before it arrived, I will have spoken to him and emphasized that we have higher up authority to keep him billeted until his plane is fixed. Further, I will tell him that we can't get the plane fixed until we ship the damaged engine back for teardown and get a new engine to him. Once the plane is fixed, Casey will be out of the colonel's hair.

I then added, "Oh, by the way, Wiplinger said you will be getting your old engine they took out of the 206. It has already been sent to Alaska."

Over the next several days there were a myriad of small details to cover. I would remain in Seattle until November 11, after which I would head to Bartlesville and then back to New York. I stayed in Seattle the extra time to make sure we had the resources (staff) in place to respond to all the media queries and also to help with logistics. We had to deal with many requests during that week.

Early morning on November 6, I got a call from Hammond at Phillips. He was pissed. "Where the hell is my quote in the most recent news story by you guys? Who took it out?" he demanded. He was referring to a news story we sent out on November 5 that detailed that a Minnesota company (Wipaire) would provide a new engine to Casey. It seems that in the original draft of the news release Hammond had a quote in the story which stated the following: "Because this flight is testing a new engine technology, we want to tear down the engine immediately to determine the source of the mechanical problem."

It had continued, "Jack Hammond, manager of aviation, further added that all the necessary repairs to the original could not be done on Shemya. From a safety standpoint, replacing the engine helps ensure that Casey will successfully complete this flight."

I told Jack I would call him back. I called New York – apparently, Hirsch again had caused a major conflict with the client. He on his own decided to cut out all of Hammond's quote. Why did he do such an asshole thing? Hirsch thought Hammond's quote was ineffective and inappropriate. Also, he thought the quote in the release would have made the news release sound too commercial.

Upon calling Jack back with an explanation, he just screamed at me. "Coleman, we need to tell the truth. What the fuck are you doing?" I then relayed Hammond's displeasure with our company to my boss in New York City. Hirsch drafted a memo to me regarding this issue. (The memo didn't make any sense at the time, nor does it today when I re-read it – sorry, Al.)

Subsequently, Geiger (after Hammond and I spoke with him) sent a handwritten note to Hirsch which read: *"Just talked to Coleman on the most recent Tom Casey release. I asked him why there was no quote from Jack Hammond on safety. We need this in the story next time. Would have liked it this time. It pays well to do the right thing. — Tom."*

Of course, Dennis Boggs had wanted to tell the whole truth that it was catastrophic engine failure. He, too, called me and was really pissed and called us cowards for putting out that incorrect information to the media. "Unplanned water landing? What a bullshit statement that was. Imagine if the National Transportation Safety Board said something stupid like that?" said Boggs.

# Forty

# A Long Autumn Nap On Shemya

*"I feel we are all islands — in a common sea."*
— **Anne Morrow Lindbergh**

At this point in the story, we'll let Casey take over the narrative ...

"I finally got a good night's sleep on November 6 and, frankly, the next day vertigo had set in and it was hard for me to stand up at all. I stayed in my room except for three trips to the mess halls. Later that evening, I got several beers at the NCO club, but mainly concentrated on getting my life in order after my splashdown in the Pacific. One of the most memorable events was when my new friends at the bar welcomed me to Shemya by presenting me a T-shirt. This was no ordinary shirt — it left a favorable impression for years to come. The front of the T-shirt read: *"Welcome to Shemya, not the end of the world, but you can see it from here."*

"Nice breakfast at the mess hall. Boy, the U.S. Air Force knows how to treat the stomach right. Had a real appetite today — I haven't wanted to eat the past several days. I did have some protein bars in my plane that I consumed during the seven hours I sat awaiting rescue and Captain O'Brien gave me a hearty meal on board his vessel.

"I had a meeting scheduled with the base commander on the 8th, which I was not looking forward to – it was my 'come to Jesus meeting' with Colonel What's His Name? The meeting went as expected. He wanted to kill me.

"How I was even allowed on his base was a mystery to him. 'Plus this snafu (Situation Normal: All Fucked Up) of helping you to put your plane back in working order really pisses me off,' he said.

"He insisted that he had the power to throw me and my aircraft off a cliff — into the sea — and no one would ever miss me. Further, if I made any overtures to his base personnel to assist me in any way, he would make sure that I suddenly disappeared forever. He yelled at me and said this was not an idle threat.

"He was not going to provide me any help with my plane. In fact, he issued a standing order that no Air Force Base personnel could be seen working on my plane. I begged for some assistance to take off my damaged engine as we were trying to make plans to have it shipped to the manufacturer for evaluation. Also, we were trying to have my new engine flown here with Reeve Aleutian Airways. Reeve flew a four-engine DC-6 cargo aircraft and had seats to carry military personnel.

"When he heard that, the colonel seemed almost to tip his office chair over backwards but caught himself at the last second. He just balked at my details about the possible use of Reeve Airways and firmly stated that my old or new engine would never get on that airline during its regularly scheduled runs to his base. The colonel further explained that these were operational runs made by Reeve and would not to be interfered with by some civilian whim.

"Now almost totally red-faced to the neckline, the colonel grabbed his chest as if he was having a heart attack and shouted that the airline only handles his requirements and use of that airline to get either the old one off or the new engine here was not this base's priority. He emphasized that I had better find another way. He suggested that maybe I could hire someone in Anchorage to fly the engine here.

"Now here is the best part — as the colonel slammed his fist on the top of his desk, laughingly he told me that if I did find some sucker to fly the engine here, that individual would need to have a Top

Secret clearance. He quipped that that scenario won't happen in this century. He indicated, in a smiling way, that I was fucked, and for me to have a good day."

\* \* \*

Several hours after that meeting. Casey called me in Seattle and relayed the results of the session with the colonel in gruesome detail. "That's the story, Bill," he said. "What do you recommend?"

I calmed Casey down by telling him everything was under control. I already had been in touch with the owner of Reeve Aleutian Airways. He put me in touch with his dispatcher. I assured Casey that his engine would be coming. "Casey, as always," I said, "Money talks."

I related to Casey that now I needed to get the buy-in on shipping the engine to Shemya from other Air Force sources there. My other big dilemma, after getting the engine there, was having Casey find a way to remove the damaged engine from its hangar and then move the new engine from the airfield back to the hangar. I told him to stand by as I would alert him when I received the go-ahead to make the engine delivery.

But before I could hang up Casey threw me a huge curveball. Had he told me this earlier in the conversation, we could have dispensed with the whole mini-story on his meeting with the base commander.

"Hey, I almost forgot. Here is some good news," Casey interrupted. "After my ass chewing from the base commander, I went back to the hangar where my plane is located and standing next to my plane was a gentleman in an olive drab flight suit. He had an Eagle on each shoulder and one on his fore and aft cap. He asked if I was the pilot so many people on the base were talking about. I said yes."

"He said, 'I am Colonel Dave Johnson, and I am the officer in charge of the Cobra Ball aircraft operation. I assume you know what I am talking about.'

"Colonel Johnson was pointing to the two aircraft in this hangar. Bill, it turns out that he is the head honcho here and he can get things done even if it means stepping over the head of the base commander. I immediately trusted this gentleman. Colonel Johnson's voice was firm and resolute. He stated that he wanted me to know that if I needed anything he would make it happen.

"I thought, no time like the present, so I asked. Colonel, I need some help getting my plane back to working order. And, my immediate need was dismantling my damaged engine and loading it on an upcoming Reeve Airways flight, possibly on November 10. Also, my handler is trying to have my new engine shipped on the same flight.

"The colonel then told me he would lend me the services of a carpenter that worked for him. And if I needed any support from any of his mechanics or wanted to borrow any equipment, all I had to do was ask. Bill, I have help here and we are in business."

And with that issue apparently resolved, our conversation turned to other topics. I asked Casey what the facilities on Shemya were like. He explained that the main administration complex included a cafeteria, recreation room, his sleeping quarters, barber shop, and a bank. All the Air Force intelligence gathering activities emanated from there as well.

"This horizontal, two-story building stretches more than two football fields," Casey went on. "At each end are wings and that is where the administrative staff is located. My hangar, where my plane was billeted, is huge. We are not far from the runway.

"Imagine that inside this hangar are two really big 707 aircraft, maintenance equipment, and my tiny 29-foot aircraft. Talk about being invisible.

"Other buildings on base include the movie theater, crafts shops, and living dorms for enlisted personnel. It turned out that the big hangout for everyone is the Cobra Den where the main bar, pool tables, and a fast food outlet are located. It's a great place to go after 1700 when everyone lets their hair down and rank is not an issue. On the weekends, live bands are brought in by Reeve Airways from the mainland. But, the best part is that top-shelf booze is only a dime a drink and beer is a nickel a glass.

"As for my new home for the next month, from what I read Shemya is about two miles wide and four miles long. We are about 200 miles from Russia. Most Air Force folk have referred to Shemya as 'the Rock'. It is so windy on this island that you have to grab onto someone to just stay upright. I am about 1,500 air miles from Anchorage.

Here, there is a joke that one of the air force guys shared with me: The International Date Line bends around Shemya and on a clear day one can see tomorrow.

"This island is between the Pacific Ocean and the Bering Sea. The island's meteorologist told me that since both bodies of water meet each other and are not attracted to each other, that this phenomenon of nature has been the cause of hurricane-proportioned winds and waves on Shemya. Ain't that cool.

"The weather keeps changing. One day it snowed and the wind blew all the snow away, and then it snowed again. There is always precipitation and the temperature remains about 40 degrees Fahrenheit during the day and 30 degrees at night.

"When I relocated my ass on Shemya, I was impressed by the incredibly blue water. I didn't realize that real water could be that blue. Someday I would like to take a long walk around the island. Everyone has warned me about stepping on mines or landing in a foxhole dug by the WW II forces. The rock on Shemya is molten lava and is very dense and black — thus the other nickname, the 'Black Pearl of the Aleutians.'

"As I said, I am in a hangar with two super large aircraft. I was told they are the RC-135S Cobra Ball aircraft. Colonel Johnson told me they are a militarized version of the Boeing 707 civilian airliner and are equipped with a sophisticated array of optical and electronic sensors, recording media, and communications equipment.

"At the bar, I quietly asked several new Air Force acquaintances of mine about the aircraft. They said these aircraft were a national asset uniquely suited to providing America's leaders and defense community with vital information that cannot be obtained by any other source. They were strictly suited to fly from the Aleutians and collect intelligence. Well, I shut my mouth and never asked another person another question. I didn't want to give the base colonel any reason to throw me off this island. They might have thought that I was a Russian spy."

At this point in our conversation, I cut Casey off and explained to him the good news that both his Wipaire engine and the ECI engine crate were in storage at the main Reeve Aleutian Airways hangar in Anchorage. I emphasized that right now, even with Colonel

Johnson's support, I still needed to obtain approval for his engine and empty crate to reach Shemya. I had Reeve on board but now needed the base command to approve its landing while carrying non-essential cargo.

I told Casey that I wanted to bypass the base commander and hopefully speak to someone with a bit of empathy regarding the difficulties we were facing regarding bringing the new engine aboard. My choice was going to be the base commander's adjutant. Thus, Air Force Captain Mike Compton, the second-in-command at Shemya, was my next call for help.

Compton and I subsequently discussed the disposition of the two engines. He said if I worked a deal with Reeve to transport the crated engines to and from the base during non-critical operational hours (preferably the weekend), he would give permission for the exercise. So that is how I lined it up with Reeve Airways. All Casey had to accomplish was to steal a forklift or bribe a forklift operator to move both engine crates and we were in business.

I called Casey again in the early morning on November 9 and told him I had approval from the base's second in command, plus I had contracted with Reeve for a flight mid-afternoon on Saturday, November 10, to deliver the empty crate in which to secure the damaged engine. The flight would also bring the new Wipaire engine. This flight would then return to Anchorage with the crated damaged engine. From there, Reeve would have it sent by air to Engine Components in San Antonio.

Casey's responsibility would be to dismantle the damaged engine off his aircraft, crate it, and then deliver it to the airport so it could be loaded onto the Reeve aircraft. Casey also was to help offload the new engine and have it taken back to his hangar, to be later secured onto his plane.

Later in the day on the 9th, Casey called me in the hotel. He was out of breath in anticipation of telling me all the events of the day. "Oh my God," he said, "At first I thought when you previously spelled out the deadline, I would wind up having to take this engine off the aircraft all by myself.

"But the fates were good to me and the Cobra Ball commander's carpenter and his friend showed up and helped. All I had to do was tell them what not to do. I quite emphatically yelled at them that I had less than ten hours to get this blasted engine off the aircraft. Then, I had to find someone to bring the empty crate from the airport to this hangar and then back to the airport. I kept thinking that hopefully there would be no screw-up and the new engine would also arrive when you told me it would.

"Need to hang up as I need to get back to my hangar to make sure we are ready for the Reeve flight tomorrow." Casey, true to form, remained a bit flustered and grumpy.

Before he could hang up, I interjected, "Wait a second Tom, I have more questions." I told Casey that as far as I was concerned everything on my end would go like clockwork. So, I wanted to know how he actually dismantled the engine.

Casey, now acting like an engine powerplant instructor, replied, "One of the first steps before we could remove the engine was finding the all-important tail stand. We needed to put this in place before we could actually release the engine from its mount. The stand compensated for a tail-heavy condition. Luckily, we found this piece of equipment in the hangar by one of the 707s.

"Second, we had to empty the engine of any fluids. Mostly, we were concerned about the oil, and once that was removed we could start stripping away the vital parts.

"Third, we unbolted the prop. Remember, a constant speed propeller may be impacted by wear if there was a cylinder detonated. Also, the prop must be flushed out and inspected. My dynamic Mc-Cauley propeller will have to be re-balanced prior to it being placed back on the new engine.

"We wrapped the prop in a weatherproof canvas and cushioned it with rubberized military packaging material. Then we marked it for delivery to Dominion Propeller, a certified service center for Mc-Cauley Propellers in Anchorage. Reeve would carry this prop back to Anchorage along with the damaged engine.

"Last, we carefully took off the engine cowling so we could attack the engine itself. We carefully moved the engine controls aside so they were not bent too sharply or damaged in any other way. We carefully moved away the woven material around the sump and in between the cylinders. Then came the hard part: actually lifting the engine away from the firewall.

"In the hangar where our two roommates (the Cobra Ball aircraft) lived, we found a chain pulley mechanism. This meant we could attach both ends of the pulley bar extension chains to the top of the engine. Then once we unbolted the engine, they could manually lift the engine off the engine mount and safely free it away from the aircraft. There were many lines that needed clamping and special care had to be taken to examine the propeller shaft for bits of metal.

"The steel tube engine mount and its welds are often taken for granted, and having the engine off gave us the opportunity to remove the mount for closer cleaning and inspection. Once this had been completed, the engine mount would be painted and mounted back onto the repaired firewall in preparation for the new engine. With the engine free, we were assured we could pack the damaged engine into the crate and transport it to the airport.

"Here was another tricky part of this operation: getting someone with a forklift to move both engines. My carpenter's friend paid the janitor at the airport $100 — monies I got from the base bank — to operate the forklift."

Following that long-winded response, I thanked Casey and asked that he call me the next day once both engines were safely where they should be. And late on the afternoon of November 10, Casey called: "All done, boss. Once the Reeve aircraft arrived here today, the lift operator had the empty crate delivered to the hangar and we secured the damaged engine inside and sealed the crate. The operator then took this crate plus the prop back to the airport and stowed them aboard the aircraft.

"Next, he off-loaded the new engine from the Reeve aircraft and brought it back to my hangar. Just about the time the forklift operator reached our hangar, the Reeve aircraft was en route back to Anchorage." All told, I paid more than $3,000 for the trip. Bernie Coleman paid for his end and so did Wipaire.

Later that evening I received a call from the Shemya base commander at the hotel. He was totally pissed. "How dare you usurp my orders?" he demanded. "I told you that Casey would sit here forever and that you shouldn't try and help him. I saw the news story about his Minnesota company's willingness to supply him with another engine. But I left word with Reeve Airways that they were not to carry this engine to my base." By now he was stammering.

I responded, "Listen colonel, we paid Reeve good money to get that engine to Casey when your U.S. Air Force Base had no operational exercises that would involve Reeve Airways. Plus, we paid special attention to determine if there were any special base necessities that would take precedence over our little engine being transported to your base. I verified these facts with your executive officer and he approved my sending the engine."

"Mr. Coleman, I have dealt with him," he countered, "And promise that Casey will never get off this rock." His character traits now changed over from Colonel Klink in "Hogan's Heroes" to Captain Queeg from "The Caine Mutiny".

Deep within the recesses of my mind, I thought that I was not going to have this bass-ackwards colonel threaten me. At this juncture in our conversation, I told the colonel that I was going over his head right to the Air Force Chief of Staff, General McPeak, at the Pentagon. I promised I would have his ass hanging from the nearest yard-arm.

"Go ahead, you asshole," he said. "What are they going to do with me? Send me to Shemya? This conversation is over."

The next morning I called General McPeak's office. I spoke with his adjutant who very nicely said not to worry as I hadn't usurped any Air Force regulations. "Fixing Casey's plane and getting the new engine to Shemya was the perfect thing to do," she said. "We will call Shemya and get the ol' boy off the ceiling. Have a good day, Mr. Coleman." The adjutant's sweet sounding voice was a perfect morning pick-me-up.

That accomplished, I left the hallowed grounds of Seattle and headed straight back to New York without a stopover in Bartlesville.

I had made all the appropriate calls to all the invited guests and the media. My apologies were far-reaching and for the most part everyone sincerely wished us good luck. Further, everyone knew that Casey was safely on Shemya Island and we would have to wait patiently for him to fix his aircraft before he could be on his way again.

Now that this latest episode in the ongoing Casey saga had passed, it was time for a bit of reflection. In truth, it was almost like a small glitch in the grand scheme of his around the world journey. Yes, Casey was once again delayed, but at least this time we knew exactly where he was. (No screaming out *"Where the hell is Casey?"* was necessary.)

\* \* \*

Now back in New York on Monday November 12, the day started out like so many other days in this maddening adventure. I was busy going through mounds of mail and trying to keep everyone, and I mean everyone, out of my office. My boss kept bursting in asking for all the billing hours for the last month so he could bill Phillips 66. I hadn't figured them out and told him so. God, he could piss me off.

All I really wanted to do was quietly speak with coworkers Tim and Kyle to determine our next strategies (homecoming, news releases, etc.). Remember, we had left Bukota in charge in Seattle and he didn't have the balls to push back at Casey like I did. But before any strategy meeting took place, there was a sharp knock on my door. Kyle held up a fax and appeared a bit shaken. Or perhaps she was suffering from lack of sleep, like most of us.

"Bill, Casey's insurance has been canceled. Wipaire never paid the premium as promised," she said dryly. I looked at the letter. It was self-explanatory:

> *Dear Tom:*
> *This letter is to verify to you that effective November 14, 1990 at 1201, all coverage under London Cover Note No. AV050373 will cease.*
>
> *Original premium coverage from 5/14/90 to 8/14/90. Additional premium for extension and War Risk from 8/14/90 to 11/14/90.*
>
> *Current Balance due: $21,373.26*
>
> *Mr. Wiplinger verbally agreed to the net payment of your*

*original premium of $19,800, less 40%, or $11,880. We
have not received that premium.*

*Lloyd's of London is reluctant to extend coverage without
full payment. Also, please be advised that your 11/1/90
claim cannot be processed prior to full premium payment.*

*Regards:
Susan Gerk, Forbes Westar, Inc.*

That letter got my attention. I called Susan Gerk and she verified that no monies had been received from Wipaire and she wondered
why. I then called Wipaire and it was explained to me by Wiplinger's
accountant that they had just sent Casey his original engine from the
Cessna 206 aircraft. And the engine they had provided Casey for this
trip was one they had loaned him. They also said he owed them for the
floats and that they only agreed to pay the premium if Casey made it
back before November 14.

I countered by saying that they had promised me in a previous
conversation to pay the premium when Casey was in Saudi Arabia.
The accountant countered by saying that nothing was ever in writing
regarding that supposed promise. "And, as far as I am concerned,"
said Wiplinger's accountant, "When and if Casey makes it back, he
had better fly Liberty II to our place and surrender the plane as payment for all the debt he owes us."

Well, this day was really going well. I finally got Casey on
the horn and repeated my conversation with Wip's accountant and
acquainted Casey with the fact that this dude was at the OK Corral
with his guns drawn. Casey didn't catch my drift at first, but finally
admitted that he owed Wipaire all this money. He had hoped that
the Smithsonian Institution would purchase his plane once he made
it back to Seattle. With that money he felt sure he could clear up his
debt with Wipaire.

I asked him what the hell was he thinking and why had he
never said anything to anyone about his financial problems? He responded that he didn't want anyone to know since that bit of information would have deterred any potential sponsorships. His game plan

once he left Japan was to be back in Seattle before November 14 and, by doing so, his insurance would have still been good.

I asked Casey if maybe there was a base psychiatrist he might talk with; and, if so, for God's sake use the couch. "Listen to yourself," I said. "In Forbes Westar's letter they said, and I repeat, that your claim of 11/1/90 cannot be processed. So how the hell would your coming home before November 14 have done you any good? You still owed the money for the policy and you couldn't have raised funds that fast. So it looks like Wipaire gets your plane."

Casey acknowledged, "I have no money to clear up this debt. Maybe Phillips 66 will help financially. As for having the insurance to cover my plane, once it is fixed and ready to go, I plan to call AOPA and see if I can arrange for a short-term policy. I have some money you gave me on my credit card. That is my only way out. I will call you later when I have worked it out.

"Oh, I almost forgot," Casey added, "When I got here on Shemya, I really had a bad case of vertigo. It happened once I stepped on land at the base. I was very dizzy and my vision was blurred. Hell, at one point, I couldn't even stand up. Further, I also got a terrible ear infection. But the base medic gave me some great medicine and the Scotch really helped cure that ailment." All at once, Casey seemed to be back in the driver's seat. (I never again broached the subject of Phillips 66 financially bailing him out.)

Later that afternoon, I called Bernie Coleman with the news that the engine was on its way. Bernie wanted to know what kind of fuel Casey got at Attu. Maybe, Bernie thought, that the engine failed because Casey had used the wrong fuel. Bernie thought Casey may have taken on some kerosene. I assured Bernie that was not the case. To support that claim, I explained to Bernie that Casey's aircraft always had an emergency supply of avgas in its left tip tank. Bernie said that he and Boggs would tear down the engine once it got to Texas.

# Forty-one

# The Install; a Temporary Hold; Then Cleared for Takeoff

Casey spent the rest of November just getting familiar with his surroundings and repairing his plane in order to leave Shemya and continue on his world record flight. During this period, he also obtained the short-term aircraft insurance from AOPA (Aircraft Owners and Pilots Association) as he had enough money on his credit card to cover the premium.

There were all the comforts of home on 'the Rock.' He got a haircut during the week for only 25 cents, plus saw three recently released movies for nothing. When he finished working on the plane in the evening, Casey would visit the Cobra Den. Generally all the base personnel, after a tough workday, would spend their off-duty time there. It had a bar, fireplace, and even a hot tub.

Initially, the carpenter said he wouldn't be available during the base's normal working hours from 0800 to 1700. But after the engine arrived on November 10, Casey and the carpenter seemed to work 14-hour days. Casey wondered how he was going to pay this fellow for all the hard work. (This was a matter that was never resolved.)

There also remained a question about one of the subsequent events following the forced landing that continually haunted Casey. What happened that caused his strut, attached to the float, to snap like a wooden twig breaking in half?

Looking back on the whole episode, Casey could only think of one event that may have caused his strut to break. It seemed that during the rescue, when his plane was lifted from the Pacific Ocean, it was accidently dropped rather hard onto the deck of the Judy B by the vessel's boom operator. This incident had a dramatic negative effect on the aircraft. The concussion generated by the aircraft hitting the deck actually snapped the aircraft's left strut in two and filled the air with a very loud cracking noise. Thus this same strut could no longer support the aircraft's left pontoon.

The most damaging result of this accident followed after the strut snapped. One end of the strut shot upwards and punctured a large hole in the aircraft engine's firewall. But the good news was that it didn't damage any part of the engine itself. Not only did Casey need to have a new strut sent to him by Wipaire, but he also had to fabricate a large patch to cover the puncture in the firewall. The latter was a daunting task.

Before Casey could repair the punctured firewall as well as the damaged pontoon, he had to siphon out the remaining fuel. Luckily, he had dumped most of his avgas while he was adrift for seven hours in the ocean waiting for rescue. With the Cobra Ball colonel's assistance, he procured an empty 55-gallon drum to store the remaining fuel.

Casey called me more than ten times during the succeeding weeks to provide a status report on what he had accomplished. This included repairing the firewall; replacing the left strut that secured the left pontoon to the aircraft; repairing the damaged left float; hanging the new engine; putting on the overhauled prop; and finally running up the new engine to ensure he had enough power to take off.

First, to repair the firewall, they had to create the patch; the carpenter – now his best friend on the island — had the initial task of finding material to be used for the patch. In the Cobra Ball maintenance area, they found a 4x8-foot sheet of stainless steel.

They measured the square footage of the damaged area on the firewall and this allowed them to create the shape of the patch. Once this was determined, they cut out the patch design from the large stainless steel sheet. Steel cutters were used to create the patch. Edges were smoothed out on the Cobra Ball mechanics' machinery, and once they had the exact size and thickness they riveted it onto the aircraft's firewall. The finished job looked just like it had come off the original manufacturer's assembly line.

Second on his repair list was the repair of the left float. The sidewall portion of the left float's forward section had a four-inch gash above the waterline that was made when the prop was windmilling after the ditching of the aircraft. The gash in the float happened when the left pontoon jutted upward following the very hard landing in the ocean. The prop actually cut into the float. They welded the gash and made sure it had watertight integrity.

Third, he needed to install a new strut to support the left float. On November 13, a new strut arrived from Wipaire by way of Reeve Airways. To replace the strut, his carpenter friend and three other Air Force mechanics jacked the aircraft off the ground so they could fit a new strut onto the aircraft's wall and attach it to the pontoon. They had to elevate the aircraft because they needed to have the left float free from having to support any weight. With a lot of elbow grease, they subsequently replaced the broken strut.

Fourth in the lineup was getting the new engine hung on the bird. Casey used the same chain mechanism as before when taking off the damaged engine. The mechanism held the engine in place and, manually, the carpenter connected all the appropriate hoses and wires. They then lowered it onto the refurbished mount. Finally, the engine was bolted and the engine cowling fit like a glove.

The last critical maintenance issue was replacing the prop. The prop hub and crankshaft had been cleaned and inspected. The refurbished prop arrived on the 15th. The hub was now ready to accept the prop. Both men manually held each end of the newly refurbished and rebalanced prop and slipped it on.

Nearing the end of these arduous tasks, both men slapped each other on the back and in celebration drank down half of a bottle of good Scotch. They took the aircraft outside the hangar by putting it on mechanic's dollies. Liberty II was run up more than ten times, all the time checking the instruments.

Casey had stashed away three cases of Phillips X/C oil that had been sent to him on the Reeve trip to Shemya. He made sure that once the engine run-ups were completed, he changed the oil. Superstitious as he was, Casey would change the oil once more before leaving Shemya. The engine was running smoothly, instruments were in the green, and it was ready to go.

Later at the Cobra Den with Colonel Johnson, Casey would relate, "All I need now is to get the engine certified airworthy. Following that step, I need to obtain 200 gallons of avgas. Last, I need my special five-foot long specially built dollies. Each of the dollies has ten-inch front and eight-inch rear wheels — like a skateboard. These are needed so that they can be placed under the floats in order to facilitate my aircraft taking off from land." The colonel just smiled as he had now been an integral part of this journey.

Meanwhile, back in my New York City office, life was about to go from mildly complicated to really bad on November 15. I had checked with Casey every so often to determine the disposition of his aircraft. This was mostly driven by Hammond and Boggs who wanted to know how Casey was progressing in fixing his aircraft and its engine. Both also had been alerted that the damaged engine was on its way to Bernie in San Antonio. Boggs would be there for the teardown once it arrived.

However, corporate political unrest was now going to rule the day. The Casey project would be declared dead in the water. The promotions manager at Phillips had Tom Geiger send us a fax that stated:

> *"Effective 1000 central time on November 15 all activity on the Casey project has stopped. I asked Bill to cancel this project after he talks to George Bukota, G+A's West Coast vice president. Bukota's orders will be simple: tell George to notify the media when Casey finally arrives back to Seattle. There will be no charge for this service and there will be no press conference."*

From our perspective at G+A, Bukota could handle this task as he exemplified a 1970's philosophy professor at Southern Cal. He was so laid-back that he would only do the bare minimum. He was still in the Hippie age. He loved the John Lennon quote: *"If everyone demanded peace instead of another television set, then there would be peace."*

Geiger's message went on to say ...

*"... that this project had been handled in a professional manner and in good faith by all concerned. It is our firm belief that Bill Coleman is an asset to our group and Phillips 66. We are all disappointed with how this project has evolved. Even with all the twists and turns, we at all times did what was required."*

I, of course, responded to Geiger. In my note back to him I acknowledged that all future work would not be billed. But the promotions manager was on the warpath. Once he received a copy of my note, he immediately scribbled a hand-written note right below my typed note and sent it flying back by fax to us in New York. His cryptic comments began:

*"Understand that this was not a good program. It was not well managed by us or by you. Need your help to control this type of thing in the future. We feel like the meter was allowed to run unchecked. Any future billing on Casey will be absorbed by you."*

It was signed by a drawing of a sad face.

Casey received an ASAP call from me regarding the bad news. From now on, he could talk with George in Seattle. Casey asked me, "What is the origin of the name George?" I said it comes from the Greek name Georgios, meaning "farmer." Casey then retorted that he would now be handled by a farmer instead of an aviator. With that, he added, "I don't want to talk to him. Do you hear me? George is useless and you never know if he understands what you are talking about, or maybe he is just throwing up a smokescreen. I won't have my journey screwed up by him."

I told Casey that George is a good man and that he could handle his requests. But if there is a specific question having to do with the flight, the aircraft, or money, please call me. Casey was now on his own. George, often kept in the dark, never really knew what was happening with Casey.

Meanwhile, I also finally got the chance to speak with Dick Eason at the State Department. It had been two months since we spoke and I thanked him for his help in Karachi, the Philippines, and Japan.

Said Eason, "Sorry to hear about your pilot but I understand he got a new engine and should be on his way again. We would like to send a representative to Seattle when he returns. Can you keep me abreast, so we can be there in time?"

I told Dick, "No problem," and again thanked him for the assistance that State had provided to Casey. By alerting all the ambassadors and clearing the way for Casey to fly through and over various countries — in some very hellish circumstances — State had gone way above the norm. There was nothing else to ask for as Casey was back in the United States.

Back in D.C., Knight was still helping in the trenches. I spoke to him about the 'ceasefire' at Phillips and he was truly taken aback. During our call, David put me on hold and came back in about five minutes. Admiral Engen, it seemed, was hopping mad. Knight said Engen picked up the phone and called Hammond. The latter assured Engen not to worry because the person that gave the order — the promotions manager at Phillips 66 — would have a very short-lived career.

Knight later called me back and commented that Admiral Engen was thinking of calling Mr. Silas, the chairman of Phillips Petroleum. "Ouch," I said.

Knight also said he drafted a letter that day to Admiral William Kime, Commandant of the U.S. Coast Guard. In the letter, Knight reviewed for the admiral the events leading up to Casey's rescue and his current exile on Shemya. Knight said Casey now had a new engine and spare parts and would soon be ready to continue on his quest for a world record. The only ingredient missing was fuel. Knight asked the commandant if they could supply fuel to Casey. Knight humbly made a request: "There were three barrels on Kodiak but we needed a way to get them delivered to Casey. Could the admiral's people in District 17 get the fuel to Casey?"

On November 21, Knight heard back from the admiral and the Coast Guard said it had to decline in helping get fuel to Casey. That meant it fell on my shoulders.

Casey had mentioned that if we could reach Tom Wardleigh, who was associated with the Alaskan Aviation Safety Foundation, maybe he knew of a way to get the avgas to Shemya. I reached out to Wardleigh and he was aware of Casey's plight. He promised me that if at all possible he would get the fuel to him on Shemya.

I spoke again to Wardleigh on November 22, and he said he now had in his possession five 55-gallon drums of avgas, which his foundation paid for. I told Tom to get the fuel over to Reeve Airways at the Anchorage airport and I would take the matter from there. After speaking to Reeve's dispatcher, he said they would deliver the fuel on Saturday, November 24.

The monies again flowed out the door. Reeve would be paid another $5,000 for transporting the fuel. This also included payment for an earlier trip to deliver the refurbished prop. I called Hammond with the news about the fuel, and then at the end of the conversation explained that it had cost him almost $10,000 to help get Casey off 'the Rock'.

Casey was also alerted about the situation, and he said that now two further steps were needed to be accomplished before he could fly. The first step was to have a set of undercarriage float dollies sent to him. Dollies? I inquired what they were.

Casey said that he had previously had them built and that they fit underneath each pontoon. The dollies, in the shape of the floats, had steel ball bearing rollers attached to the underside. The aircraft floats would sit atop the dollies and the weight of the aircraft would hold them in place. Thus, the dollies were directly under each float and served as the mechanism to allow him to take off from land. Without them, Casey could not push the floats over the concrete runway. Once he had left the runway, the dollies would just run off the runway and settle in the grass.

I called Tim Tometz, a flight controller and friend of Casey, on November 26. Tim said he knew where the dollies were. We both agreed that if he could get them shipped to McCord Air Force Base, I could help arrange to have them brought out to Shemya on a C-130 transport. The colonel for the Cobra unit had advised Casey and me that he would make all the arrangements at McCord. Tim got them there and the C-130 flew them out to Shemya.

The only one who objected to the use of the dollies was the base commander. And he was going to make an issue of this.

It was my understanding that at the exact moment the base commander heard about Casey's plan to use dollies on his runway was when he became apoplectic. At 2200 on November 27, I received a call from the base commander (Colonel Klink) as well as some general attached to Chief of Staff McPeak's staff in D.C.

The base commander started by yelling at me in an attempt to make sure the general would understand his plight. He claimed that I had been "smuggling" goods to the uninvited pilot who had crashed off his island a month ago. The smuggled goods were aircraft parts, a new engine, and a sundry array of other items. In addition, he claimed that I wanted to provide Casey with dollies that would be employed under his floats so as to facilitate him taking off from the airfield.

"General," the colonel said, "When that blasted seaplane takes off, the dollies will fall off and then they will shoot down my runway, destroying all the runway lights. We estimate the cost to our base to replace the broken runway lights would conservatively run more than several hundred thousand dollars. Who is going to pay for this catastrophe? Phillips 66? I doubt it.

"We want to haul his ass down the mountain and put his plane back into the sea. Casey, the pilot, said the waters around Shemya were too rough and that it would swamp his aircraft. General, make a decision," the colonel pleaded.

Before the general could comment, I said putting him directly into the sea wouldn't work, as Casey had predicted. Also, this approach may cause more damage to his plane, leading to him being "your" visitor on Shemya through Christmas.

The general asked me if the colonel's dire tale was true. I explained to the general that I was not an expert and couldn't comment. I did say that Casey explained to me that the dollies should drop from the floats just as he lifted off from the runway.

"At this point during his takeoff, the dollies should slide off the floats and glide off the runway and go directly onto the grass," I said. "Casey further explained to me that he would only be traveling about 85 to 100 miles per hour on takeoff and as such there would be no imminent problem to damaging the runway lights."

"Ok, colonel," said the general. "The takeoff with dollies is approved."

The colonel wanted the last word. "General, there is a lot of betting going on whether Casey will make it off safely or crash. Seems my base underground betting pool is split 50/50. There has to be more than $50,000 at stake."

"Do you have a bet?" asked the general. "No," said the colonel, "But if I hurry, maybe I can get a hundred down — anything for you, general."

"Yes put me down for five hundred that Casey makes it off safely from Shemya," the general laughed. "Bill?" the general asked.

"No I'm neutral on this one," I said. "Don't forget, I have been witness to the whole party and frankly anything could happen. I just want to see our boy come home."

The general seemed to be pacified and wanted to know when Casey would be leaving. I estimated early in December as we had a few more tasks yet to take care of. The general then told the base commander to cool his jets and trust the briefing that Casey had provided him.

"We need to send this pilot on his way," he said. "General Mc-Peak wants this chapter of Air Force support to come to an end very soon. Do you understand me, colonel?" The general didn't wait for a response and just hung up. So did I.

Truth is, I hadn't the faintest idea what would happen when the aircraft took off, with the dollies subsequently scattering to the wind. My evaluation of the 'dollies' scenario was fairly simple. I was only guessing. And, my rationalization for this response to the general was clearly intended to employ whatever means possible in getting Casey off 'the Rock'.

Our next step was shipping out an airframe and powerplant (A&P) mechanic to Shemya to inspect the installation of the new engine, as well as to sign off on the airworthiness of other repairs to the aircraft which included the prop, firewall, float, and strut.

My job was to get the A&P mechanic to Shemya. I asked Wardleigh to recommend a mechanic. I immediately contacted the one he suggested. Then, I made arrangements with Reeve Airways for the mechanic to be flown out to Casey at least four to five days before Casey was set to depart.

We now had a possible date for Casey's departure — December 7. Hell, why not Pearl Harbor Day? After all, everything else in this journey was bizarre.

Meanwhile, back at Command Central (my office in New York), politics were running rampant. My boss, big Al, wanted to write a note back to the Phillips 66 promotions manager and basically fall on his sword. I was against that tactic and informed 'big Al' that Geiger and I would figure out what our response needed to be.

Geiger and I tried to draft a letter that big Al would accept. But no, he was a coward and totally went against what Geiger and I had proposed. Geiger had just gotten an infusion of cash from Hammond of $100,000, but that fact didn't dissuade Al. Geiger and I did not want to pander to the promotions manager, but big Al did.

Anyway, he constructed the following letter (sorry Al):

*Friend, in response to your note, we agree the Casey project did not come off exactly as planned. At present, we are aware from phone conversations originated by Casey to us, that his plane is fully repaired. Aviation fuel is being obtained and he intends to leave for Seattle during the week of December 7, depending on weather.*

*As requested, we will keep promotions alerted to Casey's estimated arrival time in Seattle.*

*If and when Phillips 66 determines that Jack Hammond will be present to meet Casey and you feel there is a need for our support in Seattle, we will willingly cover this event at our expense. Our support would be to assist Jack Hammond with media relations and control what Casey says or doesn't say to the media and other people.*

*Regards—Al*

This letter was sent in the morning and by the afternoon the whole matter took a new twist. Hammond's budget allocation earmarked for supporting the Casey project showed up on Geiger's books. This was a game changer.

Wow, by the afternoon of November 29, Geiger and Ron Stanley, Geiger's new manager, had both agreed that I should be in Seattle with Hammond once Casey arrived. Hammond had made an issue of my being there and even though one dissenter didn't like it, Hammond and Stanley won.

Moreover, Lorraine Dix, general manager, Aviation and Specialty Products at Phillips, told this dissenter (the promotions manager) to suck it up and she made the final decision and approved for my being in Seattle as well as the holding of a homecoming press conference.

But here is the irony. The promotions manager called big Al late that same afternoon and told him that he would hold Al to completing the Casey homecoming at our agency's expense. Yet, Geiger had agreed that all the agency's out-of-pocket expenses would be paid under the Casey project code. Al now looked to me to find a way to salvage our billing. These would be the hours spent for the remainder of the Casey project. In other words, find out how we can get paid. His peace offering was a Japanese lunch. God, I love politics.

Dennis Boggs also called me later in the day. The day before, I had drafted a presentation for him to make before Lorraine Dix on the sales performance of X/C oil. He said his presentation to marketing management on market share for Phillips 66 aviation oil was well received. Key in the presentation was the important fact that sales of X/C oil, since the Casey project began in early 1990, had risen 22 percent compared to the same timeframe in 1989. And Boggs was strong on letting management know that Phillips 66's image was gaining positive feedback in the aviation community.

After his presentation, Boggs shared with me that Lorraine Dix said Philips 66 will get positive results from the Casey project. She then gave Dennis an 'Atta Boy.' Everything seemed to be smoothing out by day's end. All we had to do now was wait for Casey to leave Shemya. We would then be in Seattle preparing to welcome Casey back.

It was now December 1 — day 171 of Casey's odyssey. I spoke

to Casey that Saturday to inform him that there would be several surprises on Reeve Airways' trip to Shemya on Sunday, December 2. Aboard would be an A&P mechanic to do an inspection of his aircraft, plus five 55-gallon drums of avgas. There would also be many letters wishing him well on the last leg of his journey.

Casey alerted his forklift operator friend and had him standing by at the airfield to meet the Reeve aircraft. He also asked his Cobra Ball colonel friend if he could borrow some of his men to help off-load the fuel.

Later, with the fuel and mechanic now secure in the hangar with his plane, Casey watched patiently as the A&P did his initial inspection. As it was close to chow time, the A&P informed Casey that it would probably take him an extra day to complete the inspection.

By December 4, the A&P gave Casey's plane a clean bill of health and the mechanic left for Anchorage. All Casey had to do was obtain some manpower from the Cobra Ball colonel to fit on his dollies and then upload the avgas to his aircraft.

Next stop for Casey was a visit to the meteorologist. After a two-hour weather briefing, Casey was now confirmed that he would be leaving 'the Rock' on December 7.

# Forty-two

# The Pursuit of a Record Continues

*"A single event can awaken within us a stranger totally unknown to us. To live is to be slowly born."*
— *Antoine de Saint-Exupéry, writer & aviator*

Casey successfully took off from Shemya at 1055 on December 7. It seemed all too appropriate that his return to gaining a world record would coincide with none other than Pearl Harbor Day.

Shortly after Casey took off, the Shemya base commander called me and inquired if Phillips 66 was prepared to reimburse him for 30 destroyed runway lights. "As I predicted, Mr. Coleman, your pilot took off in 45 mile per hour crosswinds and once airborne his float dollies each went in a separate direction. What happened next? Well, each one careened out of control and proceeded to smash into about 30 of my runway lights on either side of the airfield. After knocking out most of the lights, the dollies finally ended up smashing into two emergency vehicles, which I had strategically positioned adjacent to the runway in case Casey needed them. Do you think Phillips will pay? That is all I ask," the colonel said.

"How much?" I asked.

"Maybe several thousand dollars — just for the lights," was the response.

I wanted to laugh but didn't have the nerve. Here the poor bastard had had his base invaded by Casey and now he had to close his airfield until he could get his runway lights fixed. Once again, Casey had a unique way of putting an exclamation point on how he would be remembered upon departure.

Before I could respond to him about whether Phillips 66 would pay, I asked if he could calm down a second and perhaps provide me a briefing on how Casey's takeoff actually went. The base commander started by saying that the Cobra Ball commander, Colonel Johnson, was primarily responsible for helping Casey make it off Shemya. "The colonel helped guide Casey's plane from the hangar to the airfield. You also have to realize that his aircraft engine was idling as it pushed towards the edge of the runway's west end — runway 28.

"Here is the scenario on how he got to the runway. Casey had a long rope tied onto the aft end of his aircraft. The other end was tied to the bumper of Colonel Johnson's truck. All the roads leading to the runway and the runway itself had a quarter-inch sheet of ice on them.

"Since there was such a strong crosswind, Colonel Johnson's rope tied to his bumper actually helped stabilize Casey's aircraft. The colonel just kept the rope taught and maintained almost a straight line hook-up. This prevented Casey's plane from skidding off the icy roads. All who were present — maybe 300 people — wondered if Casey could pull this off.

"When Casey reached the runway's end, he unhooked the rope and then turned his plane 180 degrees so it faced forward into a takeoff position. We saw the colonel exit his truck, grab the rope, and begin to retie onto Casey's plane. But before he could manage to retie it, Casey was headed down the runway. I am sure Casey thought the colonel had control of his plane's aft end, but he didn't. I asked the colonel what he said to Casey on his handheld radio that the two were communicating on. The colonel said he just told Casey that he was on his own now and that he wished him good luck.

"It was my understanding that Casey was going to head off to the west. He was heading back to Attu, where he would land and then take off again. He was restarting the last leg of his journey all over again. And the funny part was looking at Colonel Johnson just standing by his truck, some hundred feet from runway 28, holding the end of a long rope attached to his bumper.

"Now for the takeoff. Casey seemed to shove his engine throttle full forward to gain maximum power. His aircraft lurched forward almost like a diesel train leaving the yard and in what seemed like a matter of seconds, he was airborne.

"We had all the fire and emergency equipment stationed along the airfield. Also, there were more than 300 spectators that were evenly divided on each side of the runway. Interestingly, one side was rooting (betting) that Casey would take off successfully, while the other side bet he'd fall off the runway into the ocean. The last tally was that more than $60,000 had been wagered. You missed out, Bill. Hey, if you ever are in the vicinity, stop in for a cup of coffee."

I found his response surprising. In the end, the colonel seemed pleased he had gotten rid of his surprise guest. I responded, "Will do, colonel. I'm just glad Casey made it off safe and sound."

Also, I asked if he could put in writing his request for Phillips 66 to pay for his lights so I could personally deliver it to Chief of Staff General McPeak. That was the last I ever heard from the colonel.

***

Moving on, the following is Casey's version of the day's events ...

"The takeoff was magnificent. I took no more than 100 feet to get airborne. Colonel Johnson really helped. I promised to tell the world about his support. Now back to Attu where I could land and then turn back to the east and head home.

"I contacted Attu and said, 'This is Liberty II and I want to make a landing and takeoff in Casco Cove. I need to restart my journey. I had a brief delay, as you know, on Shemya Island where I was helping the Air Force with gathering top secret information. Ok, I also had a bit of engine trouble, too. But, everything is ship-shape now. Pursuit of my round the world record is still my focus, over.'

"The Coast Guard operator came on and said, 'Liberty II, we

approve you using our harbor and all hands wish you the best. We are happy you got the opportunity to start over. The record is yours.'

"I touched down in Attu's waters at 1115 and was quickly airborne again and heading to Dutch Harbor. I flew back toward Shemya and made a relatively low pass near the airfield control tower. My intention was to do a fly-by and wave my wings in thanks to all the folks who helped me there.

"All of sudden I thought I was in the Tom Cruise movie, "Top Gun". As I got right over the middle of Shemya's airfield, my radio crackled, and a voice came on: 'This is your friendly base commander and you had no permission to take off. Mr. Casey, I am putting you on report!'

"Before the colonel had the opportunity to add to the most stupid comment anyone had ever uttered, I had long passed Shemya and was on my way east.

"If I wanted to reach Dutch Harbor, I would need to fly about 850 miles. As there were only some seven hours of daylight in the Aleutians this time of year, I knew I wouldn't make Dutch Harbor until long after dark. Landing on water in the dark is not a recommended procedure for a floatplane due to a lack of depth perception. In addition, there was a massive snowstorm hovering over Dutch Harbor at the time and the weather folk at Shemya had warned me against landing in that mess.

"So my alternate was Atka, which was only 543 miles from Attu. I had a great tailwind and figured I would reach Atka in 4 hours — just about the time the sun would be setting. Safer flying, indeed.

"At Atka, I parked my aircraft on the shoreline and had just enough room to pull almost three quarters of my plane out of the water. To my left was a derelict fishing vessel just rotting away and looking like a ghost ship. I passed the vessel and walked up to a house with a large satellite dish anchored in the front yard. I knocked on the front door, or so I thought.

"Now you have to realize there are only about 100 people living on Atka Island and most are Native Americans. A second story window opened and a gentleman stuck his head out and asked very nicely what I wanted.

"Where can I get accommodations for the night, plus a good

meal?" I asked. 'What is accommodations?' came the reply.

'Just a place to sleep and eat,' I said.

"He said, 'See that red building about 100 yards from here? That is our local eatery and they can give you a bed. And they have good beer there.' He then went back inside his house and closed the window.

"I would spend a restful night in Atka. That night I sat in on an Eskimo Bingo game. Hell, I won $175.00, much to the dismay of the locals. The next day I would head for Dutch Harbor, where I could refuel.

"The next morning, December 8, I taxied out for a takeoff at 1030 and lo and behold, my left magneto started to backfire. That meant I couldn't attain maximum takeoff power; so, I had to abort my mission and went back to the beach area in Atka. All my inner emotions freaked. Not again, I thought. Not another engine problem. I tried to find some help. What was facing me this time? I pulled open the cowling and checked my plugs and other lead lines to the engine. I tried turning over the engine again and it backfired again. By now it was close to 1400. At that point, I just gave up for the day.

"On December 9, I asked anyone and everyone if they knew of an engine mechanic on the island. I finally met with one gentleman who knew boat engines but not aircraft engines. I asked if he could read my engine manual. He then studied my engine and pulled some wires and plugs, like I had done the previous day, but nothing seemed to work.

"The next day, I finally was able to find a phone which I could use to call the mainland. Turns out, the phone had been at the eatery all the time, but no one wanted me to use it because a long distance call cost a lot of money. Once I said I would pay the charges for the call, they let me use the phone. Amen.

"I got hold of my mechanic, Tom Barr, at the Harvey Airport in Snohomish, Washington. After some discussion he said that the part I needed would take maybe ten days to arrive on Atka. So, we chose the most expeditious means to get me flying again. He advised me to disconnect the 'P lead' on the left magneto.

"The P lead was the wire that went from the starter switch to the magneto. It is attached to the magneto coil's primary windings

— hence the name 'P lead'. This lead grounds out the magneto – or, turns it off.

"Now here is what my mechanic at the Harvey Airport said: 'You want no one near your prop. Why? Should the propeller be moved by hand, without the P lead connected to the magneto, you will have a functional hot magneto. That means the engine could fire and the prop would become dangerously alive and harm someone permanently. In layman's terms, the prop could whack the shit out someone if the engine came alive.'

"I spent the rest of the day unhooking the P lead and turning my engine over to make sure it didn't backfire. My string of bad luck remained the same because the next day there was really bad weather and not suitable for takeoff.

"I continued to use the phone and called a few friends at the various destination points I planned as stopovers on my way back to Seattle. These friends could provide me a place to sleep, shower, and a good meal. I also mentioned that they might call the media and alert them of my planned arrival. I figured the closer I got to Seattle, the more interest there would be generated by the media."

\* \* \*

On December 12, Casey made his way to Dutch Harbor.

Dutch Harbor is a harbor on Amaknak Island in Unalaska, Alaska. This 337-mile leg was intentionally short as he needed fuel and had friends to see. He departed Atka at 1250 and arrived at Dutch Harbor at 1620.

The flight was only 2 hours and 20 minutes, but his arrival was one hour longer as he had passed through a time zone. He flew the distance at heights of 800 to 1,200 feet to avoid the bad weather that seemed to be following him since he left Atka.

"The island was surrounded by beautiful white-capped mountains and the sea was shimmering blue," he would later relate. "I landed in the harbor area near the town and was met at the dock by several seaplane buddies. I tied up at the town's fishing pier located just off Delta Way road. There must have been more than 100 fishing vessels either off-loading fish at the fish terminal or still anchored in the harbor.

"Here is a great bit of trivia friends of mine told me. Dutch Harbor is considered to be the largest fishing port in Alaska. It also was the location of the Battle of Dutch Harbor in June 1942, and is one of only two American areas to be bombed by the Japanese in WW II. The other of course was Pearl Harbor."

Sunrise on December 13 came at about 0930. "After a hearty breakfast, I went down to the Dutch Harbor PBS station for an interview," he later explained. "The gentleman was excited to hear about my many adventures. He kept on asking me what made me keep on going in the face of so many adversities. I told him that I personally had to beg and plead for all my clearances as I was only getting minimal support from the State Department and Phillips 66. Along the way, the Air Force helped me a bit; the Navy didn't like it much when I went to say hello to all the guys on the aircraft carrier USS Independence in the Gulf of Oman.

"On Shemya I had great help from the spy plane head, but no help from the base commander as he hated me." Yet again, Casey was letting his emotions get the better of him.

The one-hour interview (which aired all over Alaska) sounded as if he didn't think this was a real taped interview. He seemed very blasé. Casey went on to tell about both the typhoon and tropical storm he survived as well as the almost 1,600-mile endurance flight over the North Pacific Ocean to Attu. The interviewer just let Casey talk. Casey added that he had become an expert in diplomatic relations, plus a booking agent for all his lodging, fuel, and money.

Casey left Dutch Harbor on December 13 at about 1130 and arrived in Kodiak at 1538, which meant his flying time was 4 hours and 38 minutes, covering some 823 miles.

"The trip was wild. I must have encountered at least two major snowstorms on my way there. I would try different altitudes and even deviated to the west to try and get out of this mess. But it seemed the snow wanted me. I prayed I would reach Kodiak at all," he later recalled.

A third major snowstorm awaited Casey some 50 miles out from Kodiak. This was a horrendous storm and, once inside the storm, he realized that he was flying in blizzard conditions. Winds of 50 to

60 miles per hour whipped around him. He was buffeted by both up and down drafts. The storm conditions forced him to deviate from his flight plan and head south about 70 miles in an attempt to circumnavigate the weather.

Casey contacted the Kodiak tower and was given landing instructions to land in the bay about three hundred yards from the airport. Yet, over the radio he could hear an Alaska Airlines pilot abort his landing at Kodiak because of the severe crosswinds on the runways. Recognizing that he might face a similar scenario, Casey quickly hammered out an alternative plan. He thought he could make a safe landing and avoid the high crosswinds by landing farther outside in the bay, rather than land close to the base of the airport's runway.

But once he set his craft down, he was immediately surrounded by "willy winds" (waterspouts). These appeared as funnel-shaped twisters that touched the waterline but were actually connected above to towering cumulonimbus clouds.

He had a helluva time trying to navigate; the willy winds actually spun his aircraft around twice. The tower told him to look for a ramp to secure his aircraft. He finally managed to taxi toward a boat ramp on the shoreline that sat adjacent to the airport's runway. Once there, he gunned his craft up onto a concrete ramp. No more than five minutes after securing his craft, he was met by the Kodiak fixed base operator (FBO – an aircraft services company). He and another gentleman, fighting winds of up 60 knots, positioned the floats securely onto a boat trailer. The low-slung trailer, especially made to transport float planes in Alaska, was pulled by truck to the safety of the FBO's hangar.

Casey stayed the night at the home of a friend, Dave Kinney. He later had time to visit with members of the local Lions Club and said he would return and give a talk on his adventure.

Meanwhile, back in New York on December 13, I had just hung up the phone with Jack Hammond. He was delighted to hear that Casey was well on his way to Seattle. I didn't want to bring Hammond up to speed until I was sure Casey had made it off Shemya and had made it successfully to Dutch Harbor, where there was actually a real civilization in the Aleutians. Casey at this moment was well on his way to Kodiak.

I had reviewed with Hammond Casey's original planned itinerary after he left Shemya. He had forecasted a planned landing in Seattle on December 13. That brought a chuckle from Hammond, since today was the 12th, and he doubted that would happen. We realistically could expect him by December 18.

I also mentioned that Casey had a left magneto problem with his engine, which he had called and told me about when he was in Atka. He was able to fix it himself based on the long distance phone advice of his mechanic at Harvey Airport near Seattle. "Jack, if anyone fools with his prop, they will get a close haircut," I joked. Hammond was more than complimentary of the effort our agency (G+A) had put forward with the Casey project overall.

"Bill, we will have a great reunion in Seattle and those in power at Phillips know that you have done this whole damn thing very well. I want you at my side when that turkey gets back to the starting point," Hammond said. "I am paying (out of his budget) for this project and if anyone, and I really mean the promotions manager, tries to malign you, then I will go right to the Chairman of the Board.

"You made this flight happen, and if it hadn't been for your perseverance, he probably wouldn't have made it past India. Both Admiral Engen and myself are proud of what you and David Knight have done.

"Instead of Phillips 66 having egg on their face for sponsoring this event, you brought us glory. Keep me up to speed and let's hope he makes it home by Christmas." With that remark, Hammond started to laugh out loud.

I also spoke with Boggs at Phillips and reviewed Casey's plans. Boggs laughed at the magneto problem, but added that he had no intention at present of discussing with the media what caused Casey's engine to fail. We would only say that our investigation was ongoing and the circumstances were under evaluation.

A complete summary of that evaluation would be released to the media sometime in January. Dennis wished Casey well and said he was sure he would make it back alive and hopefully in one piece.

I subsequently informed Knight of the kind words Hammond had said about him. In the meantime, David had sent a letter to Sig Rogich, the assistant to President George H.W. Bush for activities and initiatives. Knight briefed Rogich on Casey's adventure and told him that the pilot was due back at Sand Point Naval Air Station (now NOAA Western Regional Center on Lake Washington) on December 18 at precisely 1000.

In Knight's two-page, extremely well-written letter, he clarified that "the flight took much longer than expected due to a wide variety of challenges (bureaucracy, health, logistics, the threat of war, weather, etc.). It read:

> *"The flight shows the resourcefulness of this American pilot, his performance and, frankly, his pilot skills and commitment to completing an enormously difficult task which will probably never be attempted again in this century or the next.*

> *"The flight also represents a massive cooperative effort between the private sector that included a variety of aviation companies, led by Phillips 66, working together with the public sector (State Dept., FAA, USIA), the military (USN, USAF), the U.S. Coast Guard, and the people and governments of 20 nations, the most pivotal being Saudi Arabia, where he was welcomed by the Minister of Defense just prior to the Iraqi invasion of Kuwait, and allowed to leave during Desert Shield."*

Knight added several other key paragraphs having to do with media exposure and a few highlights of Casey's journey, concluding:

> *"President Bush has demonstrated his strong belief in international cooperation to achieve more than just the possible. He also promoted the achievements that can be gained by public/private sector collaboration.*

> *"As well, many of us in aviation know him as a pilot who identifies with the stamina and commitment needed to complete such a mission."*

David inquired if the President could call Casey or send him a letter of congratulations.

Knight also informed me that Admiral Engen had contacted Craig Fuller as well. Fuller served for eight years in the White House as Assistant to the President for Cabinet Affairs for President Ronald Reagan and then as Chief of Staff to Vice President George H.W. Bush.

In preparation for the big event, I left for Seattle on December 14 and staff-mate Tim McCormack was to follow by December 15. He was busy drafting the final 12-page news story for pre-event release.

I stayed at the same hotel I had stayed at back when Casey had his engine failure. Now, I would just sit tight and let Casey give me a call from other stopovers he landed at while heading back to Seattle.

That afternoon, the Dutch Harbor PBS interview with Casey aired and those that heard it wondered why Casey was taking all the credit. Hammond called me about it and I told him that I hadn't the faintest idea what he was doing, but again would talk to him about the tenor of his future interviews. All I could imagine was: What the hell would Casey say to the media once he returned to Seattle on the 18th?

Meanwhile, George Bukota, our man in Seattle, had made progress in getting NOAA back on board and the site of our news conference would be the same place where he took off the first time on May 20 (east to west) and then again when he restarted on June 14 (west to east.)

It seemed so long ago since the day he left. What a journey this had been. If and when he made it back on December 18, this journey of perseverance will have taken him 188 days to travel more than 29,000 miles. Hurrah.

In the subsequent days we found ourselves tied to the end of the phone receiver in my hotel room. I had two other phone lines and a fax machine put into my suite so we could respond to the many incoming inquiries and handle outgoing responses.

The guest list for the event on December 18 would include dignitaries from the 'World's Who's Who List,' including: the Governor of Washington State; Senator Slade Gorton; two Congressmen;

members of the U.S. State Department; and ministers from Saudi Arabia, Thailand, the Philippines, and Japan. We would also have representatives from the U.S. Navy, Air Force, and Coast Guard. Also, a representative from the National Aeronautic Association (NAA) would be present to award the record.

Our pilot was on his next leg in the trip back to Seattle. On December 14, Casey departed at 0914 for Ketchikan, but realized he would never reach his appointed destination in the daylight. The severe snowstorm that seemed to be following him had again hunted him down in Kodiak was now fast on his tail as he headed for Ketchikan.

He was now crossing the Gulf of Alaska with 60-mile per hour headwinds buffeting his plane. So, instead of Ketchikan he chose the closer destination of Juneau, which was only a leg of 653 miles. He contacted the Juneau tower at around 1500 and it directed him to land in the channel that went from the edge of the International Airport to the town of Juneau.

He taxied several miles and purposely lined up in the middle of the channel to avoid coming close to any anchored tankers or freighters. With the help of the tower he located a wooden ramp. A gentleman in another aircraft adjacent to Casey secured his aircraft at the seaplane dock and then provided assistance in getting Liberty II up on the ramp and securing it to the dock.

The following day, December 15, he continued on his journey towards Ketchikan. But he wanted to make an intermediate stop. After departing at 1100, he flew just 166 miles to Petersburg to visit an old friend. He touched down in Frederick Sound and navigated south down the channel. After several miles, he took a right hand turn into a back channel inlet that led to the town of Petersburg.

He was met by Mac McGugan, an old mechanic buddy. The two had known each other for many years and Casey just wanted to share with his very close friend the excitement of him actually completing the record trip. During their conversation, Mac told Casey that he really never thought Casey would make it. Mac told Casey, "You kept disappearing off the face of the map and then all of a sudden you appeared again. But I prayed a lot and I hope that helped." Mac seemed overjoyed at seeing Casey alive and well.

Casey left Petersburg at about 1400 and flew another 100 miles straight down the inland waterway to Ketchikan and arrived at about 1500. "I had a bird's eye view of Alaska's top wilderness regions from the air," he would recall.

"The land below was still lush and green. About 35 miles north of Ketchikan lay the Misty Fjords National Monument. From books I've read, Misty Fjords encompasses more than two million acres of alpine wilderness. Misty Fjords features an overwhelming array of different-sized valleys surrounded by sheer cliffs and spectacular flowing waterfalls.

"The moose were in great abundance, and I did notice many bears feasting by the rivers in anticipation of a long winter. When I have brought tourists here, I really enjoyed the almost glass-like water landings on many of the lakes or fjords in the area."

Casey landed in the large harbor adjacent to the city of Ketchikan. He chose not to tie up to the massive piers where during the summer months there are at least three passenger ships disembarking some 6,000 tourists to visit a small town selling souvenirs. "I taxied past the massive piers and pulled into the boat dock used to tie up yachts and seaplanes," he later explained. "At this point in the journey, I got my agonizing taste of being back in the United States.

"Right away, as soon as I was secure inside a hangar, the Immigration and Customs officials approached me and told me that I had not cleared Customs anywhere in the U.S. I immediately tried to explain that I had come from Attu, stayed on a top secret Air Force Base on Shemya where I had been checked by either Immigration or Customs. I added: Why now?

"But these dudes were not listening. They asked me to actually strip the interior of my plane of all my belongings. I secretly concluded that they were probably looking for drugs and couldn't care less even if I was the President of United States. The whole exercise took more than four hours to offload and re-load all my gear onto Liberty II. When they finally completed their wild goose chase, it was very dark.

"The officials looked at my passport and inquired why I had been to so many countries. They were especially interested in the length of time I spent in Karachi, India and in Thailand. When I told them what I was trying to accomplish, they simply stamped my passport and told me to have a good day.

"What was really not funny was that this whole episode took place in front of two TV station cameras and several newspaper reporters. I guess it was good news, as they had found no contraband in my plane."

Casey met with his close friend Don "Bucky" Dawson and had a great meal and lots of laughs and praise from Bucky to Casey regarding his accomplishments.

On the 16th, Casey was getting closer to the end of this tedious and amazing journey. He left Ketchikan in the mid-morning and flew some 370 miles to Port McNeill on Vancouver Island in British Columbia. Casey had come down from Ketchikan flying over Queen Charlotte Sound and there were high winds coming over the tops of the mountains to the left of his aircraft. They were banging the hell out of his plane. Overall, he experienced 80-knot crosswinds for several hundred miles, and he was anxious to find safe harbor near Port McNeill.

Canadian Air Traffic Control had Casey line up in the center of the harbor adjacent to the town. Recalled Casey, "After having conveyed to ATC my needs, they advised me to line up in the center of the harbor leading to Port McNeill. They warned me to stay away from any shipping traffic.

"On lining up to land in Port McNeill, I first flew over Port Hardy and then actually took more of an easterly direction and passed outside Port McNeill. I then turned south and flew several hundred yards behind the docks (the breakwater) where all the fishing boats were parked.

"I didn't want to be trapped by the heavy winds from the south, so at this point I reversed course and made a pass directly over the Port McNeill administration building. My "Top Gun" skills were at work as I made a 90-degree turn heading west. This turn set me down short and right at the gas dock for private boats. I tied up where most floatplanes are docked. One great thing about this last part of my journey is that most of these stopovers had avgas readily available.

"I was met by 100 rousing, cheering fans. All had a beer in their hands, so I presumed my landing must have been the highlight of the month. They presented me a T-shirt with the front inscription, 'Touched Down at The Breakwater.' The person who presented me the T-shirt said my landing hadn't been attempted in over 20 years. Equally, the T-shirt looked like it had been stowed away for 20 years."

Port McNeill sits on the northeast side of Vancouver Island and it lies surrounded by the staggering grandeur of mountains, rainforests, and the islands of the archipelago. Casey stayed at his friend Coleen's home for the night. She was the secretary for the local FBO and a long-time friend. Casey complained that he rarely saw a woman on Shemya, and he observed that some other islands he visited were only inhabited by the Aleut people.

That night quite late, Casey finally contacted me and verified he was still alive and where he was. He explained that the media reports he'd seen should have given me a good hint as to his location. More than once during our conversation he repeated for me what I had called his mantra: 'Where the hell is Casey?' I just laughed and cautioned that if he addressed the media like he did at the PBS station, then he would seriously see everyone abandon him.

Quickly changing the subject, he said, "There were both severe headwinds and crosswinds in my path and in spite of these challenges, I made some spectacular landings. This major snowstorm, hitting the whole coastal area of Alaska, had a will of its own and kept following me. I can't ever remember such high winds and being buffeted so much in a neck of the woods so familiar to me.

"I had to make a sensational landing earlier today at Port Mc-Neill. I tried to make the story very vivid to those who greeted me at the dock by describing all my twists and turns I had to make. One of the head dudes of all these spectators that watched me land presented me with a commemorative T-shirt."

I told Casey to stay in Friday Harbor in the San Juan Islands on December 17, prior to his big ceremony outside Seattle, and that his official Seattle landing date was December 18. We wanted him to land at 1000 hours.

It was now Day 187 of his trek around the world. The trip from Port McNeill to Friday Harbor was a simple jaunt of 230 miles. He left around noon and made it to Friday Harbor by 1400. He flew VFR at about 1,200 feet most of the way. He then docked at the boat ramp where most seaplanes tie up.

Recalled Casey, "Friday Harbor has a tranquil and slow-paced atmosphere. My friends and I enjoyed a charming long walk and it was pointed out to me that the town had been built on a hill leading up from the harbor where my plane was docked. There were small friendly stores and restaurants and a refreshing absence of fast-food chains. What I really liked about Friday Harbor was that most of the coffee shops offered large lounge chairs to sit and watch the port's activities, and cars have been replaced by horse-drawn buggies."

When Casey called me from Friday Harbor, I related that all the preparations had been made for his landing at Sand Point and that much of the world media would be there. In addition, the governor may be there as well as many dignitaries from state and foreign countries. That got him really excited.

Casey said that he would be leaving Friday Harbor about 0830 and would fly the 76 miles to Seattle, landing on Lake Washington at 1000 on December 18. I told him that we wanted him to come out of the clouds, if possible, and make a grand entrance. He was now set for the homecoming of his life.

Later relating how that day began, he said, "I arose early and had a really great home-cooked breakfast. Walked to the aircraft, got fuel, and left Friday Harbor by 0830. It was snowing lightly when I left, but as I got closer to Lake Washington the snow intensified and became blinding. I did my first 180-degree turn and deviated westward towards Whidbey Island and looked for clearer weather. I was now over Puget Sound with a 200-foot ceiling. The tankers below seemed to almost touch the underbelly of my aircraft, so I went higher to about 600 feet.

"I dipped a bit lower, leaving Puget Sound behind and as I broke through the cloud cover, right directly in front of me was the carrier USS Nimitz (CVN 68). I was directly in its flight path and didn't want another call from Admiral Dunleavy. I rocked my wings and radioed the ship, asking that they please tell Admiral Dunleavy that I didn't need another emergency landing as I was now home. Then I rolled off and headed to Seattle."

As Lake Washington came into view, he alerted NOAA that he was lining up to land. Casey swooped out of the clouds at about 1,000 feet and was still in a heavy downpour of snow. Liberty II looked to all like a giant bald eagle coming through the mist. His aircraft steadied itself at about 100 feet off the deck and the crowd below just seemed to all at once make an "ahhhh" sound. Casey made one very low pass over Sand Point in his red, white, and blue Cessna 206 and came around and slid his floats gently onto the lake in order to make a very smooth landing. He taxied for about 600 yards and gracefully slid his aircraft up to a dock of the National Oceanic and Atmospheric Administration Regional Headquarters.

Casey landed at 1030, December 18, 1990. Stepping out of the left side door of his plane at dockside, Casey excitedly addressed a welcoming crowd of over 500 people. "Sorry I'm late," he said. In attendance was his son, whom he immediately hugged. At that moment, tears rolled down both men's faces.

\* \* \*

*"All big men are dreamers. They see things in the soft haze of a spring day or in the red fire of a long winter's evening. Some of us let great dreams die, but others nourish and protect them, nurse them through bad days till they bring them to the sunshine and light which comes always to those who sincerely hope that their dreams will come true."*

**— Woodrow Wilson**

# Forty-three

# An Unrequited Success

*"I would challenge you to a battle of wits, but I see that
you are unarmed."*

**— William Shakespeare**

The day prior to Casey's historic landing our PR team had
all huddled in my room. We were going over every detail for Casey's
homecoming the following day. Boggs had arrived in the early afternoon as a replacement for Hammond, who had some crucial company
business that needed his attention. Boggs was the perfect alternative
as he knew the value of this historic journey and would be an excellent spokesperson for Phillips 66.

We had discussed strategies with Knight previously and
thanked him for sending the President's letter of congratulations to
Casey. Knight had surely pulled a proverbial 'rabbit out of the hat' in
suggesting to the President's advisors the importance of drafting this
letter of congratulations to Casey.

Knight also had confirmed with me that Admiral Engen
would be calling Casey the next evening, following the successful
landing of our hero. To make sure Engen knew where Casey would be
at that hour, Knight had asked me to call him early in the afternoon
with that info. As always, David got me laughing when he said, "I bet

you a million bucks he will have pissed off someone by the time the day is over. I hope it's not Phillips 66."

Knight didn't stop there: "And, to think, my career is not resting on the line like yours. Maybe next time you will listen to me. I told you (only kiddingly) that you should take a vacation in all of December." At this point, Knight was roaring with laughter.

My response: "Thanks, and I bet your excuse for not being here was that you had planned to be at another event way back in 1989!"

He said, "I am sorry I cannot be there. Good luck Bill, the eyes of Phillips 66 and the rest of world are upon you. And that is not a new song."

Fact is, Knight wasn't far off in his comment. My ass was indeed hanging out in the wind as I would be the master of ceremonies and I also was responsible for what Casey would be saying to this august group of well-wishers. That meant trying to keep Casey's ego in check, while at the same time extolling to the media as well as dignitaries the value of this hero's accomplishment.

We had more than 20 news agencies planning to attend the event. That included all four Seattle TV stations (three networks), four major radio stations, eight newspapers, and several wire services (including the biggies — Reuters, AP, *USA Today*, *The Washington Post*). CNN and Good Morning America planned on doing live feeds. Some 30 other news outlets had requested press materials.

Included in our presentation were two news stories which McCormack had prepared. This day, December 17, we had released the news story telling the world that Casey would be home tomorrow after flying more than 29,000 miles, and landing more than 75 times in oceans, bays, harbors, lakes, and rivers in some 20 countries. The second news story would be released the next day. It encapsulated Casey's perseverance, and featured all the newsreel highlights of his journey.

Nothing, it seemed, was being left to chance. Casey had been alerted that he was to arrive by 1000 at Sand Point. Meanwhile, the weather people were calling for the storm of the century the following day. Frankly, this type of weather event would fit perfectly into the legend of this story. Why? Because it seemed a perfect way to cap off a journey that had been thrown so many curveballs by fate along the way.

I spoke with the caterers and they were all set up for a lavish spread to be laid out at NOAA's headquarters. I figured once Casey landed we could adjourn there for lunch and let the media have their go at Casey.

There were also the TV folks to consider. I knew they would want footage of Casey's landing and would also want to interview him planeside. The weather would dictate how this all was going to shake out. I just told myself that I was going to calmly let all the events happen as they may. Frankly, if I tried to control everything, then something surely would go wrong. Yet, despite my own reservations about what would occur, FUBAR became the norm of the next day.

My suite was well stocked with over 20 bottles of booze plus wine and beer. I knew many of the guests might want to have a drink after the formalities were over.

That evening, dinner went well and Boggs just laughed the entire meal. He just couldn't imagine how Casey had skirted so many disasters and actually finished the journey across the North Pacific with an engine hanging on a wing and a prayer. "That's it!" he exclaimed while shaking his head in disbelief. "A wing and a prayer — that had to be the answer!"

The Phillips 66 team included Kurt Maurer, the company photographer, who was ready to take photos of every facet of Casey's landing and press briefing. Kurt and I had been on many previous assignments together since 1985. He always proclaimed to everyone at Phillips that when working with me, one should get hazardous duty pay. Kurt was in his early 50s and stood about 5-foot-5. He was German-born to the core, spoke with a distinct German accent, and came to the U.S. when he was 19. Early in his 20s, he worked for Phillips as a graphic designer, only later becoming a world famous and accomplished photographer. His award-winning photos have appeared in many prestigious magazines and galleries.

Kurt had become a close friend, too, and often was giving me advice. He was right about 90 percent of the time. He thought Casey was an extremely brave person but a bit of a screw-up. "There has never been a dull day with this pilot," Kurt said. "He just keeps on moving. The 'Energizer Bunny' took a cue from Casey."

Among the graphics we had created for the press briefing was a giant world map, detailing Casey's historic flight. At the ceremony, we wanted Maurer to take a great photo of Boggs and Casey holding it together.

December 18 came early at our hotel – 0500, to be exact. We all met in my suite at 0630 for breakfast and a rehearsal. Boggs wanted to know what he should say. I gave him some remarks I had prepared the night before. "Just welcome him home and tell everyone how proud Phillips 66 is of him in that he had persevered and completed this journey. Emphasize the courage he exhibited on this arduous trek. Tell everyone that Phillips 66 is extremely proud to have been his sponsor," I explained.

We then left for Sand Point. Upon arrival, we found George Bukota setting up the podium and sound system. It was about 30 degrees Fahrenheit and snowing heavily; I hoped we could complete all the outside festivities in about two hours. I checked that we had ample coffee and breakfast items for the media and dignitaries in NOAA's lounge area. And, I spoke with the caterers and was advised that they would be setting up for a buffet lunch for 40 people in the conference room at 1230.

I welcomed Washington Governor Booth Gardner, U.S. State Department officials, and Senator Gorton, as well as several dignitaries from both the Saudi Arabian and Philippines embassies. I visited with the media and promised the TV networks good close-up angles for filming Casey's descent onto Lake Washington. The print media asked for interview times and I promised each of them exclusives during lunch.

The prep work was almost done. It was now about 1010 and far in the distance we could hear the roar of an aircraft's engine heading our way. At approximately 1015, Casey dropped out of a sleet-filled sky; made a pass over the crowd; shot out to a safe distance over Lake Washington; made a left-hand turn, and then landed magnificently. What a smooth landing.

He taxied to NOAA's dock and then, in what seemed like one continuous motion, he jumped out from his aircraft while simultaneously yelling to the crowd. "Sorry I'm late, but I'm here!" Casey blurted out with great exuberance. He then secured his aircraft, turned, and greeted his son. After hugging his son, he turned his attention to the media throng around him. Lots of footage was being taken and he was deluged by what seemed like thousands of questions. Almost oblivious to his surroundings, Casey just kept saying, "I've set the record and I'm here to prove it."

# Historic flight ends after circling

Associated Press    921A

# globe landing only on water

Associated Press

After landing his Cessna 206 float plane, pilot Tom Casey waves to a crowd gathered to greet him Tuesday on the shore of Lake Washington at Seattle.

Casey almost ran to the podium and, even before I could introduce him or welcome him back, stood facing the almost 400 people, smiling like a Cheshire Cat, and then spoke like a true victor. "Wow," he exclaimed, "To be back in one piece and see all of you here to greet me. What a wonderful sight! I need to say a special thanks to my sponsor, Phillips 66, for all you have done for me."

At that point, I quickly stepped to the podium. "Excuse me Tom, but before you continue I have a few simple points of interest I want to share with everyone," I said, now addressing the crowd. "Casey's round-the-world feat was a historic event that likely will never, ever again be repeated in this century or the next. We have a host

of dignitaries here today as well as many worldwide media representatives. Thank you for coming. And after Tom speaks to you, Dennis
Boggs of Phillips 66 would like to officially welcome Tom home."

Our pilot stepped back to the podium. As if on cue, he began
to thank one and all for their support. "A special thanks to my handler
and his staff," he said, extending out his hand to shake mine. Most of
all thank you Vice Admiral Don Engen who brought everyone together to make this flight happen."

"Without them, I wouldn't be here today. And, let's not forget
the State Department, who helped pave my way through the countries
I visited. I understand the Saudis have a representative here today. I
would have been lost without their support in healing me. All in all,
there are so many I want to thank and I will be sending a personal
thank you to each of you."

Casey also wanted to tell everyone about his harrowing trip
this day from Friday Harbor. "It was just me and the seagulls, since
I had to fly low below the clouds," he said. "The last 60 miles from
Friday Harbor were probably the toughest of the journey. Also, the
carrier Nimitz almost got an unexpected guest as I broke out of the
snowstorm about 100 yards from her deck. I did apologize to the
ship's captain over the radio.

"Overall, this journey took longer than I thought it would,
but the extra time only makes finishing the flight even more satisfying.
It will be great to stay at home for a little while," Casey said, offering
a broad grin to the crowd.

The crowd laughed and moved to gather around Casey at the
podium. I asked that they stand back some as I had several other
speakers I wanted to introduce. I told everyone that we had a conference room for the rest of the media interviews and also a place for
Casey's close friends to congregate.

Most of the TV folks wanted to do their interviews with
Casey by his plane. I told them Casey would be available right after
comments from Phillips 66 and a few photos. Before Boggs spoke,
Casey again extolled the audience by stating, "Phillips 66 has done a
great job. Because of them, I had great media coverage everywhere I
stopped. They really coordinated all my activities with the U.S. Navy
and Air Force."

Casey then challenged other Americans to go out and test themselves. "People should go out and try to break records," he said.

I introduced Dennis Boggs and acknowledged that he was the guru of lubricants technology at Phillips 66. He had been responsible for tracking Casey's engine performance by the collection of oil samples at various points along the journey; those samples were then shipped to Bartlesville for in-depth analysis.

Boggs officially welcomed Casey home and said he was an example of keen perseverance and heroism. "In one sense it was a demonstration," said Boggs. "We wanted to show the world how safe and versatile general aviation is and how far aviation technology had come in the years since the original round-the-world flight."

He confirmed that the actual cost to Phillips 66 for sponsoring this record performance had not yet been tallied, but he estimated it would be in the hundreds of thousands of dollars.

"Flying 29,000 miles in temperature extremes from zero degrees Fahrenheit in Alaska and Iceland to higher than 120 degrees in Saudi Arabia made the Liberty II flight a great test of an engine's mechanical endurance," he continued. "We will analyze the effects of this strain put on his engine as well as how Phillips 66 X/C multiviscosity aviation oil helped to make this flight successful. We are examining the engine that earlier failed in the Aleutians and we will provide our industry groups and the media with a detailed report, possibly in late January.

"The individual Liberty II flight segments are similar to those flown by an average general aviation pilot. The almost 1,600-mile segment from Japan to Attu was a real test of Casey's seasoned piloting skills and would be more difficult for the average pilot. We believe Tom's success proved to the public that improved aviation technology is available and that general aviation flying is safer than ever." By this point, Boggs had the audience captivated.

Following those comments, Casey and Boggs posed before the giant world map that outlined Casey's journey. Then Casey went back to his plane and the TV media followed, asking many question while shooting their coverage.

Casey's journey had followed the flight path of the original around-the-world flight decades before, although he flew in the opposite direction. The first circumnavigation had been completed by two of the original four Douglas World Cruisers that departed Seattle in April of 1924. Those single-engine planes used floats and wheels to complete the trip and burned up more than 30 engines in the process. Casey, of course, had only landed and taken off on water.

Before we left the dock area, I worked out an arrangement with NOAA to have several of the maintenance people upload Casey's plane onto a special flatbed for seaplanes. It was to be stowed in the old Naval Air Station's hangar for safe keeping. I told Casey what I had arranged for his aircraft, and also told him that we had arranged for him to have a room at our hotel. That seemed the best approach as Casey had an interview with KOMO, ABC Channel 4 in Seattle, the following day.

At about 1230 I directed everyone to head back to NOAA's lounge area and invited all to join us for lunch. I explained to the media they could continue inquiring about Casey's journey during that time. During lunch, Governor Gardner personally praised Casey — both verbally and in a citation — for his record. He also read a letter he had sent to Jack Hammond at Phillips 66:

*Dear Mr. Hammond:*

*Thank you for the participation of Phillips 66 Company in the successful record setting flight of Liberty II around the world by floatplane. This arduous journey covered more than 27,000 miles, and landing only on water once again proved that the spirit of man can accomplish anything when combined with the proper equipment and support.*

*Such a bold undertaking would have been impossible without the support of businesses such as Phillips 66 Company. Your participation demonstrates the vital role the business community has placed in reaching new aviation achievements throughout history.*

*Sincerely*
*Booth Gardner*
*Governor*

In the NOAA lounge, Casey was asked about his dealings with foreign governments and how much support he received from the U.S. State Department. "State was always on my side, except for a few glitches, where I had to become something of a diplomat. In those very few instances, I was forced into the position of having to cajole foreign officials for permission to fly into and out of their countries.

"In Pakistan and Greece, I encountered horrible delays. Getting into Egypt was only achieved through perseverance and the State Department pulling a few strings." Casey said all of this while acknowledging the presence of two State Department officials in attendance.

He said his most bureaucratic snafu was gaining clearances to enter India from Pakistan. "I had to wait in Karachi more than 20 days. My phone bill in trying to gain a flight clearance was more than $2,000." He rubbed his thumb and middle finger together.

At this point, while Casey was recounting how he got clearance into India, I interrupted him. I wanted to tell the media the back story of what actually happened in Karachi, India, and Burma. "Casey was held in Karachi for more than 20 days at the bidding of the U.S. State Department," I explained. "Why? On the playing field was a need to determine, by both the State and Defense Departments, which countries would choose to align with the U.S. Coalition or take sides with Saddam Hussein during the Desert Shield crisis.

"Further," I said, "State had told the U.S. Embassy in Pakistan that Casey was not to be given a clearance to fly to India for that reason. Once Pakistan had determined it would line up with the U.S.-led coalition, Casey was given permission to leave Pakistan and head onto India. And, we needed to provide the Indian aviation ministers with some incentives to gain approval for him to fly in and out of both Bombay and Calcutta.

"Further, at the same time, since the U.S. lacked diplomatic relations with Burma, Saudi Arabian Airlines stepped to the plate and they designated Casey's plane as Saudi Special Flight #2, so he could fly over Burma."

The editors thanked me. I also told them that most of Casey's flight clearances had been handled through us. I reiterated that we were in constant contact with all the U.S. embassies and foreign governments from Greece to Japan. Those officials in turn approved all movements of Casey to and from their respective countries.

"We also had direct contact with the U.S.S.R.," I explained, and told the story of my late night call to Premier Gorbachev. The media thought that was really one heck of a diplomatic encounter. (By now, Casey was listening but not fully paying attention. As far as he was concerned, he had flown the record – not me or anyone else. What else was there to discuss?)

The Reuters reporter asked me if all the negative news coverage I personally received in Japan was viewed as a negative aspect for this historic record. I explained that we had worked closely with the U.S. FAA in Japan and that's how we chose to gain Casey's flight clearances. Our efforts were all very transparent and aboveboard.

I further elaborated that "it was just that certain Japanese officials were somewhat annoyed as to how these clearances were obtained. Also, there was a bit of miscommunication — a language barrier — between the Japanese and myself. I finally worked out the wrinkles, but not before the Japanese newspapers claimed it was my fault personally that an unauthorized American civilian was flying through Japan and had severed the SOFA agreement between our two countries. By the time Casey had made it to Misawa, the Japanese press was on our side. Moreover, there were no personal repercussions as a result of my actions from any official in Japan or here in the States.

"Frankly," I said, "Probably the most interesting aspect of this journey was that we always knew there would be another adventure ahead when he took off for another country."

Casey was then asked about his engine failure off the Aleutians. He went on to explain that this was the low point in his journey — when he made an emergency landing in the Pacific Ocean off of Kiska Island. Casey reinforced that this event had occurred after his successful long flight from Japan.

"For a moment," he said with his arms extended over his head, as if he were orchestrating a symphony, "I thought the trip was over, but then I realized with the help of my friends and sponsor I could repair the damage to the plane and continue for the record."

"Didn't you have to get a new engine?" one journalist inquired. Casey responded that he could have fixed that engine on Shemya, but he wanted to be sure nothing else needed repair, so he obtained another engine. He also commented that there was only minor damage to the plane.

"That was the best landing of my life as far as I'm concerned," he said.

Other questions had to do with various portions of the trip and each answer by Casey was a story of its own. These were tales of bravery and tenacity. Admiral Engen would have been proud of how Casey, undaunted in his quest, exemplified the positive side of general aviation.

"My will to succeed was enormous," he continued. 'My hope is that those hearing about my record-setting journey and its many hair-raising tests will want to try their hand at learning to fly. Remember, I was only flying a 29-foot long (39-foot wingspan) aircraft through some pretty hectic encounters, during which nature and my training and piloting skills allowed me to succeed. My many years of general aviation flying were a prelude to making this dream come true." Casey now appeared totally in command as he sat half-on and half-off the conference room table.

During all of this, I was watching Boggs' eyes the whole time. He on several occasions just smiled as if to say, "Glad you made it in one piece, lad. You certainly had me worried as well as most of Phillips Petroleum."

Stepping in front of Casey, I informed the guests in the lounge area that I had received two letters from the heads of the Seaplane Pilots Association. Executive Director Robert Richardson's long letter could be summed up by one key sentence: "I salute you for the dogged determination which you have exhibited."

President Kenneth Fulton equally saluted Casey for his deeds and this sentence summed up his letter: "Tom, please accept my salute to the courage which you have displayed in getting this world record for seaplanes."

Further, I informed everyone that I also wanted to read the letter sent by President George H.W. Bush to Casey. "In the letter the President also gave equal accolades to Phillips 66 for all their efforts in ensuring that Casey finished this journey." (I wanted to make sure that Phillips got due credit.) The letter read:

> *I am delighted to send warm greetings to everyone gathered to welcome Tom Casey to Sand Point Naval Air Station. My hearty congratulations to Tom upon the successful completion of the historic global flight of Liberty II.*
>
> *Nearly a century ago, Orville and Wilbur Wright ushered in the age of aviation with one brief, bold flight over the beach near Kitty Hawk, North Carolina.*
>
> *Tom's historic worldwide flight by seaplane — to advance new ideas in aviation technology — is in keeping with the great legacy of the Wright brothers. I salute Tom for his perseverance and for his courage, and I congratulate the many volunteers and the generous sponsor who helped to make this record-setting flight possible.*
>
> **— George Bush**

The editors thought all this attention was exemplary and applauded accordingly. Meanwhile, I waited patiently for the representative of the National Aeronautic Association (NAA) to officially give Casey the record. I went over to him and asked if there was a problem.

"Yes," he said. "Casey's flight didn't qualify for the record."

I asked why and he explained that Casey's flight was interrupted. I explained that I had previously spoken with NAA officials in Washington, D.C., and NAA's president had acknowledged that the interruption of his flight and his stay on Shemya didn't adversely affect the overall record. The NAA headquarters confirmed that the record remained intact once his plane had been fixed; he went back to his last recorded landing spot after Japan (Attu Island), and restarted the journey.

The NAA rep also stated that Casey didn't have enough

mileage to qualify for the record. I countered by saying that he only needed 24,960 miles for the record, and that he had flown 26,579 miles since he restarted his journey on June 14. If his initial Alaska round trip had been included, he would have flown more than 29,499. His mileage was all verified in his logbook.

No sooner had these words slipped from his lips, then bingo, the NAA rep got up from his chair and left the NOAA building. I was flabbergasted. No record! I felt betrayed and horribly bad for Casey at that moment.

It was nearly 1700 hours when we all packed it in and headed back to our hotel. Casey slumped into a big lounge chair, popped the cap on a bottle of Scotch, and proceeded to pour himself a well-deserved drink.

At the first opportunity, I called Knight and gave him a blow by blow account of the press briefing. Knight laughed several times, but in general he expressed how happy he was that Phillips 66 and the State Department were singled out by Casey for their support. He wanted Admiral Engen to hear about Casey's successful homecoming personally. The admiral would be placing a call from his home at about 1900.

I mentioned that Casey acknowledged he would still be on Shemya if not for all of our support — like getting him a new engine, fuel, an A&P mechanic, dollies, and all the efforts working with the U.S. Navy and Air Force.

Knight was pleased the media conference went so well and said he would brief Engen. "I imagine Hammond will be pleased, too," David said. "Good luck on everything else, my friend. Cheers."

It was about 1800 when the phone rang. It was Admiral Dunleavy. The admiral was in good spirits, much different from the time we talked after Casey had crashed. "Hey, is our boy there?" the admiral asked. "Yes," I responded. I handed the phone to Casey and his eyes seemed to open wide like a deer in the headlights of an oncoming car.

"Yes admiral, I'm back," he said. "Great trip, and I said hello to the captain of the Nimitz. No, I plan to have a long rest before I start on the speaking circuit. I will see you back in D.C. when I come east. Coleman will be lining up my speaking engagements and I want to address Congress, too. Thank you admiral; yes, it was an arduous trip. I told everyone whom I came in contact with that you were my mentor. Yes, Captain Harry Smith was great. Said he worked for you once. He should be promoted to admiral and maybe you can make that happen. Hey, say hello to General McPeak for me. Thank you for everything, admiral." At that point, Casey seemed to fade away into his lounge chair.

I got on the phone and explained to the admiral that Casey was exhausted. In the call, Casey never bothered to specifically thank him for saving his ass in Greece; for his not getting shot down in the Gulf of Oman; and for his great accommodations in the Philippines. Again, I thanked the admiral for all of his support and told him we couldn't have made it happen without him in his Pentagon chair.

The rest of the evening went well. Admiral Engen called Casey and praised him for his dedicated spirit of adventure. As always, Engen was the perfect gentleman and bent over backwards praising Casey for his accomplishment. "General aviation gained a real hero today, Tom. You have a lot to be proud of and we are most certainly proud of you," Admiral Engen told him.

Later, Casey retired to his room after we all returned from dinner. It was still snowing hard and Seattle could expect snow and sleet to continue all night — maybe two feet of accumulation. God forbid we had to drive to downtown Seattle the next day and be at KOMO-TV for a 1200 live interview.

As might be expected, the next day turned out to be totally bizarre. The snow and sleet had turned Seattle into an icy mess. Casey was at the wheel of our rent-a-car; he had insisted that he knew where we had to go, and said the trip might be hazardous considering the conditions.

It began with our having to cross a bridge that was covered with ice. We skidded the whole length of the bridge span; luckily, we were the only car trying to cross during our out-of-control driving lesson by Casey. Boggs, sitting in the back seat, was sweating. I was frozen to my seat and I think I screamed several times.

After finally arriving at KOMO studios, Casey was met by several of the station's producers. He was ushered into the studio, introduced to the anchors, seated, and the red light on the camera blinked.

They were now live on the air.

Casey was asked many questions. One of first was regarding what had happened to his aircraft engine. "It just quit and I made the landing of a lifetime," was his response. He used his hands to serve as the actual aircraft and in one motion went through the acrobatics of how he had made the emergency landing happen.

"But, to live up to my safety standards, I decided to completely replace my engine. Wipaire in Minnesota provided me the new engine. Phillips 66, my sponsor, had the new engine shipped to me on Shemya. In fact, my handler — who worked for Phillips 66 — got me fuel sent and had a mechanic flown out to Shemya to check my work on the aircraft. Phillips paid for all the expenses." With that, Casey smiled to Dennis and me through the TV studio glass that separated it from the waiting room.

As the TV folks continued with their questions on the set, Casey offered the viewers multiple anecdotes and spell-binding tales. Overall, Casey kept acknowledging the support by the State Department; Phillips; and all embassy people he encountered. He also built up his image in an attempt to garner future speaking engagements. He was hoping this interview would land him some paying gigs.

After the interview was completed, we headed back to the hotel. Along the way, Boggs informed Casey that I had some very important news for him. Back in my suite I said, "Tom, Phillips 66 has decided to help you gain some speaking engagements. We will determine at a future date to what extent you might act as their official spokesperson for their aviation oil. And, we understand you want the recognition and spoils, like speaking engagements, movie rights, and maybe a book deal. Tom, you can proceed with all of these and we will try to support your efforts."

Casey explained that he had always wanted to carry the general aviation banner and have everyone acknowledge his flying prowess. He was also looking to get some paying appearances and wanted to get a movie made of his adventure. He admitted he always knew Phillips 66 did great things for him, but never knew what had happened behind the scenes.

"Hell, I never knew of all the twists and turns Coleman had to handle," he said. "I was too busy flying the plane. It gets very lonely up there and I spent a lot of the time wondering if I would even make it. So when people asked me questions about my journey, I would often say I just had to persevere to make it this far. But, really, when evaluating everything that happened, I had to fly the blasted plane to gain this record.

"And I am proud of that fact. The damn NAA is blowing smoke and that really pisses me off!" Casey stuck his finger in the air wanting to emphasize the importance of that statement.

I attempted to reinforce the gravity of the moment. "Tom, without our help, the State Department, or the U.S. Navy, the Air Force, and FAA, you would have never made it," I said. "With all this help you got clearance to enter major metropolitan areas such as Alexandria, Karachi, Pattaya Beach; and countries like India, Brunei, the Philippines, and Japan. You had to have the support of the U.S. Defense Department to fly through Saudi Arabia during Desert Shield. After all, who the hell was running the war? And, remember in Jeddah, your ass was lucky that you and your plane weren't shipped back to the U.S. when you had back trouble. Throughout, you had Dunleavy and Engen pulling strings, especially when you had to be put on Shemya." I wanted to be sure Tom knew firsthand the role others had played in making his journey a success, whether or not it was officially recognized by the NAA.

"Tom, think about this. Where did all the money come from? Not Dan Hood at Pan Am or any of your friends. No, it was Phillips 66 who bankrolled you. In one simple move, they paid $24,000 for you to make it through India. John King at Saudi Arabian Airlines admitted he didn't have the stroke to get you cleared through India — we did."

I told Casey that once back in New York, I was going to further explore why the NAA didn't award him the record.

"Tom," I said, "I am heading back to New York in the morning. Dennis is going back tonight to Bartlesville. And, I would advise you to go home. I will make it a priority to schedule you several speaking engagements and then I am going to look into finding a publisher for a book on your adventure." Casey smiled at that, and we spent the rest of the day laughing about some of the astonishing exploits he encountered on his historic adventure.

The next day as I was leaving the hotel for the airport, Casey hugged me and I thought he wasn't going to let go. "Thanks, Bill, for everything," he said.

Yet, unable to curb his ego he calmly added, echoing a bit of the Irish leprechaun inside of him, "I am a hero and the world will want to hear from me." Now that was Tom Casey, full of bravado to ...

**The End.**

\* \* \*

**Fast forward to 2015.** I have written this account of one of the greatest adventures of all time because the world needs to know and appreciate the accomplishments made by Tom Casey during the year 1990.

He deserves it. We are hoping that NAA one day will present Casey with the record. He deserves all the accolades that come with flying this round-the-world adventure. Yes, he is as good a pilot as Lindbergh and perhaps even better, since he flew much farther and had to land and take off only on water.

In life there is much that is bittersweet. Such is the case with Tom Casey, who pursued and completed an aviation voyage for the ages.

*Casey and Dennis Boggs of Phillips 66 with a map of the
completed journey.*

# Final Analysis of Casey's Failed Aircraft Engine

**Following the forced landing due to engine failure on the
Liberty II aircraft in the Aleutian Islands on Nov. 1 1990, Phillips 66
performed an in-depth analysis to determine the cause of the mechanical problem with Tom Casey's IO-550F Continental engine. Here's what
they found.**

Once the pilot and plane were safely on Shemya Island,
Phillips 66 immediately recommended replacement of the aircraft's
engine. With WipAire's generous offer of providing a replacement engine, Phillips 66 used every resource available to assure Casey received
maintenance parts and support, fuel, and other needed supplies to
help him continue on his arduous world record.

Phillips 66 was then eager to determine the cause of the mechanical problem in the original engine. As such, Phillips 66 teamed
with Engine Components, Inc. (ECI), the manufacturer of the Cermicrome-processed cylinders used in the engine, to conduct tests at ECI's
facility in New Braunfels, Texas.

Engineers from both companies inspected Casey's damaged
engine using a procedure similar to a FAA certification check. Each
engine part was meticulously examined and evaluated to determine
the cause of the engine malfunction. The results of this examination

were completed in late December, 1990 and are explained in the following Q&A:

**What caused the Liberty II aircraft engine to fail while en route from Attu to Dutch Harbor in the Aleutians on Nov. 1, 1990?**
After a thorough examination of all engine parts, Phillips 66 and ECI determined the engine failed due to a burned No. 6 piston. The piston burned because of pre-ignition.

**What was the cause of pre-ignition in the engine?**
In any investigation, analysis of the engine parts provides most of the reasons for the engine failure, but there often remain some unanswered questions. In the case of Liberty II, specific operating parameters during many segments of the flight may have induced additional stress to the engine usually not experienced by the majority of general aviation piston-powered aircraft in use today.

Liberty II experienced many environmental extremes during the flight. Variable temperatures as high as 120 degrees Fahrenheit in the Saudi Arabian desert, and as low as 20F in Alaska and Iceland, placed high stress on the engine. Further, water takeoffs required long taxiing time to build up speed, and water landings sometimes necessitated shock cooling, putting enormous torque on the engine. After a thorough examination, it was determined that the combination of a possible air induction leak and/or air constriction in the intake system limited takeoff power at various times during the trip. The resulting low manifold pressure placed additional stress on the engine.

Because of an imbalance in the air/fuel mixture, high ambient temperatures, and long taxiing times, it was often necessary for the pilot to run a rich mixture. At cruise, when the pilot chose to lean his engine, the adjustment was always sensitive to the demands of the No. 6 cylinder.

Attempts to compensate for low manifold pressure, maximum load takeoffs, and extreme operating parameters may have started a chain of small, systematic pre-ignitions which began to erode the No.6 piston crown. In effect, the leaning process, used to gain more complete combustion in the engine, could have increased the stresses on an already hot No.6 piston.

**Was oil or the Cermicrome process in any way the cause for engine failure (a key consideration for both companies)?**

No. Examination of the engine revealed that all oil-wetted parts were in excellent condition, except the limited area which was damaged by piston failure. The critical analysis by Phillips 66 and ECI verified that the oil and Cermicrome-processed cylinders provided maximum protection in spite of the demanding engine operating parameters during the flight.

Most importantly, there was no scoring on the No.6 cylinder. In addition, no rust was present on any cylinder, which is often an adverse side effect with floatplane engines.

Also, the plane's engine performance had been monitored closely by Phillips 66 technicians during the journey. Following a prescribed schedule to change the engine oil, Casey was required to send oil samples to Phillips 66 for evaluation. Each sample that was received was then analyzed so as to monitor the condition of the IO-550F engine.

**When was it determined that Casey's engine was showing elevated wear, which may have resulted in total engine failure?**

After review of the oil analysis sample from an oil change Casey made in Subic Bay, Phillips 66 lubricant technical specialists (in Bartlesville, OK) became concerned about a sudden increase in wear metals in the oil. Analysis revealed indications of a possible engine failure. Phillips 66 immediately notified the pilot in Hokkaido, Japan, of these results.

An on-site mechanic was secured to investigate for engine damage. The mechanic did compression checks on all cylinders and verified that they were at specified limits. The rocker cover was pulled to investigate for metals, and none were found. Oil was drained through a cheesecloth strainer and no metals were apparent. After five hours of mechanical review, Casey made a pilot-in-command decision to fly to Attu in the Aleutians. He then safely completed that leg of the flight. It was after he departed Attu that the engine failure occurred.

# Jack L. Hammond

In 1990, Jack L. Hammond was the Phillips 66 manager for aviation sales, a position that oversaw virtually every aspect of the company's involvement in aviation. A 34-year Phillips 66 employee, he was an integral force in the general aviation community for more than 30 years.

According to *Flying* magazine in 1993: "Jack Hammond, Phillips' main man in aviation fuels, solidly built and was totally behind his company's aviation fuel delivery network." He came to Phillips 66 in 1960 with a B.A. degree in economics from the University of Colorado. He moved into aviation product sales in 1962, working for Billy Parker, company founder Frank Phillips' first pilot and holder of pilot license #44. Thus, Jack learned the ropes from a man whose career paralleled the very development of the airplane. Billy and Jack were the only rated pilots in the company's aviation division.

A licensed pilot since 1954, he flew a Beech Duke; Cessna 310; a Baron; a Bonanza; his dad's Twin Bonanza; and just about any other general aviation aircraft. All told, Jack was a multi-engine instrument-rated pilot for more than 33 years, amassing more than 15,000 hours.

After opening many aviation market areas for Phillips 66 as a member of the company's "Flying Salesmen", Hammond became assistant manager of general aviation sales. Soon afterward, Hammond was promoted to product manager before becoming manager of aviation sales in 1983.

Hammond retired from Phillips in 1994 and now splits his time between his homes in Upper Michigan and Bartlesville, OK. He is married to his wife Patricia.

*Jack Hammond peers into the cockpit of Liberty II.*

# Dennis Boggs

In 1990, Dennis Boggs was the Lubricants Technical Director for Phillips 66. He oversaw all technical training, aviation oil manufacture, and sales. He was highly regarded by the general aviation community as an authority on aircraft engine operating performance and longevity. His achievements in aviation oil development are well documented.

Boggs joined Phillips in 1958 and worked in various positions in warehousing, sales, training, and the technical service of fuels and lubricants.

In 1964, Boggs moved into the Phillips 66 marketing division and for more than 30 years held several positions in the lubricants product group. He personally oversaw all aspects of product development and quality control.

A native of West Virginia, Boggs studied engineering at the Citadel, a military college in Charleston, SC, and served in the U.S. Marine Corps.

Boggs was a member of the Society of Tribologists and Lubrication Engineers. He also served on the SAE Aviation Piston Engine Oil Subcommittee TC-8. He retired from Phillips 66 in 1997. He is married to his wife Joy and they reside in Broken Arrow, Ok.

*Addendum: IV*

# OUR PILOT – Tom Casey

Thomas P. Casey was four years old when World War II began, and among his earliest memories are those of seeing the huge flying boats in the water near his parents' home in New York City. Thus armed with an enthusiasm for flight, he would go on to earn his private and commercial licenses, adding seaplane, instructor, and instrument endorsements by the age of 25.

In 1963, he graduated from Temple University and, subsequently, worked in aviation as a multi-engine aircraft sales representative for Cessna Aircraft Company. For several years, he served as an instructor for instrument flight and "Weekender" seminars for the AOPA Air Safety Foundation, traveling around the U.S. from his Everett, Washington home. During the 1970s-80s, Casey turned to the skiing industry, becoming a designer and manufacturer of ski apparel and equipment as well as the marketing director for Sportscaster, Inc.

His 1990 west-to-east world record flight, detailed herein, was in his Cessna 206 aircraft. For this adventure he gave the aircraft the name 'Liberty II'. Why? Explained Casey, "Liberty II meant freedom and independence without restraint. This clearly defines a typical floatplane pilot."

Casey left his homecoming celebration on December 20, 1990 in Seattle and flew back to his home in nearby Everett. He wanted a long rest but his father's health precluded that desired goal. His father was slowly dying and for the next three months he went back and forth to New York City to be by his dad's bedside.

In between these trips, he put together all of his flight data — as best he could — and sent this information and other materials to the NAA in Washington, D.C., in pursuit of that organization's recognition of his record-making achievement. A deadline had been missed, as recounted in this book, and the official recognition was never given by NAA.

Along the way, we continued to work with Casey in pursuit of speaking opportunities and getting his story told in a book. All the while, Casey continued talking to the media and aviation groups (Seaplane Pilots Association, AOPA, and others who recognized Casey's record) — while minimizing the support he had received from Phillips 66 and the U.S. State Department, among others. Because of this, Phillips' executives, who maintained their continuing admiration for Casey's round-the-world achievement, decided to pull the plug on a continuing relationship with him. When I later related this news to Casey, it broke my heart.

\* \* \*

Prior to the publication of this book, I contacted Casey for an update on his activities following the severing of ties by Phillips 66. Here is his response ...

"After I was cut from my sponsor Phillips 66, I found I was deeply in debt and had to sell my plane. I flew Liberty II to WipAire and sold it for $180,000. I paid Wip the monies I owed him; paid off my insurance invoice I owed Lloyd's of London; and finished paying off all of my personal loans I had taken to bankroll this historic journey. Frankly, I was broke.

"Over the past 25 years, I really haven't done much of anything. I was too old to go back into the ski equipment business, so I spent time speaking at local high schools and colleges about aviation and my historic trip. I also gave flying lessons and enjoyed seeing young aviators get their licenses.

"I remember about 20 years ago, I saw Coleman at Sun 'n Fun

and we had a chance to talk. I said that in time I finally understood what he meant about giving all the credit to my sponsor. We saw each other several times after that over the years and kept in touch by phone.

"I had some speaking engagements at aviation groups over the years and kept in touch with Harry Smith and my buddies at the Seaplane Pilots Association. My son, John, now lives in Alaska and every year I go there and see him and my friends.

"Life has been a bit hectic with several health issues and also having to have back surgery several times. The surgeon in Saudi Arabia had warned me that recurrent surgery might be warranted over the years and he was so right. Speaking of the Saudis, I had the excellent chance of meeting with Director Abdullah Mejallid several times. We saw each other the last time about ten years ago. He always wondered why the National Aeronautic Association would never give me the record. Must be political, he said.

"When Coleman said he was going to write this book, I just couldn't believe it. Imagine, we now have a book on the 25th anniversary of my historic flight. Hurrah."

— W.C.

# THE RECORD

Tom Casey may be the only pilot to ever make a historic flight and never get credit for it. To date, his accomplishment has never been recognized by any official sanctioning body. He was stonewalled, and what a shame that remains. Why?

When Casey made his triumphant return home after his record-setting journey, the National Aeronautic Association (NAA) was very hesitant about awarding Casey the world record for being the first person to fly around the world while landing only on water. This disclosure became very evident at the December 18, 1990 Casey homecoming at Sand Point in Seattle, Washington. Art Greenfield, the Records Representative for the NAA, abruptly walked out of the homecoming press briefing and announced that Casey did not qualify for this record.

Casey had complied with the stipulations to set this record, including the 24,960 verifiable miles needed to be flown to qualify in circumnavigating the globe. His flight was interrupted several times but he always regained the steadfastness to continue on with the journey. It took 188 days and he flew more than 29,000 miles.

Casey petitioned the NAA and was told that he had three months from the date of his return to provide NAA with a copy of his logbook, maps, and other pertinent information such as flight clearance approvals and his U.S. passport, indicating where each country's

Immigration and Customs had stamped permission for Casey to be in their country.

During this same period, Casey was fraught with financial considerations, forcing him to sell his plane to pay off liens by creditors. Also, his father was very sick in a New York City hospital at the time and Casey was constantly at his bedside.

Both of these traumatic events precluded Casey from getting his materials to NAA at the agreed upon deadline. According to Casey, he failed to get all the necessary papers to the NAA prior to the three-month deadline.

Again according to Casey, he did get his materials to NAA five days following this deadline. And, when Casey called to verify the status of his record, Greenfield told him he was too late. Casey then asked for all of his materials to be sent back to him, as he wanted to personally resubmit these same documents in person to NAA's President. Casey related that Greenfield told him that the materials had all been tossed out or had been lost. Thus, Greenfield told Casey that he would not get the record.

Now 25 years later, we again have approached the NAA to determine if this record can finally be awarded to Casey. We will see if Casey's dream comes true and the NAA awards him the record.

Casey's entire journey is recounted in this book. The story was taken from his logbook, interviews with all the people who came in contact with Casey, plus memos, letters, and detailed handwritten notes from U.S. Embassy and foreign officials (during the actual journey), as well as the author's own personal recordkeeping.

Lindbergh just had the wireless — we had the world to verify Casey's historic feat.

# A Reflection on the Tom Casey Experience

This story of Tom Casey flying around the world in a float-plane in 1990 is the story of a rebel pilot with a dream and a public relations (PR) man named Bill Coleman, who supported the dream in every conceivable way, even after almost everyone else had parachuted or bailed out. (Both metaphors are apt for a floatplane story, especially this one). Tom Casey was a lot to handle in terms of personality and sticking to the script. Somehow, Bill knew that it took just this kind of self-centered, independent spirit to achieve something as challenging as flying around the world in a single-engine plane landing only on water.

I was 25 years old and working at G+A Communications in New York when I was assigned to work with Bill on the publicity campaign for the flight. As we stood on the dock in Seattle with a small group of supporters and a few members of the press corps, I can attest that there were already Casey doubters, even in our own office. The problem was not when Casey was flying, it was more when he was on the ground.

Less than a week later, we orchestrated a perfect press conference to watch Casey's landing on the Potomac with the Washington Monument looming in the distance. We had played up the angle of the independent American spirit that was clearly represented in the plane's name, Liberty II, and the lone, adventurous pilot. All the major TV stations and newspapers were there to capture the scene.

But Casey was late, and because he had limited landing and departure clearance on the river, we had to hustle him up the dock to the podium and then to individual interviews. When we started to hint to him that he needed to be on his way, Casey looked over at the restaurant bar and the spread of food and said that he was starving and that he had not had breakfast or lunch. I am not sure if he knew how tight his flight window was, but the next thing I knew his entire PR team was wrapping up sandwiches in napkins and stuffing them in his pockets before nudging him back down the plank to the plane. The independent adventurer needed logistical support.

The Casey project consumed our small PR agency for most of a year. Our client, Phillips 66, had a long history of supporting aviation and we were thrilled to work with them to promote this record-setting achievement. Since most of us on the team were so young, we had just the right amount of naïveté and energy for this project. Under Bill's direction, we would work with U.S. and foreign media by telephone and fax machine into the late hours of the night, and then come to the office the next day bleary-eyed with the question: "Where is Casey now?" As he trekked across Europe the excitement grew along with the number of Casey stories. A lot of it was fun stuff, like him giving away all of the client's Phillips 66 hats or not paying his gas bill before flying off. Bill cleaned up every mess and we laughed about them all.

Things started to slow down after Europe and Casey was grounded for weeks when he was denied clearance to fly through India and Pakistan. Each time, eventually, he would get to fly on. Bill had a world map in his office and we would stick little dots on the map to mark Casey's progress. I remember looking at the dot on Saudi Arabia, wondering if that would be the last one, while Bill talked on the phone to the consulate there inquiring about the state dinner they had held in Casey's honor and the subsequent back surgery for an injury we imagined occurred on the dance floor.

To explain all of the detours and delays, Kyle MacDonald and I would sit in her cubicle writing and rewriting press release copy to convey incredibly complex aviation airspace rules or diplomatic meddling in short crisp sentences, while giving credit to the sponsor and not overdoing the drama. We would take it into Bill who would make some changes, add some information, and send it back. We would then bring it in to Alan Hirsch, the president of the agency, who would "red line" whole sections, and we would rewrite again — and again. In some ways it was the hardest writing I have ever done in my life, with our editors scrutinizing every bit of our information, as well as every sentence and comma of our style. I learned a lot about audience, storytelling, tone, and how to make complex ideas read simple from this work. It was an education I still use today.

As the timeframe lengthened and the stories piled up, we had to cut the budget for the project, and Phillips 66 wanted to pull the plug entirely. Ever relentless, Bill kept talking them into staying on board at least until the next stop. Then he would pick up the phone and convince some Navy admiral or foreign-service ambassador to arrange clearance for Casey to fly through a no-fly zone. It is an underestimation to say that if Casey flew 30,000 miles on his flight, Bill Coleman spoke ten times that in words, persuading his sponsors for funding, persuading government officials to let Casey fly through or land, and persuading the media that this story was worth covering. Coleman did PR like Casey flew, never fazed by a change in plans and relentlessly optimistic.

Bill and I took separate flights to Seattle for Casey's homecoming because it was agency policy that we should never have more than one person on the same plane in case the plane was delayed, diverted, or went down, a policy that still makes me laugh considering the story we were covering. We landed without incident and then found out that Casey's plane had crashed into the sea 20 miles from Kiska Island, in the western part of the Aleutian island chain. Casey was an excellent pilot — how else to explain successfully landing a seaplane in ten-foot ocean waves? But he was also lucky, since a fishing boat was close enough to go pick him up and even use its fishing net boom to lift his sinking plane out of the water.

From a storytelling point of view, this latest travesty added to what was already a full plot; from a public relations point of view, we had quite a bit of work to do. Bill and I sat in hotel rooms in Seattle, talking to media on multiple phone lines and taking apart press kits that marked the completion of something that was not quite done. On the side, Bill convinced our client to send Casey a new engine, explaining that perhaps the engine "trouble" was caused by Casey's hardest leg the day before, a windy, 13-hour, 1,500-mile trip across the Bering Strait from the Japanese island of Hokkaido to the Aleutian island of Attu. We couldn't give up on this pilot now, Bill explained.

Six weeks later we were back in Seattle, and along with the press and his family we watched as Casey landed and glided up to the dock as if he had just flown in from 20 miles away. (He actually had stayed only an hour away to make this last leg trouble-free.) I took the photos as he emerged from the plane, since our photography budget had been cut to nothing. I remember being surprised that both he and the plane looked good; and though there was cheering, it should have been louder and more sustained. Like a good PR man, Bill stood off to the side.

In retrospect, I like to think of Casey as a talented, strong-willed risk-taker like Steve Fossett, only with a lot less money and a lot less fanfare. At this point in history, an increasing number of adventurers have climbed Everest, been to the North Pole, or circled the globe in a plane. It's not big news anymore. Yet, there is still only one person in that latter category to do it all on water. The around-the-world floatplane record stands as testament to what happens when one person is independent enough to dream up such a challenge and then cavalier enough to carry it all the way through to the finish. It was a damn good story to tell and I am glad Bill Coleman has told it right to the end.

**Tim McCormack**
**Tappan, NY**
**2015**

*(Tim McCormack left the world of Public Relations in 1995 to earn his Ph.D. in English from the Graduate Center of the City University of New York. He is now a professor of English at John Jay College of Criminal Justice in New York, where he teaches writing and research, directs the writing program, and is Deputy Chair of the English Department. He does not write about airplanes anymore, although he is prone to slip in aviation metaphors whenever the chance arises.)*

# Addendum: VII

# Liberty II Log

| Arrival Date | Landing Site | Distance | Purpose/Duration |
|---|---|---|---|
| May 20 | Anchorage | 1,460 | 20 Days |
| June 13 | Seattle | 1,460 | Overnight |

*(Casey returns to Seattle as U.S.S.R. would not give clearance to travel through its territory. He decides to reverse course, going west to east.)*

| Arrival Date | Landing Site | Distance | Purpose/Duration |
|---|---|---|---|
| June 14 | San Diego | 1,089 | Overnight |
| June 15 | Oklahoma City | 1,148 | Overnight |
| June 16 | New Orleans | 602 | Fuel stop |
| | St. Augustine | 510 | Overnight |
| June 17 | Lancaster, SC | 418 | Overnight |
| June 18 | Washington, D.C. | 346 | Press conference |
| | Hackensack, NJ | 211 | Father in hospital |

| Arrival Date | Landing Site | Distance | Purpose/Duration |
|---|---|---|---|
| June 19 | East Haddam, CT | 108 | Repairs |
| | Halifax, Nova Scotia | 497 | Overnight |
| June 20 | Goose Bay, Labrador | 640 | Overnight |
| June 21 | Narsarsuaq, Greenland | 785 | Overnight |
| June 22 | Reykjavik | 772 | Stopover |
| | Keflavik, U.S. Naval Station | 18 | Overnight |
| June 23 | Ayr, Scotland | 878 | Overnight |
| June 24 | Ayr, Scotland | — | Strut repair |
| June 25 | Foynes, Ireland | 277 | Visit relatives |
| June 28 | Lake Como, Italy | 935 | Missed U.K. Press conference — Overnight |
| June 29 | Lake Como, Italy | — | Awaited clearance to Athens |
| June 30 | Athens | 926 | Awaited clearance |
| July 5 | Souda Bay, Crete | 140 | Awaited clearances |
| July 28 | Alexandria, Egypt | 435 | Fuel stop |
| | Jeddah, Saudi Arabia | 897 | Extended stay — back operation |
| Sept. 10 | Bahrain (plus 150 miles) | 950 | Overnight |
| Sept. 11 | Dubai | 301 | Overnight |
| Sept. 13 | Karachi | 741 | Extended stay — State Dept. edict re: Desert Shield |

| Arrival Date | Landing Site | Distance | Purpose/Duration |
|---|---|---|---|
| Oct. 3 | Bombay | 510 | Awaited clearance; paid flight to Calcutta |
| Oct. 10 | Calcutta | 1,022 | Overnight |
| Oct. 13 | Burma | — | Overfly |
| | Bang Reservoir, Thailand | 1,036 | Hosted by Thai Gov. |
| Oct. 15 | George Town, Penang | 554 | Overnight |
| Oct. 16 | Singapore | — | Overfly |
| | Brunei | 1,093 | Overnight |
| Oct. 17 | NAS Cubi Point | 787 | Awaited Japan clearance |
| | Subic Bay, Philippines | — | Moved to protected harbor |
| Oct. 21 | Kadena, Okinawa (+150) | 1,120 | Awaited Japan clearance |
| Oct. 23 | Kasumigaura Bay, Japan | 1,060 | Overnight |
| Oct. 24 | Misawa AFB, Japan | 321 | Weather delay |
| Oct. 30 | Memanbetsu, Japan | 285 | Overnight |
| Oct. 31 | Attu, Aleutian Islands | 1,587 | Engine inspected |
| Nov. 1 | Kiska Island | 205 | Engine failure; rescued, taken to |
| Nov. 2 | Shemya Island | — | Shemya for repairs |
| Dec. 7 | Attu | 52 | Restarting Attu leg |
| | Atka Island | 544 | Magneto problem |
| Dec. 12 | Dutch Harbor, AK | 337 | Overnight |
| Dec. 13 | Kodiak, AK | 823 | Overnight |

| Arrival Date | Landing Site | Distance | Purpose/Duration |
| --- | --- | --- | --- |
| Dec. 14 | Juneau | 653 | |
| Dec. 15 | Petersburg, AK | 117 | Stopover |
| | Ketchikan, AK | 114 | Overnight |
| Dec. 16 | Victoria Island, BC | 379 | Overnight |
| Dec. 17 | Friday Harbor, San Juan Islands | 231 | Overnight |
| Dec. 18 | Seattle | 125 | End of record flight |

**Total miles traveled — global round trip starting from June 14: 26,579**
**Total miles flown — initial round trip to/from Alaska: 2,920**

**Total miles flown: 29,499**

# A Final Word from David Knight

**Dear Readers:**

I was so eager for you to meet all of the people involved in the flight of Liberty II, and who crossed my path during this unique and unforgettable journey. So many people were involved in every one of the 27,000 miles flown, but my personal recollections primarily emanate from three people: the late Vice Admiral Donald D. Engen, U.S. Navy (Ret.); Tom Casey himself; and Bill Coleman. Recapturing this voyage, as Bill Coleman has done, immediately proves how refreshed one's memory can become regarding all the lessons learned that, at the time, you had no idea you were learning.

I recall it all as if it were just yesterday when "the Admiral" called me into his office to introduce me to Tom Casey, who had gained the admiral's interest in Liberty II. The admiral said, as the then-president of the AOPA (Aircraft Owners and Pilots Association) Air Safety Foundation, that he wanted us to help this pilot in any way we could to set this record. Sure, he wanted it done safely, but in his heart he wanted to prove, yet again, what could be accomplished through all the multi-faceted capabilities of an aviator.

Too, it was the admiral's long-time desire to always have aviation records set, and challenged. It was that conviction, combined with Tom's considerable sales ability, which secured the admiral's commitment to this aviation adventure. The admiral even convinced Jack

Hammond, head of aviation at Phillips 66, to become Casey's sponsor. In the end, it was Phillips 66's generous support that paved the way for Casey's success.

Admiral Engen loved breaking aviation records. But he never bragged about any of his own staggering list of firsts, either as a U.S. Navy test pilot or a Fleet Admiral. He had an amazing "we can do it" attitude, which led to such things as world altitude attempts; a spectacular military record; CEO of Piper; the NTSB; the FAA; and the Smithsonian Air and Space Museum.

The admiral's sign-off on Casey's flight led to his contacting powerful friends in D.C., the U.S. Navy, the FAA, the airlines, the State Department, general aviation, and beyond. He gathered the support of people we needed in order to secure the mission's credibility and to smooth out so many of the problems we would encounter every step of the way.

Also, along the way came a lesson on the word tenacity. Joining Tom in the day-to-day lead were two strangers who would become strong allies and friends during this escapade of Casey's around-the-world flight — myself and the author. Over the next six months, Bill and I would attempt to uncover, time and again, "Where (fill in the blank) was Casey?" That, coupled with wondering what had he done lately to upset the balance of diplomatic stability needed to maintain world order (a bit of tongue in cheek, here, of course).

And finally, to be the PIC (pilot-in-command) in this adventure required at least two deeply developed attributes. The most obvious is the confidence and skill it takes to pilot a small water-dependent aircraft in such long, varied, and many times dangerously challenging circumstances. But, maybe that was comparably the easy part. Tom Casey had within him a contagious and adventurous charm that could befriend anyone, and such a personal, totally dedicated commitment to achieving this flight (also contagious). Yes, he had a huge amount of help. But, in the end, it was he alone in the left seat of that airplane that made it happen. He proved that at the core of any such attempt comes a dedicated and knowledgeable airplane driver. Oh, and by the way, throw in a healthy dose of bravery.

**David Knight**
**Brunswick, Maine**